DEEP ROOTS

DEEP ROOTS

Rice Farmers in West Africa and the
African Diaspora

EDDA L. FIELDS-BLACK

INDIANA UNIVERSITY PRESS
Bloomington and Indianapolis

This book is a publication of

Indiana University Press
Office of Scholarly Publishing
Herman B Wells Library 350
1320 East 10th Street
Bloomington, Indiana 47405 USA

iupress.indiana.edu

Telephone   800-842-6796
Fax   812-855-7931

First paperback edition 2015
© 2008 Edda L. Fields-Black
All rights reserved

♾ The paper used in this publication meets the minimum
requirements of the American National Standard
for Information Sciences – Permanence of Paper for
Printed Library Materials, ANSI Z39.48-1992.

Manufactured in the United States of America

The Library of Congress has cataloged
the original edition as follows:

Fields-Black, Edda L.
    Deep roots : rice farmers in West Africa and
the African diaspora / Edda L. Fields-Black.
    p. cm. – (Blacks in the diaspora)
    Includes bibliographical references and index.
    ISBN 978-0-253-35219-4 (cloth)
1. Nalu (African people) – Agriculture – Guinea.
2. Baga (African people) – Agriculture – Guinea.
3. Rice farmers – Guinea – History – 18th century.
4. Rice trade – Guinea – History – 18th century. 5. Slave
trade – Guinea – History – 18th century. 6. Rice – South
Carolina – History – 18th century. 7. Rice – Georgia – History – 18th
century. 8. Slavery – South Carolina – History – 18th century.
9. Slavery – Georgia – History – 18th century. I. Title.
    DT543.42.F54 2008
    633.1'80899632 – dc22
                                                2008007846

ISBN 978-0-253-01610-2 (paperback)

2 3 4 5   20 19 18 17 16 15

To
D.J.F., E.L.F., and K.L.F.
on whose shoulders
I stand

Contents

Maps

Tables

Orthography

i-	"s<u>ee</u>"
ɪ-	"s<u>i</u>t"
e-	"w<u>ei</u>ght"
ɛ-	"b<u>e</u>d"
a-	"<u>a</u>pple"
u-	"c<u>oo</u>p"
U-	"c<u>ou</u>ld"
o-	"r<u>oa</u>d, fl<u>ow</u>"
ɔ-	"l<u>aw</u>, c<u>au</u>ght
ŋ-	"si<u>ng</u>"
NY-	"<u>ign</u>ame"
θ-	"<u>the</u>"

Acknowledgments

According to the Haya in Tanzania, "Many hands make light work." More people, institutions, and funding agencies on three continents than I could possibly name have supported me over the past ten years as I researched and wrote my dissertation and subsequently my first book. While the work was never "light," it would have exceeded my capacity without the support of so "many hands."

I am most grateful to Steven Feierman and David Schoenbrun for the shaping of my dissertation, which provided the archives of linguistic data and the testing ground for the comparative method of historical linguistics used in this study. First, as my adviser Steven took on the challenge of training a young head-strong Africanist whose research interests extended into the African Diaspora—before the African Diaspora and the Atlantic World were popular fields of historical inquiry, particularly among Africanists. Steve not only trained me in asking new and interesting questions on both sides of the Atlantic, encouraged my use of interdisciplinary sources and methods and desire to write to a broader audience, and strongly encouraged—i.e., forced—me to think about my own future when political instability persisted in Sierra Leone whose pre-colonial history was initially the subject of my dissertation. Steve had the vision and David Schoenbrun helped me to work out the details. David's passion for historical linguistics has always been infectious. And his willingness to share and teach what he knows in tutoring sessions in Gainesville, FL, Athens, GA, and Evanston, IL, has influenced countless graduate students, some of whom were not his advisees. Lastly, David has probably read more drafts of this project than anyone else. For his patience and willingness to give feedback promptly, I am also eternally grateful. Any remaining errors are truly my own.

During my fieldwork, countless people in Guinea, Conakry, Kamsar, Kukuba, Monchon, Binari, and Kawass; and in France, Paris and Aix-en-Provence, supported my research. Appendix 1 lists the names of all of the farmers in the aforementioned villages whom I interviewed. A list will never be enough for me to repay the generosity of these elders and their families in telling me their

xiv Acknowledgments

stories, opening their homes, fields, and granaries to me, and making me an honored part of their families. Several colleagues in Conakry, Djibril Tamsir Niane, at the University of Conakry, Ishmael Barry and Aboubacar Toure, and in Boké, Sory Kaba (formerly the archivist of the regional archives in Boké), deserve special mention for their support throughout my research. My fieldwork would also have been literally impossible without my research assistant Mohammed Camara, who handled the logistics of our travel between the four coastal villages throughout the rainy/rice cultivation season, made it possible for me to negotiate the uncomfortable terrain of being a young, (then) unmarried woman living and traveling without male relatives in a conservative Muslim society, and transcribed scores of tapes. I will never be able to repay Mohammed or his family. My fieldwork would have been less pleasant without Guinean families who adopted me: Dr. and Mme. Ibrahima Bah-Laliya, Dr. and Mme. Abdul Radiya-Bah, and Mr. Alhassane Tangue-Bah in Conakry and Dr. and Mme. Camara in Kamsar, and American missionaries and linguists specializing in the (Baga) Sitem language, Marty and Tina Ganong (of Kawass), who befriended me. Last but not least, researching and writing the dissertation would not have been possible without funding from Annenberg Pre-Dissertation and Mellon Dissertation Fellowships (University of Pennsylvania), a Fulbright-Hays dissertation research fellowship, a travel grant from Bremer Stiftung für Geschichte, and a dissertation-writing fellowship from Oberlin College Departments of History and African-American Studies.

A number of people have played critical roles in the reconceptualization of this project as a book. My mentors at Carnegie Mellon, Tera Hunter (now at Princeton) and Joe Trotter have selflessly nurtured me through this process, supported me as I made difficult decisions about the book, and read draft after draft. It is humbling how much time and energy they have both invested in my family and me, my book, and my career. Judith Byfield (formerly the series editor for Indiana University Press's Blacks in the Diaspora series) played a critical role in convincing me that the series would be the vehicle for my book to reach audiences interested in African, African-American, and African Diaspora history and in getting the manuscript under contract. My colleagues who specialize in the Rio Nunez region have also been indispensable sources of feedback over the years: Vickie Boimba Coifman, Marie Yvonne Curtis, Bruce Mouser, Ramon Sarró, as well as colleagues who work in other regions of the Upper Guinea Coast: Judith Carney, Walter Hawthorne, Martin Klein, and Olga Linares. I am especially grateful to Bruce Mouser for reading many drafts of this project and turning them around very quickly on short notice, despite many more pressing responsibilities and to Walter Hawthorne for giving unvarnished feedback on an early draft that helped to shape future revisions. To the historians and anthropologists, I must add the linguists who specialize in Atlantic languages, Marie-Paule Ferry, Konstantin Pozdniakov, and Guillaume Segerer (all are affiliated with LLACAN, Langage, Langues, et Cultures d'Afrique Noire of CNRS in Paris where I have also received temporary affiliation) and G. Tucker Childs. Valentim Vydrine, who specializes in Mande languages was also a helpful resource. Colleagues from southwestern Pennsylvania, West Virginia, and New Jersey in the African Studies Research Group, particularly Patrick Manning and Cymone Fourshey, played an important role in putting finishing touches on the manuscript. Friends and colleagues in South Carolina helped me to remember the totality of my audience and gave me several opportunities to present aspects of my work: Timothy Brown and Donald West (Trident Technical College), Alpha Bah (College of Charleston, Department of History), and Curtis Franks (Avery Research Center). Research and travel for the book were funded by The Woodrow Wilson Foundation Career Enhancement Fellowship, Ford Foundation Post-Doctoral Fellowship, and Berkman Faculty Development Grant and the Faulk Fund both from Carnegie Mellon.

I want to thank my husband Samuel Black for inspiring me to locate images for the book that help to illustrate the diversity of the coastal environment, material culture, rice-farming techniques, and rice farmers with whom I worked. Sam also supported my decision to use an original painting for the cover and tapped his colleagues in the Association of African American Museums. Deborah Mack, also a member of AAAM, suggested John W. Jones's work and along with Elaine Nichols of the South Carolina State Museum put me in contact with the artist himself. I sincerely enjoyed collaborating with John W. Jones. As a South Carolina artist, his artistic vision of the West African Rice Coast complements my narrative, which is rooted in the pre-colonial history of the Rice Coast and which looks across the Atlantic at slave ships disembarking in South Carolina and Georgia. When IUP experienced technical difficulties with the digital file of Jones's painting, Sam came to the rescue with his colleague from the Senator John Heinz History Center, Brian Butko, who magically reconfigured the digital file to make it fit the publisher's specifications. I am grateful to my student, Laura Miller, for allowing me to use two of her original images of the slaving vessels that disembarked in South Carolina and Georgia from the West African Rice Coast and West-Central Africa.

In addition to inspiration and professional consultation, I thank Sam for keeping the home fires burning while I devoted a tremendous portion of my time to finishing my book. His rock-steady patience enabled me to keep one foot on the ground throughout this long process. Our son Akhu is an amazingly curious, energetic, and authoritative five-year-old who was fascinated with the tales of Mama's work in the rice fields and the alligators, snakes, crabs, and cane rats that I encountered there, rather than the thought of Mama spending so many hours away just writing a book! Thanks to Akhu for reviving my imagination and reminding me that I can move over and around obstacles rather than always using force to go through them. I am especially grateful to everyone who cared for my son while I traveled and finished the book, including my brother- and sister-in-law Gloria and Michael Evans, our friends Mariama Farma, Robert and Phyllis Goode, Akhu's devoted principal, Dr. Carol Taylor, and teacher, Collette Taylor Matthews, and my student Abiola Fasehun who were always willing to help, even on very short notice. My parents and my husband also traveled with me when I was nursing Akhu, holding, chasing, and spoiling him while I presented papers, gave lectures, conducted research, and attended conferences. As a family, we are eagerly awaiting the next chapter of our lives.

Outside of CMU, we have a rich network of friends whose support has been indispensable: Mama Kadiatou Conte and Baba Forte, Terrance Hayes and Yona Harvey, Robert and Phyllis Goode, Christina Springer and Norman Numley, Aaron and Terry Washington, family, Charles Jenkins and Aunts Judy Jenkins and Eloise Alston, and the Highland Park Play Group. Reassuring conversations and "play dates" with my girlfriends, Terry Crump, Bernadette Davis, Yona Harvey, and Terry Washington have also helped me to remain sane, pedicured, and balanced. My cousins Cleveland and Valerie Frazier and Jonas Fields (in Green Pond, SC) and my in-laws John and Edna Black, Sadie Utley, Eloise Alsten, Judy Jenkins, and Charles Jenkins helped me to stay connected to our roots in South and North Carolina. Lastly, thank you to Ura-tu, Shekhem-u, and Sheps-u for the tools to make lasting change in our lives and the lives of others. Completing this book took many "hands" indeed.

The book is dedicated to my parents, Dorothy Jenkins Fields and Eddie L. Fields for their sacrifices to provide my big sister Katherine and me with the best education available and to instill in me the will to do whatever I set my mind to do and the self-discipline to always finish what I start.

DEEP
ROOTS

Introduction

The Bagos are very expert in Cultivating rice and in
quite a Different manner to any of the Nations on the
Windward Coast The country the[y] inhabit is chiefly
low and swampy. The rice they first sow on their dung-
hills and rising spots about their towns[.] when 8 or 10
Inches high transplant it into Lugars made for that
purpose which are flat low swamps, at one side A they
have a reservoir that they can let in what water they
please[;] other side B is a drain cut so that they can let
of[f] what they please. The Instruments they use much
resembles a Turf spade with with [sic] which they turn
the grass under in ridges just above the water which by
being confind Stagnates and nourishes the root of the
plant. Women & girls transplant the rice and are so
dexterous as to plant fifty roots singly in one minute[.]
when the rice is ready for cutting they turn the water
of[f] til their Harvest is over[;] then they let the Water
over it and lets it stands three or four Seasons it being
so impoverished Their time of planting is in Sept and
reaping. [sic].(Bruce L. Mouse, *A Slaving Voyage to Africa and Jamaica: The Log of the Sandown, 1793–1794*,
75–76)

In 1793, despite his years of experience as a slave trader,[1] Captain Samuel Gamble found himself in the wrong place at the wrong time—stranded on the mosquito-infested West African Rice Coast for the entire insalubrious rainy season. The *Sandown* departed from London in April of that year and arrived in the Cape Verde Islands three months later. Eight days into its refueling, crew members of the ship were stricken with dysentery, malaria, and Yellow Fever. While the slavers may have contracted the illness in the Cape Verde Islands, the ship's water supply and bilge water may also have been contaminated with mosquitoes carrying the virus.[2] When they arrived in the Iles de Los located near Conakry—the present-day capital city of Guinea—Gamble and the crew of the *Sandown* found that war between France and England had eroded neutrality along West Africa's coast. The necessity of protecting his cargo and his vessel from capture by French privateers may have prompted him to seek refuge in the smaller rivers and ports in coastal Guinea. From this location, he used a smaller vessel to travel north up the Nunez River in present-day Guinea to Doctor Walker's factory—Walkeria— and south to Bance Island off the coast of present-day Sierra Leone to purchase 250 captives.[3] In coastal Guinea, Gamble and his afflicted crew became figuratively and literally stuck in the mud.

Unfortunately for them, 1793–94 was "recorded as the second most unhealthy year on the coast."[4] Though the mangrove swamps of the Rio Nunez region provided protection from enemy war boats and pirates, they also served as a breeding ground for mosquitoes and mosquito-borne disease, particularly malaria and Yellow Fever. The rainy season brought torrential downpours, tornadoes, and fever annually between June and October. Disease routinely spread on the trading ships that traveled from port to port along the coast and on caravans from the coast to the interior. After the majority of his crew became incapacitated, Gamble had no choice but to spend the rainy season in coastal Guinea, waiting in port for nearly nine months as the crew recovered. Ultimately, the wait was in vain. By February 1794, before the *Sandown* left the coast, eight members of Gamble's crew and nine captives had succumbed to disease. Because the ship's doctor had deemed the remaining crew unseaworthy, Gamble hired eight new crew members to guide the ship back across the Atlantic.

Disease and death continued to plague the *Sandown* as it passed through the Middle Passage, for slaver and enslaved alike. The experienced captain made an emergency landing in Barbados after an additional nine captives perished from disease, ten captives either committed suicide or were killed in an insurrection, and the ship's new crew was driven to mutiny because of illness and diminishing water supplies. In Barbados, ten more enslaved Africans perished from illness, bringing the number of casualties due to illness up to

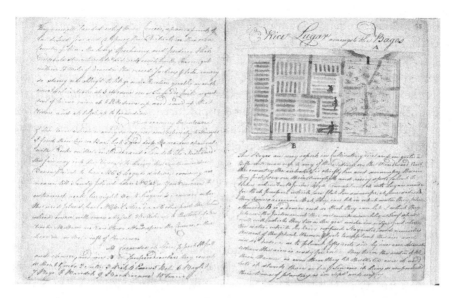

FIGURE INTRO.1. "Rice Lugar amongst the Baga," in "The Log of the Sandown, 1793–94."
Copyright National Maritime Museum, London.

thirty. The crewmen hired in West Africa subsequently absconded, secured legal counsel, and demanded back wages. Before the *Sandown* was impounded, Gamble and a skeleton crew set sail in the middle of the night, limping to Jamaica, the voyage's intended destination.

Although Gamble's hiatus in coastal Guinea proved costly in human life and suffering, his journal provides an unparalleled glance at coastal inhabitants, telling of their flora, fauna, and wildlife, as well as their cultural, ritual, and even agricultural practices. The purpose of Gamble's travel to the "Baga" Sitem villages located in coastal Guinea's Rio Nunez region and surrounding the commercial center of Kacundy/Boke is unclear—possibly he was looking for provisions.[5] Later on in his sojourn in coastal Guinea, Gamble purchased for the return voyage across the Atlantic both red rice—husk rice produced by coastal farmers and routinely acquired by European traders for consumption while in port and aboard ship—and clean polished rice.[6]

On Tuesday, September 24, 1793, Samuel Gamble unknowingly recorded the earliest existing and most detailed description of irrigated rice cultivation among farmers in the Rio Nunez region of coastal Guinea.[7] During his tour of (Baga) Sitem villages, he witnessed firsthand coastal inhabitants turning the water-logged soil in their fields, sowing rice seeds in nurseries, and transplanting the seedlings to mounds and ridges within their rice fields. The description recorded in Gamble's journal is not the earliest for West Africa's coastal littoral.

North of the Rio Nunez region, however, Portuguese traders had observed and described mangrove rice fields and cultivation techniques as early as the mid-fifteenth century. For example, in 1456 Diogo Gomes left accounts of trade in red salt that had been produced on abandoned mangrove rice fields along the Sine-Saloum estuary north of the Gambia River. In 1594 André Alvares de Álmada recorded a detailed description of mangrove rice-farming along coastal estuaries south of the Gambia River, a farming system which included embankments, ridges, and canals.[8] For coastal Guinea, however, detailed descriptions of coastal agriculture do not exist prior to Gamble's sojourn along the Nunez River more than three hundred years after Diogo Gomez.[9]

Though one cannot deny the historical significance of Gamble's detailed account of mangrove rice-farming technology, historians have been misled by it for a variety of reasons. Most importantly, in coastal Guinea's Rio Nunez region, this first written account appears to have emerged out of a vacuum. A thorough examination of travelers' accounts for the region is revealing.[10] Not one trader traveling in the Rio Nunez region before the late eighteenth century described anything resembling the comprehensive tidal farming system that Gamble observed. Instead, though travelers took careful note of the amounts of rice that farmers produced and traders bought and sold, they did not pay similar attention to the methods by which coastal farmers cultivated rice. This absence of written documentation does not denote an absence of technology before the late eighteenth century. Understanding the reasons for the omission necessitates understanding the motivations of the traders who produced the region's first written documents.

Beginning in the late fifteenth century in coastal Guinea's Rio Nunez region, as in other parts of West Africa's coastal littoral, "Portuguese" traders recorded the first written documents for the area. This date stands in contrast to that of recordings about interior regions in West Africa's savanna, where Berber traders came across the Sahara Desert from North Africa and recorded the first documents more than five hundred years before the Portuguese arrived in coastal West Africa.[11] Many of the early European traders who traveled to the coast of West Africa were not actually Europeans by modern-day standards: they defined their "Portuguese" identity based on occupation, Catholicism, and language—first Portuguese and subsequently the Portuguese-based Creole known as Criouo. In the late fifteenth and early sixteenth centuries, the first generation of lançados—as they were known—migrated from Portugal, lived for extended periods in coastal villages, and even married African women from the local host societies. Some *lançados* settled initially in Cape Verde, establishing a base from which they traded with ports between Senegal in the north and Sierra Leone in the south. By the end of the sixteenth century, unions between *lançados* and women from coastal West African societies produced a second generation of Luso-Africans whose culture blended African and European traditions. As cultural intermediaries, Luso-African traders employed extended family members and fictive kinship networks to maintain a monopoly over trans-Atlantic trade, a monopoly that they held until the mid-eighteenth century. In decentralized societies that lacked state apparatuses to generate captives and to control commerce, they manipulated their kinship networks to produce captives from within their own societies, sometimes even from within their own families.[12] This class of Luso-African traders also wrote many of the first historical sources for West Africa's Rice Coast region.

Luso-African traders looking for goods to export to the New World and to other West African coastal ports gathered and recorded information about raw materials and crops, riverine trade along the coast, and caravan trade from the interior to the coast. In coastal Guinea-Conakry as in coastal Guinea-Bissau to the north, European traders were generally not attracted to the coastal regions, because they lacked large indigenous trade centers. Politically centralized states located primarily in the interior controlled these entrepôts. Throughout West Africa's history, a distinct correlation emerged between political centralization and interregional trade.[13] For example, the formation of the West African kingdoms of Ghana, Mali, Songhay, and Kanem-Borno was integrally connected to trans-Saharan trade, just as the formation of the West African coastal states of Allada, Whydah, Dahomey, and Oyo was integrally bound to trans-Atlantic slave trade. These are the most well-known, but certainly not the only examples. In Guinea, Futa-Jallon became a centralized state in the eighteenth century and controlled trade on the coast and in the interior.[14] Coastal peoples who were overwhelmingly "stateless" or lacking in centralized political authority—such as those inhabiting the Rio Nunez region—did not control coastal trade. Most European traders frequented commercial centers.

Portuguese and Luso-African traders frequented coastal ports—among them the Iles de Los where Samuel Gamble landed—which were bulking centers for the slave trade. Located south of the Rio Nunez region near the present-day border between Guinea and Sierra Leone, the Iles de Los possessed many features attractive to foreign traders. It was easier to access, as it lacked both the sandbars that lined the mouths of the Nunez River and the rivers to its north, and the "bottom-ripping reefs" that lined Cape Verga.[15] The mangrove swamps had been cleared around Factory

Island for agriculture, thereby reducing the mosquito population and the spread of mosquito-borne disease. Ironically, though Samuel Gamble's crew was ill upon arrival, the Iles de Los had the reputation of being one of the healthiest places in the coastal region. It possessed an abundance of fresh water, food for sale by local inhabitants for subsistence—agricultural produce, fish, domesticated and wild animals—and commodities for trade such as ivory, hides, beeswax, palm oil, malaguetta pepper, and captives. Lastly, the local population was a source of skilled workers who were available for hire: pilots to navigate vessels up the coast around sandbars and reefs, as well as carpenters, sail makers, rope makers, joiners, and blacksmiths to repair ships.[16] Hence, the Iles de Los was an attractive port for European and Luso-African traders to conduct trans-Atlantic trade efficiently. The Rio Nunez region, in contrast, was not.

Even among stateless societies, however, the Rio Nunez region was particularly isolated. Upriver Kacundy and Deboka/Boké became the center of interregional trade. Here caravan traders brought abundant quantities of slaves, gold, and ivory from the interior to exchange for salt produced on the coast.[17] Unlike Senegambia further north or Sierra Leone further south,[18] most traders arriving in coastal Guinea traveled from coastal port to port primarily during the dry season, spent limited time at each stop, and ventured inland only occasionally and only far enough to investigate the source of caravan trade and to report on the goods that caravans brought. Factories within these ports were built beyond the limits of the mangroves to shield European traders from mosquitoes and mosquito-borne illnesses.[19] Also, prior to the end of the eighteenth century, many traders had more direct contact in the Rio Nunez region with Susu traders from the interior—who acted as intermediaries between commerce in the interior and on the coast—than they had with coastal inhabitants.[20] Thus, Samuel Gamble's visit to coastal Baga villages and recorded observations are truly anomalous.

In addition to Luso-Africans' interests and motivations, the nature of the coastal environment also profoundly affected the travelers' accounts on which historians have relied so heavily. Gamble's own voyage in 1793–94 exemplified the hazards traders faced during the rainy season on West Africa's coast. Torrential rains and flooding characterize that season, creating conditions in which traders risked languishing in coastal ports for long hiatuses as they waited for more favorable weather or risked losing their lives if they persevered. Even with today's modern technology—a motorized boat as opposed to a dugout canoe—travel in coastal Guinea and commercial activity are greatly suppressed until the rains subside. Torrential waters and floods also produce stagnant water, a haven for mosquitoes and mosquito-borne diseases. Until the invention of quinine—the first pharmaceutical malarial prophylactic—in the late nineteenth century, this area of West Africa's coast was appropriately known as the "white man's grave."[21] In addition, the presence of sandbars along the rivers in coastal Guinea limited Cape Verdean and Luso-African traders' ability to navigate the Nunez River throughout the year, not just in the rainy season. Prior to Gamble's 1793–94 journal, references to the rainy season, to torrential rains, tornadoes, and floods were in conspicuously short supply in travelers' accounts of the region, because the beginning of the season also marked the end of caravan trade from the interior.[22]

Almost one hundred years after Gamble's ill-fated voyage, a second European visited villages in the Rio Nunez region. The commander of the *Goeland*, Lieutenant André Coffinières de Nordeck, was charged with touring coastal villages inhabited by the "Baga" and Nalu ethnic groups; he aimed to convince their chiefs to sign treaties bringing them under the protection of French sovereignty and thereby halting the influence of English colonial power in the region. Coffinières de Nordeck's journal cites anecdotes from the voyage to enable his readers to vicariously visit the Rio Nunez region and familiarize themselves with its inhabitants without experiencing the "fevers." In one passage, he vividly describes tornadoes,[23] gusts of wind, and thunderstorms that typically preceded heavy downpours at the beginning of the rainy season:

> It was impossible: the air was heavy and saturated with electricity; the greatest calm reigned in the woods, but we soon heard the increasing crackling of lightning, announcing the arrival of a tornado. . . . [24]

Further south in the Sierra Leone estuary, Father Baltasar Barreira—a Jesuit missionary living on the coast of Sierra Leone who traveled into the interior—reported the hardships of traveling by foot and canoe through swamps "surrounded by mangroves . . . impenetrable" during the season of "rain and contrary winds." According to Barreira, travel for Europeans unfamiliar with the challenges of the region and the rainy season was only possible with the assistance of local guides and porters who were familiar with the coastal region:

> In the early stages this form of travel was irksome to me and I was eager to regain dry land, thinking that it would be less tiring to travel that way. But it was not so, for as the rain was continuous, not only were we almost soaked, but we came upon such large lakes that much time was spent in passing through them, which I did on the shoulders of a black, a tall man whom I chose so that I should not get wet . . . [25]

Unlike traders whose tenure on the coast was dependent on commercial activity during the dry season, several missionaries remained on the coast throughout the rainy season, some, like Barreira, traveling into Sierra Leone's interior.[26]

Though the flooded swamps of the rainy season were death traps for European traders and sailors, they are ideal conditions for rice. Under torrential rains, coastal farmers planted rice in the mosquito-infested swamps. The floods inundated the soils with freshwater, washing away salt, which would otherwise kill off the rice and ruin the subsistence base of the coastal farmers. Cape Verdean and Luso-African traders, who traversed the coast in the dry season when the weather was conducive to travel and when trade flourished in coastal ports, missed the rice-planting periods of the agricultural cycle altogether. They missed bearing witness to the agricultural innovations used by coastal farmers to produce the rice that the traders purchased in coastal ports during the dry season. Both these rice farmers and their innovative agricultural technology have "deep roots" on West Africa's coast, extending into the ancient past, millennia before the trans-Atlantic slave trade and before the expansion of rice cultivation in the eighteenth century to cater to the Atlantic trade.

This study examines the evolution and impact of innovative rice farmers on both sides of the Atlantic, in the swampy, salty coastal regions of West Africa and in the African Diaspora. It traces the origins and evolution of tidal rice-growing techniques by farmers in West Africa's Rice Coast region, and investigates the export of captives from West Africa's Rice Coast region and their transmittal of tidal rice-growing technology to the New World.

On the African side of the Atlantic, innovative methodology—historical linguistics—reveals the antiquity of coastal dwellers' agricultural technology. The study focuses on the millennium prior to the arrival of European traders and slavers along the Rice Coast. During this period, coastal farmers made key innovations in their rice-farming and land-use strategies. The confluence of linguistic evidence reveals that inhabitants of the coastal region fashioned rice-farming techniques and material culture to suit the coastal environment. They also borrowed elements from inhabitants of the interior to extend their coastal rice-farming systems into landscapes that had been previously uncultivable. In analyzing the African side of the Atlantic, the study presents new scientific evidence on the diversity of mangroves and the role of mangrove rice-growing techniques as integral parts of coastal land-use systems. It underscores the importance of understanding the environment in reconstructing the past of pre-colonial Africa. In the Rio Nunez region, tidal rice cultivation had for centuries produced commodities for inland markets and for

coastal African trade before rice and rice-farmers became important commodities in the trans-Atlantic slave trade.

On the opposite side of the Atlantic, this study also follows slaving vessels,
which purchased both rice and captives in West Africa's Rice Coast region,
through the Middle Passage. Enslaved Africans—some of whom originated
in the Rice Coast—played important roles in the development of commercial
rice industries in colonial South Carolina and Georgia. It examines the impact of West African rice farmers in producing provisions for slaving vessels
and the impact of enslaved laborers who originated in the West African Rice
Coast on the commercial rice industries of South Carolina and Georgia.

My work builds on the pioneering research of Peter Wood, Daniel Littlefield, and Judy Carney, who recast the way scholars look at African rice, indigenous knowledge systems, and the transfer of technology from West Africa to the New World. Wood's *Black Majority* was the first study to suggest
that enslaved laborers on South Carolina rice plantations were skilled, not
just brute, laborers. Their experiments planting rice in provision grounds laid
the foundation for South Carolina slaveholders and plantation owners' experimentation with rice in coastal environments and concentration on commercial rice production. Based on census data, Wood also demonstrated a
correlation between the formative period of South Carolina's commercial rice
economy and the importation of enslaved Africans as the majority of the
colony's population. Wood's critical examination of slaveholders' documents
reveals that technological change—the introduction of floodgates—saturated
the colony with stagnant water, creating a breeding ground for mosquitoes
and mosquito-borne illness. This pestilential environment turned owners of
rice plantations and slaveholders into "local" absentees[27] during the hot,
rainy, and humid summer months, leaving enslaved laborers to till the soil
with little supervision or interference from slaveholders.

Building on Wood's study, Daniel Littlefield's *Rice and Slaves* pioneered
the examination of the African background of enslaved laborers on plantations in South Carolina and Georgia, locating the origins of their agricultural
contributions in West Africa's Rice Coast region. Littlefield distinguished
tidal rice cultivation as central to Diaspora history—so central that this
coastal rice-growing technology drew the attention of European slave traders,
particularly Samuel Gamble. Littlefield concluded—based on an analysis of
slave-trade records and advertisements for runaway slaves—that South Carolina's slaveholders preferred captives from West Africa's "Rice Coast" region.

The publication of Judith Carney's *Black Rice* expanded the discussion of
enslaved Africans' transmission of rice-rowing technology to include Texas,
Louisiana, and Brazil. Carney argued that West African farmers' dependence
on rainfall, which fluctuates annually, necessitated their development of a

diverse agricultural system to reduce the risks of famine and crop failure. Over time, they developed a diverse and complex system of planting rice along a landscape gradient in distinct microenvironments, which receive varying amounts of rainfall at different points in the agricultural cycle. Carney coined the term "West African rice knowledge system" to describe this diverse and flexible indigenous knowledge system, which also includes a highly structured, gendered division of labor and techniques for processing cereals.

Like Wood and Littlefield, Carney demonstrated how South Carolina slaveholders refused to acknowledge enslaved Africans' contributions to the colony's commercial rice economy. Slaveholders also assumed that Africans— enslaved and free—were incapable of skilled labor. Their mindset contributed to historians' lack of understanding of Africans' critical role in the transfer of agricultural technology from West Africa to the New World. Based on a wealth of knowledge of the geography of West African rice-farming regions, Carney noted that historians of South Carolina have looked for correlates in West Africa of rice-farming technology practiced on South Carolina rice plantations without understanding the principles underlying West African rice-cultivation techniques. Thus, Carney counted the transmission of the West African rice knowledge system—land-use principles, gendered division of labor, and processing techniques—as one of enslaved Africans' chief contributions to the New World.

Now that historians have established the importance of West African rice-farming technology to the plantation economies of the U.S. South, the next logical step is to discern the antiquity of the West Africa rice-knowledge system within West Africa's history. The unique contribution of this study is its use of the comparative method of historical linguistics to trace the "deep roots" of this indigenous knowledge system in West Africa's Rice Coast region. It will also trace the development of tidal rice-farming technology as part of a coastal land-use system. Finally, the study will suggest that the antiquity of coastal farmers' strategies for adapting to the constantly fluctuating coastal environment—land-use strategies that pre-date the incorporation of rice—is evidence of the evolution of a multiplicity of highly specialized and localized West African rice-knowledge systems.

The Comparative Method of Historical Linguistics

Though Gamble's account of tidal rice-growing technology in the Rio Nunez region does emerge out of a vacuum, the technology it describes did not. To date, however, historians could not recount the early history of coastal dwellers' indigenous agricultural revolution because it was not recorded in written sources—European travelers' accounts like Samuel Gamble's journal—on which historians have almost exclusively relied. The lack of documentation represents the limits of the written sources and the historical inquiry based on the sources heretofore available. It presents the historian with a methodological challenge. By and large, the lack of documentation for coastal Guinea's early pre-colonial history is not unusual when compared to other regions of West and West-Central Africa.

However, a lack of sources for historical reconstruction is acute for West Africa's coastal regions, for a number of reasons. First, little archaeological research has been conducted in West Africa's coastal societies. According to Olga Linares, who has examined the archaeological remains left by Jola rice farmers in the Casamance area of present-day Senegal, the acidic nature of coastal soils favors decomposition of many fossilized materials. In addition, agricultural practices in which coastal farmers cyclically turn over the soil have resulted in the disruption of fossils and artifacts interred in the earth.[28]

Second, archaeological studies and European travelers' accounts are not the only sources lacking for West Africa's coastal region. Historians have collected and interpreted oral traditions to reconstruct the history of many parts of Africa and for early time periods in African history for which written sources are not available. The overwhelming majority of these studies were conducted among states in which oral traditions played a critical role in legitimizing political authority. Among stateless societies, the oral traditions preserved are fragmentary because stateless societies lack a single locus of political authority and thus lack social institutions for orally transmitting historical information.[29]

In coastal Guinea for example, young men learned historical information from their male elders in the "Sacred Forest," the institution in which elderly men socialized boys in the rites and responsibilities of adult men and heads of households. As a result of a violent Islamization campaign waged in 1956–57 by Sekou Toure—the first independent president of the Republic of Guinea—the institution of initiation no longer functions as it once did. When I conducted fieldwork in 1997–98, I interviewed some of the few remaining elderly men who had been initiated into the "Sacred Forest." Recent work by David Berliner is an important first step toward identifying and repairing the chain of transmission in Guinea's coastal societies.[30]

Indeed, the state of written sources for pre-colonial coastal Guinea is but a minute example of a much larger methodological vacuum in the history of pre-colonial Africa and of some periods in the history of the African Diaspora. With so many obstacles and challenges, it is no surprise that the early history of rice farmers in West Africa's Rice Coast has not been told. Without it, historians have an incomplete understanding of what skills enslaved Africans who originated in the Rice Coast region contributed to plantation economies in the New World.

For historical periods pre-dating written sources, the problem may at times seem insurmountable. Africanist historians, such as Christopher Ehret, Jan Vansina, David Schoenbrun, and Kairn Klieman, have turned to the comparative method of historical linguistics to reconstruct the early pre-colonial history of East, Central, and Southern Africa.[31] Their pioneering scholarship has led to a proliferation of archaeological research in the region, consequently leading to more historical linguistics studies, a very productive cycle indeed. Telling historical narratives pre-dating written sources, which would otherwise be lost, is what drives this historian to adopt linguistic methodologies.

For several reasons, this study is the first to apply the comparative method of historical linguistics to reconstructing the early pre-colonial history of West Africa's coastal region.[32] First, the overwhelming majority of Atlantic languages spoken in Guinea's coastal littoral are understudied and poorly documented in comparison to the Bantu language group of Eastern, Central, and Southern Africa where a plethora of research using historical linguistics has taken place. When I conducted fieldwork in 1997–98, only a handful of researchers and missionaries had previously recorded coastal Guinea's Atlantic languages.[33] Second, historians employing linguistic methodologies in other regions of Africa have compared their findings to those of independent archaeological studies, very few of which are available for the coastal littoral of West Africa's Rice Coast region. The lack of archaeological studies conducted in coastal West Africa south of Senegal places limits on what the comparative method of historical linguistics can tell a historian about coastal dwellers' ancient past. Thus, many of the independent streams of evidence that historians of Southern, East, and Central Africa have compared to linguistic evidence are absent for coastal Guinea. For all of these reasons, the practice of using historical linguistics to reconstruct West Africa's early history remains in its infancy. It is hoped that this pioneering effort will inspire other scholars of all disciplines—particularly archaeologists, botanists, and marine biologists—to conduct independent studies that will enable future historians to add flesh to these bones.

Having established why the comparative method of historical linguistics is essential to the telling of this story and how it makes this study unique, the remainder of this section will be devoted to a discussion of theories underpinning the method. To historians employing the comparative method of historical linguistics, words are sources for every facet of society for which its members have designated a name. Clusters of vocabulary words give historians clues about who an ancestral speech community was, where and how they lived, what kinds of things they were familiar with, what they valued, which other groups they interacted with, and how they transformed their practices, institutions, and worldview in response to internal and external factors. For some parts of the world and for the earliest periods of history, including the early history of stateless societies of West Africa's coastal region, words are currently the only sources available to reveal these otherwise unrecoverable stories.

Because linguistic evidence is comprised of words from the mouths of generations of people, the speech communities which spoke the words in the past and present are the central actors in any study employing the comparative method. Their words contain a fascinating indigenous and inherently social history. By analyzing words spoken by present-day speech communities and published in dictionaries, ethnographies, and travelers' accounts, historians use linguistic tools to reconstruct the social history of the distant past.

Languages are particularly powerful tools of historical reconstruction, because each language is comprised of its own system of sounds. The human vocal cords are capable of producing a limited number of vowel and consonant sounds. At some point in time, speakers of each individual language subconsciously select an even smaller number of vowel and consonant sounds with which to communicate with one another. They also select their own set of rules governing the combination of these sounds. No two languages possess an identical set of sounds and rules. These are the basic building blocks of every language.

Throughout the evolution of a language, its speakers will alter both the sounds and the rules. The choices of a language speaker or a speech community—people who communicate with one another or are connected by chains of speakers who communicate with one another[34]—to change the systems governing their language are usually subconscious acts[35] with profound implications. These subconscious choices are usually precipitated by decreased contact and communication among speakers of the same language. If, for example, a group migrates and/or otherwise loses frequent contact with villagers who speak their language, the language will evolve differently in the separate locations. This process results in dialect divergence. At that stage, however, the two groups can still understand each other. After the passage of more time during which the two dialects evolve separately, the two dialects cease to be mutually intelligible. Two separate languages are born. A historical linguists' work can then begin.

An explanation of the technical operations of the method follows, drawing on the familiar example of Indo-European languages to demonstrate key concepts of the method. Readers must always keep in mind a principle difference between Indo-European languages and language groups in Africa and between applying the comparative method of historical linguistics to Indo-European languages—as it was initially intended—and applying it to language groups in other areas of the world. Indo-European languages possess long histories of written documentation, with versions of the languages dating back more than one millennium. Comparative linguists use these written documents for language classification. However, when dealing with unwritten languages, such as the Atlantic languages in West Africa's coastal region, written forms, when available, were recorded by missionaries and colonial officials in the last two or three hundred years. We must rely heavily on collecting samples from fieldwork among present-day speakers.[36] Thus, this comparison is in no way meant to equate Indo-European and Atlantic languages. Instead, its purpose is to give nonspecialist readers a familiar point of reference.

The historical linguistic method can only be applied to genetically related languages descended from a common linguistic ancestor. Portuguese, Spanish, Italian, and French, for example, are descended from the same ancestral language, Latin. Old High German, Old Saxon, Old Low Franconian, and Anglo-Frisian (which diverged into Old English and Old Frisian) are descended from an ancestral Germanic language.[37] In West Africa, the genetic relationship of "Atlantic" languages is less straightforward. Since the 1960s, linguists have debated whether or not "Atlantic" is a genetic, merely a typological, or a geographic grouping. Most of the debate is centered on the low cognate percentages exhibited by many Atlantic languages.[38] The latest research, however, has confirmed a genetic relationship among the languages in question and has produced better documentation and detailed morphological analyses of subgroups within the Atlantic language family.[39] This study will not delve into the debate on the genetic relationship among Atlantic languages spoken in the Rio Nunez region, as that topic has received in-depth treatment in other publications.[40] The Nalu, Mbulungish, Mboteni, and Sitem languages, whose speakers inhabit the Rio Nunez region and whose words are the foundation of this study, are part of the Atlantic language group.

Since a group of genetically related languages by extension descended from a common linguistic ancestor, the languages in question also share their building blocks, a system of sounds, and regular rules of sound change. A preponderance of evidence from languages worldwide reveals the existence of regularities in sound changes in genetically related languages. Language speakers often subconsciously change sounds that are more difficult to articulate in the mouth to sounds requiring less effort to produce. These small adjustments make languages more efficient.[41] As individual languages diverge from their common linguistic ancestor, the regular sound changes among them correspond to the sound changes in other languages to which they are genetically related.[42] Sound correspondences provide a genealogy of how daughter languages have changed.

Because language groups possess their own set of sounds and their own rules for combining them, sound change will also be specific to the language group in question. Linguists analyze a small sample of "core" vocabulary words in order to identify words with similar meanings and sequences of sounds, shared by pairs of languages—*cognates*—and to determine a language group's regular rules of sound change and sound correspondence.[43] "Core" vocabulary words are common grammatical words *(the, and, is)*, numerals *(one, two, three)*, kinship terminology for close family members *(mother, father, brother)*, parts of the body *(head, neck, mouth)*, elements in nature *(rock, rain, cloud, tree)*, and common verbs *(to eat, drink, sleep, die)*, to name a few examples. Cross-culturally, these core vocabulary words are less likely to be changed or borrowed from neighboring languages and are thus the most stable words in a language.[44] Because of the paucity of documentation for the languages of coastal Guinea, I collected core vocabulary lists from Nalu-, Mbulungish-, Mboteni-, Sitem-, Landuma-, Temne-, Susu-, and Jalonke-speakers during my fieldwork. See Appendix 1 for a list of my fieldwork interviews.

Throughout their evolution, languages develop different sets of sound correspondences and other grammatical features. Linguists begin to categorize genetically related languages possessing remnants of a common ancestral language, a set of regular sound correspondences and cognate vocabulary, as linguistic subgroups. Linguists use these grammatical features and sets of sound correspondence to distinguish linguistic subgroups within an ancestral language's genealogy. For example, Germanic languages inherited an inflectional system from their Proto-Indo-European ancestral language. Languages in the Germanic linguistic subgroup used inflected word endings to denote case distinction, gender, and number, but its Old English daughter languages lost these grammatical features.[45] Atlantic languages spoken in the Rio Nunez region are classified in two separate linguistic subgroups: Nalu, Mbulungish, and Mboteni languages forming the "Coastal" subgroup, and Sitem, Temne, and Landuma forming the "Highlands" branch of the Mel subgroup.

Linguistic subgroups have intrinsic historical reality and profound historical importance because their language speakers possessed common practices, values, and institutions at a distant period in time. Historians can search linguistic evidence, archaeological and botanical studies, oral traditions, travelers' accounts, ethnographies, and other available interdisciplinary evidence to reconstruct the social history of speech communities who spoke languages in a particular linguistic subgroup. This study will reconstruct the strategies for surviving in the coastal environment innovated and shared by Coastal and Highlands linguistic subgroups, the linguistic ancestors of present-day speech communities in the coastal Rio Nunez region.

After performing these technical operations, historical linguists then examine a second set of words, "cultural" vocabulary, for regular sound correspondences. According to a preponderance of cross-cultural evidence, cultural vocabulary words name such phenomena as social, political, cultural, and ritual institutions and practices. In contrast to core vocabulary words, cultural vocabulary is more vulnerable to change when language speakers no longer find the information described by the words relevant to their present condition and/or when they come into contact with speakers of another language.

Because of the paucity of published sources for coastal Guinea's languages, it was necessary for me to collect cultural vocabulary lists of approximately three thousand words each in Nalu, Mbulungish, Mboteni, and Sitem, and smaller vocabulary lists in Landuma, Temne, Susu, Jalonke, and Balanta languages during the course of my fieldwork. Reports of these interviews are also listed in Appendix 1. When it was available, I also supplemented my own data with published and unpublished wordlists and dictionaries. To elicit the cultural vocabulary related to coastal rice technology, I traveled to coastal villages inhabited by Nalu-, Mbulungish-, Mboteni-, and Sitem-speakers for each stage of the rice-growing process, where I became a student of elderly rice farmers, male and female. When men's associations prepared the rice nurseries and fields, the strict gendered division of labor did not permit me to participate, so I observed and asked questions. In addition, I labored with women and girls as a part of work associations sowing, pulling up, and transporting the germinated rice seedlings; transplanting them into the fields; guarding the rice from predators; harvesting; and processing the rice. I collected the cultural vocabulary through participation observation and fieldwork—and I mean this literally—under either blazing sun or blinding rain, standing in stagnant water sometimes up to my knees with my lower back bent at a most unnatural angle, and removing blood-sucking leeches from my fellow female farmers' legs as the conditions necessitated. (I cannot even begin to describe the mosquitoes!) This study examines cultural vocabulary related to, but not limited to, the coastal environment and rice cultivation.

Depending on whether or not it possesses regular sound correspondence, a cultural vocabulary word, such as those of the examples I collected in coastal Guinea, falls into one of three categories. It is either inherited from a linguistic ancestor, innovated by a linguistic subgroup in the language's genealogy, or borrowed from another language. Each category of words possesses intrinsic historical value because it provides clues as to how the speakers' practices, values, institutions, and relationships with neighboring groups have changed over time.

First, when daughter speech communities find that the information the words describe is relevant enough to their present situation to keep, they retain inherited vocabulary words. These inherited words usually possess regular sound correspondences. For example, the presence of inherited vocabulary words for *plow* and *furrow* among some Indo-European languages sparked a debate over whether or not proto-Indo-European-speakers were agriculturalists. Traditionally, scholars viewed these distant linguistic ancestors of modern English-speakers as nomadic or semi-nomadic people who possessed some domesticated animals and wheeled vehicles. This view was based on the existence of inherited vocabulary words for domestic animals and their by-products, parts of vehicles, and an absence of vocabulary for agriculture.[46] An examination of words that Nalu-, Mbulungish-, and Mboteni-speakers, on the one hand, and Sitem-speakers, on the other, inherited from their proto-Coastal and proto-Highlands linguistic ancestors respectively illuminates their processes of adapting to, and thereby transforming, their coastal and upland environments.

A second category of cognate vocabulary, which does not possess regular sound correspondences, may have been innovated by a linguistic subgroup in the language group's genealogy. Daughter speech communities internally generate new vocabulary. For different reasons—migration, environmental change, warfare, and disease are but a few examples—speech communities choose to break with the past and to create new institutions, practices, and material culture. For historians, innovations are important signals of the kinds of change societies have undergone. An examination of cultural vocabulary words reveals the development of a coastal rice knowledge system and its relationship to ancient coastal land-use strategies. The innovated words describe agricultural technology that Nalu-, Mbulungish-, Mboteni-, and Sitem-speakers fabricated together.

Finally, borrowed vocabulary is an important source for determining the nature of interaction between speech communities. When speech communities come into contact with one another, they exchange institutions, material culture, and practices, as well as the words used to name them. For example, the English language borrowed vocabulary at various stages in its evolution. In the early Old English period, it borrowed a number of words from Greek and Latin related to Christianity. During the Viking conquest, Old English-speakers borrowed a small number of ordinary vocabulary words from Scandinavian languages, even core vocabulary words for body parts, common nouns, and family relationships. During the Norman Conquest, the Old English language borrowed a larger number of French vocabulary words. As opposed to employing commonly used core vocabulary borrowed from the Scandinavians, Old English-speakers borrowed vocabulary words of a cultural, political, and social nature from French-speakers. The difference in the everyday words Old English borrowed from Scandinavian and the prestige words Old English borrowed from French reflects differences in the interaction between Old English-speakers and Scandinavians as equals versus the interaction of Old English-speakers as cultural and political subordinates to French conquerors.[47] In the Rio Nunez region, loanwords are evidence of contact between Atlantic speech communities, inhabitants of the coast, and Mande speech communities, which migrated to the coast from the interior.

These are the building blocks of the comparative method of historical linguistics. Chapters 2 through 5 will use these tools to reconstruct the deep roots of the coastal rice knowledge system in West Africa's Rice Coast. To begin to measure the antiquity of these roots—coastal land-use systems and tidal rice-growing systems—this study will employ a subset of the historical linguistic method, glottochronology.

Glottochronology was developed to give absolute dates to linguistic subgroups within a language group's genealogy. This chronological calibration was elaborated on the basis of European languages for which copious written records are available. It measures *the patterned accumulation of individually random change among quanta of like properties.*[48] Glottochronology uses a mathematical constant to measure the cumulative effect resulting from the individually random changes occurring on the vocabulary of a proto-language. From this figure, historians and anthropologists infer an approximate length of time since the divergence of linguistic subgroups.

Since its inception, some linguists and historians have been critical of glottochronology. Certain linguists question specific aspects of the method, such as whether the rate of word replacement could be the same in all of the world's languages from the beginning of time to the present and whether word loss and grammatical change can be measured before a particular linguistic threshold.[49] Others object specifically to lexicostatistics, cognate counts, and family trees; this school of thought argues that the time depth of language divergence can be overestimated if cognates go unrecognized because of sound change. Conversely, time depth can be underestimated if chance similarities and borrowed words are wrongly identified as cognates. These linguists also continue to question the simplicity of language trees, which do not represent the continued effect languages have on each other even after they have technically "split."[50]

Glottochronology has also become a bone of contention among historians of Africa who employ the comparative method of historical linguistics. Among Africanist historians who pioneered the comparative method, Jan Vansina objects to the use of glottochronology and to the premise that words in all languages are replaced at a steady rate. Instead, Vansina advocates using the relative chronology of language divergence that the comparative method itself yields from the genealogy of languages. Language groupings with higher cognate percentages are more closely related and diverged from their linguistic ancestor more recently. Language groupings with lower cognate percentages are less closely related and existed as one language at an earlier period in time. It is well known that languages diverge from each other slowly, taking centuries for adjacent dialects to turn into languages that are no longer mutually intelligible. Vansina advocates estimating that half a millennium elapses between one level of a language's genealogy and the next. But these estimates would remain unconfirmed.[51]

A second group of Africanist historians, including Christopher Ehret and David Schoenbrun, has continued to use and to refine the method. Ehret, in particular, demonstrated correlative chronologies from linguistic evidence and pottery traditions in languages throughout Africa. In a recent study, he reviewed empirical linguistic and archaeological data in four language families in four different regions of Africa to test for correlation between dates generated by glottochronology and dates generated by archaeology. Over a 10,000-year period, Ehret found that the two methodologies independently generated similar rough dates. Over a 1,000-year period of individual random changes, the language families in Africa shared 74 percent of their retentions. However, critics of glottochronology continue to question the underlying assumptions, because Ehret does not test his findings against a third independently generated chronology.[52]

Despite criticism of the method, dates generated by glottochronology are only one stream of data that must be compared to independent evidence from other sources. Scholars of the Bantu in East and Central Africa who use glottochronology do not use it in isolation. They rely instead on correlations between sequences of change—in the formation and dissolution of language groups; the birth, growth, and dissolution of pottery traditions; and in the pace and character of change in vegetation communities and climate regimes—dated by radio carbon and thermoluminescence studies. Whereas linguistic sources provide indirect evidence of, and relative dates for, ancestral speech communities, archaeological and environmental studies provide direct evidence and absolute dates for the historical developments of ancestral communities[53] that would otherwise be unavailable for time periods pre-dating written sources. In East, Central, and Southern Africa, this collective body of work reconstructs the social history of a large portion of the African continent for millennia before the recording of the first written sources; it does so by examining independent and interdisciplinary evidence.

At the current stage of research, the Rio Nunez region of coastal Guinea lacks chronologies from interdisciplinary data sources, particularly archaeology. Hence, this study can strictly speaking only use relative dating and can only approximate the absolute involved. One way of giving the reader at least an idea of the order of magnitude of the time spans involved is to compare the genealogy of coastal Guinea's linguistic subgroups to the European situation. For this purpose, the study will cite glottochronological estimates. Readers must realize that the dates are unconfirmed and are only comparative estimates employed to help readers visualize the time depths involved.[54] Until independent confirmation is available for the Rio Nunez region from interdisciplinary evidence, the dates generated by glottochronology must be considered provisional.

Given the authority and power of calendar dates, particularly for historians accustomed to dealing with documents, it is imperative for this historian to emphasize that the dates cited in this study and generated by glottochronology are provisional. Some readers, particularly linguists, may discount the importance of the study because of its reliance—out of necessity—on a single source of dating. Other readers, particularly historians, may discount the provisional nature of the dates, treating them as they would dates confirmed against independent sources—or worse yet, as guild historians would treat calendar dates. Neither action is desirable. The intent of the study is to begin to understand the time depths involved in coastal farmers' innovation of coastal land-use strategies and tidal rice-growing technology.

In addition to linguistic data, the forthcoming narrative presents biological and botanical studies on mangrove ecosystems and coastal land-use change whose employ is unique to the historical linguistic literature. Together, the two independent streams of historical evidence reveal the antiquity of coastal settlement and rice-growing technology in the Rio Nunez region and provide the tools to reconstruct its development. The combination of the two independent streams of evidence makes a unique contribution to an innovative body of historical research.

To historians of other regions of the world who are accustomed to dealing with dates and documents, the sources used in this study—cultural vocabulary words, sound changes, scientific studies of mangrove vegetation, and oral traditions—may seem unorthodox, nontraditional, and even anthropological. (We Africanist historians have been called worse!) The paucity of written sources discussed throughout this chapter is not at all unique to coastal

Guinea. The absence of sources written by Africans is the norm for the overwhelming majority of the continent and for the overwhelming majority of the continent's history before the colonial—if not the independence—period. Thus, out of necessity, nontraditional sources and interdisciplinary methods have become traditional among Africanists since the decolonization of African history in the 1960s.

Telling the important story of the antiquity of innovation in West Africa's Rice Coast creates an unusual opportunity for dialogue between specialists and nonspecialist readers of Africa and the African Diaspora. This study will seize this rare opportunity to discuss methodological challenges faced by all Africanist historians and the methods used by some Africanists to reconstruct history where written sources are by and large absent and/or one-sided when available. There are similarities to the challenges faced by historians of African-descended peoples in the Diaspora. Like the inhabitants of coastal West Africa, the overwhelming majority of Africans enslaved in the New World did not leave journals, diaries, or other documents about their lives, and written with their own hands. Where documentation is available, the authors' commercial interests and notions of race and gender shaped their interpretations. This lack of documentation, however, neither indicates a lack of dynamic cultures and innovative technology before the arrival of Europeans among West Africans, nor a lack of vibrant cultures and communities even under an oppressive social system among enslaved Africans. It does require historians to fashion new tools to reconstruct and understand them. Through examining new kinds of sources and employing interdisciplinary methods, this study will serve as a model for scholars of all regions for reconstructing history of historical periods and of groups that did not leave a proverbial paper trail.

Despite the tentative and controversial nature of glottochronology, which is after all a subset of the method, the application of the comparative method of historical linguistics to Atlantic languages in coastal Guinea empowers this historian to tell an important and untold story. Though the story is framed by sources written by European traders, it is not dependent on them. The comparative method reveals a relative chronology: the antiquity of coastal settlement and coastal land-use systems in the Rio Nunez region and coastal dwellers' subsequent evolution of the coastal rice knowledge system. The comparative method also provides the tools with which to reconstruct their development. Neither Samuel Gamble nor other slave traders who purchased rice and/or captives in the Rice Coast region's ports could have imagined how the area's farmers developed their agricultural technology. Nor would they imagine how coastal innovators launched an indigenous agricultural revolution whose effects were felt most keenly on the opposite side of the Atlantic

Ocean. Other histories have not unraveled the details of this important story, because written sources are not the proper tools for reconstructing the early history of West Africa's coastal region. This fascinating indigenous history has been waiting to be told.

Chapter Summaries

Chapter 1 examines the history of African rice, details what is currently known and what remains unknown, and surveys the rich literature on West African rice farmers. It argues that by focusing on one portion of the West African rice knowledge system—tidal rice-growing technology—and one environment of the landscape gradient—coastal estuaries, floodplains, and mangrove swamps—this study will provide a better understanding of how West African farmers developed the underlying principles of their indigenous knowledge system. It also discusses why the Rio Nunez region is an ideal location that allows us to expand and deepen our knowledge on innovation in West Africa.

Chapter 2 focuses on the earliest inhabitants of the coastal Rio Nunez region, proto-Coastal-speakers, and the in situ divergence of their language c. 3000 to 2000 BCE. By reconstructing inherited vocabulary related to the coastal landscape, this chapter demonstrates Coastal-speakers' establishment of the roots of tidal rice-growing technology and the genesis of coastal land-use systems. Lastly, based on areal innovations, chapter 2 argues that after the divergence of proto-Coastal, its Nalu, Mbulungish, and Mboteni daughter speech communities deepened their knowledge of the coastal environs, c. 2000 BCE to c. 500 CE.

Chapter 3 focuses on the Sitem-speaking newcomers to the coastal Rio Nunez region, highlighting their important contributions to the coastal rice knowledge system. In contrast to the in situ divergence of Coastal languages, migration was a contributing factor to the divergence of Highlands, c. 500 to 1000 CE. Proto-Highlands-speakers migrated into coastal Guinea from the forest-savanna region in the interior, bringing with them critical knowledge about the forest-savanna. Chapter 3 also presents linguistic evidence for words related to iron in the proto-Highlands language and explores the probability that proto-Highlands-speakers possessed indigenous iron ore deposits, but simultaneously lacked iron-smelting technology.

Chapter 4 highlights the collaboration of the daughter speech communities of Coastal (Nalu, Mbulungish, and Mboteni) and Highlands (Sitem) languages across linguistic boundaries, which resulted in the genesis of the coastal rice-growing knowledge system, c. 1000 CE to c. 1500 CE. Borrowed vocabulary from proto-Highlands into Nalu, Mbulungish, and Mboteni for mounds/ridges, cutting down trees, wooden fulcrum shovels, and the *D'mba* headdress, for example, suggests that Coastal daughter speech communities—the earliest inhabitants of the region—appropriated Highlands speech communities' knowledge from the forest-savanna region and applied it to the coastal region. The presence of specialized vocabulary in Atlantic languages within the Rio Nunez region is evidence that tidal rice-growing technology was an agricultural revolution indigenous to Atlantic speech communities inhabiting the coast.

Chapter 5 focuses on a stage of coastal rice-growing technology that transformed West Africa's coastal littoral: mangrove rice production. It introduces loanwords related to rice cultivation as evidence of contact between the new owners of the land, Nalu-Mbulungish-, Mboteni-, and Sitem-speakers, and Mande strangers from the interior, Susu-speakers. The interdisciplinary evidence is clear. Iron-edged tools from the interior did not define coastal rice-growing technology. On the contrary, it gave coastal dwellers the means to extend their indigenous coastal land-use system into red mangroves. In addition, the localness of agricultural technology uniquely designed by coastal farmers who spoke Atlantic languages for fluctuating microenvironments in West Africa's Rice Coast region facilitated the transmission of West Africa's rice-growing techniques to similar microenvironments across the Atlantic.

Chapter 6 discusses the importance of the West African Rice Coast to trans-Atlantic trade in provisions and captives. It begins by focusing on the expansion of markets in Rice Coast ports as a result of trans-Atlantic trade and the expansion of coastal trade in rice to meet the new demands. In addition, chapter 6 applies the largest compendium of documented and studied slaving voyages to date from *The Trans-Atlantic Slave Trade: A Database* to the question of whether a greater number of Africans who disembarked in South Carolina and Georgia originated in the West African Rice Coast region or West Central Africa. It suggests ways in which we can go beyond demographics to understand the impact of enslaved laborers who originated in the West African Rice Coast had in South Carolina and Georgia.

1

The Rio Nunez Region: A Small Corner of West Africa's Rice Coast Region

The West African Rice Coast spans the region from the Senegal River in present-day Senegal to Liberia.[1] After establishing a trading post off the coast of Mauritania and discovering the uninhabited islands of Cape Verde, Portuguese traders had become well acquainted with the region south of the Senegal River by 1460. In the minds of the European traders who shaped the first written documents of the region, trade in cereals as opposed to production of cereals defined the West African Rice Coast throughout the period of trans-Atlantic commerce. Distinct from the Grain Coast or Malaguetta Coast,[2] the Rice Coast fits within the West African region that was named the Upper Guinea Coast by Walter Rodney.[3] This study will use the terms interchangeably—*Rice Coast* when discussing rice and rice farmers and *Upper Guinea Coast* when discussing other social, political, and economic phenomena within the region.

The Rice Coast also forms a small portion of a larger West African region stretching from Senegal in the north, the lower Niger Delta of Nigeria in the south, and Lake Chad in the east. Not only do the inhabitants of this broader region consume rice as a staple crop, but they have also adapted specialized technology—shifting cultivation, intercropping, transplanting, and building embankments around and ridges within their rice fields, for example—to grow rice in eighteen distinct microenvironments. In addition, within the region where rice is grown West African farmers utilize eleven systems to irrigate their rice crop with three water sources: groundwater, rainwater, and tidal flow. As a result of centuries of experimentation before the advent of trans-Atlantic trade, African farmers have learned to manipulate this malleable plant species to flourish in a landscape gradient of challenging and constantly fluctuating tropical environments.[4]

Several environmental features are common to the coastal littoral of West Africa's Rice Coast region, an area riddled with rivers and small streams along the breadth of its coastline. Coastal soils are an enigma—they are waterlogged by brackish water much of the year as well as saturated with iron.[5] On the one hand, marine tides flood mangrove swamps and low-lying areas at the base of coastal rivers with brackish water to the point where a high proportion of the swamps are permanently saline. On the other hand, the tides also deposit fertile organic matter in the heavy clay soils, known throughout the region as *poto-poto*. Though rich in fertile alluvium, coastal soils also have a high concentration of acidity and sometimes acid sulphate. Without submersion with freshwater—in this case rainwater—coastal soils would produce acidification and mineral toxicity at intolerable levels for plant species.[6] All of these factors make the coastal littoral of the Rice Coast environmentally distinct from West Africa's interior where rice was domesticated.

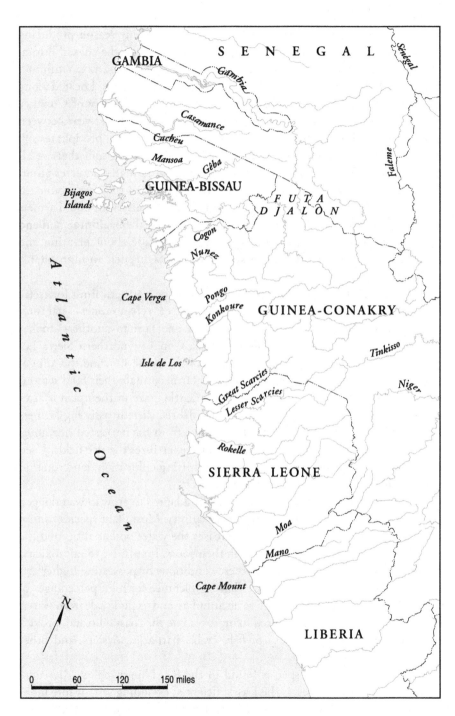

MAP I.I. Rice Coast/Upper Guinea Coast

The entire coastal farming system hinges on the rainy season producing torrential rains and seasonal flooding. In an average year, the coastal littoral of West Africa's Rice Coast region receives between 2,000 and 3,000 millimeters of rainfall in a season spanning approximately six months. Located along the coast south of the Rio Nunez region, Guinea's capital city of Conakry received an annual average of 2,079 millimeters of rainfall per year between 1982 and 1991.[7] The intensity and short duration of the season precipitates soil erosion, a process that washes away valuable nutrients from soils that are already nutrient-deficient. The timing and amount of rainfall fluctuates annually; sometimes rains are sparce while at other times they are abundant enough to kill the rice crop, ruining a farmer's precarious livelihood. Farmers are especially vulnerable when rainfall is unreliable at the beginning and end of the rainy season, when decisions are typically made about planting and harvesting.[8] Not many other plant species can grow in such an inhospitable environment.

West Africa's Rice Coast region bifurcates at the northern limit for tsetse flies and lowland mangrove forests. The presence of trypanosomes—parasites that carry and spread trypanosomiases from one host to another—makes cattle-keeping untenable in southern Guinea-Conakry, northern Sierra Leone, and central Liberia.[9] However, north of the tsetse fly zone the annual rainfall averages 1,000 millimeters, and rice farmers rotate their land seasonally between rice fields and cattle pastures. Cattle graze in the uplands after the harvest to clear the land of stubble and debris, thereby assisting farmers with preparation of the rice fields. The stubble from the harvested rice nourishes the cattle; at the same time, cattle manure fertilizes the rice fields. Used in conjunction with burning, clearing, and shifting cultivation, land rotation works to manage the fertility of upland fields.[10]

African rice and mangroves are specifically adapted to grow in waterlogged soils and to tolerate varying percentages of salinity. Most plant species cannot tolerate salinity, because its toxicity increases the water potential beyond the amount that plants can absorb through their roots. Insensitive to salt toxicity, mangroves are uniquely adapted to these conditions by possessing higher cellular water potential. All mangroves have a tolerance for high percentages of salt in their tissues and the ability to accumulate and exclude salt from waterlogged soils. The aerial roots of red mangroves line the coastal littoral, providing a habitat for a rich variety of fish, crabs, barnacles, oysters, and other marine life.

Of the two mangrove species found in the Rio Nunez region, *Avicennia africana,* white mangroves, is the least efficient at excluding salt. White mangroves secrete salt through their roots and salt glands, and then the voided salt evaporates and crystallizes. *Rhizophora racemosa,* red mangroves, the

second species common to the region, void some salt through their leafy surface, and their aerial roots have evolved to obtain the oxygen necessary for
respiration even in water-logged soils. *R. racemosa* mangroves pay a high
price, however, for their insensitivity to salinity by sacrificing rapid growth
for salt tolerance. Taking up water and excluding salt requires greater root
mass, which they grow at the expense of leaves and tall branches.[11]

Like red and white mangroves, African rice, *Oryza glaberrima,* has also
evolved to withstand a certain percentage of salinity in coastal soils. *O. glaberrima* grows in the most marginal of environments where high percentages
of salinity, iron, and acid, and low amounts of phosphorus, are found in the
soils. This is particularly important for coastal farmers whose subsistence was
and is dependent on decreasing the percentages of salinity in the soil by
maintaining a delicate balance between fresh and brackish water. Rainfall
fluctuations, which often plague the coastal littoral of West Africa's Rice
Coast, can easily tip this balance in favor of salinity. Even in the twentieth
century, some tidal rice farmers planted *O. glaberrima* in the most marginal
areas of their rice fields and were rewarded with good yields, if relentless birds
and other predators did not eat their crop first.[12] An excess of salinity, however, is the enemy of all rice. Uniquely adapted to Rice Coast soils, *O. glaberrima* has a long history within the West African Rice Coast region. It is to
this history that we now turn.

The History of African Rice:
What Is Known and What Remains Unknown

In West Africa, the story of African rice begins not on the coast, but in the
interior. *Oryza glaberrima,* the rice species indigenous to West Africa, was
domesticated in the inland Niger Delta of present-day Mali. There botanist
Roland Portères found the greatest diversity of both wild and domesticated
varieties, as well as of floating, semifloating, and subfloating varieties of *O.
glaberrima.* Based on this evidence and on the diversity and distribution of
contemporary African rice varieties, Portères identified the Inland Niger
Delta in present-day Mali as the region whose inhabitants adapted to their
savanna environment by drawing on the largest pool of potential domesti-
cates in the *O. glaberrima* species.[13] Archaeologists Roderick J. McIntosh and
Susan Keech McIntosh found *O. glaberrima* in the lowest levels of excavated
areas of Jenne-Jeno, dating back as far as 300 BCE to 300 CE. These are the first
reliable dates for the domestication of African rice.[14]

However, there is currently no consensus among scholars on how inhabitants of the savanna domesticated African rice or how farmers adapted the rice

to suit other environments. Despite its influence, Portères's work left questions unanswered about the processes by which inhabitants of the savanna domesticated *O. glaberrima*. Experimentation in the uplands and floodplains may not be unrelated to the processes of domestication. Jack Harlan, in particular, diverged from Portères's diffusionist approach, arguing instead that it is impossible to locate a center of cereal domestication in Africa because cereal domestication was an ongoing and slow process rather than a singular event. On the basis of botanical evidence, Harlan argued that cereal domestication resulted from noncentric experimentation, intensification, and manipulation of wild plants by populations in vast expanses of territory, probably over long periods of time.[15]

Cultivation was only the beginning of the domestication process that resulted in West African farmers adapting *O. glaberrima* to the diverse landscape gradient where it is cultivated today.[16] Subsequent to the domestication of *O. glaberrima* in the freshwater wetlands of present-day Mali, farmers selected traits in the rice species amenable to physical environments with different soils, rainfall levels, and vegetation types in the savanna where African rice was domesticated. Portères identified two contrasting environments as centers of "secondary diversification" where West African cultivators diversified *O. glaberrima*. In the highlands bordering present-day Guinea, Sierra Leone, and Liberia, farmers selected traits that flourished in rain-fed uplands. In the coastal floodplains and mangrove swamps on both sides of the Gambia River of present-day Senegal, farmers selected traits in the species pool that grew in soils waterlogged by brackish tides.[17] Although the story of West African rice begins with domestication in the interior, it by no means ends there.

Along the coast south of the Gambia River centuries before the advent of the trans-Atlantic slave trade, West African farmers honed their rice-growing skills in a landscape gradient ranging from dry hillsides and uplands to coastal floodplains and mangrove swamps. Through experimentation and adaptation, West African farmers learned to evaluate the quality of soil and vegetation in their fields, identify suitable rice varieties, and adapt planting and irrigation techniques to the soil, vegetation, and water level of their fields. These skills are the science behind the "West African rice knowledge system." In the coastal region alone—representing just one portion of the landscape gradient in which West African farmers grow rice—farmers have innovated seven different irrigation systems for cultivating rice in as many distinct coastal environments.[18] Though it is part of the continuum of experimentation and adaptation, coastal technology is both unique to the coastal littoral and distinct from cultivation in uplands and freshwater swamps. Thus, West African farmers' experimentation in and adaptation to the coastal littoral is an important and unique story.

Though *O. glaberrima* is indigenous to West Africa, it is not the rice species primarily grown by West African rice farmers today. *Oryza sativa*—the rice species indigenous to Asia—is. West African farmers had developed farming systems for cultivating *O. glaberrima* prior to incorporating Asian rice species into their arsenal of land-use strategies. Scholars continue to debate how African farmers gained access to *O. sativa*. According to Joseph Lauer, Muslim traders from North Africa as early as the tenth century—or Portuguese traders as late as the sixteenth—transported the first varieties of Asian rice to West Africa.[19] In contrast, Judith Carney has argued that the seeds traveled via nonhuman vectors—animals, particularly elephants, wind, and possibly water. Paul Richards suggests that the Mende, who live in northeastern Sierra Leone, tell stories about elephants dropping dung, which contained undigested grain, as they migrated throughout the region.[20]

Human agency was certainly at work, however, when African farmers experimented with new Asian rice species.[21] As seed selectors, African women in particular played important roles in choosing Asian rice species over their African competitors, primarily because Asian rice yields more. Secondarily, Asian rice is easier to process by hand or machine. The grains of many African rice species are dark red, black, or smoky in color and tend to shatter when milled mechanically.[22] Ease in processing and mechanical milling became a critical advantage when West African women and enslaved women began producing "cleaned" rice for commercial European markets. For the purposes of subsistence production, *O. sativa* has its disadvantages, however. Although it yields more, it cannot grow in the most marginal coastal soils with high percentages of salinity and acidity as *O. glaberrima* does.[23]

Recent literature on West African rice farmers highlights the social transformations that societies in one of Portères's secondary centers of diversification—the coastal floodplains south of the Gambia River—have undergone as a result of cultivating rice in mangrove swamps. According to Walter Hawthorne, making the transition from cultivating yams to paddy rice enabled the Balanta of present-day Guinea-Bissau to relocate to inaccessible swamps and to minimize the effects of slave raiding on Balanta society. The Balanta's shift in production necessitated significant transformations of age-grades, their most fundamental social institution. The labor-intensive task of clearing the mangroves became the responsibility of young unmarried men whose labor was mobilized and controlled by senior men. Cultivation of paddy rice also transformed the economy of Balanta societies, making them participants in an "iron–slave" cycle. Balanta villagers traded surplus rice to Luso-African traders in exchange for iron to make knives, swords, arrows, and spears for defensive and offensive slaving pursuits and tools for agricultural production.

Olga Linares's research among Jola rice farmers in the Lower Casamance region of present-day Senegal examines the relationship between religion and economic change. Linares found shifts occurring along various fault lines—gender, age, and status—as a result of Islamization, "Mandingization," and intensification of the cash crop economy. In the three Jola villages in which Linares conducted her fieldwork, the effects of conversion to Islam were uneven and unpredictable. The proximity of the Jola villages to Mande cultural practices deeply influenced the degree to which Islam reduced the role of spirit shrines regarding death and disease, replaced cultivation for rice subsistence agriculture with cash crop production, and circumscribed women's power in the household.

The Rio Nunez region of coastal Guinea, which is the location of this study, is also situated in the floodplains south of the Gambia River. This study traces the Rio Nunez region inhabitants' evolution of tidal rice-growing technology as an organic part of their coastal land-use strategies. The deepest roots of these processes begin millennia before the advent of the trans-Atlantic slave trade, Islamization, and Mandingization. As a result of archaeological and botanical research in the inland Niger Delta of present-day Mali, the early history of the region where *O. glaberrima* was domesticated is relatively well known. In contrast, due to a lack of archaeological and botanical research on the coast, much less is known about the early history of secondary centers in which African farmers manipulated African rice to suit rain-fed or floodplain environments. Before bringing interdisciplinary sources and methods to bear on reconstructing the early history of coastal Guinea, we will take a look in the following section at the Rio Nunez region.

The Rio Nunez Region and Its Inhabitants

This study focuses on one small corner of the West African Rice Coast, the Rio Nunez region. Beginning on the edge of present-day Guinea-Conakry, the Nunez River and its tributaries cascade to the coast from its source at the foothills of the Futa Jallon Mountains in Guinea's interior. Annually, the river swells with the torrential downpours of the rainy season, creating seasonal streams, floodplains, and inland swamps. As the Nunez River passes through the highland plateaus bridging the extremes of the mountains and the sea, it deposits rich alluvium in coastal floodplains. The mouth of the river empties out into the Atlantic Ocean, the tidal flow of which reaches almost seventy miles upriver.[24] Tidal flooding of low-lying areas deposits silt and saline along the banks of the Nunez.

During the rainy season, the flow of the tides and of the river, swollen by seasonal flooding, virtually submerge many sparsely inhabited coastal villages. Today in the dry season, many villagers travel by boat once, possibly twice, per week to regional markets where they sell surplus rice, salt, and palm oil. However, during the rainy season several consecutive days of torrential rains pound loudly enough on a tin roof to drown out polite conversation and wash away dirt roads and footpaths. Unable to travel or even to communicate with their neighbors, villages in the Rio Nunez region, particularly those still accessible only by boat or canoe, can remain isolated for significant periods of time during the rainy season each year.

Two ethnic groups, the Nalu and the Baga, inhabit the floodplains and mangrove swamps of the region. In 1993, some 40,000 Baga inhabited both banks at the mouth of the Componi River, the Nunez River, and along the coastal littoral of Guinea between the Componi River in the north and the Conakry peninsula in the south. Numbering approximately 10,000 in coastal Guinea, the Nalu live upriver on the left bank near the head of the Nunez River.[25] Their villages also stretch north into present-day Guinea-Bissau. These ethnic designations, however, belie a much more complicated reality of identity among coastal inhabitants.

Coastal dwellers who identify themselves ethnically as Baga actually speak several languages, some of which are only distantly related. Though in the past, groups who today identify themselves as Baga actually spoke up to six languages, this study deals with just three.[26] Beginning north of the Nunez River, the Sitem[27] (Baga Sitem) inhabit islands off the left bank and the mainland on the right bank. The Mboteni (Baga Mboteni) inhabit only two small villages on a peninsula at the tip of the right bank. The Mbulungish (Baga Mbulungish) are settled to the southwest of the Sitem and Mboteni between the right bank of the Nunez and Cape Verga.[28] The study will use the term *Baga* only when referring to coastal identity; otherwise, it will use linguistic terminology such as Mbulungish-, Mboteni-, and Sitem-speakers.[29]

The Nalu, Mbulungish, Mboteni, and Sitem languages, which are spoken in the coastal Rio Nunez region and whose speakers are the subject of this study, belong to the Atlantic language group of the Niger-Congo language family. Today the territory where Atlantic languages are spoken stretches from the northwest—the Senegal–Mauritania border—to the southeast—the Sierra Leone–Liberia border. Atlantic languages number approximately thirty and vary in size; for example, Fulbe, Serer, Temne, and Wolof are rapidly expanding in the interior. These speech communities possess more than one million speakers. On the coast, Banta, "Baga" Kalum, and "Baga" Koba, have disappeared or are rapidly disappearing.[30] At the time of my fieldwork in the Rio Nunez region from 1997 to 1998, I estimate that less than 100 people living in two adjacent villages—the only two villages in the world where the Mboteni language is spoken—spoke Mboteni fluently. Mbulungish

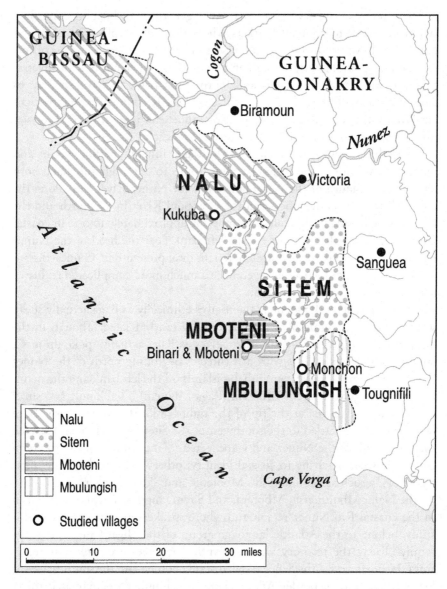

MAP I.2. Rio Nunez Region and Present-Day Ethnic/Linguistic Boundaries

probably possessed fewer than 500 speakers. Though Nalu and Sitem speech communities were slightly larger, possibly numbering a few thousand, these languages should still be considered in danger of extinction.

Language contact with rapidly expanding Atlantic and Mande languages—Mande is a second Niger-Congo language group within the Upper

Guinea Coast—has played an important role in the evolution of Atlantic languages in West Africa's coastal region. First, travelers' accounts recorded by the "Portuguese" describe the majority of Atlantic speech communities as isolated and surrounded by seas of Mande speech communities. In many areas, Mande expansion has pushed Atlantic speech communities into inhospitable and noncontiguous areas. Today, the overwhelming majority of Atlantic speech communities inhabiting the coast and the interior are separated—and in many cases surrounded—by Mande speech communities.[31] The beginning of language contact between Atlantic and Mande speech communities predates the end of the fifteenth century. Second, for speakers of Cagin spoken in Senegal and Mmani, Sherbro, Krim, and Bom spoken in present-day Sierra Leone, bilingualism in another Atlantic language—Wolof and Temne respectively—has eroded the number of children who learn these endangered Atlantic languages as their primary language.[32]

Due to this confluence of factors, extinction for some Atlantic languages within a few generations is a very real danger. For example, in the Rio Nunez region, many young people from isolated coastal villages move to cities and towns for schooling and employment and learn to communicate in Susu—the Mande language that has become the lingua franca of coastal Guinea. Not only are Atlantic languages currently dying, but a lack of traffic from European traders, missionaries, and colonial administrators means that Atlantic languages have historically been infrequently recorded or documented. Atlantic languages spoken in West Africa's Rice Coast region, including but not limited to coastal Guinea's Rio Nunez region—and the history and culture of these rice-growing people—are in danger of dying and potentially passing from the historical and linguistic record in the next generation or two.

Though Nalu, Mboteni, Mbulungish, and Sitem are distinct and endangered languages, some measure of common cultural identity unifies coastal dwellers in the Rio Nunez region.[33] In the first written sources recorded for coastal Guinea, "Portuguese" traders identified these three elements—rice cultivation, salt production, and practice of indigenous spiritual traditions—as common to the inhabitants of coastal Guinea, and juxtaposed them against the identity of Susu and Fulbe traders from the interior who had embraced Islam earlier in their history. Rice, salt, and the practice of indigenous spiritual traditions are also important characteristics among inhabitants of West Africa's Rice Coast region further north in present-day Senegal, Gambia, and Guinea-Bissau, lending credence to George Brooks's assertion: more than ecology distinguishes the Upper Guinea Coast as a region.[34]

Tidal Rice-Growing Technology in the Rio Nunez Region

Rice cultivators on the coastal littoral of West Africa's Rice Coast have adapted to waterlogged soils and brackish water, like the sprawling roots of red mangrove trees. Coastal inhabitants uniquely designed tidal rice-growing technology to maintain a vigilant balance of salinity in coastal soils by trapping fresh water and allowing it to wash the salty soils until they became "sweet." Though today coastal farmers primarily use the system with *Oryza sativa* varieties, tidal rice-growing technology was originally designed for *O. glaberrima* rice varieties indigenous to West Africa's Rice Coast region.

Samuel Gamble's 1793–94 journal describes a comprehensive and complex tidal rice-growing system dependent on tides to alternately flood and drain rice fields along floodplains of rivers and estuaries and mangrove swamps. First, Gamble observed Rio Nunez farmers planting rice seeds in nurseries located on higher and drier ground, then allowing them to germinate. Second, once the seedlings reached a stage at which they could withstand inundation and small percentages of salinity, coastal farmers replanted them in the rice fields. Third, coastal farmers constructed an intricate irrigation system of dikes and canals, mounds and ridges, to trap fresh water. They used irrigation to reduce the level of salinity in the soil, enabling the rice seedlings to flourish. Reclaiming swamps from inundation by salt water with drainage and protecting the reclaimed farmland from the ever-threatening brackish water, played key roles in the farming system Gamble described. Tidal rice-growing technology practiced today among the coastal inhabitants of Guinea's Rio Nunez region is strikingly similar to the 1794 description of mangrove rice-farming. The remainder of this section will describe the tidal rice-growing techniques that I both observed and recorded from interviews with male and female rice farmers of coastal Guinea's Rio Nunez region.

To establish a new mangrove field, male farmers use the fulcrum shovel to create "dikes," large embankments—one meter high and wide—of packed earth around the perimeter of floodplain or mangrove swamp fields. The embankments act to block the entrance of brackish water and to collect precious fresh water inside the fields. The men also manipulate the wooden shovel to dig drains, which farmers use to control the level of fresh water in the fields. The sculpted metal blade of this tool is specifically designed to cut the tangled roots of red mangrove trees and to turn waterlogged, muddy clay soils. After laying the foundation for a new rice field, particularly a new mangrove rice field, coastal farmers leave it lying fallow for several years, collecting fresh rainwater and allowing it to leach the salt out of the soil. On average, it takes five to seven years for the percentage of salinity in a mangrove field to decrease to a level tolerable to African rice species. The growth of certain weeds indicates the presence of a "sweet" swamp where rice will grow.

Today in the Rio Nunez region, farmers repair earthen embankments but seldom need to construct them, because they farm the same fields year after year unless forced to abandon a mangrove rice field due to severe rainfall shortages over several years. Instead, coastal farmers begin cultivation by clearing secondary vegetation from floodplains and mangrove swamps using the fulcrum shovel. Along the region's coastal estuaries, the beginning of the rainy season inaugurates the agricultural and ritual cycles and marks the beginning of the period of intensive fieldwork.

Though they frequently acquire small quantities of rice seeds from neighbors and family members, Rio Nunez region farmers obtain most of their seeds from the previous year's harvest. The different varieties must be carefully separated and the seeds conserved. If they are not separated carefully, the mixed varieties will mature at different times, making it almost impossible for farmers to defend their crops from birds. After the rains begin, male farmers prepare the nursery plots located in the village or in areas of the fields that do not receive an excess of sunlight or collect rainwater; they do so by clearing the weeds and turning the soil with a fulcrum shovel. When the nursery plots are ready, Rio Nunez farmers submerge the rice seeds in water overnight and then plant them in the rice nurseries. They remove the seeds the next day, spread them between banana leaves, and allow the seeds to germinate for two or three days. If the ground is soft, the women broadcast the germinated seeds onto the nursery plots. If, however, the ground is hard, they make holes in the earth with digging sticks or their fingers, drop in the seeds, and cover them by massaging the earth with their hands. The rice seeds are left to mature in the nurseries for thirty to forty days, depending on the variety. Family members take turns guarding the precious rice seedlings from predatory birds as the plants develop in the nurseries.

As the rice sprouts and begins to mature in the rice nurseries, coastal farmers start to prepare their fields for cultivation. The men use the fulcrum shovel to turn the soil inside of floodplain and mangrove fields, building "ridges," small embankments of earth within the rice fields. Farmers dig the ridges side-by-side, extending the width of the fields. As with the dikes, coastal farmers use the ridges to collect fresh water inside the fields. The men use wooden shovels to cut the weeds, to divide the small embankments of earth, and to turn the soil. If the weeds are too tall, young men and boys walk on them to press them into the earth. Working in pairs, one man picks up and turns over a heavy shovelful of wet earth, while a second man simultaneously packs the earth in place with his hands. The second man uses his hands to push the weeds into earth, and then the two men walk over the new ridges,

pressing the earth and weeds together with their feet. After the first period of clearing, farmers allow the weeds to compost in the fields for a week or two, making a natural fertilizer for the rice. Then they turn the earth and the weeds a second time, using the same methods.

After thirty to forty days, the women transport rice seedlings from the nursery to the rice fields and transplant them. First they pull up the seedlings, being careful not to damage the roots, and gather bunches of seedlings in their hands. Holding the rice seedlings in one hand and flicking their wrists in a quick downward motion, they hit the roots against their legs, shaking out any dirt or insects. Then they comb their fingers through the heads of the rice seedlings to remove any dry stems or stalks. Lastly, they tie the rice seedlings together into bundles, using a piece of cord or one seedling. In some villages, the women put the roots of the seedlings in water overnight to repair the damage done by pulling up the rice.

Young women and girls transport baskets of bundled rice seedlings to the fields for replanting. By this time in the rainy season, heavy and continuous downpours have left knee-high water in most fields, softened the soil, and facilitated composting. However, if the earth is not soft enough, older women walk on the bunds to soften them and use digging sticks to make holes in the earth. Younger women follow them, breaking apart the bundles of rice and pushing the seedlings into the earth using their fingers.

After planting, coastal farmers survey the fields almost constantly, ensuring that there is enough rainwater covering the rice, that insect and animal predators have not devastated their crop, and, most importantly, that salt has not seeped into the soils and killed their crop. If there is too much water in the fields, the men evacuate some of it by opening the drains. Approximately two and a half months after planting—depending on the variety that has been planted—the entire family chases birds from the fields. Every morning for roughly two weeks, the head of the household goes to the fields before dawn, armed with a slingshot and other weapons to scare the birds. Soon thereafter, accompanied by the children of the household, particularly babies

FIGURE I.I. *Above facing:* Photograph of "Fieldwork: Two Young Men Compete Against Each Other Turning the Soil with Fulcrum Shovels." Copyright Edda L. Fields-Black.

FIGURE I.2. *Below facing:* Photograph of "Fieldwork: Father and Son Work Together. One Turns the Soil with the Fulcrum Shovel. The Other Tucks Weeds into the Soil." Copyright Edda L. Fields-Black.

and toddlers who are still nursing, the women transport cooking pots and eating utensils to the fields. There they spend the day until dusk in makeshift huts, using bows, arrows, slingshots, and noisemakers, making scarecrows, and uttering high-pitched screams to scare birds and other predators away from the rice.

For many villagers, this period in the agricultural cycle is one of great hardship and deprivation. By this time, most households have exhausted the rice from the previous year's harvest. Yet also during this time, coastal farmers spend many hours working and have very little food to eat. For these reasons, inhabitants of the Rice Coast region call this period of the agricultural cycle the "hungry season" or the "period of suffering."

At the beginning of the rice harvest, the women of the household reap small quantities of rice by hand, just enough for one day's rations. After drying the harvested rice in the sun, the women "dance" on small piles of it, rubbing the rice against straw mats with their feet to separate the rice grain from the stalk. Then they peel rice harvested for the day's provisions with a mortar and pestle to remove the husk. Lastly, the women fan the beaten rice with woven baskets or fanners, tossing it into the wind and allowing the wind to blow away the chaff. To harvest the remainder of the rice crop, boys and girls grab bunches of rice with one hand and use sickles and knives to cut it with the other.

A month or so after the harvest, the men thresh the remainder of the rice to separate the grains from the straw. In some Rio Nunez villages, coastal farmers prepare an open area in the village or in the fields by covering the ground with clay. In most villages, however, Rio Nunez region inhabitants sweep the ground well and transport the large bunches of harvested rice to the threshing area. The younger men begin threshing the rice by swinging waist-high batons over their heads and bringing them down onto the piles of harvested rice. The elderly men follow, using similar motions, but swinging shorter, lighter batons. After the rice has been beaten, the women process it by peeling and fanning it in the same manner as they processed the daily rations.[35]

The agricultural cycle ends with the arrival of Fulbe herders and traders from Futa Jallon and their herds of cattle. Today, farmers in coastal Guinea's

FIGURE I.3. Photograph of "Sowing: Woman Pulls up Rice Seedlings." Copyright Edda L. Fields-Black.

FIGURE I.4. Photograph of "Sowing: Women Transplant Rice Seedlings." Copyright Edda L. Fields-Black.

FIGURE 1.5.
Photograph of "Temporary Shelter
Built in Rice Fields during Hungry
Season." Copyright Edda L.
Fields-Black.

FIGURE 1.6.
Photograph of "Woman Guards
Rice Fields from Birds with
Slingshot." Copyright Edda L.
Fields-Black.

FIGURE 1.7. Photograph of "Girl Processes Daily Ration of Early Rice."
Copyright Edda L. Fields-Black.

FIGURE 1.8. Photograph of "Elderly Women Fan Rice with Basket." Copyright Edda L.
Fields-Black.

FIGURE 1.9. Photograph of "Mother and Daughter Peel Rice in Mortar and Pestle." Copyright Edda L. Fields-Black.

Rio Nunez region, like their counterparts along the Casamance River in present-day Senegal, use cattle to eat the stalks remaining in their rice fields after the harvest. Rio Nunez farmers then spread the cattle manure as fertilizer in the rice fields.[36] Because the Rio Nunez region is located in the southern part of the Rice Coast region and below the tsetse fly line, it is infested with trypanosomes. This factor determines the primary difference between coastal farmers' rotation of rice fields and pasturelands in coastal Guinea and in present-day Senegal's Casamance region, located in the northern part of West Africa's Rice Coast. In the Rio Nunez region, the Fulbe arrive with their herds at the end of the dry season but vacate the coastal swamps before the first rains.

The Rio Nunez region is an interstice between the tidal rice-growing technologies practiced in the northern and southern portions of the West African Rice Coast—the Senegambian and Sierra Leonean slaving ports of the Upper Guinea Coast. The tidal rice-farming system practiced by farmers in the Rio Nunez region included and still maintains agricultural techniques found in both the northern and southern portions of the Rice Coast region. Thus, even though the Rio Nunez region is located below the limit of trypanosomes, its inhabitants practice land-use strategies found in both the northern and southern halves of the Rice Coast region.

Both the description above and Samuel Gamble's observations of the Rio Nunez region bear striking resemblance to methods used by coastal farmers throughout West Africa's Rice Coast region, particularly the Balanta of present-day Guinea-Bissau[37] and the Jola of Senegal.[38] The coastal inhabitants who have used knowledge of their inhospitable environment to design specialized agricultural technology to suit it also speak Atlantic languages. Like the Nalu, Mbulungish, Mboteni, and Sitem, most of their languages are threatened with varying degrees of extinction.[39] In these ways, the Rio Nunez region is a linguistic, cultural, and technological microcosm of West Africa's Rice Coast region.

The Rio Nunez Region and the Trans-Atlantic Slave Trade

The Rio Nunez is an important part of the West African Rice Coast region and, by extension, of the West African rice knowledge system. How important was it to the trans-Atlantic slave trade, the vehicle through which African captives from West Africa's Rice Coast region involuntarily transferred their indigenous agricultural technology to the Americas? The following section discusses this important question.

For centuries before the advent of trans-Atlantic commerce, the inhabitants of coastal Guinea engaged in salt production and traded the surplus with pastoralists in the interior. Salt, not rice, was the primary commodity exchanged in interregional trade networks for cattle, white cloth, and gold. Interregional trade networks attracted small populations of Susu itinerant traders to the region. Beginning in the sixteenth century, the Susu traded in their own locally produced commodities—iron and dyes—and acted as middlemen between coastal salt producers and Fulbe herders in Futa Jallon.[40]

The advent of trans-Atlantic commerce and the arrival of European and Euro-African traders on the coast redirected trade between the coast and the interior to the Atlantic market. The head of the Nunez River became the endpoint of caravan routes from Futa Jallon to the coast, carrying produce from the interior—ivory, rice, hides, gum, small amounts of gold, and captives. Fulbe traders bartered on the coast with European and Luso-African traders, primarily for salt.[41] European and Euro-African traders also assumed the role of intermediary in coastal commerce, exchanging locally produced commodities for manufactured goods and cloth. With the advent of Atlantic commerce, captives became an important commodity traded along the Nunez River.[42] Slavers were attracted to the region by the availability of a steady stream of captives, generated by Fulbe wars of expansion in the interior.

Local chiefs also facilitated commercial transactions by offering hospitality and protection in what scholars have come to call "landlord–stranger" relationships. Under these arrangements, local chiefs allowed traders to build or purchase a factory in their territory and gave traders freedom of movement within the area. In exchange, the stranger traders paid tribute to the landlord chiefs, entertained the chiefs at their own expense, and often produced future members of the royal lineages by marrying the chiefs' female relations or dependents. The local chief also inherited the goods of traders who died while residing in the chief's territory.[43] These social relationships—transformations of indigenous coastal customs—facilitated traders gaining relatively easy access to local commodities and became critically important to a region lacking a centralized political state to execute and regulate the trans-Atlantic slave trade.

By the early eighteenth century, the trans-Atlantic trade in captives was firmly implanted in the Rio Nunez region of coastal Guinea. Though Luso-African traders had been the first to introduce trans-Atlantic commerce to the region, a small community of factories emerged along the Nunez River beginning in the 1790s. In operation approximately between 1750 and 1791, Walkeria—in the town of Kacundy/Boké—was one of the largest factories on the river. Samuel Gamble disembarked in Iles de Los, an island off present-day Guinea, and took a smaller vessel north to Walkeria to purchase 250 captives.

A different pattern emerged fifty miles south of the Rio Nunez region along the Pongo River. European and American traders who were enmeshed in "landlord–stranger" relationships with local chiefs continued to dominate the trade. A small handful of European and American traders' descendants kept slave trading alive in the Rio Pongo region into the mid-nineteenth century, decades after the slave trade was abolished. The presence of seven small rivers and lagoons within the Rio Pongo region provided plenty of coverage for clandestine commercial activity.[44]

But overall, the sparsely inhabited Upper Guinea Coast was a minor player in the trans-Atlantic slave trade relative to densely populated regions further south along the Slave Coast and in West-Central Africa.[45] Within the Upper Guinea Coast, coastal Guinea received less direct traffic in slaving vessels compared to ports north in the Senegambia and south at the Iles de Los and Bance Island. According to the *Trans-Atlantic Slave Trade Database,* only fifteen ships are recorded as having purchased captives in the Rio Nunez between 1792 and 1837. None of these ships disembarked in South Carolina or Georgia.

In comparison, seventy-four slaving vessels docked fifty miles south along the Pongo River to purchase captives between 1794 and 1847. In the early nineteenth century, seventeen ships that embarked in the Rio Pongo transported captives to South Carolina.[46] Two prominent families have left documentation about operating plantations and producing rice in the Rio Pongo as well as in South Carolina: the Fraser family in Charleston and on Florida's East Coast, and the Lightburn family, also in Charleston.[47] It is clear that more research needs to be done on both sides of the Atlantic to understand the nature and extent of the connections between West Africa's Rice Coast region and the commercial rice industries of South Carolina, Georgia, and even Florida.

However, due to inconsistent record-keeping by slaving vessel captains, this low figure is misleading for several reasons. Historians are still not able to quantify the number of direct voyages that departed from the West Coast of Africa, where slavers purchased captives and sailed directly to the Americas. Because the ships were privately owned—not directly affiliated with companies or agents—and based in Africa, the records of some privately owned vessels were not preserved in the metropole and have been more difficult for historians to access.[48]

Second, slave vessel records frequently listed the Rio Nunez region as part of the Senegambia or the Sierra Leone region. According to the *Trans-Atlantic Slave Trade Database,* twenty-six slaving vessels voyaged to the Senegambia region and as far south as the Rio Nunez region to fill orders for captives between 1661 and 1824. Only one of these slaving vessels disembarked its captives in South Carolina, and none in Georgia. Between 1562 and 1845, 120 ships purchased captives in the Sierra Leone region from the

Rio Nunez to Cape Mesurado (in present-day Liberia). Seven ships from this southern region disembarked their cargo in South Carolina.[49] The intersection of the Senegambia and Sierra Leone at the Rio Nunez region mirrors the intersection of the two halves of West Africa's Rice Coast region in coastal Guinea.

In addition, captains of an untold number of slaving vessels that disembarked in the broader region from the Senegambia to Sierra Leone actually traveled to coastal Guinea to purchase a complement of captives. Samuel Gamble's *Sundown,* which embarked in the Iles de Los, is just one example. His slaving vessel embarked in the slave-bulking center where fresh water, provisions, skilled workers, and a steady supply of captives were usually available, and subsequently sailed north to the Rio Nunez region to fill his complement of slaves. Only after historians have culled the records of the English factories, which operated out of the Rio Nunez region, the records of direct voyages, and the private collections of descendants of trading families operating out of the Rio Pongo—if in fact such documentation still exists—will historians have a more complete understanding of the magnitude of the trans-Atlantic slave trade in coastal Guinea.

As a result of the trans-Atlantic slave and provision trades and their production and sale of surplus rice to Susu villages in the region's uplands and to European traders,[50] the Baga gained a reputation as quintessential rice farmers. The Baga's agricultural technology and one slave trader's recording of it make the Rio Nunez critical to understanding the development of the West African rice knowledge system in the Rice Coast region and the transmission of West African rice-growing and processing techniques to the New World, even though the number of slaving vessels visiting the region did not.

Conclusion

This study could draw a number of parallels to connect the Rio Nunez region of coastal Guinea to the coastal regions of South Carolina and Georgia. First, South Carolina and Georgia—plagued with their long and intense rainy seasons, which bred mosquitoes and mosquito-borne illnesses like malaria and yellow fever—could be called the "White Man's Grave" of the southern American colonies. Samuel Gamble's crew may not have fared much better had they disembarked in Charleston or Savannah instead of the Iles de Los in 1794. Second, there is contemporary evidence that the Gullah language, an English-based Creole language developed by enslaved Africans in coastal South Carolina and Georgia and their African-American descendants, has in recent history been in danger of language death, as are Atlantic languages spoken on West Africa's coast from Senegal to Sierra Leone. These important parallels will not be the focus of this study. This story is instead about the deep roots—African roots—of adaptation, innovation, and technology.

Though the Rio Nunez is just one of many rivers and ports in West Africa's Rice Coast region, coastal Guinea's Rio Nunez region is the ideal place for telling this important story. Neither its soils nor its farmers were more productive than those of other rivers within the region. This study is not claiming that the majority of African captives who disembarked in South Carolina and Georgia, and subsequently labored on rice plantations in these colonies, originated in this one, small river region. Although this subject will be discussed more in chapter 6, I must reiterate here and now that I am not at all asserting this. Why, then, is the Rio Nunez region an ideal location to trace the deep roots of tidal rice-growing technology in West Africa and the transfer of this technology to the Americas? The answer lies where the story began, with Samuel Gamble's 1794 description of mangrove rice-growing techniques among the "Baga" Sitem.

So struck was Samuel Gamble by the agricultural technology he found at the mouth of the Rio Nunez region that he made a detailed drawing of Baga farmers planting rice and of the embankments, mounds, and ridges used to irrigate their rice fields. Scholars of enslaved African and West African rice farmers have been so impressed by the similarities of Gamble's description and drawing to rice fields in antebellum South Carolina and Georgia that they have relied heavily on it. From Gamble's journal, historian Daniel C. Littlefield identified the West African origins of enslaved laborers on rice plantations in coastal Georgia and South Carolina.[51] Making reference to Gamble's description, Judith Carney illustrated the importance of mangrove rice-farming and its gendered division of labor to agricultural techniques, which enslaved Africans from West Africa's Rice Coast region transmitted and adapted to their new physical, social, and political environments on rice plantations in coastal South Carolina and Georgia.[52] Even though Samuel Gamble's slaving voyage had no direct connection to coastal South Carolina or Georgia—the captives whom he purchased were sold in Jamaica and not South Carolina or Georgia—his description and drawing of Baga farmers' agricultural technology has had a profound effect on the way scholars on both sides of the Atlantic have come to understand Africans' agency in the transfer of technology from West Africa to South Carolina and Georgia rice plantations. Gamble's influence can be traced to this: his eighteenth-century description of tidal rice-farming among the Baga is the mirror image—the "spitting" image—of tidewater rice production, which both became the colony's most lucrative crop and transformed South Carolina's coast by the 1770s. Closer examination reveals that the mirror's reflection shines in two ways.

Reflected first across the Atlantic is an image of tidal and tidewater rice production resulting from a culmination of rice farmers' adaptation to, and innovation in, a range of microenvironments from the uplands to the lowlands. Mangrove rice-farming represents a culmination of agricultural innovation because it is based on the land-use principles developed in earlier stages of experimentation and adaptation in the coastal estuaries and floodplains. Though Gamble's account of mangrove rice-growing technology appears to emerge out of a vacuum, it evolved out of West African farmers experimenting, adapting, and innovating along a landscape gradient of uplands, inland swamps, and tidal floodplains and mangrove swamps for more than a millennium.

Enslaved laborers and slaveholders in coastal South Carolina and Georgia undertook a similar process of experimentation, adaptation, and innovation with South Carolina soils, water sources, and water control. An as yet undetermined number of enslaved laborers on South Carolina plantations originated in West Africa's Rice Coast region. Their skilled labor played an important role in developing South Carolina and Georgia's commercial rice industries. In colonial South Carolina, rice production began also in the uplands, moved into the inland swamps, and culminated by the end of the eighteenth century in the salt marshes, tidal rivers, and swamps. One of this study's primary goals is to trace the earliest roots of rice-cultivation technology in a small coastal corner of the West African Rice coast region. Digging deep into coastal Guinea's early indigenous history to understand how Rio Nunez inhabitants acquired knowledge of their constantly fluctuating environment and innovated farming techniques to achieve sustainability in it holds important lessons for understanding how enslaved farmers in coastal South Carolina adapted West African rice-growing techniques in the New World.

Second, the Rio Nunez also mirrors South Carolina and Georgia in these terms: who were the innovators of tidal rice-farming technology and how have historians perceived them? After thirty years of research by Peter Wood, Daniel Littlefield, and Judith Carney, there is little credibility to notions that enslaved Africans did not play an important role in the transmission of rice cultivation and processing technology to and in the development of commercial rice production in South Carolina and Georgia's lucrative rice industries—indeed, they were skilled, not just brute laborers. Work remains to be done on understanding the processes of agricultural synthesis that occurred between enslaved Africans and slaveholders, each with their own agricultural experience and needs—for subsistence and commercial economy respectively.[53] This conclusion begs the question of whether or not African ingenuity ends when European American engineering begins.

Our study will explore this question by looking across the Atlantic and into the mirror of tidal rice-cultivation in coastal Guinea's Rio Nunez region. It will argue first and foremost that floodplain and mangrove rice farming has its deepest roots on the coast, not in the interior, and that it was developed by Nalu-, Mbulungish-, Mboteni-, and Sitem-speakers who themselves have deep roots on the coast, not by Susu-speaking migrants from the interior. Coastal dwellers' experimentation, adaptation, and innovation laid the foundation for the evolution of tidal rice-farming systems.

It will also argue that at various points in their history, groups of coastal inhabitants incorporated and collaborated with different groups from the interior uplands who spoke both Atlantic and Mande languages. In most instances, coastal dwellers tutored first Sitem- and then Susu-speaking neighbors from the interior on flourishing in the coast's inhospitable environment. In other instances, coastal inhabitants borrowed key land-use strategies first from their Sitem- and then subsequently their Susu-speaking neighbors; these methods helped them strengthen the foundation of their coastal rice-farming system. The incorporation of technology from the interior also enabled coastal dwellers to extend their tidal rice-farming system to other coastal micro-environments and to produce surplus rice for a commercial industry. By tracing the depth and antiquity of the roots of innovation in West Africa's Rice Coast, we will indicate that collaboration and borrowing with neighbors from the interior—appropriated, transformed, and perfected by South Carolina and Georgia slaveholders and overseers—does not expunge the importance of tidal rice-farming technology as indigenous to and deeply rooted in West Africa's coastal littoral.

In *Black Rice: The African Origins of Rice Cultivation in the Americas,* Judith Carney has argued convincingly that separating parts of the West African rice knowledge system and portions of the landscape gradient along which West African rice farmers adapted *O. glaberrima* obscures the indigenous knowledge system's underlying principles. This kind of segregative thinking has prohibited scholars on the American side of the Atlantic from fully appreciating Africans' agency in transferring this "indigenous knowledge system" to the Americas. In addition, it has limited scholars' understanding that African captives throughout West Africa's Rice Coast region—not just those originating in Sierra Leone or embarking at Bance Island where the surviving documents are copious and detailed relative to other ports in the region—were potentially both the inheritors and the transmitters of West African rice-growing technology.

But what if, for the sake of argument and scientific investigation, one did separate one portion of the West African rice knowledge system and one environment of the landscape gradient? In order to gain a better understanding of how West African farmers developed the underlying principles of their indigenous agricultural technology, separating one portion of the West African rice knowledge system—tidal rice-growing technology—and one environment of the landscape gradient—coastal estuaries, floodplains, and mangrove swamps—is exactly what this study intends to do. I am suggesting that the Rio Nunez region is the perfect location in which to do it. The result is a fascinating history of highly specialized and intensely localized experimentation, adaptation, and agricultural innovation, which this study will show has deep roots in the coastal littoral of West Africa's Rice Coast region.

2

The First-Comers and the Roots of Coastal Rice-Growing Technology

A Foulah [Fulbe] law protects [the Baga] from foreign violence (being the producers of salt, this is their prerogative). Salt is guarded in the Interior as one of the greatest necessities of life, and its makers are under the safe-guard of this law. (Theophilus Conneau, *A Slaver's Log Book or 20 Years' Residence in Africa*, 103

Though *Oryza glaberrima* was domesticated in the inland Niger Delta and is indigenous to West Africa's Rice Coast region, does it have deep roots in West Africa's coastal floodplains? Can its cultivation be traced to the earliest coastal settlement? Millennia before the advent of the trans-Atlantic slave trade, the linguistic ancestors of present-day Nalu-, Mbulungish-, and Mboteni-speakers inhabited the coastal Rio Nunez region. This chapter will discuss their settlement of the coast and will consider whether or not the region's first settlers possessed knowledge about "Black rice."

Throughout West Africa's Rice Coast, the evolution of coastal rice-growing techniques is embedded in the indigenous history of the region. In addition to evolving out of pre-existing land-use systems, coastal agricultural innovations also grew organically out of the movement of the region's speech communities, the physical changes that the micro-environments underwent, and the speech communities' adaptation to, and interaction with, these micro-environments. Reconstructing coastal farmers' development of coastal rice knowledge systems requires digging deep into the indigenous history of West Africa's Rice Coast region.

As the indigenous history of Atlantic speech communities in coastal Guinea is currently written, it privileges migration and migrants from the interior as the vectors of change and innovation on the coast. In the Rio Nunez region, the story of coastal innovation is even a story within a story. In oral traditions, coastal "Baga" and Nalu elders claim that their ancestors migrated to the coast from the interior. However, the scholarship on West African rice farmers has attributed important aspects of tidal rice-growing technology to Mande migrants from the interior. The current literature attributes innovation on the coastal littoral of West Africa's Rice Coast region to migration and diffusion.

This chapter will examine the earliest settlement of the coast and the lessons learned about the coast by the earliest settlers of the Rio Nunez region. By examining interdisciplinary sources, the chapter chronicles coastal dwellers' development of tidal rice-farming techniques as part of an intricate land-use system designed to minimize famine and to ensure food security. It expands our historical knowledge further back in time than the period covered in European travelers' accounts, which have predominated coastal West Africa's pre-colonial historiography.

A paucity of written source materials pre-dating the sixteenth century necessitates utilizing interdisciplinary sources and methods. Linguistic evidence allows us to establish the degree of relationship among genetically related languages spoken in coastal Guinea today, to generate a chronology of the divergence of ancestral languages into daughter languages, to locate where ancestral languages were spoken in the past, and to reconstruct words from the proto-languages once spoken by the linguistic ancestors of present-day speech communities. It provides the earliest evidence of innovation for the coastal littoral of West Africa's Rice Coast Region.

From Coast to Coast: Linguistic Evidence for the Earliest Settlement of the Rio Nunez Region

In coastal Guinea, generations of scholars, both during the colonial period and after independence, have collected oral traditions among Baga and Nalu elders about the founding of their coastal villages. Major synthetic works on the history of Guinea have also based their interpretation of coastal Guinea's history on these oral traditions. In many ways, these oral narratives have established the standard for the ways that many coastal elders, colonial officers, and scholars have understood the history of Guinea's coast.

In short, the traditions consist of several interlocking elements. First, coastal elders posit their ancestors' origins in the "East." Occasionally, the traditions cite Mecca or Sudan as the homeland of the Nalu or Baga.[1] More commonly, they locate "Futa"—Futa Jallon and various villages therein—and claim that their ethnic groups were the original inhabitants—before the Jalonke or the Fulbe—of these regions.[2] Second, coastal elders claim that their ancestors were motivated to leave the east and to migrate west, because their refusal to convert to Islam precipitated a deterioration of relations between themselves and incoming groups, particularly the Fulbe, who had already converted. Recorded in the early colonial period and based on oral accounts, J. Figarol's monograph states:

> They came from Labe [Futa]. It has been around 100 or 150 years. A certain Sampeul refused to convert at once to Islam, took refuge in the Nunez and created the village Katako [which means] "I will stop here."[3]

In a second tradition, retold in the Sitem village of Kawass and recorded in 1998, an elder uses "dance" as a powerful metaphor for indigenous spiritual traditions, which Baga and Nalu villagers continued to practice until Sekou Toure's forced Islamization campaign in 1956–57:

> The Sitem left Futa, because they did not have the same religion as the Fulbe. The Fulbe were practicing the Islamic religion. Then, the Baga were not practicing Islam. They were practicing idolatry. They adored idols. They practiced fetishism. The two [Islam and "fetishism"] cannot stay together. When one

adores the unique God and the others *dance,* this cannot go together like that. So, God aided the Fulbe to defeat the Baga, because the Fulbe were right.[4]

Despite the passage of almost one hundred years—the transition from colonial rule to independence and from indigenous spiritual practice to Islamic conversion—the core elements of these traditions bear a strong resemblance to one another.

In *Art of the Baga,* Frederick Lamp drew on the meta-narrative retold by many coastal elders in his argument that the Baga brought their ancestral spirits, age-grade ceremonies, and spectacular masquerade traditions—all of which were ended, or at least driven underground by the 1956–57 Islamization campaign—to the coast when they fled Futa Jallon to avoid conversion to Islam. According to Lamp, the Temne of present-day Sierra Leone, whose language is closely related to Sitem, share similar oral traditions.[5] Lamp's influential work spurred a firestorm of scholarly interest on the subject. Ramon Sarró-Maluquer interpreted the oral traditions as evidence of the Baga defining their identity in binary opposition to Islam, slave raiding, and the pre-colonial Islamic Fulbe state of Futa Jallon, which played an important role in propagating Islam and slave raiding throughout the coastal region. Sarró-Maluquer stressed the centrality of the mangroves—though this locale is often minimized in discourse about the Baga's migration from Futa Jallon before the centralization of the state—in understanding the formation of Baga identity.[6] In a previous study, I argued that within the interior–coastal binary opposition, Baga and Nalu elders associate parts of their identity purely with the coast. For example, male elders described rice as a crop cultivated by their ancestors in the distant past in the interior, in places such as Futa Jallon. In contrast, they also described the fulcrum shovel as a farming implement fabricated by their ancestors to grow rice in the inhospitable coastal environment.[7] Scholarly attention and interrogation is complicating and even decentering the meta-narrative that claims the Nalu and Baga originated in the interior and migrated to the coast.

To be sure, even during the colonial period some researchers critiqued the narratives, pronouncing the Baga too well adapted to the coastal environment to be "mountain men," or immigrants from Futa Jallon.[8] In the most recent work to date, David Berliner argues instead that among the Mbulungish only the descendants of village founders retell traditions about migration from Futa Jallon. Other families claim to have originated in heterogeneous locales—other Baga villages, Guinea-Bissau, and Mali—from which they created the Baga Mbulungish language and culture on the coast.[9] By collecting and examining oral traditions passed down in the region's lineages throughout coastal Guinea and Sierra Leone, and not just those of village founders, scholars will better understand the dynamics of settlement and identity formation among coastal inhabitants.

Linguistic evidence paints a divergent image of the settlement of coastal Guinea. On the one hand, the key elements of oral traditions—the binary opposition between the interior and the coast, the Nalu and Baga's refusal to convert to Islam, and their indigenous spiritual practices versus the interior's conversion to Islam and the Islamic state of Futa Jallon—cohere to form a common cultural identity uniting some Baga and Nalu families. On the other hand, linguistic evidence—the core vocabulary—divides the Nalu-, Mbulungish-, Mboteni-, and Sitem-speakers into separate speech communities whose languages are not mutually intelligible. Whereas coastal elders stress their ancestors' migration from the interior, the core vocabulary is evidence that Nalu, Mbulungish, and Mboteni languages have deep roots on the coast.

Though Nalu, Mbulungish, Mboteni, and Sitem belong to the Atlantic language group, some of these languages are only distantly related. Relatively speaking, Nalu, Mbulungish, and Mboteni are more closely related to one another than any individual language is related to Sitem (the Sitem language and Sitem-speakers' trajectory to the coast will be discussed in chapter 3). Together, Nalu, Mbulungish, and Mboteni form a linguistic subgroup descended from a common ancestral language, which I have called proto-Coastal.[10] Glottochronology generates c. 3000 to 2000 BCE[11] as the approximate date when the linguistic ancestors of present-day Nalu-, Mbulungish-, and Mboteni-speakers spoke a common ancestral language.[12] The remainder of this section will examine linguistic evidence for the coastal settlement of the linguistic ancestors of present-day Nalu-, Mbulungish-, and Mboteni-speakers and the divergence of their languages.

Proto-Coastal diverged into three daughter communities between c. 3000 and 2000 BCE. Maurice Houis initially suggested that Nalu and Mbulungish were dialects of the same language.[13] Because the cognate percentages are almost equally low for all three languages—Nalu, Mbulungish, and Mboteni—I have argued elsewhere that the three Coastal daughter languages diverged simultaneously and became the present-day Nalu, Mbulungish, and Mboteni tongues.[14] Given the relative proximity of their present-day communities, the likelihood is small of these daughter communities having migrated from the interior or even having moved far to get to the present-day locations of their speech communities on the coast.[15] Because Nalu dialects extend north along the coast into present-day Guinea-Bissau, Nalu may possibly have diverged from proto-Coastal as a result of north–south movement of its speech communities along the coast, not east–west movement between the interior and the coast. In the Rio Nunez region, Nalu, Mbulungish, and Mboteni

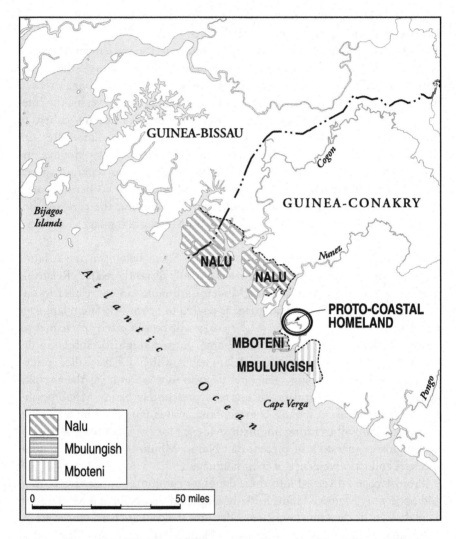

MAP 2.1. Proto-Coastal Homeland and Present-Day Locations of Coastal Languages

languages have diverged on the coast in situ. Rather than migration, two interlocking factors have likely been more important in the divergence of Coastal languages: the swampy nature of the coastal environment—divided by rivers and plagued with long and intense rainy seasons—and the isolated and remote nature of coastal settlements.

In West-Central Africa, many studies of the Bantu expansion have posited migration as the source of cultural and technological innovation.[16] However, Kairn Klieman's 2003 study of Bantu- and Batwa-speakers presents linguistic evidence of Bantu and Batwa languages diverging in situ without the earliest settlers of coastal and central West Africa moving far from the territories that they continue to inhabit today. Whereas natural boundaries, swamps, seasonal streams, and rivers likely contributed to Coastal languages diverging in situ, the introduction of new technologies and crops contributed to Bantu-speakers' economic specialization and to Bantu languages' divergence.

Klieman also proposes what she calls a "first-comer model" of interaction between Batwa-speaking owners of the land and Bantu-speaking migrants. First-comers founded frontier settlements and developed expertise about the land's flora, fauna, and territorial and ancestral spirits. Those groups who subsequently migrated into the territory valued the first-comers for their knowledge. Because migrant communities depended on the ability of the first-comers to ritualize territorial and ancestral spirits for their survival, they forged respectful relationships with the region's earliest inhabitants. Though first-comers were often incorporated into the communities of newcomers, they continued to be remembered and revered for "owning the land" and for possessing an intimate relationship with the spirits inhabiting it.[17]

As the first-comers to the Rio Nunez region, Nalu-, Mbulungish-, and Mboteni-speakers acquired knowledge of the flora, fauna, and wildlife of the region. Through experimentation and innovation, they developed subsistence strategies and ritual systems to ensure the survival of their communities in this flood-prone environment. Millennia before the migration of Sitem-speaking newcomers and Susu-speaking strangers, the coastal region's first-comers developed land-use systems that were important precursors to the evolution of the tidal rice knowledge system so eloquently described and illustrated by Samuel Gamble.

The Genesis of Coastal Knowledge:
Proto-Coastal-Speakers, c. 3000 to 2000 BCE

Given the deep roots of coastal settlement in the Rio Nunez region, much of the region's earliest history lies outside the scope of this study. However, our primary interest remains in determining whether or not these earliest coastal settlers were the innovators of tidal rice-growing knowledge systems. Does tidal rice-growing technology have deep roots in West Africa's Rice Coast region? To investigate this question, this section will examine the land-use strategies developed by coastal first-comers to survive in the harsh micro-environments of the coastal littoral and to ensure the maintenance of food security. It is left to our historical imaginations to envision the problems encountered by the earliest settlers as they faced the swampy, salty floodplains and mangroves of the Rio Nunez region—a microcosm of the coastal littoral of West Africa's Rice Coast extending north to present-day Senegal and south to Liberia. Even without historical record of their challenges, experiments, or decision-making, the end results have left imprints in both the written, linguistic, and environmental sources of this coastal region. In the absence of archaeological studies conducted in the Rio Nunez region, it is the linguistic, environmental, and written records on which we must rely, even for the most ancient history of coastal dwellers.

In his ground-breaking study, *Paths in the Rainforest,* Jan Vansina coined a methodology called "upstreaming" to reconstruct the history of a huge expanse of territory in Central Africa for historical periods before the arrival of Europeans and for which no previous historiography existed. First, Vansina used the earliest written documents for the region and oral traditions to chronicle major social and cultural features of Bantu societies before the advent of European influence in the late 1400s. Then he used regular sound correspondences to distinguish between three categories of cultural vocabulary: words inherited by daughter speech communities from their linguistic ancestors; words innovated as cultural, social, political, and economic circumstances changed; and words borrowed from their neighbors. Lastly, in this 1990 publication, Vansina used glottochronology to estimate the entrance of cultural vocabulary words into the daughter languages. Vansina used the region's first written documents as a baseline from which he employed linguistic sources to move backwards in time—swim upstream—to roughly five hundred years before the trans-Atlantic slave trade.[18]

This study employs Vansina's upstreaming approach to reconstruct the earliest history of coastal Guinea's innovators and their development of tidal rice-growing technology in the Rio Nunez region. Despite the limitations that were discussed in general in the introduction and the limitations of individual accounts that will be discussed in more detail, Portuguese travelers' accounts, the first written sources documenting West Africa's Upper Guinea Coast region, form the baseline. The study employs linguistic evidence and biological and botanical evidence of mangrove vegetation to swim upstream from the baseline to the earliest settlement of the coastal region. Inherited, innovated, and borrowed vocabulary words, in addition to environmental studies in mangrove ecosystems and land use, provide evidence for how coastal inhabitants created an indigenous agricultural revolution whose greatest effects were felt on the opposite side of the Atlantic. The study will purposefully keep the independent streams of interdisciplinary evidence separate and draw conclusions from the emerging patterns.

The trip upstream begins with salt and salinity, two of the most onerous challenges plaguing the coastal inhabitants of the Upper Guinea Coast region. Coastal soils are waterlogged by brackish water much of the year and saturated with iron levels which are toxic to many plant species. Even today in coastal Guinea, the ever tenuous balance between brackish and fresh water must be vigilantly maintained. If the rainy season begins late or the amount of rainfall is inadequate, the salt tide can creep into the rice fields, ruin the rice harvest, and destroy a family's precarious livelihood. After several years of diminished rainfall, a villager will be forced to abandon a mangrove rice field and subsequently invest large labor inputs to clear the vegetation to resume farming the field. He will then likely have to wait years before trapped fresh water decreases the level of salinity in the field to the point at which the field is "sweet" enough for rice to sprout again. Salt and salinity remain ancient threats with tangible implications in coastal farmers' everyday lives.

The trip upstream also begins with an analysis of reconstructed vocabulary, showing direct historical evidence for the ancestral speech community that spoke the Coastal language. Though they did not leave written documents and their artifacts are potentially waiting for archaeological discovery, Coastal-speakers left historical evidence in the words spoken by present-day Nalu-, Mbulungish-, and Mboteni-speakers. Using the comparative method of historical linguistics, noting words spoken by present-day Nalu-, Mbulungish-, and Mboteni-speakers, and demonstrating the patterns of regular correspondence in these genetically related languages,[19] the remainder of this section will reconstruct words from the proto-Coastal language.

-Mer (salt) is a very ancient word in the Atlantic language group. To understand how comparative linguists know this and what it means, we must go even further back in time than to proto-Coastal, the ancestral language that diverged into the Nalu, Mbulungish, and Mboteni daughter speech communities. The previous section discussed the relationship among Nalu, Mbulungish, and Mboteni languages and estimated the divergence of proto-Coastal to have occurred c. 3000 to 2000 BCE. Sitem, an additional Atlantic language currently spoken in the Rio Nunez region, is distantly related to Nalu, Mbulungish, and Mboteni. At some point in the ancient past before c. 3000 to 2000 BCE, languages ancestral to Temne, Landuma, Sitem, and additional Atlantic languages spoken today in Guinea and Sierra Leone—which constitute the Southern branch of the Atlantic language group and which will be discussed in chapter 3—shared a linguistic ancestor with languages ancestral to Nalu, Mbulungish, Mboteni, and additional languages spoken today in Guinea, Guinea-Bissau, and Senegal—which comprise the Northern branch of the Atlantic language group.[20] Tables 2.1 and 2.2 illustrate cognates, which exhibit regular sound correspondences, for *-mer* in languages from the

Table 2.1. Inherited Forms for "Salt" in Northern Branch Atlantic Languages

	Banyun	Limba	Mbulungish[1]	Mboteni
Salt	*mu-mmer*[2]	*meci*[3]	*mbes*	*ɔ-mbɛl*

1. All cultural vocabulary words that are not cited come from linguistic interviews, which I conducted during my fieldwork. Please see Appendix 1 for a complete list of dates, including topic, date, location, and name of interviewee.
2. Charles Lespinay, "Dictionnaire baynunk (gu[ny]un-gujaxer-guhaca-gubòy): français," unpublished, December 1992 version.
3. Mary Lane Clarke, *A Limba-English Dictionary or Tamp ta ha Talu ta ka Hulimba ha in Huikilisi ha* (Freetown, Sierra Leone: Printed by the Government Printer, 1929), 36.

Table 2.2. Inherited Forms for "Salt" in Southern Branch Atlantic Languages

	Temne	Landuma	Kogoli	Kalum	Sitem
Salt	*m-mer*		*mɛɛr*[4]	*mɛr*[5]	*mer*

4. Marie-Paule Ferry, unpublished Konyagui/Kogoli wordlist.
5. Sigmund Koelle, *Polyglotta Africana* (London: Church Missionary House, 1854), 81.

Northern branch of Atlantic and languages from the Southern branch of Atlantic. Thus, the ancestral language, proto-Northern-Southern, would have been spoken long before proto-Coastal began diverging into its daughter languages, c. 3000 to 2000 BCE. Speech communities throughout the Upper Guinea Coast region not only inherited knowledge of salt from linguistic ancestors, but found it important and relevant enough to their contemporary situations to retain it. The written sources give us some clues as to why.

Throughout the Upper Guinea Coast, coastal inhabitants innovated a diversity of techniques for harvesting salt, which were witnessed by Cape Verdean and Luso-African observers. André Donelha, a Luso-African trader who was born and raised in Cape Verde and who traveled to the Upper Guinea Coast thrice in his lifetime, described Baga villagers making salt by boiling sea water over a fire.[21] Further south in Sierra Leone, villagers used a second salt-harvesting technique to collect salt deposits from mangrove leaves, but produced low yields. From these rudimentary methods, coastal salt producers fabricated a third method, in which salt producers collected and evaporated sea water, leaving a saline crust. They then dissolved the crust in warm salt water, added a small quantity of wood ash, and separated out the ashes by straining the solution with a cone-like apparatus made of palm leaves. Finally they used clay ovens with tin or iron basins specially constructed for this purpose, to evaporate the water and produce dry salt.[22] Salt production and salt harvesting were prevalent in the coastal reaches of the Upper Guinea Coast, but lacking in the interior.

Luso-African travelers also surmised that a lack of salt in West Africa's interior played an important role in the evolution of trading networks between inhabitants of the interior and of the coast. Multiple European traders repeated what has become known as the infamous and exaggerated "salt legend": ethnic groups from the interior went to great lengths to acquire salt and suffered dire consequences for their overindulgence upon obtaining it. A second Portuguese trader, Francisco de Lemos Coelho, who traveled between Cape Verde and Sierra Leone but never visited the Rio Nunez region, recounts one version of this coastal legend: "many of them [the Bassari in present-day Senegal] have never tasted salt in their lives, and when they reach our ships laden with salt, they gorge themselves on it, and die."[23] Another version of the coastal legend retold by André de Alvares de Álmada—a contemporary of André Donelha who was born in Santiago Island and traveled the Guinea coast between 1560 and 1590—highlights the scarcity of salt and its importance as a coastal commodity in interregional trade:

> There is so little salt that there is not enough for the people of the interior, and some nations and people never see or eat salt, for instance, those in the land of the Limbas [in present-day Sierra Leone], which never ever has any or eats any. Hence, if these Limbas go to other parts and eat salt there, they immediately swell up and die from it.[24]

Though it is an exaggeration, the tale reveals an ancient conundrum for Upper Guinea Coast inhabitants. Coastal dwellers could not live with salt in the soils where they planted crops or in the water nourishing their crops, but inhabitants from the interior could not live without it.

A symbiotic relationship between inhabitants of the coast and the interior was a partial solution to this problem and the impetus to the establishment of some of the oldest trade networks between North and West Africa and within West Africa.[25] Prior to the advent of trans-Atlantic trade, salt was the primary commodity produced by Nalu-, Mbulungish-, Mboteni-, and Sitem-speakers for interregional trade with Fulbe pastoralists in the interior, who needed salt for their herds.[26] After the end of the rainy season and after the rice harvest, Fulbe traders traveled in caravans from Futa Jallon to the Rio Nunez region to buy salt—more so even than rice—in exchange for hides, rice, wax, ivory, cola nuts, and small amounts of gold.[27] Historians cannot determine how old the salt trade is in the Upper Guinea Coast, in part, because Portuguese and Luso-African traders kept silent about it to keep their competitors in Cape Verde from gaining control.[28]

What historians do know comes predominantly from English slave traders, who frequented the region by the mid-seventeenth century. In 1794—the same year when Samuel Gamble witnessed tidal rice cultivation in Baga villages—James Watt conducted an expedition from Boké, the commercial center in the Rio Nunez region, to Timbo, a commercial district in Futa Jallon. Watts reported Fulbe caravans traveling to Kacundy to purchase salt, using bar-salt as currency in the Rio Nunez and Futa Jallon regions.[29] According to the nineteenth-century log of slave trader Theophilus Conneau, who worked as a clerk for John Ormond (one of the largest factory owners in the Rio Pongo region), Fulbe traders protected the Baga in the Rio Nunez from becoming commodities in the trans-Atlantic slave trade because of their critical role as salt producers.[30] Salt production on the coast, and Fulbe herders' dependence on it, may have been factors in the Nunez River playing a minor role in trans-Atlantic slave trafficking relative to the role of the Pongo River and Sierra Leone estuaries to its south.

Reconstructed vocabulary provides a relative chronology of innovation in the coastal Rio Nunez region. On the one hand, such vocabulary reveals that salt, salt production, and trade in salt have deep roots in the coastal littoral of West Africa's Upper Guinea Coast region. These roots cannot be traced directly to proto-Coastal, the linguistic ancestor shared by Nalu, Mbulungish, and Mboteni, because present-day speakers of one of these languages, Nalu, do not retain cognates of *-mer. Mbulungish and Mboteni do, sharing this ancient word and its regular sound correspondences with present-day languages throughout the Upper Guinea Coast. Thus, knowledge of salt can be traced to the Atlantic language group, more ancient than the existence of the Coastal linguistic subgroup.

Though *-mer, the ancient word for salt in Atlantic languages of the Northern and Southern branches, cannot be reconstructed to proto-Coastal, the remainder of this section will reconstruct other words related to the coastal landscape to proto-Coastal, the linguistic ancestor of present-day Nalu, Mbulungish, and Mboteni languages. In order to be reconstructed to proto-Coastal, a word must satisfy two criteria: Nalu and Mbulungish, the two Coastal languages whose speech communities inhabit noncontiguous villages located the furthest distance apart, must possess cognates of the word; and the cognates must exhibit regular sound correspondences. These words give the historian clues of the knowledge Nalu-, Mbulungish-, and Mboteni-speakers inherited from their linguistic ancestors about exploiting micro-environments found along the swampy and salty coast.

The earliest settlers of the Rio Nunez inherited a word, *-yop, for two species of mangroves (*Avicennia africana* and *Laguncularia racemosa*) found along the coastal littoral as far north as Senegal. Table 2.3 lists the forms for

Table 2.3. Inherited Forms for *"Avicennia Africana"* in Coastal Languages

	Nalu	Mbulungish
A. africana (white man-groves)	-yof	-yɔp
Rice cultivated in the white mangroves		mal biyɔppon/ cimal ciyɔppon

-yop in Coastal languages. In contrast, *-mer* could not be reconstructed to proto-Coastal, because Nalu did not retain a cognate for the word. Present-day Nalu-, Mbulungish-, and Mboteni-speakers inherited *-yop* directly from their linguistic ancestors and used it to name a feature of their coastal environment that became a critical part of their coastal land-use system. With glottochronology, we can approximate the introduction of *-yop* to the proto-Coastal vocabulary back to the period between c. 3000 and 2000 BCE. These shards of linguistic data are direct evidence of the antiquity of knowledge about white mangroves possessed by the first-comers of the Rio Nunez region. Reconstructed vocabulary for red mangroves is conspicuously absent from Coastal-speakers' arsenal.

-Yop is a unique innovation of the Coastal subgroup, because no other Atlantic language from Senegal to Sierra Leone possesses a cognate of the word. The presence of this unique innovation in the Coastal linguistic subgroup is not evidence that speech communities north and south of the Rio Nunez region lacked knowledge of white mangroves. It may, however, reflect the highly localized nature of the mangrove ecosystems.

As early as the sixteenth century, European accounts described how white mangroves played a critical role in food security along the coast. In the Rio Nunez region and along West Africa's coast as far north as present-day Senegal, coastal dwellers cured mangrove seedlings by soaking or cooking them in water. If not cured properly, the seedlings remained poisonous. But once cured properly, coastal inhabitants often ate white mangrove seeds during periods of famine. Among the "Baga" in Cape Verga, André Donelha described the germinated seeds, propagules, of *A. africana*,[31] reporting that "their food is rice, *funde* [fonio], seeds of white mangroves-which they cure like lupines but under the mud in rivers."[32] The region's first written documents describe coastal dwellers incorporating the seeds of white mangroves into their arsenal of food-security strategies. In addition to the absence of cognates for red mangroves in the proto-Coastal vocabulary, descriptions of curing the seeds of red mangroves are conspicuously not present in the first written sources of the region.[33]

According to biological and botanical research on mangrove ecosystems, in coastal Guinea's mature mangrove forests, red mangroves (*Rhizophora racemosa*) bordered coastal estuary channels. A mixture of white mangroves (*Avicennia africana*) and *Rhizophora* followed, with a layer of *Avicennia* situated behind.[34] And further north in the Lower Casamance region, Olga Linares describes red mangroves growing along the mouths of estuaries and a different species of white mangroves (*Avicennia nitida*) growing in more sandy and better-drained inland soils.[35] Both mangrove ecosystems exhibit a classic pattern of zonation for West African mangroves as far north as Senegal. From the riverbank to dry land, the progression goes as follows: "*Rhizophora*, dense *Avicennia*, clear *Avicennia*, *Avicennia* and *Laguncularia*, prairie to *Philoxerus* and *Sesuvium*." It is illustrated in Figure 2.1.[36]

Biologists and botanists attribute several factors to patterns of mangrove zonation. Though it is not the only factor, the different species' ability to adapt to waterlogged soils with high levels of salinity is a contributor. *A. africana* typically occupy zones closer to dry land, because their roots are not equipped to flourish when submerged under water for long periods of time.[37] *A. africana* also possess "pneumatophores," a rooting system adapted to the waterlogged soils of the coastal region, which originates at the base of the tree and grows horizontally through the soil substrate. Usually the only visible portions of the pneumatophores on top of the soil are the short, pencil-like branches extending off the horizontal roots, spaced at regular intervals. Unlike aerial roots of *R. racemosa*, pneumatophores are equipped with lenticels and gas spaces to procure oxygen from underground. These pneumatophores can only obtain adequate oxygen from shallow waters.[38] Thus, the presence of white mangroves growing in sandy, better-drained soils and located closer to dry land enables them to take in oxygen from the atmosphere.

Unlike red mangroves (which will be discussed in chapter 5), whose aerial roots are designed to be submerged under brackish water for relatively long periods of time, white mangroves' pneumatophores are not equipped to survive under these conditions. Scientists have experimented with applying Vaseline to pneumatophores to seal the lenticels. As a result, the concentration of oxygen in the white mangrove trees fell low enough to asphyxiate the underground roots. From experiments such as this, scientists have concluded that even high tide covering the lenticels can cause oxygen levels to fall and carbon dioxide levels to remain steady, effectively halting the oxygenation process, eventually killing the root and subsequently the tree.[39] It is thus unlikely that soft and spongy pneumatophores of white mangroves would require iron-edged tools to be chopped down, uprooted, and cleared away.

In reconstructing the history of West African rice and rice farmers, scholars have not taken into account the botany, biology, and diversity of

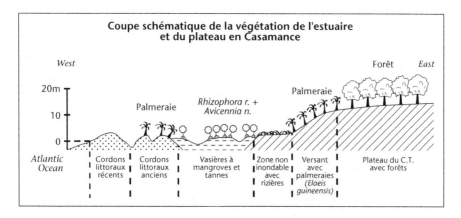

FIGURE 2.1. Illustrates the progression of *Rhizophora racemosa, Avicennia africana,* and non-inundated rice fields located between the coastline and sandy plateau. Graphic of "A Schematic Section of a Mangrove on Hardened Lateritic near Conakry (Republic of Guinea)" reprinted with permission from M. Sow, et. al., "Formations végétales et sols dans les mangroves des rivières du Sud," in Marie-Christine Cormier-Salem, ed., *Dynamique et usages de la mangrove dans les pays des rivières du Sud* (Paris: ORSTOM éditions, 1994). Copyright ORSTOM éditions.

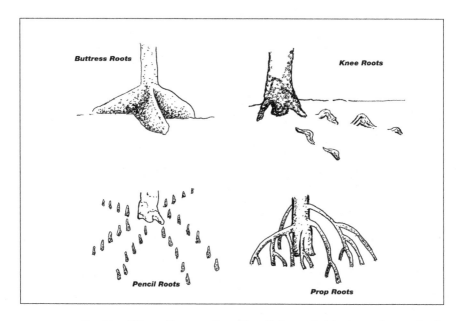

FIGURE 2.2. Graphic of "Some Common Root Types." Copyright The State of Queensland Wet Tropics Management Authority Website, www.wettropics.gov.au.

FIGURE 2.3. Photograph of "The Pneumatophores are the Respiratory Organs of *Avicennia Africana* Mangroves." Copyright F. Blasco/ CNRS Photothèque, Terrestrial Laboratory of Ecology (CNRS, France).

mangrove flora and fauna. The botanical and biological literature is clear: mangrove trees and their roots are not one and the same. The shallowness and sponginess of pneumatophores distinguishes them from tangled, impenetrable aerial roots. It also makes white mangroves more vulnerable to climatic and tidal fluctuations. If white mangroves were submerged by water, particularly brackish water, for long periods of time, their pneumatophores and subsequently the trees themselves could die. Red mangroves may also have been vulnerable to fluctuating levels of fresh and brackish water. In zones of *Rhizophora racemosa* in the Gambia located along the coast north of Guinea-Bissau and bounded on three sides by Senegal, the process of "mangrove death" is an important component of desalination and swamp reclamation in the present day. Gambian farmers achieve "mangrove death" using the following techniques: they construct an embankment around the perimeter of their rice fields; alternately, they leave a band of mangroves in place. Both the natural and the man-made barriers restrict the flow of brackish water into, and trap fresh rainwater inside, the rice field, "thereby initiating mangrove death."[40]

In both scenarios, coastal farmers may have been able to uproot the shallow rotten roots with wooden fulcrum shovels fabricated before there was access to iron, stone tools, or digging sticks. Clearing mangrove vegetation may also not have required large organized labor inputs. The differences in the oxygenation systems of white and red mangroves, as well as the possibility of asphyxiating mangroves with brackish or fresh water, are evidence of diversity within mangrove ecosystems. Future research is necessary to better understand the diversity of land-use strategies employed by coastal dwellers to manage mangrove ecosystems, as well as to determine whether or not these aspects of coastal land-use systems have deep roots.

Coastal dwellers first encountered white (*A. africana*) mangroves growing in sandy soils closest to their villages and only later gained knowledge of red (*R. racemosa*) mangroves closer to coastal estuaries and salt water. The following section will show that the region's earliest written sources also describe red mangroves along the coast. The reconstructed vocabulary traces knowledge of white mangroves back to the proto-Coastal language and proto-Coastal-speakers' earliest settlement of the region.

The linguistic sources reveal an absence of evidence of coastal first-comers cultivating rice at the earliest settlement of the coastal Rio Nunez region. Instead, the interdisciplinary sources show that coastal dwellers laid a foundation for agricultural innovation, which can be traced back to their earliest settlement of the region. In becoming familiar with the challenges of salt and salinity, coastal inhabitants acquired knowledge of vegetation and daily tidal patterns in micro-environments along the coast. By incorporating white mangroves into their subsistence regimes, coastal dwellers exposed themselves to an entire ecosystem, rich in flora and fauna. This knowledge was critical to the development of coastal land-use strategies, particularly the development of tidal rice-growing technologies. Though terminology and technology specific to rice were still absent from the arsenals of coastal first-comers by c. 3000 to 2000 BCE, knowledge of salinity and white mangroves was an indispensable prerequisite in the evolution of the coastal rice-growing technology observed by Samuel Gamble.

Gaining Mastery over Coastal Lands: Nalu-, Mbulungish-, and Mboteni-Speakers, to c. 1000 CE

As the owners of the land, Nalu-, Mbulungish-, and Mboteni-speakers inherited knowledge of salt and white mangroves. After the divergence of the Proto-Coastal ancestral language, Nalu, Mbulungish, and Mboteni speech communities gained more intimate knowledge about their coastal environment. They innovated words that demonstrated historical evidence of the lessons they learned. Gaining mastery over the challenges of the coast represents the next step in the development of tidal rice-growing technology.

Table 2.4. Areal Innovations for *"Rhizophora racemosa"* in Coastal Daughter Languages

	Nalu	Mboteni
R. racemosa	*m-mak/ a-mak*	*-ma, e-ma/a-ma*

The words coined by Nalu, Mbulungish, and Mboteni daughter speech communities cannot be reconstructed to the Coastal ancestral language, because they do not meet two basic criterion: present-day Nalu and Mbulungish languages—the two Coastal speech communities separated by the greatest distance and least likely to have had sustained contact—do not retain cognates of the words. In addition, the words do not possess regular sound correspondences. Instead, they are "areal innovations," evidence of language contact between speech communities in intermediate linguistic subgroups, the daughter communities of the Coastal language. Areal innovations often occur among language speakers whose villages are located in close proximity. But in this case, Sitem villages are located nearer to Mboteni and Mbulungish villages than to Nalu villages. Yet Sitem-speakers—whose languages are distantly related to Nalu-, Mbulungish-, and Mboteni-speakers—do not possess cognates of these cultural vocabulary words.

Like all forms of historical evidence, areal innovations are limited in their value as historical sources. For example, it is impossible to use glottochronology to date the entrance of areal innovations into a language, because they do not adhere to regular sound correspondences or belong to a particular linguistic subgroup, such as Coastal.[41] In these cases, the areal innovations entered Coastal languages after the divergence of Proto-Coastal c. 3000 to 2000 BCE. Nalu and Mboteni share one set of innovations; Mbulungish and Mboteni share the second set. Because the Sitem language does not possess cognates of these terms, they likely entered Coastal languages before the migration of Sitem-speakers into the Rio Nunez region c. 1000 CE.

To illustrate, though a word for red mangroves, *R. racemosa*, was conspicuously absent from the proto-Coastal language, two of its daughter communities innovated the word after the divergence of their common linguistic ancestor. In the Rio Nunez region, the introduction of a term for red mangrove, however, cannot be traced back to the earliest settlement of the coast. Table 2.4 lists outstations for *R. racemosa* in the Nalu and Mboteni languages.

The previous section discussed the findings of biological and botanical literature on mangrove ecosystems that red mangroves, *Rhizophora racemosa,* grew in different zones from white mangroves, *Avicennia africana,* along the coastal reaches of the Upper Guinea Coast. Whereas white mangroves grew

Table 2.5. Areal Innovations for Coastal Features in Nalu and Mboteni
Daughter Languages

	Nalu	Mbulungish	Mboteni
Oil Palm	*m-siis/ a-siis*		*yiis*
Seasonal Stream		*i-palla-ppalleŋ*	*pɔl/sam-pɔl*
Large Seasonal Stream			*pɔlmeni (meni=*large*)*
End of Rainy Season	*m-kaak kiyoŋ* *tenah/a-kaak kiyoŋ* *tenah (kaak=*rain*)*		
Rainy Season			*kuiyoŋ*

in sandy, better-drained soils, the red mangrove species grew along the mouths of coastal estuaries. The aerial roots of *R. racemosa* may be covered with salt water during high tide, because the above-ground nature of the aerial root allows a portion of it to be exposed to the atmosphere for a portion of the day. They provide a unique atmospheric oxygenation system to obtain the necessary oxygen from the waterlogged soils of swamps. This rooting system has evolved over time to equip red mangrove trees to grow in the most marginal of coastal environments.[42] Their stilt-like roots are uniquely designed to obtain the oxygen required for respiration from water-logged soils, such as those found at the mouths of coastal estuaries. Chapter 5 will explore the implications of these phenomena in more detail.

By 1000 CE, Nalu- and Mboteni-speakers had acquired knowledge of additional aspects of the coastal region. Words for oil palms were introduced, though there is no evidence that harvesting palm nuts and/or processing techniques for making palm oil, black soap, or palm wine date back to the Coastal daughter speech communities. As their knowledge of the coastal environment became more intimate, Nalu- and Mboteni-speakers learned by necessity about the torrential rains of the rainy season. They gained knowledge of *marigots,* seasonal streams created by the collection of rainwater in low-lying areas. In addition, Nalu and Mboteni speech communities also coined terminology to describe the end of the rainy season and of the agricultural cycle. Table 2.5 lists these areal innovations in Nalu and Mboteni.

After the divergence of proto-Coastal, Nalu and Mboteni speech communities were not alone in deepening their knowledge about the coastal Rio Nunez environment. Mbulungish and Mboteni also share unique innovations that spread areally after proto-Coastal diverged. These two daughter speech communities also learned about the challenges of the rainy season. In particular, they coined a new word for mosquitoes, which are prevalent in the stagnant water

Table 2.6. Areal Innovations for Coastal Features in Mbulungish and Mboteni

	Mbulungish	Mboteni
Mosquito	ɔ-bolɔ-bolleŋ	a-bɔ
Crab (Generic)	i-nep, e-nep, ɛnippel/ɛ-nippel	a-nep/ a-neppel
Type of Crab	i-laŋ/ayel-laŋ	a-laŋ/alaŋŋel

pools produced by the rainy season's torrential downpours. Lastly, Mbulungish and Mboteni learned about shellfish, an important part of the mangrove ecosystem. Table 2.6 lists these areal innovations in Mbulungish and Mboteni.

In the interdisciplinary sources, red mangroves are typically associated with shellfish, particularly oysters. For example, in Senegal's lower Casamance region, mangrove oysters that grow on the aerial roots of *R. racemosa* were found in archaeological deposits dating back to 200–300 CE according to radio carbon dating.[43] André Alvares de Álmada nicknamed red mangroves "oyster trees," because the environment was home to hordes of sea creatures: "trees growing by the waterside with the stalkes full of oisters, and great periwinkles and crabbes amongst them [*sic*]."[44] By c. 1000 CE, the language evidence suggests that red mangroves and the shellfish found therein were also becoming a key micro-environment for supplying sources of critical nourishment in coastal dwellers' arsenals for food security.

Although the shards of linguistic evidence are fragmentary, the reconstructed cultural vocabulary and the biological and botanical studies are direct evidence of the strategies developed by Nalu, Mbulungish, and Mboteni speech communities for adapting to, and flourishing in, micro-environments along the coast. Without archaeology, at this stage of the research it is the earliest evidence available for coastal Guinea. More data would allow us to add flesh to these bones.

Why isn't more linguistic data available? Though the majority of Atlantic languages are underdocumented and understudied, the problem is particularly acute for languages in the Coastal subgroup spoken in the Rio Nunez region. If extensive dictionaries of the dialects of each language were available, and if the data had been collected over a period of centuries—since the recording of the first written documents or the arrival of the first European traders, for examples—historians and historical linguists could reconstruct more of the region's early history. As it stands now, though, large portions of this story may be permanently lost to the historical record.

In another sense, the absence of cultural vocabulary words that can be reconstructed to the Coastal language is evidence in and of itself, and in spite of itself. The lack of inherited vocabulary yields a number of historical possibilities. First and foremost, the bulk of Nalu-, Mbulungish-, and Mboteni-speakers' adaptation to the coastal environment took place after the divergence of the Coastal language. Instead of inheriting Coastal words, Nalu, Mbulungish, and Mboteni daughter speech communities created new cultural vocabulary to name elements of the coastal environment.

In addition, Nalu, Mbulungish, and Mboteni speech communities likely experienced relatively little contact after the divergence of the Coastal language. Given the nature of the coastal swamps—the challenges of navigating the sinking soils on foot or the seasonal streams by dugout canoe, and the sparseness of coastal settlements—contact between groups on the coast is limited even today when torrential rains and floods turn many villages into virtual islands. If contact between villages was limited during other periods of the year, it was further curtailed during the rainy season. Thus, even if communities all along the coast encountered similar challenges in this flood-prone region and created similar strategies to adapt to these challenges, they may have created new strategies and accompanying vocabulary in virtual isolation. This state of affairs certainly has implications for how coastal dwellers in the Rio Nunez region created tidal rice-growing technology and rice terminology.

The shards of linguistic evidence, however, do reveal the antiquity of a coastal land-use strategy. In addition to the absolute chronology generated by glottochronology, the linguistic evidence reveals an important relative chronology for the history of the coastal Rio Nunez region. Knowledge of salt is the most ancient component of the coastal land-use system, followed by knowledge of *A. africana*—white mangroves. Knowledge of other aspects of the coastal environment, including *R. rhizophora*—red mangroves—oil palms, shellfish, seasonal streams, and mosquitoes followed. Words for *rice* cannot be reconstructed to the Coastal language or to its daughter languages. Rice, whether it was grown in the mangroves, floodplains, or uplands, still remains conspicuously absent from the linguistic record of the earliest settlers of the Rio Nunez region.

Conclusion

This chapter has presented by far the earliest evidence available to date for any portion of West Africa's Upper Guinea Coast region. In the absence of archaeological studies conducted in the coastal Rio Nuñez region, the linguistic evidence is the vehicle that enables this study to reconstruct historical periods pre-dating written sources. In comparison to other regions of the Upper

Guinea Coast, which have been studied by archaeologist Olga Linares and historian Walter Hawthorne, the linguistic evidence presented for the Rio Nunez region presents a unique picture. This conclusion will compare and contrast the earliest known evidence for the Lower Casamance, coastal Guinea-Bissau, and coastal Guinea's Rio Nunez regions.

Linares's analysis of pottery, mollusks, bone remains, and iron artifacts found in shell middens in present-day Senegal's Lower Casamance also digs deeply into the history of that coastal subregion—back to 200 BCE—but not quite as deep as the glottochronological estimates for the divergence of the proto-Coastal language—c. 3000 to 2000 BCE. Linares found the first-comers to the Lower Casamance region were sparsely settled on low, sandy ridges and were not yet adapted to coastal life. An absence of mollusk shells and animal or fish bones is negative evidence of specialization among the earliest settlers of the coastal environment. Linares also suggests that the first-comers to the Lower Casamance region were unlikely to have cut down or uprooted mangroves, built embankments, or otherwise reclaimed the coastal lands—covered with mangrove forests—for rice cultivation.[45]

Though even more fragmentary than the archaeological record, the linguistic evidence for the first-comers of the Rio Nunez region in many ways exhibits patterns similar to Linares's findings. First, reconstructed vocabulary suggests that Coastal-speakers were settled in sandy areas where they would have encountered white, as opposed to red, mangroves. Only after the divergence of the Coastal language into its daughter languages did Mbulungish and Mboteni speech communities innovate terms for red mangroves and the shellfish that inhabit their aerial roots. There is no evidence of Coastal-speakers nor their Nalu-, Mbulungish-, or Mboteni-speaking daughter speech communities possessing specialized knowledge of the coast or specialized technology to exploit its micro-environments before c. 1000 CE.

Because of stark differences in the time period covered by the two studies, it is somewhat difficult to compare my findings to Hawthorne's for the earliest settlement of the Upper Guinea Coast region. Whereas my and Linares's studies focus on the "pre-history" of the Rio Nunez and Lower Casamance regions, Walter Hawthorne's study of the Balanta focuses on the period of trans-Atlantic trade. It is also based primarily on travelers' accounts by European and Luso-African traders and oral traditions. According to travelers' accounts, the Balanta are relative newcomers to the coast and to coastal rice-growing technology. The earliest Portuguese and Afro-Portuguese traders to document the region described the Balanta living in the uplands and farming a variety of crops, including yams and millet.[46]

On the contrary, in the Rio Nunez region, the region's first written accounts describe the "Baga" and Nalu inhabiting roughly the same territory that they continue to occupy today. Linguistic evidence confirms the divergence of the "Baga" languages—Mbulungish and Mboteni—as well as the divergence of Nalu on the coast, not as a result of migration from the interior. Second, there is no written or oral evidence of coastal farmers of the region subsisting on any other foodstuff than rice. Coastal dwellers most certainly continued to fish, hunt, and gather fruits and vegetables to supplement their diet. Unlike the Balanta, the earliest European chroniclers associated the Baga and Nalu with salt and rice production and characterized these ethnic groups as rice farmers even in their earliest written references.

An examination of linguistic sources does not allow us to reconstruct the coastal rice knowledge system to the ancient history of the Baga or the Nalu. It is important to remember that the earliest dates that we currently have for the domestication of *Oryza glaberrima* in present-day Mali's Inland Niger Delta are 300 BCE to 300 CE, a few thousand years after the divergence of the proto-Coastal language, c. 3000 to c. 2000 BCE. The language sources do, however, reveal the much longer and deeper history, dating back to the earliest settlement of the Rio Nunez region, that underlies the agricultural technology witnessed by Samuel Gamble in the late eighteenth century. Though Gamble's detailed description of coastal rice-growing technology appears to emerge out of a vacuum in the written sources, the tidal rice-growing technology grew organically out of coastal dwellers' adaptation to their salty and swampy environment. Reconstructed vocabulary is evidence, therefore, of coastal dwellers developing the tidal rice-growing technology out of a coastal land-use system, which had deep roots in the Rio Nunez region and along the littoral of West Africa's Rice Coast.

In coastal Guinea's Rio Nunez region, Nalu-, Mbulungish-, and Mboteni-speakers were not the only groups to lay the foundation for tidal rice-growing technology. Sitem-speakers and their linguistic ancestors would also make important contributors. It is to their story that the next chapter will turn.

3

The Newcomers and the Seeds of Tidal Rice-Growing Technology

The greatest fatigue they undergo is clearing the ground, which is done by merely cutting down the trees, the small ones close to the surface, and the large ones a few feet above it. No care is taken to remove the stumps, nor even the trunks of the larger trees, but where each falls, there it is suffered to remain. This labour is performed during the dry season; and a short time before the rains are expected, the whole is set on fire, and the ground is thus rendered as clear as the flames can make it, the unburnt wood being left strewed over the field. (Thomas Winterbottom, *An Account of the Native Africans in the Neighbourhood of Sierra Leone*, 47–48.)

The first-comers—Nalu-, Mbulungish-, and Mboteni-speakers—established sparse settlements along the coast of the Nunez River in present-day Guinea-Conakry and Guinea-Bissau, where their knowledge of the coastal environment had deep roots dating back to antiquity. From their settlement of the coastal Rio Nunez region, they forged an intimate relationship with coastal micro-environments by developing adaptive strategies, such as harvesting salt and gathering shellfish in the roots of red mangrove trees, to provide food security in the face of rainfall fluctuations. Growing rice in coastal estuaries, floodplains, or mangroves was not yet a part of their ancient arsenal. The diversity of their languages within this relatively small region reflects the antiquity of their settlement along the coast. Though they were the pioneers in the coastal littoral, by c. 500 to c. 1000 CE they were no longer alone.

Approximately five hundred years before the first European and Luso-African traders arrived in coastal Guinea, a second Atlantic speech community came to inhabit the Rio Nunez region. The newcomers, Highlands-speakers, originated in the interior of present-day Guinea, a region with higher levels of elevation and lower levels of rainfall. Highlands-speakers had many lessons to learn about the wet, salty, and swampy coastal environment. But they also had lessons to teach, new strategies applicable to surviving and flourishing in the coastal environment, which Highlands-speakers had honed in the forest-savanna region.

Thanks to the newcomers, the coastal land-use strategies that laid the foundation for the evolution of tidal rice-growing technology entered another stage of development. With their migration to the coast, Highlands-speakers had a profound impact on coastal dwellers' evolution of land-use strategies in this corner of the Rice Coast region. More than eight hundred years before Samuel Gamble observed tidal rice-growing among "Baga" farmers, the migrants to the Rio Nunez region sowed the seeds of the coastal rice knowledge system. This chapter will dig deeply once again into the indigenous history of coastal Guinea. Proto-Highlands-speakers, whose daughter speech communities— Sitem-, Mandori-, Kakissa-, Koba-, and Kalum-speakers—were the second stream of speech communities from the Atlantic language group to inhabit coastal Guinea's Rio Nunez region. It will trace their origins in the interior, strategies for adapting to the forest-savanna environment, and migration to the coast, highlighting Highlands-speakers' forest-savanna survival skills that helped to transform the coastal environment.

Settlement Chronologies: Locating Highands-Speakers' Homeland

Today, Sitem-speakers inhabit the mangrove swamps and floodplains of coastal Guinea along with Nalu-, Mbulungish-, and Mboteni-speakers. In conjunction with their Mbulungish- and Mboteni-speaking neighbors, Sitem-speakers share an ethnic identity called *Baga*. However, the languages spoken by coastal dwellers who are identified and who identify themselves as part of the Baga ethnic group are distantly related. An examination of language sources reveals a picture of Sitem and its ancestral language, proto-Highlands, which is genetically, albeit distantly related to, Nalu, Mbulungish, Mboteni, and their ancestral language, proto-Coastal. The divergence of proto-Highlands into its daughter languages was unlike the divergence of proto-Coastal, whose daughter languages have "deep roots" on the coast extending back in time several millennia. Before reconstructing words for the skills that Sitem-speakers brought to the coast and contributed to coastal land-use systems and to tidal rice-growing technology, we must first know more about their origins in the interior.

Although the earliest reference to the Baga was recorded in 1573,[1] subsequent Portuguese and Luso-African observers often used a variety of terminology—Tyapi, Sapi, Sape, and Baga—when referring to coastal inhabitants between the Rio Nunez region in present-day Guinea and the Sherbro Islands in present-day Sierra Leone. By the 1590s, Portuguese traders used *Baga* to refer specifically to the coastal inhabitants of the Rio Nunez region and *Sape*—a name for the Landuma in the Fulbe language, which was derived from "Tyapi/ Chapi"[2]—to refer generally to inhabitants south of the Nunez region on the coast and sometimes in the interior. Portuguese and Luso-African observers' usage of *Sapi* evolved: initially, they employed the ethnonym in reference to Landuma, Baga, and Temne speech communities inhabiting Guinea and Sierra Leone; progressively, they included Bullom languages from coastal Sierra Leone and then subsequently extended the usage of Sapi to include speakers of Mande languages in the immediate interior to the villages inhabited by Atlantic speech communities.[3] When Portuguese and Luso-African traders first encountered Guinea and Sierra Leone's coastal inhabitants who spoke Atlantic languages, they emphasized two elements in their travelers' accounts—the relatively close relationship between their Atlantic languages[4] and the coastal Atlantic groups' complex interactions with Mande neighbors from the interior.[5] Foreign traders' deployment of *Sape* to identify linguistic, cultural, and political groups in the late sixteenth century—sometimes interchangeably and specifically in reference to linguistic, cultural, geographic, and political groupings—was emblematic of their uneven knowledge of the region. It also bore some resemblance to present-day Mbulungish-, Mboteni-, and Sitem-speakers identifying themselves as Baga, despite their linguistic differences, mirroring the overlapping and fluid nature of linguistic, political, and cultural identities in the coastal littoral of the Upper Guinea Coast.

This section will focus on the first of these two distinguishing characteristics, the relationship between the "Sape" languages: Temne, Landuma, and (Baga) Sitem. The relative closeness of the Highlands language group stands in stark contrast to the distant relationship among the Coastal subgroup of languages: compared to Coastal languages, the proto-highlands daughter languages diverged relatively recently and some remain mutually intelligible. In contrast, Nalu, Mbulungish, and Mboteni languages ceased being mutually intelligible nearly five millennia ago and are distantly related to each other. Sitem, Kalum, Temne, Landuma, and so on are their even more distantly related "cousins." An examination of language sources will reveal how proto-Highlands' daughter languages—Sitem, Landuma, and Temne—spread from the interior to the coast.

Nalu, Mbulungish, Mboteni, and Sitem languages belong to two separate branches of the Atlantic language family. Nalu, Mbulungish, and Mboteni— which I argued in chapter 2 are descended from a common ancestral language called Coastal—belong to the Northern branch of the Atlantic language group. Northern-branch languages extend as far north as Senegal. Sitem is part of the Southern branch of the Atlantic language group, whose other languages extend as far south as Liberia. The Sitem language is closely related to the Mandori, Kakissa, Koba, and Kalum spoken in coastal Guinea, Landuma spoken in Guinea's interior, and Temne spoken both along the coast and in the interior of Sierra Leone.[6] Sitem and its closely related languages descended from a distinct ancestral language, which I have called proto-Highlands.[7] The Highlands language and additional tongues spoken in Sierra Leone and Liberia descended from a more distant linguistic ancestor, which has been called Mel. Millennia before c. 3000 BCE, proto-Coastal and proto-Mel also shared a common linguistic ancestor. Present-day northeastern Sierra Leone, between the Little Scarcies and Rokel Rivers, is the homeland of proto-Mel, the linguistic ancestor of Atlantic languages spoken in present-day Guinea and Sierra Leone, including Kalum, Sitem, Landuma, and Temne.

By the period between c. 1 and c. 1000 CE, Mel languages had already differentiated into the daughter languages spoken today in southern and southwestern Sierra Leone and northwestern Liberia. The remaining Mel speech communities began to speak languages significantly different from proto-Mel and were no longer mutually intelligible. By c. 500 to c. 1000 CE, dialects spoken in the forest-savanna of Guinea, bordering the coastal region west of the Konkouré River, were differentiating into the Highlands language. Highlands dialects spoken in the forest-savanna and along the coast of Sierra Leone became the Temne language. Dialects spoken further north in the forest-savanna of Guinea became the Landuma language. Finally, dialects

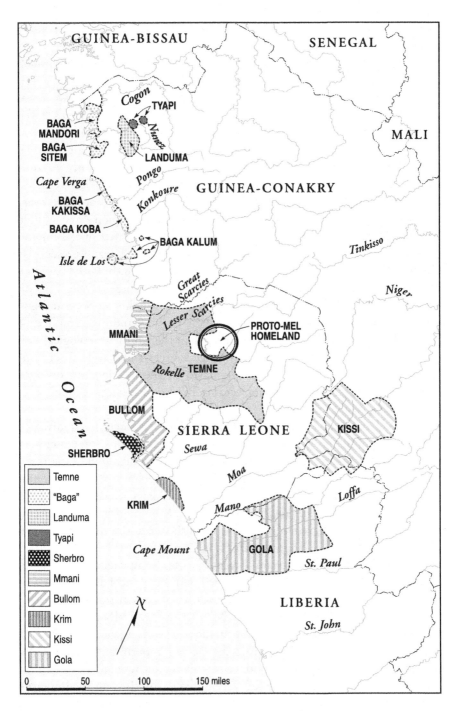

MAP 3.1. Proto-Mel Homeland and Present-Day Locations of Mel Languages

spoken along the coast of present-day Guinea became the Sitem, Mandori, Kakissa, Koba, and Kalum languages.[8]

Though it is based on a different evidentiary base, the settlement chronology based on linguistic evidence gives a more detailed picture of a general schema sketched by the late Paul E. H. Hair. Hair's incomparable work was based primarily on his own translations of a large number of European travelers' accounts for the Upper Guinea Coast, particularly those written in Portuguese, on which historians of the region still rely. Some of Hair's translations also included data from coastal, local, and predominantly Atlantic languages. Hair found the following: since Portuguese travelers recorded their location first in 1573 until the present, the "Baga" had not moved very far; at a point in time pre-dating the recording of the region's first written sources, the linguistic ancestors of the modern Baga existed in the interior between the Bullom of present-day Sierra Leone and the Baga of present-day Guinea. Their coastward movement originated in the south; lastly, based on Hair's analysis of the language data recorded by Portuguese travelers, the divergence of Baga, Landuma, and Temne occurred roughly 2,000 years ago.[9] Though by Hair's estimate the divergence of "Baga," Landuma, and Temne occurred approximately 1,000 years earlier than the glottochronological estimates, independent evidence from language sources and travelers' accounts concur that Highlands languages originated in the interior and diverged more recently relative to other subgroups in the Atlantic language group, including the Coastal subgroup.

Temne, Landuma, Kalum, and Sitem daughter languages likely diverged from proto-Highlands as a result of population movements, processes very different from the divergence of proto-Coastal into its daughter languages. By c. 500 to c. 1000 CE, Nalu, Mbulungish, and Mboteni speech communities already inhabited the coastal littoral of present-day Guinea-Conakry and Guinea-Bissau. Since the ancient past, Nalu, Mbulungish, and Mboteni speech communities have not moved far from the territories they continue to inhabit today. However, linguistic ancestors of today's Sitem-speakers settled in the Rio Nunez region much more recently. The swampy nature of a coastal environment divided by rivers and plagued with long and intense rainy seasons, as well as the isolated and remote nature of coastal settlements likely played a role in the divergence of Nalu, Mbulungish, and Mboteni languages. In contrast, population movement likely fueled the divergence of Highlands languages. Both patterns of linguistic change had important implications for coastal dwellers' development of tidal rice-growing technologies.

The two social processes also left very different imprints on the linguistic sources and very different traces for historians using the comparative method of historical linguistics to reconstruct the early history of the region. On the

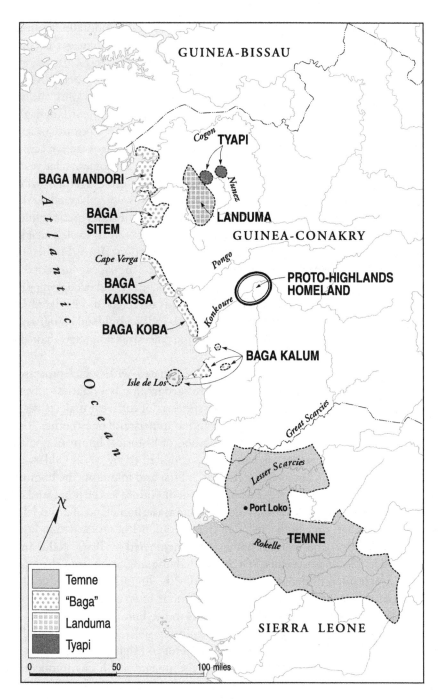

MAP 3.2. Proto-Highlands Homeland and Present-Day Locations of Highlands Languages

one hand, the distantly related Coastal languages are not mutually intelligible, though speakers of Nalu, Mbulungish, and Mboteni languages occupy similar ecological niches and inhabit villages located relatively close to one another. Proto-Coastal diverged into its daughter languages—Nalu, Mbulungish, and Mboteni—in situ. Because millennia have elapsed since the divergence of proto-Coastal, the Nalu, Mbulungish, and Mboteni languages possess relatively few cognates, which can be reconstructed to proto-Coastal.

On the other hand, the closely related Highlands languages stretch across a large expanse of territory and encompass different ecologies, relative to other languages in the Atlantic language family. The forest-savanna region inhabited by some Highlands speech communities was not subjected to the long and intense rainy seasons plaguing the coast. Ease of travel and communication enabled villagers to exchange sound changes and to exploit neighboring ecological niches in times of climatic fluctuation. Thus, Highlands dialects became the Sitem, Landuma, and Temne languages—to name a few—each remaining mutually intelligible with the other and occupying different ecological niches. Because proto-Highlands diverged into its daughter languages approximately a thousand years ago, today Highlands languages possess many more cognates of their common ancestral language than do Coastal languages.

Although language divergence cannot be equated with social processes such as migration, movement across natural geographic boundaries—rivers and mountain ranges—can contribute to speakers of different dialects ceasing to have regular and sustained contact and to understand one another. The linguistic sources and the comparative method of historical linguistics point to a different kind of social process than was described by coastal elders in oral traditions, as was discussed in chapter 2. First and foremost, the linguistic evidence identifies the forest-savanna region of Guinea as the homeland of proto-Highlands and northeastern Sierra Leone as the homeland of proto-Mel languages. Though they both existed in the interior, neither is located in Futa Jallon, the political and cultural homeland remembered by Baga, Nalu, and Temne elders. Second, the causal factors underlying migration from the interior are much more difficult to ascertain from the linguistic sources, unlike the refusal to convert to Islam, which generations of coastal elders claim in their oral traditions motivated their ancestors to flee Futa Jallon.

However, a careful analysis of interdisciplinary sources suggests that climate change may have been a contributing factor to Highlands speech communities' movement to different micro-environments. Both environmental fluctuation and movement across geographical boundaries may have contributed to the differentiation of Highlands dialects and to the settlement of Sitem-speakers in the coastal Rio Nunez region. The changing environment may also have played a significant role in how Highlands speech communities adapted to micro-environments in the forest-savanna and the coastal region.

Environmental Change in the Forest-Savanna Region

In terms of the amount of rainfall, the type of vegetation, and the strategies developed by inhabitants to exploit the two environments, the forest-savanna and coastal region are a sharp contrast. Today, both regions and their inhabitants, however, are dependent on rainfall. This section will first describe the characteristics of the forest-savanna; then it will discuss scholars' hypotheses about the effects of rainfall fluctuations over long periods of time on the Atlantic and Mande groups inhabiting the forest-savanna region.

As in the coastal littoral, the duration and intensity of rainfall play significant roles in determining the limits of forest growth in the forest-savanna region. However, whereas the coastal areas of West Africa's Upper Guinea Coast region receive in excess of 2,000 millimeters of rain per year, the forest-savanna receives between 1,000 and 2,000 millimeters. Rainfall in the forest-savanna, as on the coast, is concentrated in one intense rainy season, typically lasting between four and six months and whose beginning and ending are highly variable from year to year.[10] The forest-savanna gets its name from the combination of vegetation blanketing the region—ranging from moist deciduous and secondary forests to shrubs and grassy savannas. This is definitely not the place of coastal estuaries, floodplains, or mangrove swamps.

Insect-borne disease is also a defining characteristic of the forest-savanna region. The introduction of this study discussed the role played by mosquito-borne diseases—malaria and yellow fever—in Samuel Gamble's 1793–94 slaving voyage to coastal Guinea and on European traders and colonizers traveling to West Africa before the late 1890s. A second insect-borne disease, trypanosomiases, makes cattle-keeping in large areas of western Africa untenable, including on the coast and in the forest-savanna regions. The distribution of tsetse flies corresponds with two factors: the distribution of different types of vegetation in Africa and the spread of tsetse animal hosts inhabiting the vegetation. Several species of tsetse flies infest the southern portion of West Africa's Upper Guinea Coast region: the *Glossina fusca* species are found in the forest-savannas at the edge of moist tropical forests and the *Glossina morisitans* group—the *Glossina longipalpis* and *Glossina pallidipes*—infest thickets and forest-edge areas. Forest-savanna vegetation is an optimal environment for tsetse flies and trypanosomiases.

Tsetse flies act as vectors carrying *Trypanosoma* parasites that live in certain types of vegetation and feed on the blood of a diverse variety of animal hosts. For example, reptiles, bushbuck, bushpig, forest hog, warthog, buffalo, giraffe, kudu, elephant, rhinoceros, and hippopotamus are among tsetse flies' preferred primary hosts for blood-meals. For a variety of reasons throughout the life cycle of the insects, trypanosomes can come to depend on secondary hosts—domesticated animals such as cattle, sheep, goats, horses, pigs, and dogs—or even human hosts. When tsetse flies transmit *Trypanosoma* parasites from wild animal hosts to human hosts, humans develop trypanosomiases. This debilitating and eventually fatal disease is called "sleeping sickness," because the afflicted falls into a coma during later stages of illness. According to John Ford's classic study, *The Role of the Trypanosomiases in African Ecology: A Study of the Tsetse-Fly Problem,* destruction of the vegetation and dispersal of the hosts has been unsuccessful for ridding certain regions of tsetse flies; this is because tsetse flies are remarkably adaptable to artificial secondary hosts.[11]

Historically, inhabitants of the forest-savanna and coastal regions have not kept cattle because trypanosomes are lethal to camels, horses, sheep, and zebu cattle. Smaller in stature and resistant to trypanosomes, the shorthorn breed of *ndama* cattle can be herded in areas infested by tsetse flies.[12] The savanna and sahel regions of Guinea—where Fulbe-speaking pastoralists and their herds roamed—are located north of the area of infestation. Language evidence presented later in this chapter will suggest that in coastal Guinea's Rio Nunez region, daughter speech communities of the Highlands linguistic subgroup linked the coast and forest-savanna to the savanna and sahel through their interregional trade networks with Fulbe-speaking pastoralists. The incorporation of cattle grazing was critical to the development of tidal rice-growing technology for coastal dwellers—speakers of both Coastal and Highlands languages.

Human activity, including land clearing and crop cultivation, also played a critical role in the forest-savanna, particularly in determining whether the region tended to be sterile savanna or arable forest. Today, in the interior of Guinea, Sierra Leone, and Liberia, two forms of cultivation predominate: shifting cultivation and intercropping. In shifting cultivation, farmers clear and burn the land, cultivate it for a fixed number of years, and then allow it to lie fallow. Usually lasting five to seven years, the fallow period is determined by the length of time necessary for the land to regain fertility. During the years when the land is cultivated, forest-savanna farmers typically vary the crops planted in order to vary the nutrients required by the crops from the soil.[13] In intercropping, or mixed cropping, forest-savanna farmers plant more than one crop in the same field during the same planting season. Farmers use both shifting cultivation and intercropping to replenish soil nutrients. Both techniques allow farmers to minimize risk and to maximize yields in their micro-environments and thus to maintain food security.[14] In contrast, burning and fallowing are not necessary on the coast, because alluvial floods deposit silt in floodplains and mangrove swamps, constantly replenishing coastal soils with nutrients.

According to James Fairhead and Melissa Leach, ecologists have read the environmental history of the forest-savanna region of Guinea-Conakry backwards. Since the colonial period, ecologists have assumed that pristine forest once blanketed the region and that African farmers' shifting cultivation and land-clearing techniques, particularly slash-and-burn agriculture, have resulted in forest degradation and soil erosion. Oral interviews with farmers about the history of their forest settlements, aerial photographs of the region from various time periods, and descriptions of the landscape recorded in travelers' accounts paint a different picture. Based on this confluence of interdisciplinary sources, Fairhead and Leach concluded that uncultivated land in the interior of the forest-savanna region tends to be savanna. Through careful land-management techniques, including but not limited to controlled burning and careful cultivation of certain plants and trees, farmers in the region convert the infertile savanna tinderboxes into productive forest islands with fertile soils.[15] These land-management skills would have been critical to Highlands-speakers facing periods of climate fluctuation in the forest-savanna and would also facilitate Highlands-speakers' adaptation to the coastal environment.

Historical studies of climate change in western Africa have shed new light on the diffusion of cultigens, settlement and migration patterns, and interregional trade networks, particularly in the forest-savanna region. As is the case with the comparative method of historical linguistics, studies of climate change have the potential to transform what scholars know about the early pre-colonial period of western Africa's history for which written sources are absent. Both climate-change studies and glottochronology, the latter being just one tool of the comparative method of historical linguistics, provide chronologies for the coastal and forest-savanna regions of Guinea and Sierra Leone, pre-dating written sources and allowing historians to periodize early African history independently of European-derived chronologies.[16] Only after independently analyzing both sets of interdisciplinary data do we get a clearer understanding of the peopling of the forest-savanna region and of the climate changes that may have contributed to the migration of some Highlands speech communities from the forest-savanna to the coast.

The ever-present problem of available sources for pre-colonial African history looms large in reconstructing western Africa's climatic history.

Meteorological data recorded in Africa is absent from before the early twentieth century. Recent scholarship bases its analyses on historical and geographical sources recorded by the earliest "Portuguese" travelers to West Africa. These earliest primary sources contain a range of descriptions of rainfall, floods, drought, agricultural cycles, vegetation, abundant or lean harvests, lake and river levels, and insect and animal populations. The earliest Cape Verdean and Luso-African travelers in the region did not originally record the early journals and ship logs for the purpose of reconstructing the historical climate. Foreign traders' descriptions related to climatic conditions are the only evidence available for historical climatic reconstruction in pre-colonial West Africa, particularly, but not limited to, the Rio Nunez region. For coastal Atlantic societies, the climate data are no more or less plentiful than the linguistic data, travelers' accounts, or oral narratives.

The historical and geographical sources can be fraught with inconsistencies. Because many are based on oral traditions and second-hand information, inaccuracies may exist for the dates when, and places where, chroniclers made their observations. In addition, the historical and geographical sources lack a standard for accurate comparison. Each chronicler had his own definition of what he described, perhaps bearing scant resemblance to a twentieth- or twenty-first century idea of the same phenomenon. In addition, because the overwhelming majority of the travelers—the same population of foreign traders who recorded the first written records for the Upper Guinea Coast—did not spend extended periods of time in the region, they could not credibly compare what they saw to what existed one year, not to mention one decade, before.[17] In order for it to be useful to historians, the climate data must also be interrogated and interpreted carefully—a charge equal to the other traditional and nontraditional historical sources discussed and employed in this study.

Despite the unevenness of the historical and geographic data, climatologist Sharon Nicholson has employed it skillfully as part of a two-pronged methodology to reconstruct western Africa's climatic history. First, Nicholson compiled long-term continuous data on specific climate-related variables to establish absolute trends in the region's climate over time. By examining the long-term data, Nicholson determined whether western Africa's climate in past periods was wetter or drier than today's climate. Second, she gained insight into long-term trends from reports of short-term regional climate anomalies—such as droughts—reported in the historic and geographic sources. By corroborating the dates of climate anomalies described in the historical sources with more than one source, Nicholson used the dates to make the chronology of long-term trends more precise. Climatologists can use the regional data to determine what may have caused long-term climate changes. Finally, she combed travelers' accounts for descriptions not only of climate variations in regions visited by European traders and explorers, but also of how the region's inhabitants responded and adapted to their changing physical environment, which is of particular interest to this chapter's focus on Highlands speech communities in present-day Guinea's forest-savanna region.[18]

Building on Nicholson's work, historian George Brooks established a provisional schema for periodizing West African history based on patterns of climate change. His plan aimed to understand the history of climate change in, and its effects on, western African societies. Brooks chose a thirty-year period in the relatively well-documented twentieth century to establish the mean rainfall level. He then measured past rainfall levels against this mean, hypothesizing that western Africa experienced 20 percent more or less rainfall than the mean in wet and dry periods respectively.[19] He found that between 1000 and 1860, western Africa experienced the following periods of climatic change: the final phase of a long wet period beginning in c. 700 and ending c. 1100; a long dry period from c. 1100 to c. 1500; a brief wet period from c. 1500 to c. 1630; and a dry period from c. 1630 to c. 1860.[20] This schema can be applied both to regions inhabited by Highlands-speakers and to their daughter speech communities—the forest-savanna region and the coastal littoral of present-day Guinea-Conakry.

According to interdisciplinary studies of climate change in western Africa, beginning c. 1100 to 1500—approximately one hundred years after proto-Highlands began to diverge into its daughter languages—western Africa underwent a period of climatic fluctuation. Decreased rainfall levels and increased aridity resulted in the southward movement of ecological zones within the region. Coastal rainforests shrank, and inhabitants of the forest-savanna region, a transitional environment largely affected by human activity, responded in a variety of ways in order to maintain their food security. Certain groups followed flora and fauna from the forest-savanna as the ecological zone moved further south. Alternatively, others moved deeper into the forest-savanna region. Climate change likely prompted Highlands-speakers to find new ways of adapting to the changing environment by, for example, forming trade relationships with groups in the savanna and sahel regions and incorporating wild and domesticated animals into land-use systems.

At first glance, the forest-savanna survival skills developed by Highlands speech communities appear completely unrelated to the coast. The homeland of proto-Highlands-speakers was located in West Africa's forest-savanna region, just beyond and perched on the edge of coastal floodplains and mangrove swamps. Because of their peripheral location, Highlands speech communities probably learned valuable lessons about these two dissimilar physical environments; these lessons facilitated their ability to adapt to climatic change. Chapter 4 will show that in the coastal Rio Nunez region, Highlands-speakers' strategies for managing the forest-savanna environment planted the seeds for coastal dwellers' indigenous agricultural revolution.

Today the coastal region is riddled with mangroves, seasonal streams, and floodplains, while the drier forest-savanna region is spotted with hills and shrubs. In about c. 1000 CE, western Africa was on the cusp of a period of rainfall fluctuation and transition from a period of increased humidity to one of increased aridity. To understand how these climate changes manifested in the forest-savanna of present-day Guinea and Sierra Leone and to see which strategies the inhabitants used to manage their changing environment, we must examine the linguistic sources and the earliest available historical sources. Linguistic evidence presented in the next section provides clues to how Highlands-speakers adapted to the changing forest-savanna environment. Though the current available linguistic and archaeological sources suggest that the migration of the newcomers pre-dated the incorporation of rice-growing into coastal land-use systems, Sitem-speakers honed skills in the forest-savanna region, which would act as important precursors to tidal rice-growing technology and its material culture on the coast.

Swimming Upstream: Reconstructed Vocabulary for Highlands Speech Communities and their Forest-Savanna Skills, c. 500 to c. 1000 CE

For the interior regions of Sierra Leone and Guinea, written sources do not exist for the time period when the proto-Highlands language diverged, when some of its daughter speech communities migrated towards the coast, and when ecological zones in western African moved southward as a result of increased aridity. To counteract this evidentiary vacuum, this section examines direct evidence—reconstructed vocabulary from the daughter languages of the Highlands linguistic subgroup. It also offers indirect evidence in the form of the earliest written sources for the region. As in chapter 2, this section uses the region's first written sources to establish the major social and political features of Highlands societies at the period of initial contact with European and Luso-African traders. It also makes use of regular sound changes, reconstructed vocabulary words, and glottochronology to trace the evolution of these institutions in Highlands societies. The result is the second historiography of West Africa's forest-savanna to pre-date Europeans.[21]

Highlands languages provide three kinds of sources for the historical period dated approximately five hundred years before the arrival of the

Portuguese and the advent of written sources for coastal Guinea. On the one hand, Highlands-speakers inherited words from their linguistic ancestors; these related to social organization, climatic features, animals, and adaptive strategies in the forest-savanna region. The inherited vocabulary serves as direct evidence for the knowledge retained by Highlands speech communities about their ancestral homeland in the interior of present-day Guinea. After the divergence of proto-Highlands, daughter speech communities innovated cultural vocabulary related either to the forest-savanna or the coastal regions. These innovated words are direct evidence that Temne, Landuma, Sitem, and Kalum daughter speech communities drew on the knowledge of their linguistic ancestors to develop new adaptive strategies in the regions where they settled. Lastly, Highlands daughter communities also borrowed vocabulary words from other unrelated speech communities inhabiting the savanna and sahel regions. The borrowed words are evidence of another adaptive strategy developed by Highlands daughter speech communities in the forest-savanna: they reflect trade relationships with Fulbe-speaking pastoralists from the savanna and Sahel regions.

Through the vocabulary of present-day Sitem-, Landuma-, and Temne-speakers, we can reconstruct the Highlands ancestral language. A word that can be reconstructed to proto-Highlands must meet three criteria: it must be cognate, that is, possess a similar meaning and phonological shape; it must exhibit regular sound correspondences in noncontiguous languages that were unlikely to have experienced regular or sustained contact. Cognates exhibiting regular sound correspondences and that are present in Highlands languages spoken today on the coast—Sitem or Kalum for the purposes of this study—and Temne meet these criteria.

An examination of cultural vocabulary for the Highlands language reveals a politically and socially stratified society, one that stands in sharp contrast to most of the societies in coastal Guinea's Rio Nunez region. Words such as *-bɛ (king, chief, and chiefship) reveal centralized political authority. The presence of reconstructed vocabulary, such as *-car (male slave) and *-ɔrɛnta (chain, fetters), suggests the existence of dominant and subservient statuses within this hierarchical society. The gender specificity of *-car (male slave; the word for female slave is a derivative of *-car) suggests that mostly men were relegated to this servile status, probably as a result of capture in warfare. Social stratification and political centralization among Highlands-speakers can be traced back at least as far as c. 500 to c. 1000 CE.

The European and Luso-African travelers' accounts also depict socially stratified Highlands' societies. When Portuguese and Luso-African traders described the "Sapes"—which was how they referred to the Atlantic speech communities in the interior of present-day Sierra Leone and Guinea—they

Table 3.1. Inherited Forms for Social Organization in Highlands Languages

	Temne	Kogoli	Landuma	Kalum	Sitem
King	o-bai/a-bai[1]	o-bɛŋ[2]	o-bɛ/ a-bɛ[3]	i-bɛ/ a-bɛ[4]	
Kingdom, government, Office of the King	ra-bai/ca-bai[5]				
Chief		o-bɛŋ[6]			wi-bɛ/ a-bɛ
Chiefship					dɛ-bɛ
Very elderly and respected man	o-tem/ a-tem[7]		o-tem		wi-tem/ a-tem
Stranger, visitor	-cik/ a-cik[8]	o-cig[9]	wo-tik/ a-tik[10]	i-cik/ a-cik[11]	
Male slave	u-car/ a-car[12]	o-car[13]	o-car/ a-car[14]	i-car/ a-car[15]	
Slavery, bondage	ra-car[16]				
Female slave	u-car u-bɛra[17] (-bɛra =woman)		o-car o-rani[18] (-rani =woman)	i-car i-rani[19]	
Chain, fetters	kɔ-rɛnta/ tɔ-rɛnta[20]		ko-ronti[21]	ɛ-kɔrɛnta[22]	ɛ-kɔrɛnta

1. The Reverend C. F. Schlenker, *A Collection of Temne Traditions* (London: Church Missionary Society, 1861), 147.
2. Marie Paule Ferry, unpublished vocabulary list, Konyagui and Kogoli/French.
3. Sigmund Koelle, *Polyglotta Africana* (London: Church Missionary Society, 1854), 26.
4. Ibid., 27.
5. Schlenker, *A Collection of Temne Traditions*, 147.
6. Ferry, Unpublished vocabulary list.
7. Schlenker, *A Collection of Temne Traditions*, 256.
8. Koelle, *Polyglotta Africana*, 24.
9. Ferry, unpublished vocabulary list.
10. Koelle, *Polyglotta Africana*, 23.
11. Ibid., 24.
12. Schlenker, *A Collection of Temne Traditions*, 273.
13. Ferry, unpublished vocabulary list.
14. Koelle, *Polyglotta Africana*, 27.
15. Ibid.
16. Schlenker, *A Collection of Temne Traditions*, 273.
17. Ibid.
18. Koelle, *Polyglotta Africana*, 26.
19. Ibid., 27.
20. Ibid., 98.
21. Ibid., 97.
22. Ibid., 98.

usually designated them as the "kingdom of the Sapes" and sharply delineated them from the "Baga" that inhabited the coast. On the one hand, "kingdom" referred to a group of mutually intelligible languages, similar cultures, and societies, which by the 1590s had also seen an influx of migrants that spoke Mande languages. On the other hand, it also refers to the internal social dynamics of Highlands speech communities in which a king and chiefs presided over a centralized political and judicial system, as André de Álmada describes:

> Government and justice among these nations of the Sapes are conducted the following way. . . . In this place, the king is joined by the *solateguis,* who are the chief men of the kingdom, either in secret session, or in order to administer justice to the parties seeking it. . . . [22]

In addition, Álmada describes access to captives as a vehicle of wealth, prestige, title accumulation, and social stratification:

> Those who are condemned to death they sell to persons who buy them in order to kill them and become titled persons. For it is the custom among these people that they become persons of rank or title by killing others in wars or in fights; . . . And those who have not attained these honors in person buy condemned men at low price, paying not more than five or six gold cruzados, and kill them and become honoured men.[23]

Álmada uses broad terminology—"Sape"—although his point of reference is rather specific; he is referring to the Temne in the Scarcies River region of present-day Sierra Leone.[24] These social and cultural traits of Temne society are a far cry from descriptions of the Baga as lacking centralized political authority[25] and uninvolved in the trans-Atlantic slave trade—particularly according to slave trader Theophilus Conneau's observation (discussed in chapter 2) that the Fulbe protected the Baga from enslavement because Fulbe pastoralists' were dependent on salt produced by the Baga. Institutions of domestic servitude within Atlantic societies in Guinea's Rio Nunez region—the coast and the interior—and the transformations that they underwent as result of the trans-Atlantic slave trade are important subjects deserving future study.

However, the social and political stratification of Highlands' speech communities was not entirely dissimilar from all Atlantic speech communities in the Rio Nunez region. Colonial officers, including André Coffinières de Nordeck (who will be discussed more fully in chapter 5), reported negotiating with Nalu chiefs as he worked to secure France's sovereignty over the region. As the written sources suggest, centralized political institutions were relatively recent innovations among the Nalu, who became politically centralized in the late eighteenth century as trans-Atlantic trade in the Kacundy/Boké region intensified.[26] The independent language sources concur. Nalu-speakers borrowed -tem, or "elder," from their Landuma-speaking neighbors, re-defining it to mean "chief," "queen," and "king." The absence of indigenous terminology in the Nalu language for politically centralized institutions is likely evidence of the relative recentness of the institutions among the Nalu. A semantic shift in the Mbulungish language—political authority among the Mbulungish became centralized in the mid-eighteenth century—associating the proto-Highlands word for *chief* with slaveholders is a potentially rich avenue for future investigation on relations between coastal stateless societies and their politically centralized neighbors.

As European and Luso-African traders traveled further into the interior of present-day Guinea and Sierra Leone, they recorded rich observations of the forest-savanna physical environment at the end of the period of diminished rainfall. André Donelha, a Luso-African, had extensive experience in present-day Sierra Leone and with inhabitants from both Mande and Atlantic language groups. Sapes from Guinea and Sierra Leone sought refuge from what some scholars have termed the "Mane invasions" in the Cape Verdean community where he grew up. In the 1560s, Donelha's father, who then resided in Sierra Leone, purchased three enslaved "Manes" and allowed them to be baptized and to receive Christian names. Later in his life, the three Manes became Donelha's informants, providing him with information about the Mane invasions, or movement of Manes and Sumbas into Sierra Leone. During his time in Santiago, Donelha also befriended Ventura Sequeira, another "Sape" refugee who converted to Christianity and who some historians have speculated invited Donelha to return to Sierra Leone to live. Before 1574, Donelha also traveled to Sierra Leone, embarking with Governor Antonio Velho Tinoco's fleet and sailing to Cape dos Mastos and Sao Domingos/Cacheu, Grande de Guinhala, and the Sierra Leone Rivers. Years later, the new governor of Sierra Leone planned to send Donelha to Sierra Leone to convert the inhabitants to Christianity and to build a fort for defense against the Dutch. Donelha rewrote and embellished notes from his youthful travels for the new governor. His goal was to describe the richness of the countryside, identify locales in Sierra Leone where Cape Verdeans and Christians could settle, and for entice interested parties to emigrate.[27]

From his residence in Sierra Leone and his Mane informants, Donelha described the sparsely inhabited landscape as a combination of savanna and forest: "The largest part of this region is desert, and if there are any villages, one cannot count the few inhabitants, because the forests are immense and the entire country is covered in trees."[28] The region was blanketed with oil

Table 3.2. Borrowed Forms for Social Organization in Coastal Languages

	Nalu	Mbulungish
Chief	ma-θem, m-θim/ be-θem, bɛ-θim	
Chiefship	ma-θemnɛ/ a-θemnɛ	
Queen	m-θem θai/ bɛ-θem θai	
Slaveholder		i-bɛ/ ɛ-bɛllɛŋ

palm trees producing palm nuts, wine, and oil; different species of fruit and nut trees—some of which the Portuguese introduced, such as coconuts and sugar cane—and pepper; kola nuts; and gum copal. In addition, the forest-savanna was inhabited by a variety of wildlife: buffalo, large antelopes, gazelles, hogs, stags, and porcupines. It was also home to leopards, lions, hyenas, chimpanzees, various additional species of wild cats, poisonous snakes, boa constrictors, iguanas, many different species of fish, and crocodiles.[29] Donelha included detailed descriptions of hippopotami, sea horses, and unicorns to satisfy the imaginations of prospective "Portuguese" emigrants.[30] By the late 1500s, the region's inhabitants were hunting and trapping game, fishing in freshwater rivers and streams, and gathering fruit—subsistence strategies diverse enough to minimize risk in the event of rainfall fluctuations and to increase the likelihood of maintaining food security.

The reconstructed vocabulary provides independent evidence that Highlands-speakers had assembled an arsenal of knowledge about the dry, grassy, and hilly forest-savanna and the large and small animals inhabiting the region. Examples include *-sem (animal, quadruped, wild animal, meat, venison, or beef), *-cir (blood), *-na (cow), *-ir (goat), *-bamp (bird), and *-buk (snake). Sitem, Landuma, and Temne daughter speech communities also inherited a word for ivory,*-sik (lit., tooth), from proto-Highlands—possibly signaling that ivory had become a valuable commodity in interregional trade networks and therefore had increased in value in Highlands societies. Highlands-speakers also innovated a term for oil palm trees, *-komp, in the forest-savanna regions bordering the coast. Like the proto-Coastal language, proto-Highlands did not develop terms for palm nuts, palm oil, palm wine, or black soap. Highlands-speakers had also developed strategies to survive and flourish in the forest-savanna regions by c. 500 to c. 1000 CE. They used bows, *-bencira, as weapons for hunting and/or warfare. Trapping and catching birds and venison, *-wul, provided Highlands-speakers with important sources of protein, as did fish, *-rup, from freshwater streams. Lastly, proto-Highlands-speakers also became well acquainted with different

Table 3.3. Inherited Forms for Forest-Savanna Features in Highlands Languages

	Temne	Kogoli	Landuma	Kalum	Sitem
Meat, beef	ɔ-sɛm[1]	a-sɛm[2]	a-sɛm	a-seam[3]	
Wild animal, venison, a beast of the chase, quadruped	a-sɛm[4]				
Blood	ma-cir[5]	ma-ciir[6]	ma-cir	ma-dsir[7]	me-cir
Goat	w-ir/ c-ir[8]		w-ir/ t-ir	w-ir/ c-ir[9]	
Bird	a-bamp/ ɛ-bamp	a-bamp[10]	a-bamp/ ya-bamp	a-bamp/ ɛ-bamp[11]	
Serpent	a-bok/ ɛ-bok[12]		a-bok/ ya-bok	a-bok/ ɛ-bok[13]	
Ivory	ra-sek/ ra-runk[14]		da-sik/ ya-sik[15]	da-cenka[16]	
Tooth	ra-sek/ ɛ-sek[17]	ɛ-sik/ya-sig[18]	da-sik/ ya-sik	da-sek/ ɛ-sek[19]	
Oil palm	a-komp/ ɛ-komp		a-komp/ ya-komp	a-komp/ ɛ-komp[20]	a-komp/ ɛ-komp
Bow	a-benta/ ɛ-benta[21]	a-mbuntsura[22]	a-boncira/ ya-boncira[23]	am-boncera/ ɛ-boncera[24]	
Trap					ta-wul/ ma-wul
Loop, noose trap to catch venison and birds in	a-wul/ ɛ-wul[25]				
Fish	ka-lop/ ɛ-lop[26]	a-lop/ ya-lop[27]	a-lup/ya-lup	ku-rɔp/ɛ-rɔp[28]	
Rainy season	ra-ran/ na-ran[29]		da-ran[30]	da-ran[31]	
Rain	k-ɔm/c-ɔm[32]	-koom[33]		k-oam[34]	
Dew	k-ebi/ c-ebi[35]	kubi[36]	kebi[37]	kebi[38]	

1. Schlenker, *A Collection of Temne Traditions*, 246.
2. Ferry, unpublished vocabulary list.
3. Koelle, *Polyglotta Africana*, 80.
4. Schlenker, *A Collection of Temne Traditions*, 246.
5. Koelle, *Polyglotta Africana*, 54.
6. Ferry, unpublished vocabulary list.
7. Koelle, *Polyglotta Africana*, 54.
8. Ibid., 120.
9. Ibid.

Table 3.3 Footnotes (*continued*)
10. Schlenker, *A Collection of Temne Traditions*, 149.
11. Ferry, unpublished vocabulary list.
12. Koelle, *Polyglotta Africana*, 128.
13. Schlenker, *A Collection of Temne Traditions*, 156.
14. Koelle, *Polyglotta Africana*, 128.
15. Ibid., 136.
16. Ibid., 135.
17. Ibid., 136.
18. Schlenker, *A Collection of Temne Traditions*, 245.
19. Ferry, unpublished vocabulary list.
20. Koelle, *Polyglotta Africana*, 34.
21. Ibid., 102.
22. Ibid., 70.
23. Ferry, unpublished vocabulary list.
24. Koelle, *Polyglotta Africana*, 69.
25. Ibid., 70.
26. Schlenker, *A Collection of Temne Traditions*, 289.
27. Ibid., 202.
28. Ferry, unpublished vocabulary list.
29. Koelle, *Polyglotta Africana*, 128.
30. Ibid., 90.
31. Ibid., 91.
32. Ibid.
33. Ibid., 90.
34. Ferry, unpublished vocabulary list.
35. Koelle, *Polyglotta Africana*, 91.
36. Ibid., 92.
37. Ferry, unpublished vocabulary list.
38. Koelle, *Polyglotta Africana*, 93.
39. Ibid., 94.

forms of precipitation, the key climatic feature of both the coastal and the forest-savanna region, *-kɔm (rain), *-ran (rainy season), and *-ebi (dew). The language evidence reveals that important aspects of Highlands-speakers' forest-savanna survival skills can be traced back to c. 500 to c. 1000 CE.

The cultural vocabulary also provides evidence of Highlands-speakers' early agricultural pursuits in the forest-savanna region. For example, the presence of *-fat, a cognate term for "iron," is direct evidence that Highlands-speakers possessed knowledge of this precious mineral. The presence of *-unt and *-ima, cognates for "coal" and "smoke" respectively, suggests that Highlands-speakers may have been burning wood, though there is not additional evidence that Highlands-speakers burned trees to clear the landscape. By c. 500 to c. 1000 CE, the linguistic ancestors of present-day Temne-, Landuma-, and Sitem-speakers had acquired knowledge about, but had not yet specialized in, the forest-savanna region.

Independent interdisciplinary evidence also attests to the presence of iron in the forest-savanna region inhabited by proto-Highlands speech communities

Table 3.4. Inherited Forms of Pre-Agricultural Features in Highlands Languages

	Temne	Kogoli	Landuma	Kalum
Iron	*a-fac*[1]	*a-fac*[2]	*a-fac/ ɛ-fac*[3]	*a-fac*[4]
Iron cooking pot	*a-fac*[5]			*kɔ-fac/cɔ-fac*[6]
Coal	*k-unt/ t-unt*[7]		*k-anc/ c-anc*[8]	*ku-anc/ cu-anc*[9]
Smoke	*k-ima*[10]		*k-ima*[11]	*k-ima*[12]

1. Schlenker, *A Collection of Temne Traditions*, 166.
2. Ferry, unpublished vocabulary list.
3. Koelle, *Polyglotta Africana*, 63.
4. Ibid., 62.
5. Schlenker, *A Collection of Temne Traditions*, 166.
6. Koelle, *Polyglotta Africana*, 66.
7. Ibid., 92.
8. Ibid., 93.
9. Ibid., 92.
10. Schlenker, *A Collection of Temne Traditions*, 188.
11. Koelle, 93.
12. Ibid., 92.

and raises the question of how early forest-savanna dwellers in the Upper Guinea Coast used iron tools in agricultural production. Archaeological excavation of rock shelters in Kamabai and Yagala in northeastern Sierra Leone yielded iron tools dating back to c. 700 to 800 CE, and large numbers of furnaces and slag heaps—evidence of iron smelting.[31] Several of the earliest travelers' accounts—including André Alvares de Álmada, Manuel Alvares, and André Donelha—reported the presence of indigenous iron and iron weapons on the coast, particularly among the Temne in the Scarcies River region, and suggested that the iron was brought to the coast from Sierra Leone's interior.[32] This state of affairs will be contrasted in chapter 5 to coastal Guinea's Rio Nunez region where iron was described as a commodity that coastal Atlantic dwellers acquired from the Susu in exchange for salt.

However, other early Portuguese and Luso-African observers make conflicting claims about the presence of iron in Sierra Leone: the inhabitants lacked iron-smelting technology; iron indigenous to Sierra Leone was of an inferior quality; and trade in its products may have been curtailed by the movement of Mande groups from the interior toward the coast of present-day Sierra Leone and Liberia. In the 1780s, John Matthews—a slave trader who traveled throughout coastal Guinea and Sierra Leone—reported as follows: "In the interior country, south of Sierra Leone, they have white iron, very malleable, of which they make knives and sabers. . . . How they smelt and refine it from the ore I never could learn."[33] Archaeological research is necessary to confirm whether iron ore in Sierra-Leone's forest-savannas was of poor or good quality, and whether or not proto-Highlands-speakers possessed iron-smelting technology.

Evidence of proto-Highlands speech communities' access to indigenous sources of iron, centuries before the establishment of trade networks with Mande groups from the interior, complicates what historians think we know about the association of iron with Mande groups in the interior and the role of both iron tools and Mande groups in developing mangrove rice-growing technology. Chapter 5 will discuss this debate in more detail, chapter 4 will show that in the Rio Nunez region, knowledge of iron was one of the forest-savanna survival skills transmitted to the coast by Sitem-speakers—the daughter speech communities of the proto-Highlands speech community. Sitem-speakers' collaboration with Nalu-, Mbulungish-, and Mboteni-speaking neighbors, who possessed an intimate and ancient knowledge of the coastal landscape, bore fruit in the coastal rice knowledge system.

In addition to reconstructed vocabulary, loanwords also provide important evidence of contact between Highlands daughter speech communities and the inhabitants of the savanna and sahel regions. Both the savanna and the Sahel are located beyond the zone of tsetse fly infestation. Inhabitants of these regions keep cattle and other domesticated animals without the risk of exposure to trypanosomiases. Foreign travelers' accounts agree that Rio Nunez residents who possessed cattle obtained them from Fulbe-speaking traders. The presence of loanwords—$c\jmath l$ (herding, shepherd tending cattle herds, grazing), borrowed from the Fulbe language in Temne and Sitem—suggests that Fulbe-speaking pastoralists brought cattle from the savanna and Sahel to the tsetse fly-infested forest-savanna region. According to linguistic evidence, the development of a symbiotic relationship between farmers and pastoralists[34] may be traced back to the transitional forest-savanna region after the divergence of proto-Highlands, c. 500 CE to c. 1000 CE. The reconstructed vocabulary may provide the earliest evidence available for the development of indigenous interregional networks in this corner of the West African Rice Coast.

European observers frequently described cattle in the Rio Nunez region as belonging to, or brought to the coast by, the Fulbe.[35] The Fulbe language is part of the Northern branch of the Atlantic language group and is distantly related to Nalu, Mbulungish, and Mboteni, and even more distantly to Sitem. Álmada declared: "There are no cattle bred there [south of coastal Guinea's Cape Verga], since the blacks of these districts are not in the habit of breeding them; but this does not hinder some arriving there by way of the Fulos."[36] During the seventeenth century, much of the northwest section of Futa Jallon was converted to pasture land, a factor that contributed to dramatic increases

Table 3.5 Loanwords for "Herding" in Highlands Languages

	Fulbe	Temne	Sitem
Livestock breeding			*ki-cɔl*
To "rear (as cattle), tend, mind, attend to, take care of (as of cattle, or also of men)"		*-col*[1]	
"Reared, reared up (as cattle); tended, minded, taken care of"		*-col*[2]	
"One tending cattle, herd's man, shepherd"		*ɔ-col* / *a-col*[3]	
"When cattle return to the watery pasture"	*sol-t*[4]		
"Restrain (a cow, a bull), by a rope attached to a log, or stump, or from neck to foreleg"	*tol-*[5]		

1. Schlenker, *A Collection of Temne Traditions*, 275–76.
2. Ibid., 276.
3. Ibid.
4. Christiane Seydou, *Dictionnaire pluridialectal des racines verbales du peul: peul-français-anglais* (Paris: Éditions Karthala, 1998), 644.
5. Ibid., 722.

in the size of the Fulbe's herds. Thus, salt produced on the coast and fresh pasture lands became valuable commodities to Fulbe pastoralists.[37] Traveling through coastal Guinea in 1794, the same year as Samuel Gamble, James Watt described the Fulbe of Labé in Futa Jallon rotating their upland rice fields with pasture lands:

> . . . we set out for Laby . . . passing over plains of exceedingly rich land, on which were 60 or 70 acres of rice field. From the appearance of the stubble, we concluded the crop had been good, & from the quality of the soil it could scarcely be otherwise, which is much enriched by the pains taken by the natives to collect the dung of the numerous herds of cattle pastured on it. This they heap up and when dry burn on the ground. . . .[38]

Land rotation—alternating between rice fields and pasturage—was also a key feature of coastal land-use systems north of the region of tsetse fly infestation and in the northern portion of West Africa's Rice Coast region. In addition to clearing the land, cattle manure provided natural fertilizer to the often acidic soils. Herders needed fresh pasture lands for their herds and farmers needed fertilizer for their soils.[39]

Archaeological research among the Jola in the Lower Casamance region of present-day Senegal identified cattle bones dating back to AD 200 to 300. The earliest evidence of *Arca senilis*, bi-valve mollusks, and *Gryphea gasar (Ostrea tulipa)*, small conical oysters that attach to prop roots of *Rhizophora racemosa*, also dated back to this period. All three of these findings pre-date the earliest evidence of rice cultivation and the rotation of pasture lands and rice fields in the region.[40] The Jola have also engineered twentieth-century innovations by using a diverse group of farm animals to perform tasks, including cows, goats, ducks, and pigs (among non-Muslims). During the dry season after the rice harvest, cattle were allowed to roam free in the rice fields and to graze on the stubble of the previous year's rice plants. Women and children also gathered the animals' dung, saving it for use in their fields. Before the rainy season began, Jola women usually burned the dung, spread the ashes in the rice fields, and mixed its organic matter into the soil during fieldwork.[41] This symbiotic relationship benefited both parties.

By c. 1000 CE, Highlands-speakers possessed an arsenal of diversified strategies, including hunting, fishing, trapping, and gathering, for managing the forest-savanna environment. Their arsenal of adaptive strategies helped provide food security in periods of varying rainfall. Depending on the amount of rainfall, they exercised these skills in different micro-environments within the forest-savanna.

After the divergence of proto-Highlands, its daughter speech communities became specialists in either the forest-savanna or the coastal environment. Proto-Highlands-speakers innovated *-cap*, which Temne-speakers applied to felling trees. Chapter 4 will present evidence that Sitem-speakers inherited a cognate for -cap, but transferred their ancestral knowledge— honed in the forest-savanna region—and shifted the meaning of this inherited vocabulary word to their new environment: coastal estuaries, floodplains, and mangrove swamps. Historians will need more data from not only Sitem, and to a lesser extent Landuma and Kalum which are discussed in this study, but also Mandori, Kakissa, and Koba, which are not. In the Rio Nunez region, these virtually undocumented and understudied—and extinct in the cases of Kalum and Koba—languages could hold the key to scholars comprehending the details of how the inhabitants of the coast and forest-savanna who spoke Highlands languages adapted to their fluctuating environment.

Table 3.6 Inherited Forms for "Cutting Trees" in Highlands Languages

	Temne	Sitem
To chop, wound, fell	-cap[1]	
To cut trees on the bottom before shoveling (with fulcrum shovel)		ki-cɛpis yika

1. Schlenker, *A Collection of Temne Traditions*, 272.

By the time European traders encountered Highlands daughter speech communities and recorded the region's first written sources, Temne- and Landuma-speakers on one hand, and Kalum- and Sitem-speakers on the other, had already specialized in either the forest-savanna or the coastal region respectively. Quoted at the beginning of this chapter, Thomas Winterbottom, a physician for the Sierra Leone Company who resided in the colony of Freetown in the 1790s, describes indigenous peoples—as opposed to colonists—from the hinterland of Sierra Leone (which became the Sierra Leone Protectorate in 1896) clearing the landscape by cutting down and burning large trees, stumps, and vegetation during the dry season and just before the rains began.[42] Given the rarity of European and Afro-Europeans traveling into the interior or visiting coastal villages, foreign travelers recorded descriptions of slash-and-burn agriculture with relative frequency, reinforcing the anomalous nature of Samuel Gamble's detailed description of tidal rice-farming in a Baga Sitem village, witnessed during the rainy season.

This chapter has traced the historical relationship between Highlands speech communities that inhabit the coast and their linguistic ancestors that inhabited the forest-savanna of Guinea and Sierra Leone to their common ancestral language. Although today the homeland of the proto-Highlands language is located on the frontier of the coast, the proto-Highlands' strategies that have survived in and been retained by its daughter languages are overwhelmingly related to the forest-savanna region. As aridity increased and the location of the forest-savanna region shifted southward, some Highlands daughter speech communities migrated southward and continued to practice land-use systems honed in the forest-savanna region. By c. 500 to c. 1000 CE, proto-Highlands-speakers had developed a diverse arsenal of strategies for managing their forest-savanna environment. The transition from increasingly humid to increasingly arid periods, c. 1100 CE to c. 1500 CE, marked the point after which Highlands speech communities began to specialize in particular ecological niches.

Though the Proto-Highlands homeland is located adjacent to the coast, after c. 500 to c. 1000 CE its daughter communities came to inhabit one region or the other. In the Rio Nunez region, for example, the Landuma took their place in the rocky hillsides of the interior, while the Sitem carved out their niche in the floodplains and mangroves, joining the Nalu, Mbulungish, and Mboteni first-comers along the coast. Chapter 5 will show that the blossoming of coastal rice-growing knowledge was borne by the Nalu-, Mbulungish-, and Mboteni-speakers who possessed deep roots on the coast, and the Sitem-speakers whose migration to the coast transmitted skills from the forest-savanna region.

Conclusion

In the absence of archaeological evidence, the reconstructed vocabulary is the earliest evidence available for inhabitants of Guinea and Sierra Leone's coastal and forest-savanna regions. It reveals a picture of politically centralized, socially stratified, and highly mobile Highlands societies. This picture stands in stark contrast to the acephalous and isolated Nalu, Mbulungish, and Mboteni societies, well-entrenched in the floodplains and mangrove swamps of the coastal littoral and uniquely adapted to the coastal environs. Nalu-, Mbulungish-, and Mboteni-speakers were agents of continuity who established a tradition of coastal land-use systems. Highlands-speakers were agents of innovation, communication, and transformation who were adapted to the savanna and familiar with iron. They also founded the symbiotic and interregional relationships between farmers and herders that became critical to connecting the interior to the coast. In the ancient past, Nalu-, Mbulungish-, and Mboteni-speakers had established the roots of tidal rice-growing technology. By c. 500 to c. 1000 CE, Highlands-speakers' pre-agricultural pursuits sowed the seeds of an indigenous agricultural revolution.

Prior to the coastward migration of forest-savanna dwellers, whose dialects would evolve into the Mandori, Sitem, Koba, Kakissa, and Kalum languages, Guinea's ancestral Atlantic speech communities—Highlands and Coastal—seemed to have very little in common. However, closer examination has demonstrated that both groups successfully adapted to difficult and fluctuating environments. As a result of their migration, Sitem- and Kalum-speakers came to cultivate the same swampy terrain inundated by brackish water as Nalu-, Mbulungish-, and Mboteni-speakers. Their struggles for subsistence in these similar coastal estuaries, floodplains, and mangroves in Guinea's Rio Nunez region and the challenges of subsistence therein brought Coastal and

Highlands speech communities together. The Nalu-, Mbulungish-, and Mboteni-speakers' deep roots on the coast, and the Sitem- and Kalum-speakers' innovations in the forest-savanna region, laid the foundation on which the region's new owners of the land subsequently invented tidal rice-growing techniques several centuries before they were recorded by Samuel Gamble.

4

Coastal Collaboration and Specialization: Flowering of Tidal Rice-Growing Technology

In the present day a person going over this immense area of rice fields . . . will be struck with wonder at the mighty work, the persistence, the intelligence these men of old exhibited in order to reclaim from the waters this great body of land and reduce it to cultivation.

What skill they displayed and engineering ability they showed when they laid out these thousands of fields and tens of thousands of banks and ditches in order to suit their purpose and attain their ends! The outside banks, of course, followed streams and conformed to their meandering, but the "check" banks, which divided field from field, are as straight as mathematical exactness could make them, and divisions are accurately placed so as to separate higher from lower lands. As one views this vast hydraulic work, he is amazed to learn that all of this was accomplished in face of seemingly insuperable difficulties by every-day planters who had as tools only axe, the spade, and the hoe, in the hands of intractable negro men and women, but lately brought from the jungles of Africa. . . .

(David Doar, *Rice and Rice Planting in the South Carolina Low Country*, 8)

Unlike coastal farmers in the West African Rice Coast region or their counterparts enslaved on South Carolina and Georgia's rice plantations, plantation owners and slaveholders left a plethora of documentation about the evolution of South Carolina and Georgia's rice-growing technology and the rise of the colonies' commercial rice industries. As enslaved laborers experimented with rice varieties and reclaimed rice fields from wilderness swamps, planters documented their challenges, struggles with the environment, and strategies for surmounting them. In doing so, plantation owners and slaveholders created a body of knowledge, particularly about tidewater rice production and swamp reclamation, which is unprecedented for similar undertakings on the opposite side of the Atlantic. Not only did they share this knowledge among neighbors and pass it down to their descendants, but they also inadvertently passed it along to scholars, including but not limited to historians, who would write the rice story.

David Doar exemplified planters' production and dissemination of knowledge about South Carolina's rice industry and its technology. Doar was one of South Carolina's last large commercial rice planters on the Santee River, one of the colony's most productive rivers, particularly during the peak years between 1850 and 1860. As the rice industry ground to a halt in the 1930s, Doar reflected on its rise and fall, and wrote about the planters integral to its success and their world. In addition to recording his own experiences to share with his neighbors and descendants, he solicited and included in his narrative the reminiscences of fellow planters.[1]

Doar and the planters whom he interviewed shared a vision that glorified their class and the plantation economy. He exalted planters for creating superior agricultural technology in the more than 150 years since the introduction of rice to South Carolina; their techniques surpassed those of other cultures that had practiced rice cultivation for hundreds of years longer: "Our people have accomplished more during that period, in the cultivation and preparation of this grain, more than has been done by any Asiatic nations, who have been conversant with its growth for many centuries."[2] That Africa did not even make the elder planter's list of ancient and productive rice cultures is not surprising. In addition, Doar advanced another popular view among planters: visiting European engineers taught aspects of tidewater rice-growing technology, particularly the construction of dams, trunks, and gates, to South Carolina's planters, who, in turn, tutored enslaved Africans:

> Tradition says there was in olden times a Dutch engineer, by the name of Van Hassel, who first taught the planters how to overcome these quicksand breaks [in trunks]. There are many of these "half moons" on Santee and the negroes always speak of them as "Ben Horsal." They also speak of a stump, so large that

a ditch or drain had to go around it, as a "Joe Fuller," although why so called, I have never been able to find out.[3]

To Doar, enslaved Africans were more likely to call the material culture, which they toiled over every day, by the name of a European "expert." It was not apparent to Doar that the slaves themselves could have possessed or played a central role in the development of rice-growing expertise.

Doar was not alone. Generations of scholars had been deluded by the planters' records, which record only the slaveholders' version of the rice story. It is a story in which intelligent, ingenious, and industrious planters were the architects of the "hydraulic machine" that irrigated rice fields in coastal South Carolina and Georgia. Planters provided "the skilful engineering and patient, intelligent supervision that went to the successful result" and "worked with [their] brains on an extended scale."[4] Enslaved Africans worked with their brawn. Rather than considering some of the enslaved Africans as skilled laborers from West African regions specializing in rice production, they were thought to be "of the most unskilled character, African savages fresh from the Guinea Coast."[5] Doar's account exemplifies the prevailing view among antebellum rice planters and slaveholders, a characterization that considered the enslaved Africans to be unskilled laborers and perpetually remedial students.

The planters' rhetoric was full of racially biased overtones in its juxtapositions of their intelligent class against what they assumed to be inept, enslaved foil characters. Slaveholders who recorded the documents about rice production in South Carolina and Georgia have portrayed South Carolina's rice industry as developing *in spite of* enslaved Africans. The role of the white overseers and black drivers who acted as supervisors was also truncated. The reliance on one-sided sources produced a story weighted heavily in favor of slaveholders and rice planters.

Even though planters such as David Doar could not imagine Africans possessing the skills on which the South Carolina and Georgia rice industries were pioneered, scholarship by Peter Wood, Daniel Littlefield, and Judith Carney has worked to establish the connection between the West African rice-knowledge system and the South Carolina and Georgia rice industry. One could argue that the reclamation of West African rice-growing technology as a knowledge system indigenous to West Africa has accomplished more for the history of enslaved Africans laboring in the New World than it has for African farmers inhabiting the Rice Coast region, particularly as it concerns the history of farmers inhabiting the coastal region. The story of enslaved Africans' role in transmitting rice-growing technology to the New World is thus being told. Nonetheless, the story of how

West African farmers developed their indigenous knowledge system has remained unexplored. In the tidal floodplains and estuaries, coastal Atlantic farmers' ingenuity has been marginalized and attributed to a group of "strangers"—
Mande migrants—who arrived at the coastal region from the interior. This
chapter tells the story of coastal farmers who spoke Atlantic languages.

Evolutionary Models: Mande vs. Atlantic, States vs. Stateless Societies

While the literature on the African side of the Atlantic is not laced with the
same racial biases as is the literature recorded by slaveholders and rice plantation owners on the American side of the Atlantic, it does draw attention to a
set of assumptions about coastal dwellers who speak languages in the Atlantic
language group, and their neighbors from the interior who speak Mande
languages. The interactions between these two diverse and dynamic
groups—Atlantic and Mande—as well as historians' assumptions about
them, have shaped the historiography of the Upper Guinea Coast during the
pre-colonial period. Accordingly, if Africanists' assumptions are not racially
biased, how else can they be explained? Before examining the role of coastal
dwellers in the evolution of tidal rice-growing technology, we must address
these important issues.

In the latest study of rice farmers in West Africa, Walter Hawthorne argued that Mande traders along the Gambia River had access to iron tools and
grew mangrove rice before the arrival of Portuguese and Luso-African traders. Hawthorne drew on a seventeenth-century account of Sieur Michel Jajolet de La Courbe, a French traveler to the Rio Cacheu region in present-day
Guinea-Bissau, located north of the Rio Nunez region within the West African Rice Coast region. Written more than one hundred years before Samuel
Gamble's account of tidal rice cultivation among the Baga of coastal Guinea's
Rio Nunez region, La Courbe recorded the first written description of irrigated rice production among the Manjaco, or Brame, inhabitants of the Rio
Cacheu region: ". . . Resembles prairies; I see some lagoons of rice all along
the side of the river. The fields are traversed by little causeways, from space to
space, to prevent the running off of water; in the first place, after it rains they
sow rice that grows in the water."[6] Based on an examination of the documentary evidence of mangrove rice cultivation south of the Gambia River, Hawthorne presented three hypotheses: first, the Brame—whose villages neighbor
the Balanta in the Rio Cacheu region—learned their irrigated rice-growing
techniques from the Floup in the seventeenth century; second, Mande groups
from the interior had developed paddy rice-farming techniques in the coastal

regions of the Upper Guinea coast before the mid fifteenth-century arrival of Atlantic merchants; and third, Atlantic speech communities inhabiting the coast did not.[7]

Before Hawthorne, Joseph Lauer had interpreted La Courbe's description of inundated rice production among the Manjaco and Brame inhabitants of the Rio Cacheu region in present-day Guinea-Bissau. Lauer depicted Manjaco rice fields as poorer in quality than rice fields found further north among the Floup—what Portuguese traders such as André Alvares de Álmada called the Jola, whose villages stretch along the mouth of the Casamance River in present-day Senegal to the Cacheu River in present-day Guinea-Bissau.[8] The quality of the agriculture—as described by La Courbe—and the presence of a thriving rice trade between Portuguese and Luso-African traders and the Floup, but not the Manjaco, led Lauer to conclude that irrigated rice-growing was not "well established among fifteenth century Manjaco."[9]

Though they were assumed to be Mande, the Manjaco, Brame, and Floup speech communities, producing rice in the mangroves before the advent of trans-Atlantic trade, all belong to the Atlantic language group. Linguists have not come to a consensus on many questions concerning the Atlantic language group, but there is general agreement that the languages spoken in the Rio Cacheu region—Manjaco, Brame, and Jola—as well as some of the languages spoken in the Rio Nunez region—Nalu, Mbulungish, and Mboteni—are all members of the Northern branch of the Atlantic language group.[10] More than a century before Samuel Gamble toured Baga villages and recorded the first description of mangrove rice farming in the Rio Nunez region, La Courbe actually documented the tidal rice-growing techniques of Atlantic speech communities in the Rio Cacheu region.

In the process of establishing the West African rice knowledge system, Carney made inroads into understanding the role of coastal farmers who spoke Atlantic languages within it:

> These earliest inhabitants of the coastal littoral who grew rice included the Baga, Bainouk, Manjak, Nalu, Balant, and Jola. The Atlantic secondary center of rice diversification may well represent innovation from contact between two distinct farming systems—one Mande, based on fresh-water floodplains; the other West Atlantic [sic], located along marine estuaries influenced by salt water.[11]

The presence of salinity, and irrigation technology developed by coastal farmers to reduce it, distinguishes tidal rice-growing techniques practiced by Atlantic speech communities from freshwater techniques practiced by Mande speech communities in the inland Niger delta. Coastal dwellers designed their farming systems to control the flow of water by impounding—lowering the water level after seedlings have successfully germinated—and flushing out brackish water by controlling the flow of fresh water in and out of mangrove fields. These same fundamental principles distinguish West African from Asian rice knowledge systems. Though Carney was on the correct path, the question of just how West African farmers developed coastal rice-growing technology remains unexplored.

As this study has shown, the first-comers of the coastal region possessed deep roots on the coast, dating back to antiquity. From these deep roots, Coastal daughter speech communities developed expertise in managing salt and white mangroves extending back to their earliest settlement of the coastal region. They incorporated red mangroves, shellfish, and seasonal flooding into their coastal land-use systems. Armed with this ancient knowledge, would then the owners of the land be at the mercy of their challenging environment for millennia until "strangers" from the interior migrated to the coast and instructed them to exploit the ecological niches? What is the likelihood that groups from the interior—which had traded in, but had not lived with, harvested, or eked out a living in spite of salt and salinity—possessed a wealth of expertise to offer about salt and salinity in the first place?

Several factors are embedded in the ways that scholars have framed discussions of the earliest history of West African rice and rice farmers. First, archaeologists and botanists have gathered much of the evidence for the domestication of West African rice in the interior, particularly in the Inland Niger Delta where African rice was domesticated. As was discussed in the introduction, the physical geography of the coast and the agricultural practices of its inhabitants—the cyclical turning of the soil and potential disruption of archaeological deposits—adversely contributed to the dearth of archaeological studies conducted in West Africa's coastal region south of present-day Senegal.

Second, many of the questions scholars have asked about the development of rice cultures are embedded in larger issues of urbanization, interregional trade, and political centralization—social processes that in the Upper Guinea Coast's history have historically been characteristic of Mande societies located in the region's interior, not Atlantic societies on the coast. The Mande in the Upper Guinea Coast were once tributaries to the ancient empire of Mali, founded in West Africa's interior along the Rivers Niger and Gambia. Beginning in the late twelfth century, the Mali Empire spanned from present-day Senegal in the east to present-day Niger in the west. Trans-Sahara trade in gold gave the empire early contacts with North Africa and early exposure to Islam via Muslim traders, who transported the precious commodity across the sea of sand, but never learned its source in the savanna. From the thirteenth to the fifteenth centuries, the Mali Empire was the most powerful state in both the western African region, called "Sudan" by Muslim traders, and the Senegambia.

In contrast to the Mande societies in the interior of the Upper Guinea Coast, Atlantic societies on the coast are predominately stateless or "acephalous." Derived from the Greek word *a kephale,* the term *acephalous* literally means "without a head," without centralized and/or permanent political authority.[12] This now classic definition of stateless societies in West Africa characterizes the loci of power as diffuse and shifting, not centralized in one person or institution:

> 1) In a stateless society, there is little concentration of authority. It is difficult to point to any individual or limited group of men as the ruler or rulers of the society. 2) Such authority roles as exist affect a rather limited sector of the lives of those subject to them. 3) The wielding of authority as a specialized, full-time occupation is virtually unknown. 4) The unit within which people feel an obligation to settle their disputes according to agreed rules and without resort to force tends to be relatively small.[13]

In addition, throughout West African history, stateless societies have exhibited dispersed settlement patterns, were usually not in close proximity to long-distance trade networks, and therefore had little direct participation in long-distance trade networks prior to—and in some cases even during—the period of trans-Atlantic trade. In the absence of concentrated political authority, power in stateless societies was dispersed among a variety of what Walter Hawthorne calls "cross-cutting institutions," such as marriage, councils of elders, age-grade societies—in which boys from different lineages are brought together, initiated into manhood, and socialized by senior men into the roles they will play as adult men in their societies—and ritual and judicial secret societies. Cross-cutting institutions function to bring people from different lineages together and act as a vehicle for diffusing conflict and enforcing codes of proper conduct with fear of ostracism. When conflict could not be resolved, fission was the last resort as long as uninhabited land was available. Members who chose not to abide by the decisions of the group could voluntarily or involuntarily leave their society, clear new land, and start their own polity.[14]

There were, however, exceptions to these rules. Dating back to CE 400, Jenne-jeno, in present-day Mali's Inland Niger delta—where the earliest archaeological remains of *Oryza glaberrima* have been found—was one of West Africa's oldest urban areas. Its inhabitants lacked permanent centralized political organization but still participated in interregional trade.[15] The Igbo became chief actors in the trans-Atlantic slave trade by the eighteenth century and played a similarly important role in the palm oil trade in the nineteenth century. Though the Igbo remained stateless, they transformed their indigenous institutions—merchant networks and the oracle of the Aro-chukwu village, a religious and judicial institution—to regulate trade and to generate captives for the trans-Atlantic market.[16] The Balanta are just one example of a stateless society that chose temporary centralization as a defensive strategy against the violence of the trans-Atlantic slave trade.[17] All of these societies defy categorization.

The fact of the matter is this: all states began as stateless societies and a range of hierarchy and complexity exists between the two poles of political organization. Like the Balanta, some stateless societies—even in the coastal Rio Nunez region—evolved into states, but not all. Those that developed centralized political authority did not necessarily retain their centralization permanently. In the Rio Nunez region political structures of the Mboteni remained decentralized: society was ruled by a council of clan elders, age grades, and masked secret societies of which all adult males were members. By the mid-eighteenth century, the Mbulungish developed centralized political authority in the form of paramount chieftaincies and kings. They transformed their political structures in response to a variety of internal and external factors that included, but were not limited to, interaction with Mande groups from the interior. In contrast, Nalu clans were formed by the descendants of the leaders who guided Nalu groups in their descent south along the coast from present-day Guinea-Bissau to Guinea's Rio Nunez region.[18] Atlantic speech communities in coastal Guinea's Rio Nunez region exhibit the full spectrum of political centralization, demonstrating that the distance between states and stateless societies during the pre-colonial period was not fixed but fluid, and represented a continuum of complexity, rather than a sharp dichotomy.[19]

A third factor underscores the first two and is deeply embedded in West African historiography, particularly in the historical literature on West African rice farmers. Implicitly and explicitly, scholarly research has infused statehood with value while marginalizing stateless societies. Ann Stahl characterizes the larger questions of urbanization, long-distance trade, and political centralization as part of an "evolutionary model" of "civilization" that originated with European history, was imposed on African history during the colonial period, and continues to pervade African history even after independence. Stahl adds iron production—which most coastal Atlantic societies in the Rio Nunez region lacked—to the list of categories by which African societies are measured. This important issue will be discussed in chapter 5. Stahl also hypothesizes that archaeologists have chosen sites based explicitly and implicitly on these criteria.[20] According to this evolutionary model, societies that do not possess these characteristics—the Nalu, Mbulungish, and Mboteni of the coastal Rio Nunez region, for example—are marginalized unless they are in contact with urbanized, politically centralized societies engaged in long-distance trade—the Mande and the Fulbe would fit these criteria—or unless they were evolving toward urbanization, political centralization, and long-distance commercial activity. The value placed on urbanized and politically centralized societies may also be operating subconsciously and internally as demonstrated in the ways that elders in Guinea and Sierra Leone who speak Atlantic languages trace their origins to regions in the interior once occupied by the Mande or the Fulbe.

Racial bias has not affected the literature on West African rice and rice farmers as it has that of the South Carolina and Georgia. However, for all of the aforementioned reasons, scholars have assumed that technology diffused in one direction, from the interior to the coast. Therefore, within the history of West African rice and rice farmers, the Mande and other politically centralized societies in the interior, whose urbanized settlements, politically centralized states, and iron-working technology most resemble the hierarchies in Stahl's evolutionary model, have been assumed to have played the role of donors. Simultaneously, politically decentralized or stateless societies, with their dispersed and fission-prone settlements, age-grades, shrines, and oracles, were the recipients. Atlantic societies have been relegated to the margins on the harsh and unfriendly environment about which they possessed deep and ancient knowledge dating back several millennia.

In this chapter, the early pre-colonial history of coastal stateless societies—Atlantic speech communities in Guinea's Rio Nunez region—moves out of the margins and into the center. The following section will reconstruct the next stage of their indigenous agricultural innovation by examining the specialized terminology innovated by the earliest groups to settle in, and by the newcomers who migrated to, the coast to describe tidal rice-growing strategies. Despite its limitations—and limitations there are—to date only linguistic evidence enables us to look at coastal dwellers' development of tidal rice-growing technology. Up until this point, there has been an absence of linguistic evidence for rice cultivation. Our study has not been able to present conclusive evidence that rice cultivation was part of the land-use strategies practiced either by proto-Coastal-speakers, their Nalu, Mbulungish, or Mboteni daughter communities, or by proto-Highlands-speakers or their Sitem daughter speech communities. As a result of collaboration of the Nalu, Mbulungish, Mboteni, and Sitem in the Rio Nunez region, the tidal rice-farming system evolved.

Collaboration in the Swamps among Nalu-,
Mbulungish-, Mboteni-, and Sitem-speakers

Limited in quantity and uneven in quality, the dearth of historical, archaeo-logical, and botanical evidence for the West African Rice Coast has led schol-ars to experiment with linguistic evidence. This research has been an impor-tant first step in defining new ways of understanding the complex social, cultural, and political processes of the Rice Coast region, as well as the spread of rice varieties and rice-growing techniques in diverse physical environments among Atlantic and Mande speech communities. This section will first ex-amine these pioneering efforts, and will then present linguistic evidence to show how Rio Nunez first-comers and newcomers collaborated to fabricate agricultural technology and to innovate terminology for cultivating rice in tidal floodplains and coastal estuaries.

The origins of the root words for *rice* in many West African languages throughout the Rice Coast, as is true of the origins of rice species and rice-growing technology, have puzzled scholars of African rice and rice farmers. In languages spoken in the West African Rice Coast region, Ro-land Portères suggested that the root for "rice"—*maro/malo*—originated in Bantu languages, whose language group covers a large portion of West Af-rica south of the Upper Guinea Coast, as well as East, Central, and South-ern Africa. Judith Carney suggested that *maro/malo* originated in Niger-Congo languages; the Niger Congo language family encompasses many language groups, including Atlantic, Mande, and Bantu, and covers much of sub-Saharan Africa:[21]

> The suffixes -lo, -ro and -o in the languages of the Niger-Congo group mean food and nourishment, while the prefix, ma-is applied to foods or liquids with the meaning of "full." Mandinka is part of the Mande linguistic [sic] group; Wolof is part of the West Atlantic language family.[22]

Given the relative recentness of the domestication of African rice, which ar-chaeological research dates to the period from 300 BCE to 300 CE, insufficient evidence exists that the root word for "rice" can be traced back to proto-Niger-Congo, which is far more ancient. After all, the Coastal subgroup of Atlantic languages—just one language group of the Niger Congo language family—diverged c. 3000 to 2000 BCE. Portères and Carney's hypotheses are valuable, however, because they help to distinguish the West African Rice Coast region, where African rice and its cultivation are indigenous, from other areas of the continent where they are not. Outside of the West African Rice Coast region, speech communities derived root words for "rice" from Arabic or Portuguese. The lack of indigenous vocabulary—not to mention the examples of specialized vocabulary for the Rio Nunez region, which this chapter will analyze, and the presence of borrowed vocabulary—supports scholars' conclusions that rice was unknown in Africa outside of West Africa's Rice Coast region prior to the arrival of Portuguese traders.[23] These pioneering efforts show that rice terminology in the Rice Coast region is rooted in the language history of West African languages. Working out the details of the history will require much more extensive work in Mande, Atlantic, and Bantu language groups.

Focusing on the Rice Coast region, where rice and rice cultivation are indigenous, and on languages in which rice terminology is derived from African languages, Portères investigated rice vocabulary to determine its derivation. Based on collections and comparisons of the root word for "rice" in languages throughout the Rice Coast, he suggested that languages from Senegal to Liberia borrowed the root for "rice," *malo,* from the Mande language group:

In West Africa, "Rice" is designated by *malo* in Bambara, Malinke and Manding. This is the nominal form particular to Malinke and adopted by Wolof, Fulbe of the West, and Tukuler (Teker), Sarakole, Serer, Kabunga, Kisi, Toma, Baga, Bassari, Coinagui, Mossi-Gurunsi, Agni-Numu and A.-Nafana, A. Kulango, Guro-Gbeing, Kassonke, etc. . . . In variations, particular under-lying forms of transposed vocalics assumes the term: Looko of Sierra Leone *mali,* Susu and Dialunke *male* and *mala,* Yalunka of S. Leone *mala,* Toma of French Guinea and Liberia *molo,* Ewe of Gold Coast *moli* et *motu,* Boko (Busa) *mole,* Tonga-San and Samo of Yatenga and of Dedougou *mela,* Gurma *mule,* Balanta of Yatakunda *malu.*[24]

Portères cited languages from a multitude of linguistic groups, including Atlantic and Mande. The Atlantic languages spoken in the Rio Nunez region of coastal Guinea appear to be no exception to Portères' rule. It seems that Atlantic languages also borrowed the Mande root *malo* as a generic word for "rice" and as the root in compound words describing different stages of harvested and processed rice.[25] Coupled with the domestication of rice in territory inhabited by Mande speech communities, the presence of this single Mande loanword in Atlantic languages spoken in many parts of West Africa's Rice Coast has contributed to scholars attributing mangrove rice cultivation technology to the Mande, who migrated from the interior, and not to the Atlantic speech communities who have deep roots on the coast.

Following Portères' example, historians have examined other words as historical evidence of Atlantic speech communities borrowing tidal rice-growing technology from Mande speech communities. According to Carlos Lopes,

Table 4.1 Borrowed Forms for "Rice" in Coastal and Highlands Languages

	Susu	Jalonke	Mende
Rice	*male*	*mala*	*mba*[1]

	Nalu	Mbulungish	Mboteni	Landuma	Kalum	Sitem
Rice	*maro*	*malɔ*	*mao*	*malu*[2]	*maro*[3]	*malɔ*

1. Gordon Innes, *A Mende-English Dictionary* (Cambridge: Cambridge University, 1969), 82.
2. Sigmund Koelle, *Polyglotta Africana* (London: Church Missionary House, 1854), 105.
3. Ibid., 104.

bolanha, meaning "rice paddy" in the Portuguese-Creole language of Guinea-Bissau, is found in Atlantic languages from Gambia to Sierra Leone.[26] Walter Hawthorne builds on Lopes's hypothesis and on the presence of Mande trade networks, which brought iron to the coast, attributing the introduction of paddy-rice cultivation to the coastal region's Mande speech communities:

> A similar word, *bulon,* and derivations of it, is found in "almost all languages" in Guinea, from Gambia to Sierra Leone. . . . Mandinga states and trade routes linked these territories and therefore would have been the most likely transmitters of *bulon* farming techniques.[27]

Many pieces of this puzzle are missing, particularly since the Atlantic languages and the Mande languages spoken in this diverse region come from different branches of their respective languages groups—the Northern and the Southern branches, in the case of the Atlantic language group—and therefore are very distantly related. *Bulon* was more likely introduced to both the Atlantic and Mande speech communities relatively recently, originating in another language—perhaps in Creole (Portuguese). Speech communities from Gambia to Sierra Leone likely borrowed cognates of the Portuguese Creole loanword through contact with Portuguese and Luso-African traders.

Hawthorne, Carney, Lopes, and Portères's contributions open up a discussion about the role of Atlantic and Mande speech communities in the innovation of agricultural technology and terminology in West Africa's Rice Coast region. But the flow of technology and terminology was not uni-directional, diffusing from the Mande and the Portuguese to coastal Atlantic societies. As this chapter will show, the inhabitants of coastal Guinea possessed both indigenous technology and specialized terminology before the arrival of Mande-speakers and European and Euro-African traders.

These studies point the way to a new and promising direction, using words related to rice production as a prism for examining the interaction between West African rice farmers on the coast and in the interior, and the interaction between West African farmers and Portuguese traders. A conundrum lies not only in the origins of the vocabulary, but also in the relationship between West Africans' innovation of terminology and agricultural technology. Though the goals and methods of our studies are expressly different, the present study builds on these pioneering efforts.

In the Rio Nunez region, both rice-growing technology and rice terminology were born after the languages spoken by Coastal and Highlands ancestral speech communities diverged, and after their Nalu, Mbulungish, Mboteni, and Sitem daughter communities inhabited the swampy and salty coastal micro-environments. Innovated by Nalu-, Mbulungish-, Mboteni-, and Sitem-speakers of the Rio Nunez region, the terminology related to tidal rice-growing technology cannot be reconstructed to either the Coastal or Highlands linguistic subgroups. These areal innovations spread throughout micro-environments in the Rio Nunez region.

After the divergence of the Coastal and Highlands ancestral languages, the daughter speech communities found themselves in the same proverbial boat. Nalu-, Mbulungish-, and Mboteni-speakers had the benefit of inherited knowledge about the coastal region. But after c. 1000 CE, they were joined by Sitem-speaking villagers who migrated into neighboring villages in coastal terrain. Most of the coastal Rio Nunez region's languages were distantly related and the daughter speech communities from the proto-Coastal ancestral language—Nalu, Mbulungish, and Mboteni—could no longer understand one another. And Coastal languages were only distantly related to the daughter languages of proto-Highlands. Though coastal dwellers spoke distantly related and mutually unintelligible languages, they often lived in nearby villages and potentially worked together to design technology uniquely suited to conditions in their micro-environments. Innovating unique terminology to name the fruits of their collective labors was a product of coastal dwellers' communication as they exchanged their newly fabricated technology.

One of the first lessons learned and shared by Nalu-, Mbulungish-, Mboteni-, and Sitem-speakers in their common coastal environment was how to trap fresh water in low-lying fields in the floodplains. Using fresh water to desalinate the soil and to reduce its percentage of salinity to a level tolerable to rice species would have been critical to creating an environment in which rice seedlings could survive and flourish. To overcome the age-old challenges of salt and salinity, coastal farmers fabricated and built mounds and ridges both to trap fresh water in, and to keep brackish water out, of their fields. The use of irrigation and water-control techniques to desalinate coastal

Table 4.2 Areal Innovations for Specialized Rice Vocabulary in Highlands and
Coastal Languages

	Landuma	Sitem	Nalu	Mbulungish	Mboteni
Mound					*e-nɛk/ a-nɛk*
Ridge	*ta-nɛk/ ma-nɛk*	*a-nek/ -nek*	*ma-nɛk/ a-nɛk*	*ɛ-nɛk/ ki-nɛk*	*e-nɛk/a-nɛk*
Small Ridge				*ta-nɛk tafɛt/ ma-nɛk mafɛt* literally, "ridge small"	
Beginning of the rainy season	*ma-lɔfɛ/ ya-lɔfɛ*		*ma-lɔɔfɛ/ ma-lɔɔfɛ*		
Rice flour	*mɔnni*		*m-mɔni*	*ki-mɔni*	

soils is a unique feature distinguishing wet, or paddy-rice, farming systems indigenous to West Africa from those indigenous to Asia.

In addition, Atlantic speech communities throughout the Rio Nunez region, whose locales encompass both the coastal and highlands environments, have retained key terminology to describe aspects of the agricultural cycle, the tidal rice-farming system, and rice processing. For example, present-day Nalu- and Landuma-speakers use *-lɔfɛ* to name the beginning of the rainy season and the beginning of the agricultural cycle when cultivators prepare their rice nurseries and rice fields in the coastal areas and highlands for sowing. In addition, the Nalu, Mbulungish, and Landuma languages also use *-mɔni* to name rice flour, an important by-product of rice processing. Table 4.2 illustrates the distributions for both sets of the words.

The distributions are significant because they incorporate daughter speech communities from both linguistic subgroups: proto-Coastal, the linguistic ancestor of Nalu-, Mbulungish-, and Mboteni-speakers, and proto-Highlands, the ancestral language of Temne-, Landuma-, and Sitem-speakers. In chapter 3 it was argued that the Temne dialect diverged from proto-Highlands first, with Landuma and Sitem dialects subsequently diverging from one another. The migration of Highlands daughter speech communities from the interior of Sierra Leone to the coast of Guinea was an important contributing factor to the divergence of Highlands' dialects c. 500 CE to 1000 CE. Based on evidence that the Landuma and Sitem languages, but not Temne, possess *-nek*, we make two hypotheses: Landuma and Sitem daughter speech communities innovated words for mounds and ridges after the diverging of the Proto-

Table 4.3 Areal Innovations for "Fulcrum Shovel" in Highlands and Coastal Daughter Languages

	Nalu	Mboteni	Sitem
Shortest fulcrum shovel	ma-kumbal/ a-kumbal	faa aŋkumbɛl	toŋ-kumbɛl/ aŋ-kumbɛl
Short shovel used to weed soil for the second time in ridges		porbal aŋkumbɛl	

Highlands linguistic ancestor and Coastal daughter speech communities borrowed the terminology sometime after the divergence of proto-Highlands c. 500 to 1000 CE. Thus, at least seven hundred years before Samuel Gamble and his crew were stranded in the Iles de Los and toured Baga villages in the Rio Nunez region, coastal farmers had begun to put into place fundamental aspects of tidal rice-farming technology.

Coastal cultivators in the Rio Nunez region did not stop here. Together, Nalu-, Mboteni-, and Sitem-speakers fabricated a key piece of material culture, the fulcrum shovel. The slight concave of the shovel's body and its rounded edge were specially designed and sculpted to facilitate separating, turning, and packing heavy water-logged soils and thick vegetation. The Nalu, Mboteni, and Sitem speech communities in the northern portion of the coastal Rio Nunez region named the shovel *ma-kumbal* while Mbulungish-speakers in the southern portion of the Rio Nunez region coined a separate term. Cultivators on both sides of the Nunez River found subtle differences in the quantity of rain water and the quality of weeds in their fields, warranting subtle variations in technological design and different terminology. Table 4.3 illustrates the distribution of *ma-kumbal*.

The existence of an indigenous word for the fulcrum shovel in Atlantic languages in the Rio Nunez region still raises the question of its origins among Atlantic languages. The noun class marker suggests it is a Nalu word. However, the possibility of *ma-kumbal* originating from Sitem cannot be completely ruled out.[28] Thus, the current evidence suggests that Nalu and Sitem speech communities along the Nunez River may have separately innovated the word *ma-kumbal*. Mboteni speech communities likely borrowed it from either Nalu- or Sitem-speakers.[29]

Though the overwhelming majority of Nalu, Mboteni, and Sitem elders agreed *ma-kumbal* is the most versatile shovel, coastal dwellers also possess shovels of varying lengths and weights, each specifically adapted to the micro-environments within their fields. According to present-day coastal

Table 4.4 Forms for "Fulcrum Shovel" in Mbulungish Language

	Mbulungish
Medium-sized shovel used to make mounds	*ki-taŋgbanyi/ ci-taŋgbanyi*
Medium-sized fulcrum shovel for use by youth who have not reached full stature	*arucupuŋ*
Long fulcrum shovel (two to four meters in length) for use when turning the earth the first time	*e-lar*[1]

1. In a personal communication (March 1998 in Paris), Marie-Paule Ferry suggested that *e-lar* may be derived from *iler*. See Jouke S. Wigboldus, "The Early History of the *Iler*: Raulin's Hypothesis Revisited," in Christian Seignobos, Yasmine Marzouk and François Sigaut, eds., *Outils aratoires en Afrique: innovations, normes et traces* (Paris: Éditions Karthala, 2000), 149–72.

farmers, they use shovels of various sizes to perform different tasks in the field, and to work in parts of fields with varying kinds of weeds, qualities of soil, and levels of water.[30] Also, men chose their shovels depending on their age, stamina, and strength. Many elders testified to preferring *ma-kumbal,* because they could use it in most fields to perform most tasks, even at later stages in their lives when longer shovels were too heavy for them to manage.[31]

Mbulungish speech communities use a fulcrum shovel almost identical in design to *ma-kumbal* to repair dikes and prepare the area for the rice nursery.[32] Yet they have coined their own terminology, illustrated in Table 4.4, to name it. Mbulungish villages are located slightly to the south of Nalu, Mboteni, and Sitem villages. Of the villages where I conducted fieldwork, the Mboteni village of Era and the Mbulungish village of Monchon appear to be the closest in proximity. Actually, Era shares its micro-environment with the Sitem village of Kawas. Present-day Nalu, Sitem, Mboteni, and Mbulungish farmers named the Mbulungish village of Monchon as one of the few locations in coastal Guinea where African rice, *O. glaberrima,* still grows. They also describe the rice fields in Monchon as possessing more water and weeds than other coastal Rio Nunez villages.[33] The environmental variations may explain subtle differences in how coastal cultivators in Monchon designed their fulcrum shovels in comparison to cultivators in villages in the northern reaches of the Rio Nunez region.

Throughout the coastal littoral of West Africa's Upper Guinea Coast, farmers adapted versions of the fulcrum shovel to the ecological niches in their habitats. Variations in the shape and size of the shovel's scoop—flatter or more curved, larger or smaller—depended on land features such as quality of soil, quality and quantity of weeds, amount of fresh water collected in the fields, and land-preparation tasks. The shovel's concave scoop is attached with vines or cords to a long handle the same height as its user. The handle height enables male farmers to rest the tool on their knees when lifting heavy loads of mud. Jola farmers in present-day Senegal use *kayendo* or *kajandu* to build bunds around, and ridges and furrows within, their low-lying rice fields.[34] Balanta farmers in Guinea-Bissau use a similar fulcrum shovel, which they call *kebinde,* to cultivate paddy rice in coastal lowlands.[35] Even today, farmers throughout the coastal littoral of West Africa's Upper Guinea Coast use fulcrum shovels to carve fertile rice fields out of the mangrove swamps.

In oral narratives, present-day coastal farmers have testified that their ancestors cultivated rice with fulcrum shovels that lacked iron blades affixed to their edges.[36] According to a Mboteni-speaking elder in present-day Guinea:

> There are three kinds of *bêche* [fulcrum shovel]. When our ancestors began this work [tidal rice cultivation], they worked only with their strength, because the first *bêche* did not have a blade. At a certain moment, God made it so that we found iron that was not worked by blacksmiths. They worked that metal in place of the blade. After that time, there were blacksmiths here. We began to go to the blacksmiths to make the blades for the *bêche*.[37]

This elderly farmer's words echo an oral tradition recorded by Walter Hawthorne and told by a Balanta elder in Guinea-Bissau: "The first Balanta *kebinde* was made without an iron end. Thus, at the end, the *kebinde* was burned with fire to make it more durable and usable in farming."[38] Despite the presence of these oral narratives, however, to date historians have not examined the possibility of coastal farmers cultivating rice in the mangroves using fulcrum shovels without metal edges. Instead, historians have projected the tangled and twisted roots of red mangrove trees found on the coast today, and the centrality of iron, into the distant past. Let us not get ahead of the story. Chapter 5 will address this subject.

Patterns in the independent streams of evidence present historians with a range of patterns and questions. It is clear from the linguistic evidence that Atlantic speech communities throughout West Africa's Rice Coast region innovated specialized terminology to name this key piece of material culture. The fulcrum shovel was indigenous to the coast and was not an introduction from the interior. The ingenuity behind its design and its fabrication were part and parcel of a continuum of experimentation and collaboration by Atlantic speech communities with deep roots on the coast and those more recently migrated to the coast from the forest-savanna. Both took place after the divergence of the Proto-Coastal and Proto-Highlands ancestral languages

FIGURE 4.1. Photograph of "Man Sculpting Wooden Fulcrum Shovel."
Copyright Edda L. Fields-Black.

into their daughter languages and centuries before coastal dwellers had access to iron through the trans-Atlantic trade. In the Rio Nunez region, Nalu- and Sitem-speakers seem to have played key roles in the process.

Did the early prototypes of the shovel have a metal blade? The linguistic evidence suggests that in the Rio Nunez region it did not. While Sitem-speakers inherited knowledge of iron from their proto-Highlands linguistic ancestors, there is still no evidence—inherited vocabulary or areal innovations—of Sitem-speakers or other Atlantic speech communities in the coastal Rio Nunez region possessing indigenous iron-smelting technology or sharp-edged tools. Could they have used softer, more malleable forms of iron, which did not require smelting, to tip their indigenously made wooden fulcrum shovels? Without iron tools, could they have cleared the sandy soils of the pencil-like pneumatophores of *Avicennia africana,* possibly suffocating these shallow and vertical roots by inundating them with salt water rather than cutting them down with iron tools? Unfortunately, without archaeology, the linguistic sources only take us so far.

After c. 1000 CE, the flowering of tidal rice-growing knowledge among Atlantic speech communities in the coastal Rio Nunez region became more localized. Sitem-speakers collaborated with single-speech communities, whose languages once formed the Coastal linguistic subgroup, about specific aspects of tidal rice-growing and processing. For example, together Nalu- and Sitem-speakers innovated new terms for transplanting and sowing rice seedlings, as well as for germinated rice seedlings, *-cɛp,* which are illustrated in Table 4.5.

Indigenous vocabulary words for transplanting in coastal Guinea's Atlantic languages underscore the importance of the landscape gradient in which West African farmers adapted *Oryza glaberrima.* Transplanting is important

Table. 4.5 Areal Innovations for Localized Rice Vocabulary in Nalu and Sitem Languages

	Nalu	Sitem
Agricultural cycle	*m-tɛm /a-tɛm*	*-tɛm*
To transplant	*ma-cɛɛp*	*ki-cɛp*
To transplant rice	*-cɛp*	*pa-cɛɛp*
To sow rice with finger	*ma-cɛɛp*	*ki-cɛp tecir*
Germinated rice seedling	*m-kicɛɛp/ aŋ-kicɛɛpa*	
Seed	*m-kofok/ a-kofok*	*a-xɔfel*
Baton for beating rice		*kɪ-gbo/ cɪ-gbo*
Short baton for beating rice	*m-kigbooŋ/ a-kigbooŋ*	

Table 4.6 Areal Innovations for Localized Vocabulary in Mboteni and Sitem Languages

	Mboteni	Sitem
To fan rice into the wind	*a-foi malɔ*	*ki-foi malɔ*
Rice fanner basket	*ki-rɛbɛ/ ci-rɛbɛrɛŋ*	*ki-rɛbɛ/ ci-rɛbɛ*
Rice flour	*ku-cɔmp*	*ki-compl/ ci-com*

to rice cultivation in both inland swamps and mangrove swamps. In the Rio Nunez region, René Caillé described Baga farmers planting seedlings first in rice nurseries in their villages, and subsequently transplanting the germinated seedlings in their rice fields.[39] Rain-fed inland swamps acted as a physical buffer zone between the dry hills of the uplands, which were dependent on precipitation, and the tidal swamps that were inundated with brackish water. Linguistic evidence suggests that rice cultivation in inland swamps—which required the construction of bunds to capture fresh water, in addition to the transplantation of germinated rice seedlings—may also have been a training ground for Atlantic farmers' fabrication of tidal rice-growing technology.

Collaboration between Mboteni- and Sitem-speakers was not only highly localized, but also became highly specialized. Mboteni- and Sitem-speakers collaborated to innovate terminology related to rice processing and its accompanying material culture. Fanning rice into the wind represents just one of the ways that present-day coastal farmers separate the grain from the chaff once the rice has been peeled. Table 4.6 illustrates the distribution of the terms that are used.

In their experimentation, collaboration, and innovation in the coastal littoral of the Rio Nunez region, Atlantic speech communities innovated words for cutting trees, building on a proto-Highlands concept that Sitem-speakers inherited. Along with Temne-speakers, Sitem-speakers retained *-cap* from their proto-Highlands linguistic ancestors. However, after the divergence of proto-Highlands, Temne-speakers used *-cap* to describe cutting and felling trees, and wounding in general. Sitem-speakers attached a modifier to *-cap* and shifted the meaning to a more narrow semantic field—cutting trees before turning the soil with the fulcrum shovel. Mbulungish-speakers played an important role in this process by borrowing the term from Sitem-speakers—unmodified—and employing this new knowledge in their familiar coastal environment. Unfortunately, without regular sound changes in this areal innovation, we cannot estimate when coastal dwellers applied this aspect of the Highlands forest-savanna knowledge to the coastal littoral.

Table 4.7 Areal Innovations for "Cutting Trees" in Coastal and Highlands Languages

	Mbulungish	Temne	Sitem
To cut, wound, fell		-cap	
To cut weeds on the bottom before shoveling	a-cappa		ki-cɛpis yika
To cut some trees and leave others	e-cappa ɛti		
To cut the earth with a shovel to make a dike	ka-cappa		

In addition to innovating terminology for essential elements of tidal rice-growing technology, Nalu-, Mbulungish-, Mboteni-, and Sitem-speakers collaborated across the coastal estuaries, floodplains, and mangrove swamps to innovate vocabulary words naming an important piece of their indigenous spiritual traditions, the *D'mba* (*N'mba* in Susu) headdress. Used by all Atlantic speech communities inhabiting the Rio Nunez region, most *D'mba* headdresses stand approximately four feet tall and weigh approximately 130 pounds. Though there can be slight variations, a true *D'mba* headdress is comprised of four essential elements:

> (1) a strongly profiled head, of which one third is occupied by the face and two thirds by the hair; (2) a long and straight neck, with a rounded knob at the back possibly used to help anchor the costume; (3) a bell-shaped chest with flat breasts (symbols of motherhood), between which there are two holes that allow the dancer wearing the mask to see; and (4) two pairs of long legs, which prolong the bust and provide its support.[40]

Hidden beneath the *D'mba*'s raffia skirt, a strong dancer wore the mask on his head, holding onto the two long front legs to keep his balance and to steer his path through the crowd. Encircling the mask and the masked dancer, villagers danced around the *D'mba* to the beat of a cylindrical, double-headed drum.[41]

Art historian Marie Yvonne Curtis and anthropologist Ramon Sarro have examined the roles played by *D'mba* in coastal societies in a smattering of historical references, accounts written by European travelers and missionaries, as well as oral narratives collected among wood-carvers and the last generation of elders initiated into the "Sacred Forest." In most

Table 4.8 Areal Innovations for *D'mba* "Headdress" in Coastal and Highlands Languages

	Nalu	Mbulungish	Mboteni	Sitem	Susu
"Masculine mask of the Sacred Forest"	*m-nimba/ bɛ-nimba-yɛ*;[1] *m-nimba/ a-nimba*[2]				
"Nimba lying down"	*m-nimba-ka wala*[3]				
"Nimba that guards"	*m-nimba-ki lɛm*[4]				
"Female masquerade headdress representing a woman who has borne many children, with large, narrow, prognathous head, long pendant breasts, the entire bust resting on two front legs"		*D'mba*[5]	*Yamban; Jambang*[6]	*D'mba*;[7] *Yamban*;[8] *Penda*[9]	*N'mba*[10]
"The Great *D'mba*— sacred D'mba of the elders, as opposed to the popular one"		*D-mba-ɛ-Tɛmil*[11]	*Yamban-Andyan*[12]	*D'mba-do-Pɔn*[13]	
"Female masquerade headdress with one eye and one breast. Grotesque and disorderly— counterpart to *D'mba*"			*Yamban-Ñach*[14]	*D'mba-da-col*[15]	

1. Erhard Voeltz and Mohammed Camara, "Lexique Nalu-Français" (unpublished manuscript).
2. Marie Yvonne Curtis, "L'art Nalu, l'art Baga: Approches comparatives" (Ph.D. Thèse, Université de Paris I Panthéon-Sorbonne, 1996).
3. Voeltz, "Lexique Nalu-Français."
4. Ibid.
5. Frederick Lamp, *Art of the Baga: A Cultural Drama of Reinvention* (New York: The Museum for African Art/Prestel Verlag, 1996), 163.
6. Ibid., 156, 167.
7. Ibid.
8. Ibid., 261.
9. Ibid., 156. André Coffinières de Nordeck, "Voyage aux pays des Bagas et du Rio-Nuñez (1884–1885)," *Le Tour du Monde*, 1, 1e semestre, 1886, 273–304.
10. Lamp, *Art of the Baga*, 262.
11. Ibid., 163.
12. Ibid.
13. Ibid.
14. Ibid., 163–66.
15. Ibid.

FIGURE 4.2.
Photograph of Baga/
Buluñits, Dance Mask
with Superstructure
(D'mba), late 19th–mid
20th century. Wood,
copper alloy tacks,
123.5 × 34 × 72 cm. The
Baltimore Museum of
Art: Gift of Alan
Wurtzburger. BMA
1957.97. Copyright
The Baltimore
Museum of Art.

villages, *D'mba* was central in ensuring the fertility of women and the fecundity of the rice fields. Among the Mbulungish in particular, *D'mba* protected both pregnant and barren women. At the end of the rainy season,
D'mba also presided over the rice harvest in most villages in the coastal Rio
Nunez region. In addition to these core functions, *D'mba* could appear and
dance to welcome important visitors to a village. In a 1930s photograph
taken by a Catholic missionary, *D'mba* danced at the funeral of the "queen"
of the Sitem village. Though the queen was probably one of the chief's wives,
the appearance of *D'mba* at a funeral was an extension of *D'mba*'s core role
in ensuring fertility and fecundity. Rather than mourning, celebrating the
life of an esteemed elder who had passed on to the ancestral world would
keep the ancestors and the unborn—ancestors who are waiting to be
reborn—intimately connected to the living and to spiritual and mundane
endeavors.[42] However, in the aftermath of the Islamic revolution, which occurred in 1956–57, the role of *D'mba* has diminished, though not disappeared,

along with most other visible aspects of coastal societies' indigenous spiritual traditions.[43]

Though *D'mba* is usually associated with the Baga, especially in museum collections in which it is exhibited around the world, its origins remain a subject of debate among the region's scholars. According to Frederick Lamp's groundbreaking work on art among the Baga, *D'mba* was one of the sculptures that the Baga originally fabricated in Futa Jallon, bringing it and other ritual pieces with them in their migration from the interior. Once the Baga settled on the coast, *D'mba* then diffused to their Nalu-speaking neighbors. Lamp draws on the mask's beaded hairstyle, a characteristic of Fulbe women in Futa Jallon—seen by many Baga men to be the epitome of female beauty—and not Baga women on the coast, to buttress this theory of migration from the interior.[44]

Curtis and Sarro propose, on the other hand, Nalu origins for *D'mba*. Still dancing the *D'mba* masquerades in the 1990s, Nalu communities throughout Guinea-Bissau did not experience an Islamic revolution as the Nalu in Guinea-Conakry did.[45] Nalu-speakers in Guinea-Bissau also do not have the history of language contact with either Sitem- or Susu-speakers, as Nalu-speakers in Guinea do. In the Nalu language, the noun class marker preceding the word is consistent with the marker used by Nalu-speakers to designate inanimate objects.[46] Moreover, among Nalu communities in Guinea-Bissau, the word *m-nimba* falls into a diversity of semantic fields of words, which include the headdress, a particular rock found in the sea, a mask placed at the entry way to guard a house, and a mask used in women's initiation ceremonies.[47] However, the presence of a word in diverse semantic fields may not be evidence of the antiquity of an institution. It could signal that the Nalu's adoption of *D'mba* masquerade is relatively recent. In this scenario, the Nalu's use of *D'mba* may have spread rapidly through Nalu society. To begin to address this important question, future research is necessary to determine whether Nalu-speakers in Guinea or Guinea-Bissau possess indigenous terminology related to *D'mba*.

However, if the *D'mba* headdress originated among the Sitem—particularly when coupled with the plethora of indigenous and specialized vocabulary that the Sitem inherited from proto-Highlands and transmitted to Atlantic speech communities of the Coastal subgroup—it would signal an innovation in Kairn Klieman's first-comer thesis, discussed in chapter 2. As first-comers to the coast, Nalu, Mbulungish, and Mboteni speech communities developed strategies to subsist and flourish in the swampy, salty, and flood-prone coastal environment. To become coastal specialists, Nalu, Mbulungish, Mboteni along with Sitem societies may also have forged relationships with ancestral spirits to ensure the productivity of the land and social harmony of the villages. This shift in ritual authority may have solidified the relationship of Sitem-speaking migrants with the owners of the land.

Wherever *D'mba* originated, the role of the headdress as a coastal institution shared by the Nalu, Mbulungish, Mboteni, and Sitem is significant. It epitomizes collaboration among the Rio Nunez region's coastal dwellers, which cuts across their linguistic differences and acts as a strategy for overcoming the challenges of their swampy and salty environment. Prior to c. 500 CE to 1000 CE, neither rice nor rice-cultivation techniques had yet become part of the Rio Nunez region inhabitants' strategies for surviving and flourishing in the coastal environment. With the building of mounds and ridges and the fabrication of the fulcrum shovel without the metal foot, by c. 1000 CE, Nalu-, Mbulungish-, Mboteni-, and Sitem-speakers had become coastal specialists. Becoming ritual specialists may have been an integral part of this process.

Pre-dating the first written sources for West Africa's Rice Coast region by approximately five hundred years, the presence of shared terminology in Atlantic languages throughout the Rio Nunez region reveals rich cultural mixing among the early settlers of coastal Guinea prior to contact with Mande strangers from the interior or European traders. In his study of Luso-African identity along West Africa's Upper Guinea Coast, Peter Mark characterized identity formation among the region's inhabitants as a continuously dynamic, flexible, malleable, and multilayered process.[48] Because linguistic evidence is at its foundation, this study has focused on linguistic identities, first Coastal and Highlands ancestral speech communities, and subsequently Nalu, Mbulungish, Mboteni, and Sitem daughter communities. It has also demonstrated that Rio Nunez inhabitants traversed linguistic boundaries to innovate new terminology related to tidal rice cultivation. Yet language is merely one aspect of coastal identities.

Shared innovation in cultural vocabulary provides historical evidence for cultural contact between the region's speech communities and for the expansion of coastal identities. Prior to c. 1000 CE, coastal identities had existed very locally. They afterwards expanded to unite coastal dwellers speaking distantly related languages, inhabiting micro-environments along the Nunez River, and designing similar strategies for managing the challenging and changing physical environment.

More than likely, rice cultivation was not the only frontier on which Nalu-, Mbulungish-, Mboteni-, and Sitem-speakers found common ground and innovated technology and terminology. Future research into the cultural vocabularies of the region's languages could help historians determine whether the roots of the Baga identity—which by the seventeenth century encompassed rice-growers and salt producers in coastal Guinea, including Mbulungish-, Mboteni-, and Sitem-speakers—lie herein. Such research will help historians to understand all of the factors shaping the contours of coastal dwellers' identities before the arrival of the Portuguese.

Conclusion

This study began with the question of whether or not tidal rice cultivation had deep roots among Atlantic speech communities in the coastal Rio Nunez region. The question posed a methodological challenge for two reasons: first, there is a paucity of historical, archaeological, and botanical sources for West Africa's coastal littoral; second, the evolution of tidal rice-growing techniques pre-dates the first written sources for the region. This study has painstakingly worked to overcome both methodological challenges and to reveal the deep roots of coastal dwellers in Guinea's Rio Nunez region and of their coastal land-use systems.

The linguistic evidence reveals the slow, deliberate, and highly localized process through which coastal inhabitants gained mastery over the floodplains, mangrove swamps, and variable torrential rains. By c. 3000 to c. 2000 BCE, proto-Coastal-speakers had knowledge of white mangroves and salt. Between c. 2000 BCE and c. 1000 CE, their Nalu, Mbulungish, and Mboteni daughter speech communities gained knowledge of red mangroves, seasonal streams, and species of crabs that inhabited the aerial roots of the red mangrove trees.

While speech communities in the Coastal subgroup acquired knowledge of the swampy, salty, flood-prone coastal region, proto-Highlands-speakers learned about the dry, grassy, and hilly upland environment. However, the daughter speech communities of proto-Highlands did not just inherit survival strategies from the forest-savanna region; they also shared strategies with daughter speech communities of proto-Coastal. Together, and in conjunction with Nalu-, Mbulungish-, and Mboteni-speakers' ancient knowledge of the region, Coastal and Highlands daughter speech communities applied the sum total of their knowledge of these two dissimilar environments to the coast.

Prior to c. 1000 CE, Coastal-speakers and their daughter speech communities and Highlands-speakers and their daughter speech communities had worked in relative isolation of each other while gaining invaluable knowledge about their respective environments. In the case of Coastal speech communities, the effects of torrential rains and flooding on transportation and communication during the rainy season contributed to their isolation. In the case of the Highlands speech communities, the migration of Landuma- and Sitem-speakers from the interior of present-day Sierra Leone to present-day Guinea, and subsequently to the coast, contributed to their isolation.

After c. 500 to c. 1000 CE, the inhabitants of coastal Guinea offer us the first glimpse of tidal rice-growing technology. Coastal and Highlands daughter communities collaborated to become coastal specialists, drawing on Nalu-, Mbulungish-, and Mboteni-speakers' deeply rooted knowledge of managing salt, salinity, and seasonal flooding, and on Sitem-speakers' knowledge of mounds, ridges, and possibly even iron. Field by field and swamp by swamp, they developed systematic knowledge for managing the onerous coastal landscape, which included cultivating rice in its tidal estuaries and floodplains. After c. 500 CE, rice cultivation became just one skill in their arsenal, and tidal rice cultivation became one aspect of this skill set.

Does tidal rice cultivation have deep roots in coastal Guinea's Rio Nunez region? Its precursors do. Coastal speech communities' knowledge of mangroves, salinity, and seasonal streams laid the foundation on which this indigenous knowledge system was built. Compared to the other groups to whom tidal rice-growing technology has been attributed—the Mande from the interior, the Portuguese, and even the Dutch—Atlantic speech communities possessed deeply rooted knowledge of the coastal region.

In the Rio Nunez region, it was the Atlantic owners of the land who specialized in the salinity of the coast. Coastal specialists shared their knowledge with incoming Mande speech communities, who in the Rio Nunez region spoke the Susu language. Susu-speakers' distant linguistic ancestors hailed from the Inland Niger Delta where West African rice species were domesticated. Rice farmers in the Inland Niger Delta cultivated the same crop in very different environmental conditions. In their corner of the landscape gradient, Mande-speakers did not have to manage salinity or alter their physical environment by building dikes and bunds, mounds and ridges to diminish its effects. Along the coastal littoral of the Rice Coast region, Atlantic speech communities had deep roots and millennia of skilled expertise at overcoming coastal challenges. Mande speech communities were strangers who lacked intimate, specialized, and ancient knowledge of the coastal environment.

From plantations to coal mines, one of the underlying questions in the literature on the history of African Americans and the history of the African Diaspora is whether or not people of African descent were skilled—or merely brute—workers.[49] This chapter has argued that assumptions about skills—whether tidal rice-growing skills diffused from Mande groups in the interior to Atlantic groups on the coast—are deeply embedded in the history of the Upper Guinea Coast. My argument and the interdisciplinary evidence that I have employed to support it make this story important and unique out-

side the small yet pioneering literature using the comparative method of historical linguistics, the regional literature of the Upper Guinea Coast, and the
fields of early African and West African history. By bringing to bear interdisciplinary evidence independent of the written sources used to generate and per-
petuate these assumptions in the first place, this study has traced the deep
roots and antiquity of skilled agricultural labor to one small corner of West
Africa. In addition, it has traced some of the deep roots of African ingenuity to
the coastal littoral and to the Atlantic speech communities who inhabited it.

Having in the last three chapters laid the foundation of Atlantic speech
communities' settlement of the coastal region and indigenous agricultural
revolution, in the following chapter this study will focus on their interaction
with Mande speech communities. It will examine what skills the Mande
brought from the interior and what Atlantic and Mande speech communities
learned from each other. Lastly, it will examine the skills Nalu-, Mbulungish-,
Mboteni-, and Sitem-speakers borrowed from their Mande stranger/neigh-
bors, and how Atlantic speech communities used these skills to enhance their
coastal rice-growing technology.

5

The Strangers and the Branches of Coastal Rice-Growing Technology

These trees, whose *adventitious* [author's emphasis] roots create such a bizarre effect, generally line all the banks of the region; when the waters are receded, they seem to have been trimmed at their lower parts by a meticulous gardener, because the leaves form a horizontal plane that corresponds to the level of the highest waters. (Lieutenant André Coffinères de Nordeck, "Voyage aux pays des Bagas et du Rio-Nuñez," *Le Tour du Monde* 1: 1e semestre [1886], 274; author's translation)

Less than a century after Samuel Gamble was marooned in the Rio Nunez region for an entire rainy season, toured Baga villages, and recorded the first written description of their rice-growing technology, Lieutenant André Coffinières de Nordeck also visited Baga and Nalu villages along the mouth of the Nunez River, recording a journal of his experiences. His diary provides an unparalleled glimpse of the Rio Nunez region at a moment of immense economic, political, and social transition. Reading between the lines, it also appears as if the region had experienced an environmental transition within its mangrove ecosystem.

In this relatively short time span between Gamble's and Coffinières de Nordeck's visits to the Rio Nunez region, the political and economic climate of the region was transformed. Portuguese and Luso-African traders no longer held a monopoly over commercial activities but had been replaced primarily by English and French traders with a few Dutch in their midst. In addition, the legal trans-Atlantic trade in slaves had ended. Along the Nunez River, English traders had established factories in towns like Victoria, where they bought raw materials—rice, rubber, and palm oil—in exchange for cheap manufactured goods and scrap metal. A few miles south along the Pongo River, contraband raiding for captives continued until the nineteenth century and may have even escalated despite the abolition of the trans-Atlantic slave trade.[1]

Wars of succession among the Nalu sparked political violence and insecurity in several Nalu villages located near the major trading centers:

> On the right-hand bank, the village of Camfarandi, behind the post Victoria, also no longer offered anything but vestiges; but the premature flight of the inhabitants had saved them from a crueler fate.[2]

These ruins, near the still-intact post, nevertheless made for a bizarre contrast. Fleeing destruction, the Nalu inhabitants of destroyed villages, including members of the royal family, sought asylum in Baga villages. The French colonial administration became a key player in the conflict, using its power and influence to end the succession struggles while simultaneously extending French suzerainty throughout the region.

Coffinières de Nordeck, commander of the steamship *Goeland,* played an important role in this process by leading a French mission to visit principle Baga villages in the Rio Nunez region. Traveling via steamship, Coffinières de Nordeck was accompanied by the French commander of the region and Dinah Salifu—the newly crowned king of the Nalu who had recently signed a treaty of submission to the French colonial administration. One of the purposes of the mission was for Salifu to convince his Nalu subjects and their

Baga allies to also submit to French authority. During the early colonial period, alliances between Baga and Nalu villages became another critical component in the forging of a common identity among the Rio Nunez region's
inhabitants.

Coffinières de Nordeck's travelers' account provides two distinct descriptions of a sturdy and tangled mass of roots of red mangrove trees, *Rhizophora
racemosa*. In the first description, which is quoted at the beginning of this
chapter, he describes the coastal landscape of the Rio Nunez region—the
tides, currents, seasonal streams, and mangroves with their massive tangle of
branching roots. The *adventitious* nature of these roots may be attributable to
a phenomenon that scientists do not completely understand. Botanical studies of mangroves show that the aerial roots of *R. racemosa* branch opportunis-
tically when the root encounters environmental stress such as extremely arid
conditions or attack by predatory insects and animals.[3]

In the second description, Coffinières de Nordeck traveled down a meandering seasonal stream toward a coastal village. Until the narrow stream
widened, his party pulled in their oars and propelled their canoes by grasping
the roots of what appear to be red mangrove trees: "For a long time already,
we had had to pull in the oars and we were advancing, pushed by the current,
while towing ourselves on the roots of the mangroves. . . ."[4] Lastly, Coffinières
de Nordeck describes what he calls "dwarf" mangroves: "In the middle of the
island there is a small tuft of dwarf mangroves which allows the furious
hunter to fire treacherously on these poor beasts [pelicans and water birds]."[5]
These dwarves were likely red mangroves growing in an extremely saline environment in which a lack of fresh water and nutrients had stunted their
growth, though red mangroves can tolerate higher percentages of salinity and
levels of toxicity than white mangroves.[6] Or this passage may refer to an im-
mature secondary mangrove forest previously cut down and in the process of
regenerating. Either way, Coffinières de Nordeck provides evidence that the
ecology along the Rio Nunez region was shifting or had shifted from white
mangroves to red.

Descriptions of white mangroves, *Avicennia africana,* with their horizontal
roots—pneumatophores—and lateral branches buried in the soil are conspicuously absent from Coffinières de Nordeck's and later nineteenth-century
travelers' observations. Along with white mangroves, descriptions of red
ones—dubbed "oyster trees" by André Alvares de Álmada for their aerial
roots encrusted with mangrove oysters and other shellfish—were present in
the earliest travelers' accounts, which were discussed in chapter 2. It appears
as if zones of white mangroves that once grew in sandy and better-drained
inland soils positioned further inland, closest to coastal villages, and between
coastal villages and *R. racemosa* had been supplanted by red mangroves,

FIGURE 5.1. Drawing of "A Seasonal Stream" by Y. Pranishkoff in Lieutenant André Coffinières de Nordeck, "Voyage aux pays des Bagas et du Rio-Nuñez," *Le Tour du Monde,* I, 1ᵉ semestre, 1886, 273–304, Copyright Bibliothèque nationale de France.

which lined coastal estuaries. Though the sources are silent on how the environmental transformation took place, more than likely human activity—specifically coastal rice farmers' indigenous agricultural revolution—was at least partially responsible.

Between 1500 and 1800, Atlantic speech communities in Guinea's Rio Nunez region truly harnessed the fertility of the region—of which Nalu-, Mbulungish-, and Mboteni-speakers had deeply rooted knowledge dating back to ancient times—for their own collective benefit and for a burgeoning rice industry. From their intimate knowledge of salinity, mangrove ecosystems, seasonal streams, and rice cultivation in coastal estuaries, and floodplains, coastal farmers added growing rice in red mangroves to their repertoire. Interacting with Susu-speakers from the interior and acquiring iron for their indigenously made fulcrum shovels facilitated the ability of coastal farmers to extend their indigenous knowledge and coastal land-use systems into the most marginal areas of the coastal landscape, the red mangrove zone.

The Role of Iron in Mangrove Rice-Farming

For the first-comers and the newcomers to the Rio Nunez region, centuries and possibly even millennia of adaptation to, and experimentation in, the coastal floodplains and mangrove swamps led to the innovation of mangrove rice-growing technology. As first-comers to the region, Nalu-, Mbulungish-, and Mboteni-speakers acquired intimate knowledge about the quality of the vegetation, salinity of the soil, and fluctuations in the levels of rainfall and flow of the tides since their earliest settlement on the coast. After the divergence of Highlands languages and the migration of Sitem-speakers to the coastal Rio Nunez region c. 1000 CE, the new owners of the land became coastal specialists who gained mastery over the coastal landscape. They collaborated to design agricultural technology and material culture to the specifications of the coastal micro-environments they inhabited. Cultivating *Oryza glaberrima* became an important strategy for coastal dwellers to use for subsisting and flourishing in a region with constantly fluctuating climatic conditions. Experimentation and adaptation taught coastal first-comers the necessity of decreasing the salinity in swampy soils to levels which indigenous *O. glaberrima*, African rice varieties, could tolerate. Coastal farmers could not have successfully grown rice in the mangroves without first becoming coastal specialists.

Currently, the literature on rice and rice farmers in West Africa focuses on the centrality of iron tools to the development of mangrove rice-farming. Several scholars have argued that iron ore, iron-smelting techniques to produce iron-edged tools, and large labor inputs were precursors to the development of mangrove rice-farming in West Africa's Rice Coast region. Walter Hawthorne's research on the Balanta, the most recent study on West African rice farmers, provides one example:

> Paddy rice cultivation in mangrove swamp areas can only be undertaken with iron-edged tools. Before iron was widely circulated, coastal people, using punch-hole planting techniques and clearing trees by girdling with stone tools, may have farmed some amount of upland rice. Or as Mariano Martinho Natidai explained, they may have "farmed rice on land where there were few *paus*," few sticks or little timber, that is, on clear uplands. Without iron, he said, the twisted branches and roots of mangroves could not have been cut. Iron was required for mangrove rice-farming.[7]

According to this elder, the Balanta could only cultivate rice in the uplands without iron tools.

Implicit in asserting the necessity of iron tools to undertake mangrove rice cultivation is the notion of mangrove roots being tangled, tough, and impenetrable, and growing several feet on top of the murky soil along the coastal littoral. Traveling today to the Rice Coast, one witnesses first-hand the knotted mangrove roots that sometimes resist even iron-edged tools specially designed to counteract their force. Present-day elders who recount oral narratives about the origins and development of coastal agricultural technology are also most familiar with a coastal landscape in which twisted mangrove roots reign. Though it may seem to defy good logic, these twentieth-century experiences, or even Coffinières de Nordeck's nineteenth-century observations, must not be projected backward into the distant past.

Today along the coastal littoral, the fortress of resistant roots is characteristic of *R. racemosa,* red mangroves. Botanists and biologists refer to the tangled roots of the red mangroves as "aerial," "stilt," or "prop" roots, because they provide the main physical support for the trunk. Aerial roots also branch off, diverging from the tree trunk as much as two meters above ground and entering the ground vertically some distance away:

> As much as 24 per cent of the above-ground biomass of a tree may consist of aerial roots: the main trunk, as it reaches the ground, tapers into relative insignificance. . . . On reaching the soil surface, absorptive roots grow vertically downwards, and a secondary aerial root may loop off and penetrate the soil still further away from the main trunk. The aerial roots of neighbouring trees often cross, and the result may be an almost impenetrable tangle.[8]

As chapter 2 outlined, mature forests of red and white mangroves occupied different zones in West Africa's Rice Coast region. Zones of red mangroves lined the mouths of coastal estuaries, while zones of white mangroves grew behind them, situated closer to coastal villages on sandy and better-drained inland soils. The aerial roots of *R. racemosa* are twisted and impenetrable, unlike pneumatophores whose pencil-like structures are spongy in texture and do not develop much secondary thickening or tangling. The above-ground nature of the aerial, stilt roots allows a portion of the root to be exposed during a portion of the day, providing a unique atmospheric oxygenation system and enabling mangrove trees to obtain necessary oxygen from the swamps' waterlogged soils. Shellfish, particularly mangrove oysters, typically inhabit the roots of *R. racemosa*. In contrast, pneumatophores are equipped with lenticels and gas spaces to procure oxygen from underground.[9] The system of aerial and stilt roots has evolved over time to equip the trees to grow in the most marginal of coastal environments. Figure 5.2 depicts the aerial or stilt roots of *R. racemosa* encrusted with mangrove oysters.

FIGURE 5.2. Photograph of "Stilt Roots of *Rhizophora* Mangroves of Senegal." Copyright
F. BELASCO/ CNRS Photothèque Terrestrial Laboratory of Ecology (CNRS, France).

In presenting independent evidence from biological and botanical studies
on mangrove ecosystems and reconstructed vocabulary, chapter 2 argued that
knowledge of white mangroves dates back to the proto-Coastal language,
which was spoken by the earliest settlers of the Rio Nunez region. These early
settlers gained their knowledge of red mangrove trees, with their thick,
twisted roots and the shellfish which inhabit them, between 2000 BCE and
1000 CE. Knowledge of salt and mangroves—first white then red—were important steps—precursory stages—in the evolution of tidal rice-farming
technology. However, coastal dwellers' small-scale innovations in the mangrove zone using wooden fulcrum shovels without metal edges would not
have been enough to transform the environmental landscape. We can infer
from the traveler's accounts that *A. africana* gave way to *R. racemosa*—i.e.,
spongy and shallow pneumatophores were supplanted by dense and knotted
aerial roots—by the nineteenth century. Though coastal farmers probably
would not have needed iron tools to clear the spongy roots of white mangrove
trees, they would have needed them to clear the twisted the aerial roots of red
mangrove trees, particularly for commercial rice production. Thus, in the Rio
Nunez region, iron-edged tools acted as the impetus for the intensification of
mangrove rice cultivation and the transformation of Guinea's coastal littoral.

Found along the Lower Casamance River of present-day Senegal, archaeo-logical evidence of bog iron dates back to a seventy-year period before or after 200BCE.[10] South of the Lower Casamance River region, however, this was not the case. Coastal Guinea, like its northern neighbor Guinea-Bissau, lacks in-digenous iron ore deposits. Its inhabitants do not have an ancient history of iron-smelting technology. In contrast, proto-Highlands-speakers from the forest-savanna region did possess iron. The linguistic and historical evidence is inconclusive on whether or not they possessed iron-smelting technology to produce iron-edged tools. By the mid-sixteenth century, approximately five hundred years after the inauguration of tidal rice-farming in the Rio Nunez region, Mande traders began settling among coastal first-comers and new-comers. Through extensive interregional trade networks, these Susu-speaking strangers brought the technology for making iron-edged tools to the coast. The following section discusses the settlement of Susu-speaking traders in the Rio Nunez region and the establishment of regional and coastal trade networks.

Settlement of Susu-speakers in the Rio Nunez Region, c. 1500 to 1800

The Susu language spoken today in coastal Guinea's Rio Nunez region is ge-netically related to the Mande language group of the Niger-Congo language family. The Susu and Jalonke daughter languages were the first to diverge from the Central/Southwestern sub-branch of Western Mande.[11] Because of the high percentage of cognate vocabulary retained by both languages, most linguists classify Susu and Jalonke as dialects of the same language, as op-posed to separate languages.[12] Today Mande languages are spoken through-out a large section of West Africa, including Mali, Senegal, Gambia, Burkina Faso, Guinea-Bissau, Guinea-Conakry, Sierra Leone, Liberia, and Ivory Coast. Today in Guinea-Conakry, Susu is spoken from Guinea's northern border with Guinea-Bissau to the southern border with Sierra Leone in the prefectures of Boké, Boffa, Fria, Dubreka, Coyah, Kindia, Forecariah, Cona-kry, and some villages of Futa Jallon.[13] In much of this region, Mande speech communities, such as the Susu, are situated near Atlantic speech communi-ties, including the Nalu, Mbulungish, Mboteni, and Sitem of coastal Guin-ea's Rio Nunez region.

Today, throughout the Rio Nunez region, Susu is the lingua franca, par-ticularly in urban centers such as Conakry, Kamsar, and Boké. Most coastal dwellers who have spent a portion of their lives in urban areas—usually to pursue education and/or to seek employment—speak and understand Susu with some degree of competency. During the early nineteenth century in

some of coastal Guinea's villages, such as Koba, the Catholic Church operated missions and schools where missionaries instructed Baga students in
Susu at the expense of their own languages. The missionaries deemed Susu to
be the one language suitable for facilitating commerce among the small Atlantic speech communities who spoke different languages, most of which
were not mutually intelligible.[14] In some coastal villages, younger generations
have continued to communicate in Susu with their parents and elders who
may not have been fluent in Atlantic languages. In all coastal villages, increasing numbers of younger coastal dwellers leave for employment and education in urbanized areas. Unfortunately, in a generation or two, some coastal
Atlantic languages, particularly Koba, may become extinct—supplanted by
Susu. Simultaneously, however, Atlantic languages have likely had an effect
on Susu as well. Interaction with Atlantic languages in the interior—Fulbe—
and on the coast—Nalu, Mbulungish, Mboteni, and Sitem—has had, and is
having, an impact on the divergence of the Susu and Jalonke dialects.

In using the historical linguistics method, one must be careful not to
equate social with linguistic processes. Migration cannot be equated with
language divergence. The Susu in Futa Jallon would have spoken Susu-Jalonke,
a common linguistic ancestor to these two present-day daughter languages.
As the result of the out-migration of Susu-Jalonke-speakers, the dialect areas
of these languages were no longer contiguous. Instead, they are now separated by large populations of Fulbe-speakers.[15] Lack of contact among speech
communities can result in their mutually intelligible dialects diverging into
separate languages. We saw in chapter 3 that migration also contributed to
the divergence of the Highlands linguistic subgroup, whose Sitem, Landuma,
Temne, and other daughter languages remain mutually intelligible today in
contrast to the Coastal linguistic subgroup. The migration of Susu-speakers
from Futa Jallon to the coast was likely a contributing factor but not the only
factor in the divergence of Susu and Jalonke dialects.

In their oral narratives, Susu-speakers trace their origins to the "East," in
the territory that is Mali today, the core location of Mande speech communities. From the twelfth century and after the fall of the Ghana Empire, the
Mali Empire became the major political force and cultural influence throughout much of West Africa. Politically, the influence of the Mali Empire contributed to political centralization and to the formation of satellite states located along tributaries of rivers throughout the region. These states also
played important roles in controlling long-distance networks from the Bure
and Bambuk gold mines in the interior to the salt-producing floodplains and
mangrove swamps along the coast.[16]

Also according to oral tradition, the Susu formerly inhabited Futa Jallon,
where they coexisted with the Pulli, Fulbe nomads who had not converted to

Islam and who themselves migrated to Futa Jallon with their herds between the thirteenth and fifteenth centuries. After the sixteenth century, this population migrated into the mountainous region from Futa Toro in present-day Senegal and Macina in present-day Mali. Trans-Atlantic trade, an Islamic revolution, and the 1725 establishment of Futa Jallon as a theocratic Muslim state had a profound impact on the region and its inhabitants. A second immigration into Futa Jallon of Fulbe pastoralists from Futa Toro, Bundu, and Macina—people who had converted to Islam and with whom the non-Muslims could not coexist—resulted in a large population of Susu fleeing the region.[17] Those Jalonke who remained in Futa Jallon were absorbed into the lowest castes of Fulbe society.[18]

Environmental change, particularly several hundred years of decreased rainfall and increasingly arid conditions, resulted in ecological zones shifting southward and played a critical role in Mande speech communities moving southward from the savanna into the savanna-woodland and forest regions.[19] Though the period of increased aridity lasted from c. 1100 to c. 1500, it is not known when the Susu began migrating from Futa Jallon toward the coast. Though the bulk of the Susu migration to the coast took place after the seventeenth century, European travelers' accounts report Susu moving out of Futa Jallon before the seventeenth century, as itinerant caravan traders. Based on oral traditions, André Alvares de Álmada described Jalonke and Susu traders bringing a variety of commodities from Futa Jallon south of the Nunez in coastal Guinea to the Rio Pongo region before the advent of European traders in the sixteenth century.[20] Álmada described Susu traders selling dyes and Jalonke caravans traveling to the Rio Nunez from Futa Jallon:

> The best dye-stuffs are those brought by the Sousos, who border the Bagas in the hinterland. From the heights of this hinterland a nation of blacks called Putazes [Jalonke] come down to these rivers. They come in caravans of 1,000 or 2,000 men, in order to buy salt in exchange for white cotton cloth, for clothes made from this cloth, for some gold, and for bows and arrows.[21]

Álmada also reported the establishment of Susu villages west of Futa Jallon, sandwiched between the coast and the Futa Jallon Mountains and situated beyond the Baga (Sitem) villages on Cape Verga in coastal Guinea.[22] As coastal Guinea was drawn into trans-Atlantic trade, Susu strangers settled on the sparsely inhabited coast among the Nalu, Mbulungish, and Mboteni firstcomers and Sitem newcomers.

Several European observers identified the region in Guinea's interior from which the Susu migrated as possessing iron deposits and the Susu as possessing the technology to extract the mineral. For example, Duarte Pereira, who was employed as a navigator for two Portuguese kings and traveled along the coast of West Africa in the late fifteenth century, commented on iron deposits in Susuland and the Susu's role in the iron trade: "Twelve or fifteen leagues from the sea inland is a race of men called Sousos; they possess much iron, which they bring to Serra Lyoa and other parts and make a good profit."[23] A second foreign visitor, Father Baltasar Barreira, the first Christian missionary stationed in Sierra Leone—from 1605 to 1609—reported: "There are mines of various metals, especially iron, but the iron procured among the Sousos is better than the sort in these parts [the coast]."[24] Barreira was one of the earliest Europeans to travel into the interior and one of few to visit a Susu kingdom—the kingdom of Bena, located 150 miles north of Sierra Leone. He may have actually witnessed first-hand iron ore in Susu territory and/or iron-smelting technology among the Susu. However, Barreira's account may also be based on André Alvares de Álmada's report, which was published a few years previously and was widely circulated around the Cape Verdean community. Whatever Barreira's sources, other European observers corroborated his testimony, demonstrating a general consensus among Portuguese and Luso-African traders that the Susu possessed both iron mines and blacksmiths to process iron ore.[25] Reports from territories inhabited by Susu-speakers do not equivocate on these issues, as did reports about the Temne of Sierra Leone.

European travelers' accounts from Guinea's coastal region are less decisive in their characterization of the Baga and Nalu and their access to iron. On the one hand, in general, they are silent on the question of whether or not coastal Guinea possessed iron ore deposits.[26] On the other, although they are duly unimpressed with the quality of their weaponry, European observers describe the Baga using weapons, particularly cutlasses and spears, made of iron. Francisco de Lemos Coelho reported: "The weapons with which they fight are spears with very long iron heads and short shafts, and buffalo-hide shields which cover their whole body."[27] The earliest of these reports dates back to the late seventeenth century, after Susu itinerant traders and caravans had a well-established trade in iron from the interior to Guinea's coast.

Some of the patterns in travelers' accounts from coastal Guinea's Rio Nunez region dovetail with similar patterns in Guinea-Bissau. Walter Hawthorne found that in the Senegambia during the pre-colonial period, iron smelting was confined to the interior. Prior to the advent of trans-Atlantic trade, the Balanta bartered dried fish and mollusks with Mande traders from the interior for iron. After the advent of trans-Atlantic trade, the Balanta traded captives for iron weapons and tools. The shift in the interregional trade networks and the increased violence on the coast prompted the Balanta to move closer to the mangrove swamps, where they used the inhospitable landscape as both a natural defense and a production site for their new staple crop—paddy rice. Iron weapons provided defense against slave-raiding, while iron tools allowed the Balanta to cultivate rice in the mangroves, which they exchanged for more iron tools and weapons.[28]

Like their counterparts in Guinea-Bissau, coastal dwellers in Guinea gained access to iron-edged tools via commercial networks with Mande "strangers" to the Rio Nunez region—Susu-speakers who migrated to the coastal littoral from West Africa's interior. However, unlike in Guinea-Bissau, some Rio Nunez region inhabitants—Sitem-speakers—possessed knowledge of iron, which they brought with them to the coast from the forest-savanna region. Based on linguistic evidence presented in chapter 4, Sitem-speakers lacked the technology to fashion iron-edged tools, which could be affixed to the indigenously made wooden fulcrum shovel.

Though Susu-speakers lacked familiarity with coastal soils inundated by brackish water, they possessed knowledge of rice and rice cultivation, albeit in dry environments. Like the Sitem-speakers who settled in the Rio Nunez region before them, they shared important lessons with the owners of the land about using technology to fully exploit the coastal region and made important contributions to the development of tidal rice-growing technology in the Rio Nunez region.

Up to this point, this study has examined cultural vocabulary words that coastal speech communities both retained and innovated to name aspects of their physical environment and their strategies for managing it. The specialized vocabulary words were indigenous to Atlantic speech communities in the Rio Nunez region. The remainder of this chapter will discuss a final set of cultural vocabulary: loanwords that Susu-speakers coined and coastal dwellers borrowed and, alternatively, words that Susu-speaking strangers borrowed from the coastal owners of the land who were their hosts. Before we examine the evidence, however, the following section will first outline the ways that historians employing the comparative method of historical linguistics have used loanwords as historical sources.

Borrowing Technology, Terminology, and Prestige: Susu Loanwords in Atlantic Languages

Loanwords are valuable historical sources that provide direct evidence of the transfer of knowledge between communities, the direction of the exchange, and the knowledge transferred.[29] Historians of the large expanse of Eastern, Central, Southern, and Western Africa where Bantu languages are spoken have examined loanwords as historical evidence of technological innovation, particularly in iron-smelting, agriculture, and trade.[30] In the Rio Nunez region, loanwords pertaining to rice-growing technology provide evidence of interaction among a host of distantly related and unrelated speech communities— Nalu-, Mbulungish-, Mboteni-, and Sitem-speaking coastal dwellers and Susu-speaking strangers—and of their interaction with a physical environment ancient to some, unfamiliar to others, and unyielding to all.

In addition to evidence of contact among speech communities, loanwords are also evidence of decisions made by Nalu-, Mbulungish-, Mboteni-, and Sitem-speakers on the one hand, and Susu-speakers on the other, to adopt innovations, both terminology and technology, introduced by speech communities of the other language group. Unfortunately, we will never know the names of the individual actors who originally experimented with using iron tools to clear mangrove swamps or to build dikes and bunds. Nor will we ever know the names of Susu-speakers who first broadcast rice fields in the Rio Nunez regions' floodplains and mangrove swamps. Historians may never be able to reconstruct precisely why some coastal farmers or their Susu neighbors chose to do so, or even why they imagined that they might succeed at growing rice in this manner. This is the limitation of linguistic evidence.

Why would either Susu-speakers or their Nalu-, Mbulungish-, Mboteni-, or Sitem-speaking hosts choose to adopt the technology of their neighbors? Susu-speakers may have chosen to adopt coastal Nalu-, Mbulungish-, Mboteni-, or Sitem-speakers' technology because of their intimate knowledge of coastal micro-environments. Given the antiquity of their roots in the region, coastal first-comers and newcomers may have chosen Susu-speakers' innovations because the new technology enabled them to more fully exploit the swampy, salty ecological niche. In an alternative scenario, loanwords from Susu into coastal Atlantic languages may represent the prestige coastal dwellers perceived the strangers to possess and the power relationships embedded in the interaction between owners of the land and incoming strangers. In the absence of written documents and archaeological studies for the period prior to c. 1500, loanwords offer a wealth of evidence for agricultural innovation occurring as a result of the interaction between Susu-speaking strangers and coastal first-comers and newcomers, as well as the important role played by Susu-speaking traders in providing iron, iron-smelting technology, and iron-edged tools to coastal farmers in the Rio Nunez region.

In order for loanwords to be reliable historical sources, historians must first confirm that the words in question are in fact borrowed from another language, and then determine the words' origins. To identify loanwords, historians pursue a two-pronged approach of examining the word's distribution and its sound changes. First, a spatial distribution of a word in two or more contiguous, related, or unrelated languages qualifies a word as a potential loanword. Second, exhibiting morphological or phonological anomalies, which deviate from the sound-change rules established by a thorough analysis of core vocabulary, confirms that a word was borrowed into a language. Lastly, by identifying the language in which the potential loanword's morphology and phonology are regular, and in which other words related to the potential loanword are present, an historical linguist can potentially pinpoint the source language that introduced the word.

Identifying loanwords and their source languages is not an easy task, because languages borrow words at all stages of their development. Thus, loanwords can be borrowed into an ancestral language and inherited by its daughter speech communities. Early loanwords borrowed before the language in question underwent regular sound changes are more difficult to distinguish from core vocabulary words, because they will also exhibit regular sound changes.[31] Though early loan words are more difficult to identify, in some ways, they are easier to date, because they may exhibit the regular morphological or phonological correspondences used by historical linguists to assign words to a particular linguistic subgroup and to date the divergence of the subgroup using glottochronology. More recent loanwords do not exhibit these regular correspondences.

In the Rio Nunez region, identifying and dating loanwords into Atlantic languages spoken in the Rio Nunez region requires a working knowledge of the morphology and phonology of Mande languages—in addition to Atlantic languages—in order to separate Susu words from words in the ancestral Susu-Jalonke language. Though a complete analysis of the Northern branch of the Mande language group—to which the Susu and Jalonke dialects belong—is beyond the scope of this study, some analysis can be made from the core vocabulary lists that I collected during my fieldwork. Present-day Jalonke words possess the definitive marker "-na, -nna" in their nominal inflections. However, Susu words do not end in "-na, -nna," because the Susu dialect dropped the inflection since it began to diverge from proto-Susu-Jalonke.[32] This study will use the presence or absence of this definitive marker to distinguish between Susu words inherited by Susu-speakers from the Susu-Jalonke language, and Susu words innovated by Susu-speakers after proto-Susu-Jalonke began to diverge.

Susu-speakers in the Rio Nunez region inherited two sets of vocabulary from their Mande linguistic ancestors before their migration in the c. 1500 to 1800 period. First, they inherited knowledge from their linguistic ancestors who spoke more distantly related ancestral languages in the Mande language group. Second, they inherited knowledge from their linguistic ancestors who spoke proto-Susu-Jalonke. Like coastal first-comers and newcomers who preceded them, Susu-speakers also created knowledge specific to the coastal environment that they encountered in the Rio Nunez region. Coined on the coast prior to the c. 1500–1800 period, this third set of Susu words is unique and cannot be traced to other Mande languages, including Jalonke. This study will use population movements of Susu-speakers from the interior to the coast as an approximate beginning point when Atlantic speech communities in coastal Guinea borrowed loanwords from their Susu-speaking neighbors. Dating the entrance of the words to various branches of the Mande language group, however, is beyond the scope of this study.

To the Rio Nunez region, Susu-speakers brought a wealth of knowledge about cereals—fonio and sorghum, in addition to rice, which was discussed in chapter 4—and material culture used to clear the savanna region, particularly short-handled hoes. *Oryza glaberrima* grows in uplands and lowlands inundated by brackish water; fonio, *Digitaria exilis,* also grows in dry and wet conditions and nonwoody environments, particularly along the upper basin of the Niger River in present-day Guinea, Mali, and Burkina Faso and west into the Casamance River valley of present-day Senegal. Though fonio is adapted to grow in neither excessively dry conditions nor in environments inundated by brackish water, it is adapted to other unproductive environments, in soils of sand, gravel, lime, pebbles, slopes, plateaus, valleys, and riverbanks.[33] These characteristics make it an important famine food in coastal Guinea today.[34]

Not grown in coastal Guinea, sorghum is cultivated in the Senegal River Valley of Mali and Senegal, particularly along the banks of the Niger and Senegal Rivers. It is one of the principle crops of *dércue*—which refers literally to the recession of waters after the floods—agriculture in which farmers sow seeds in fields moistened by flood waters. Unlike southern rivers such as the Nunez, there is an absence of salinity along the sandy, clay banks and the basins of northern rivers, making it unnecessary for *décrue* farmers to trap fresh water and use it to leach salinity out of the soils.[35] *Décrue* agriculture also differs from tidal farming systems in the types of material culture used by the regions' farmers to clear and prepare the fields.

Short-handled hoes for sowing and weeding are common tools for cultivating fonio and sorghum. Susu-speakers transmitted knowledge of hoes to coastal dwellers in the Rio Nunez region. Throughout West Africa, farmers use hoes to turn the soil in the dry, rocky hillsides of the savanna-forest and the sandy, clay soils of riverbanks in Mali and Senegal north of the Casamance River. Whereas coastal farmers vary the length and concavity of the fulcrum shovel scoop and the length of the handle depending on the ecological conditions in their rice fields, farmers throughout West Africa vary the length of the hoe's handle, the angle at which the handle is attached to the blade, and the size and shape of the blade. Inhabitants throughout West

Table 5.1 Mande Loanwords in Coastal and Highlands Languages

	Susu	Jalonke	Mende
Fonio	*fundeyi*	*fundema*	*funde*[1]
Rice	*male*	*mala*	*mba*[2]
Sorghum	*mɛŋgi*	*mɛŋgina*	
Hoe	*keri*	*kerina*	*kali*[3]

	Nalu	Mbulungish	Mboteni	Sitem	Kalum	Landuma
Fonio	*m-pindi/* *apindi*	*pundɛ/* *cu-pundɛlɛŋ*	*pundu,* *pundo*	*pundu*		*pende/* *ya-pende*
Rice	*maro*	*malɔ*	*mao*	*talɔ/ malɔ*	*maro*[4]	*malu*[5]
Sorghum			*mank/* *cu-mank*			
Short-handled hoe		*keri/ci-keri*	*keri/si-keri*	*kel/ cel*	*kara*[6]	

1. Gordon Innes, *A Mende-English Dictionary* (Cambridge: Cambridge University, 1969), 15.
2. Ibid., 82.
3. Ibid., 39.
4. Sigmund Koelle, *Polyglotta Africana* (London: Church Missionary Society, 1854), 104.
5. Ibid., 105.
6. Ibid., 84.

Africa have customized hoes, like the fulcrum shovel, to fit the topography of the land, the labor regimes of their crops, and even the strict division of labor in which men clear and prepare the soil and women weed, each gender using a different kind of hoe.[36] In the Rio Nunez region, Susu-Jalonke-speakers inherited words for hoes, sorghum, and fonio from their linguistic ancestors who spoke ancestral tongues in the Mande language group. Table 5.1 depicts the distribution of the words.

Even though Susu-speakers possessed knowledge of diverse cereals grown in dry climates, the linguistic evidence is clear: it was not *Susu* knowledge. These are not Susu words. They are Mande words that were borrowed into languages in the Atlantic language group and other language groups throughout West Africa at different stages in the language history of the region. Similar to the word for rice, they may have been introduced more than once

Table 5.2 Susu-Jalonke Loanwords in Coastal and Highlands Languages

	Susu	Jalonke
Mound	*tukunyi*	*(tukuŋma) tekina*

	Nalu	Mbulungish
Mound	*m-tukuɲi/* *atukuɲi*	*tukunyi*

to ancestral—and subsequently to daughter—speech communities. How early on the words were introduced, historians and linguists still are not certain.

Susu-Jalonke words for mounds are evidence of knowledge that Susu-speakers inherited from their more immediate linguistic ancestors prior to the c. 1500–1800 period. Table 5.2 illustrates the distributions of these words. First, Susu-Jalonke-speakers may have learned to plant crops in mounds, to decrease incidence of soil erosion. Throughout West and West-Central Africa, farmers use mounds to plant tubers, including but not limited to cassava—a high-yielding New World crop suited to forest environments and introduced to the region as a result of trans-Atlantic trade.[37] Chapter 4 presented the indigenous specialized vocabulary words innovated by coastal dwellers to describe mounds and ridges in Atlantic languages spoken in coastal Guinea's Rio Nunez region. Today coastal farmers build mounds and ridges to trap fresh water within inundated rice fields. However, building mounds as a farming technique is not limited to rice cultivation or to the coastal environment.

Though the current literature on rice in West Africa portrays the Mande predominantly as innovators, in the coastal Rio Nunez region they provided the tools for coastal inhabitants to improve upon their indigenous technology. The fulcrum shovel is a perfect example. Chapter 4 discussed the innovation of specialized terminology to describe the tool whose length and weight coastal farmers customized to fit the quality of the weeds and depth of water in their rice fields, in addition to their own stamina and physical strength. The first term spread areally among Nalu, Mboteni, and Sitem speech communities located in the northern part of the Rio Nunez region. Susu-speakers borrowed a term for the shovel from the Mbulungish located in the southern part of the region. Susu-speakers innovated a third term, a generic one, to describe all wooden fulcrum shovels. However, the owners of the land in the Rio Nunez region still customized *kɔp,* the generic Susu word for the wooden fulcrum shovel, and made it their own by combining the borrowed word with adjectives in their own languages to form compound words describing the elongated size of the shovel.

Previously, scholars suggested that since coastal Atlantic farmers in the Rio Nunez region borrowed the word kɔp from the Susu, Atlantic farmers by extension also borrowed their rice-growing technology from the Susu, or learned it from the Portuguese.[38] However, this study has found no evidence to support these claims. Kɔp is only one of many words used by present-day coastal farmers to name this important aspect of their agricultural material culture. Chapter 4 presented extensive evidence that coastal speech communities coined a host of specialized and indigenous vocabulary words related to rice production and specific to the coastal environment. Table 5.3 illustrates specialized vocabulary for tidal rice-farming—transplanting rice seedlings— and its material culture—the wooden fulcrum shovel—that Susu-speakers borrowed from their Nalu-, Mbulungish-, Mboteni-, and Sitem-speaking neighbors.

Though Atlantic farmers throughout West Africa's Rice Coast designed and fabricated the wooden fulcrum shovel based on their intimate and extensive knowledge of the coastal environment, linguistic evidence reveals that in the Rio Nunez, Susu-speakers fabricated metal blades. The story, however, does not end there. The proto-Highlands word for iron and the semantic shift of the word to include iron cooking pot, suggests that iron and some level of iron technology pre-dated the advent of interregional trade networks established by Mande traders, and was also indigenous to Atlantic speech communities. However, Susu-speakers, not proto-Highlands-speakers or their daughter speech communities fabricated the metal blades. Susu-speakers may have been influenced by knowledge from their ancestral speech communities in the Mande language group about the short-handled hoe—the essential implement for clearing brush in the savanna—in sculpting the cutting edge to fit the foot of the wooden fulcrum shovel. However, among Susu-speakers, making iron edges for coastal implements represented an innovation, which was unique to the coastal region.

Independent language evidence and biological and botanical studies of mangrove ecosystems have revealed the diversity of coastal ecosystems, as well as the diversity of coastal land-use systems—important variations that are masked by assertions of the centrality of iron. Metal-edged tools were not needed by coastal dwellers clearing the spongy, pencil-like pneumatophores of white mangroves in the Rio Nunez region, though they may have been requisite to coastal farmers clearing the twisted and tangled roots of red mangrove trees. According to linguistic evidence, Coastal and Highlands daughter speech communities—which had deep roots on the coast and rudimentary

Table 5.3 Susu Loanwords in Atlantic Languages/Atlantic Loanwords in Susu

	Nalu	Mbulungish	Mboteni	Landuma	Sitem	Susu
Fulcrum shovel (generic)	m-kɔp/a-kɔp	kɔp/ci-kɔppel	kɔp/su-kɔp	k-ɔpi/c-ɔpi		kɔfi
Long shovel	m-kɔp lanna/a-kɔp lanna	kɔp kokilannɛ/ ci-kɔppel kokilannɛ				kɔfi kuye
Medium-sized shovel used to make mounds		ki-taŋgbanyi/ ci-taŋgbanyi				kitangbanyi
To transplant rice	-cɛp				pa-cɛɛp	male siftɛ

	Nalu	Mbulungish	Mboteni	Kalum	Sitem
Blacksmith	ma-kabinɛ θɛn/ a-kabinɛ θɛn	kabi/ n-kabilleŋɛl			
Iron	m-fads[1]			kɔ-fac/cɔ-fac[2]	
Iron cooking pot				kɔ-fac/cɔ-fac[3]	
Fulcrum shovel blade		ma-fanc/ a-fanc	a-fɛnc/ e-fɛnccel		a-fɛnc/ fɛnc

	Temne	Kogoli	Landuma	Susu
Blacksmith				xabui
Iron	a-fac/ɛ-fac[4]	a-fac[5]	a-fac[6]	a-fac/a-fac
Iron cooking pot	a-fac/ɛ-fac[7]			
Fulcrum shovel blade				-fɛnsi

1. Koelle, *Polyglotta Africana*, 83.
2. Ibid., 82.
3. Ibid., 67.
4. The Reverend C. F. Schlenker, *A Collection of Temne Traditions* (London: Church Missionary Society, 1861), 82.
5. Marie Paule Ferry, unpublished manuscript.
6. Koelle, *Polyglotta Africana*, 83.
7. Schlenker, *A Collection of Temne Traditions*, 66.

knowledge of iron-working technology, respectively—took Susu-speakers'
technology—iron blades for their indigenously made fulcrum shovels—and
used it to further exploit their highly localized environments.

Having traced the origins and spread of words for the key aspects of the
coastal rice knowledge system, there are a host of other words that defy the
comparative method. This indigenous terminology related to tidal rice cultivation falls outside the categories for inherited vocabulary, areal innovations, and
loanwords, because individual coastal speech communities—Nalu, Mbulungish, Mboteni, and Sitem—individual villages, and in some cases individual
families have adapted their own strategies for managing the variable conditions
found in their rice fields. For example, in each village coastal farmers perform
countless actions associated with fieldwork. In some, the actions include walking on the weeds to bury them into the earth, turning the soil for the first and
second times with the fulcrum shovel, and catching the earth and packing it
into place with one's hands. The same is true for the actions, implements, and
rituals associated with clearing a new mangrove field, transplanting rice seedlings, surveying fields as the rice matures, harvesting, and processing the rice.
Throughout the region, coastal farmers' technology varies slightly.[39] In each
community, in each micro-niche, in each village, and sometimes in each family, coastal farmers call their localized technological innovations by different
names (see Appendix 2). The presence of this exceedingly specialized and
uniquely local terminology is direct evidence of Rio Nunez farmers who spoke
Atlantic, not Mande, languages uniquely fashioning rice technology and terminology to micro-niches and micro-environments along the coast.

Though the introduction of iron-edged tools was an important addition to
coastal dwellers' land-use strategies, these tools did not, and do not, define
tidal rice-growing technology. Rather, the technological innovations of the c.
1500–1800 period were driven by the ingenuity of coastal dwellers experimenting in, and adapting to, their environment since ancient times, and not
vice versa. The accumulation of the linguistic evidence—the inherited vocabulary, areal innovations, and loanwords—attests to the indigenous nature
of this coastal farming system, uniquely adapted to the daunting challenges
of the region by the groups whose deep roots had been planted in it, some
since ancient times. The introduction of iron improved the effectiveness of
tidal rice-growing technology and empowered coastal dwellers to extend
their indigenous knowledge system to areas of the mangroves, which had
heretofore been insurmountable.

Tidal rice-farming exists in an area larger than coastal Guinea's Rio Nunez
region, which is, after all, a small corner of the West African Rice Coast region.
Several centuries before Samuel Gamble toured Baga villages and described
their agricultural practices in detail, the first Portuguese and Luso-African

traders to visit the West African Rice Coast region and to record the region's first written sources described tidal rice production north of the Rio Nunez region along the Gambia River. The linguistic sources presented throughout this study have shown that tidal rice growing was indigenous to Atlantic speech communities in coastal Guinea, evolving organically from the deep roots of the first-comers to the coast and the innovations of migrants from the interior uplands. Not all Atlantic speech communities inhabiting the coast have deep roots in the region or histories of cultivating rice which date back to ancient times. However, future research, particularly among the Jola of the lower Casamance River, would likely show that tidal rice-growing is also indigenous to, and deeply rooted among, other Atlantic speech communities located north of the Rio Nunez region. It will also help historians, linguists, and archaeologists to understand the immense diversity of this large and understudied region and its inhabitants and the development of their coastal rice knowledge systems.

Conclusion

Language evidence and the comparative linguistics methodology have provided a unique vantage point from which to study the early pre-colonial history of the West African Rice Coast and the innovative farmers who inhabited it. In the absence of archaeological evidence south of the Lower Casamance region, language evidence and the comparative method of historical linguistics provide the earliest evidence to date for the region. It has shifted the focal point from the interior—including but not limited to the inland Niger delta where *Oryza glaberrima* was domesticated—to the coastal estuaries, one of two secondary centers where African rice was diversified. Coastal stateless societies whose languages belong to the West Atlantic language group did not typically attract the attention of Arab and European travelers, because they lacked centralized political authority, urban centers, and long-distance trade networks. Historians of the region have overwhelmingly relied on the first written sources for West Africa recorded by foreign traders. Employing language evidence and the comparative method of historical linguistics enabled this study to reconstruct historical periods predating both the available archaeological evidence and travelers' accounts.

The confluence of language evidence—reconstructed cultural vocabulary, areal vocabulary, and loanwords—has revealed that in coastal Guinea's Rio Nunez region, tidal rice-growing technology—the coastal rice knowledge system—is indigenous to the Atlantic speech communities. In its early stages, two speech communities, Coastal and Highlands, made important contributions to the coastal rice knowledge system, based on their intimate knowledge of two dissimilar micro-environments. Entrenched in the low-lying swamps, inundated by brackish water, and isolated by torrential rains, Coastal speech communities spent millennia acquiring knowledge about salinity, white mangroves, seasonal streams, shellfish, and red mangroves before Highlands speech communities migrated to the coast. From their homeland in the dry, rocky, and hilly uplands, Highlands daughter speech communities contributed knowledge of iron, planting in mounds, and cutting down trees. All of these strategies became key ingredients in the coastal rice knowledge system.

Only through cooperation did Nalu-, Mbulungish-, Mboteni-, and Sitem-speakers become specialists of the coastal landscape. As a result of collaboration, they established the foundation of tidal rice-growing technology—building mounds and ridges to block brackish water from entering, and to trap fresh water in, their rice fields, and fabricating the wooden fulcrum shovel, which they customized to suit the quality of soil and vegetation, as well as the quantity of water in their fields. The confluence of language evidence, particularly the presence of specialized vocabulary words related to tidal rice-production, in the Rio Nunez region's Atlantic languages—and their absence in the region's Mande languages—has shown that the development of the coastal rice knowledge system was highly localized and specialized among the Atlantic speech communities whose deep roots were planted on the coast.

Specialized rice vocabulary from Atlantic languages in the Rio Nunez region shows that the evolution of tidal rice-growing among coastal dwellers marked an indigenous agricultural revolution. It occurred independently of trade networks bringing iron to the coast, of Susu-speakers migrating from the interior to the coast, and of coastal dwellers uprooting the tangled, resistant roots of mangrove trees. Walter Hawthorne's research in coastal Guinea-Bissau suggests that the Balanta—who unlike the Nalu, Mbulungish, and Mboteni of coastal Guinea migrated to the coast and began cultivating paddy rice after the arrival of the Portuguese—learned their paddy-rice cultivation techniques from the Mande, from whom they also acquired iron tools. The differences lie not only in our conclusions, but also in the time periods that we study—the undocumented past pre-dating European traders and their travelers' accounts versus the period of contact between European traders and stateless societies in coastal West Africa—as well as the methods that we use to study them: language evidence, the comparative method of historical linguistics, and botanical and biological studies of mangrove ecosystems versus travelers' accounts and oral traditions. They highlight the diversity of the West African Rice Coast region and its inhabitants who spoke Atlantic languages. We both agree, however, that the Mande played an

important role in extending mangrove rice farming and thereby in transforming the coastal landscape.

By the period from 1500 to 1800, all the pieces were in place for coastal
dwellers to practice mangrove rice technology and to alter the physical landscape of West Africa's Rice Coast region. With the addition of iron to their
indigenous wooden fulcrum shovel, coastal farmers possessed all of the component parts of the mangrove rice-farming technology witnessed by Samuel
Gamble during his walking tour of Sitem villages at the end of the eighteenth
century. Armed with iron-edged tools and millennia of experience managing
the flood-prone region, the inhabitants of West Africa's Rice Coast were
poised to transform not only the physical landscape of West Africa's coastal
littoral, but also to play a transformative role in the economy of South Carolina.

Little is known about the earliest stages of rice production in coastal South
Carolina except that enslaved laborers were cultivating rice by the early seventeenth century in moist soils without irrigation.[40] Enslaved laborers grew rice
in their provision grounds to provide for their own subsistence and were allowed to sell some of the surplus. Because of a lack of documentation about
enslaved Africans during the earliest settlement of South Carolina, historians
can only speculate on what role their experimentation played in the colonists'
and slaveholders' search for a staple crop between 1670 and 1720.[41]

In the early eighteenth century, inland swamp production became the
next evolutionary stage as South Carolina planters experimented with irrigation. Enslaved laborers constructed reservoirs to collect fresh water from
streams and springs, controlling its flow into floodplain soils made rich by
decayed organic matter and swamp vegetation, but simultaneously possessing
few weeds. On some plantations, rudimentary reservoirs gave way to more
elaborate systems of embankments, dams, ditches, and drains. Downstream
dams and ditches impounded flood water, while dams and ditches upstream
controlled fresh water from the reservoir.[42] Both stages are representative of a
period of experimentation during which South Carolina planters and enslaved laborers learned about the nature of the land and the nature of the
crop. Through trial and error, enslaved Africans and the rice planters who
enslaved them learned how to trap, and when to release, fresh rainwater to
flood the rice fields, perfecting water-control techniques by the 1720s.

Most planters considered the inland swamp farming system to have lacked
the scientific precision of the tidewater system, a later stage of evolution in the
colony's rice industry. Though productive, inland swamp technology provided
inefficient water control, leaving rice plantations vulnerable to too little water
due to drought, or to too much water due to flood. By the mid-eighteenth century, runoff from land cleared in South Carolina's interior increased freshnets,

swollen streams that broke dams, flooded fields, and destroyed property. The runoff exacerbated this state of affairs to the point where inland swamp production was no longer feasible because it left the plantation economy vulnerable to steep fluctuations in the production of its staple crop.[43]

Like inland swamp rice production on coastal South Carolina and Georgia rice plantations, tidal rice-growing technology in West Africa's Rice Coast was anything but perfected. Subsistence was a constantly moving target, which coastal farmers attempted to attain each growing season by adapting to environmental fluctuations and by modifying their techniques and technology. When the salt-water tide broke through the embankments or the rains produced insufficient fresh water to balance out the salinity in the soils over a period of several years, coastal farmers were frequently forced to abandon their mangrove swamp rice fields. Once a mangrove field lay fallow for an extended period of time, the laborious process of clearing secondary vegetation and leaching salinity from the soils had to begin anew. There was no compensation, either, for the loss of a swamp field's productive yields. In the West African Rice Coast, farmers' options were limited and uncertain. After the advent of Atlantic trade, farmers in the Rice Coast could experiment with *Oryza sativa* varieties[44]—domesticated in Asia—which yielded more than *O. glaberrima* varieties. They could choose to plant more *O. glaberrima*, which was adapted to flourish in marginal environments.[45] Or they could concentrate their cultivation strategies on the floodplains. Either way, it was a gamble for subsistence.[46]

In the South Carolina and Georgia plantation economies,[47] profit and not subsistence was at stake. After 1720, rice quickly became the staple crop of South Carolina's commercial economy. With the colony's economy heavily invested in one crop, planters could ill afford to gamble or to lose. By perfecting tidewater technology to minimize the effects of drought and flooding, they ensured more consistent yields for their export economy than farmers on the coastal littoral of West Africa's Rice Coast could ever have hoped to achieve.

By the mid-eighteenth century, a major shift was occurring in the South Carolina commercial rice industry. Tidewater rice fields were beginning to line the mouths of major rivers in coastal South Carolina. The ideal location of a tidewater rice plantation was found not too close to the ocean or too far upstream, in a place where salt water acted as a dam against the stream flow and where freshwater could then be channeled to flood the rice fields. Mangrove swamp reclamation required many years and many hands to complete. Its undertaking gradually enabled planters to plant rice in small portions of the new field as the remainder of the field was still under construction, and to reap a profit sooner, rather than later.

On the one hand, historians of South Carolina have underestimated the importance of tidewater rice production by their reluctance to acknowledge two phenomenon: the fact that inland swamp rice technology was a precursor to the development of tidewater production in the colony; and the possibility that aspects of inland swamp rice production were based on land-use strategies used in West Africa's Rice Coast region. South Carolina colonists may have had experience draining swamps and using irrigation in England, but they lacked experience creating the delicate balance between fresh and brackish water so that rice would grow in the tidewaters. This unique feature distinguishes tidal-growing systems and by extension the West African rice knowledge system from all others, including wet paddy rice farming systems practiced in Asia. This study has shown that coastal specialists in the Rice Coast region possessed knowledge of salt/salinity and mangrove ecosystems which dates back to antiquity and which laid the foundation for the development of coastal land-use systems, including tidal rice-growing technology.

I am, however, also arguing that historians of West Africa have overestimated the importance of mangrove rice-growing technology, which was but a small portion of a holistic West African rice knowledge and coastal land-use system, designed by West African rice farmers who had deep roots on the coast. While mangrove rice-farming may have caught the attention of European and Luso-African traders and historians alike because of its unique material culture, technological sophistication and potential for producing higher yields,[48] its innovation was the culmination of ancient processes of coastal farmers' experimentation, adaptation, and tutelage about soils water-logged with brackish water, rainfall, and mangroves.[49] On West Africa's coastal littoral, Atlantic speech communities, not Mande, were engaged in this process.

According to planters, most of whose accounts were jaundiced by views of African inferiority, the tidewater system bears little resemblance to Samuel Gamble's description of mangrove rice-growing technology in coastal Guinea, or many other descriptions of agricultural technology in West Africa's Rice Coast region. There were certainly technological differences. For example, there is no evidence of West African farmers using hanging trunks as barriers to trap and to regulate the flow of fresh water in their mangrove rice fields. In areas of the Rice Coast north of the Rio Nunez, however, evidence exists of coastal farmers using hollowed-out trees and plug trunks to channel and control the amount of fresh water in the rice fields—precursors to more mechanized technology—and "heel-and-toe" sowing techniques used in *décrue* agriculture along rivers in present-day Mali. Future historical linguistics research could reveal how far back into the past "heel-and-toe" sowing techniques can be traced.[50] To date, there is also no evidence of enslaved Africans using fulcrum shovels in the low-lying areas of coastal South Carolina. Despite the techno-logical differences, an underlying logic—trapping and using fresh water to de-crease the percentage of salinity in the soil to enable rice species to flourish—was the basis for all technological innovations.

In the introduction, I proposed in this study to separate one portion of the West African rice knowledge system—tidal rice-growing technology—and one environment of the landscape gradient—coastal estuaries, floodplains, and mangrove swamps. The result is a more nuanced understanding of how farmers on the coastal littoral of West Africa's Rice Coast region adapted to their unfriendly and constantly fluctuating environment. The interdisciplinary evidence reveals that it is the localness of tidal rice-growing technology—uniquely designed by coastal farmers who spoke Atlantic languages for micro-environments in West Africa's Rice Coast—that made this indigenous knowledge system transmittable to new micro-environments across the Atlan-tic. Coastal farmers' ability to adapt to coastal micro-environments and to changes in the environmental conditions therein—not iron-edged tools or iron trunks—gave West Africa's rice farmers their global import and impact.

With the deep roots of coastal dwellers and the evolution of their tidal rice-growing technology firmly established, we will, in the final chapter, cross the Atlantic in the hull of slaving vessels. Chapter 6 will follow the embarka-tion of captives who originated on the coastal littoral of West Africa's Rice Coast region, examine their production of surplus rice for the trans-Atlantic slave trade, and discuss their disembarkation in Charleston and Savannah. In light of the interdisciplinary evidence for the development of Atlantic speech communities' tidal rice-growing technology revealed in this study, chapter 6 will suggest new ways of understanding the contributions made by enslaved Africans from West Africa's Rice Coast region to South Carolina and Geor-gia's commercial rice industries.

6

Feeding the Slave Trade:
The Trade in Rice and Captives from West Africa's Rice Coast

> Rice is the principal Article of Produce on this Part of
> the Coast, and Camwood and some Ivory. . . . The
> Quality of the Rice is very good, and particularly that
> which grows on the Hills and sloping Ground. The
> Quantity purchased annually for Consumption of the
> Ships and Factories may be from 700 to 1,000 Tons;
> the Average Price he takes to be from 6 l. 10 s. to 7 l. per
> Ton, and it is sometimes as high as 10 l.; but Mr.
> Mathews has bought it so low as 2 l. but then he paid
> for it in Tobacco *only*, and it was an extraordinary Year
> of Plenty [*sic*]. (Sheila Lambert, ed., *House of Com-*
> *mons Sessional Papers of the Eighteenth Century, Vol-*
> *ume 69, George III: Report of the Lords of Trade on*
> *the Slave Trade 1789, Part 1,* 66, 71.)

By 1793–94 when Samuel Gamble recorded and illustrated the techniques of Baga rice-farming, tidal rice-growing technology was no longer unique to the West African Rice Coast region. Tidewater rice plantations were thriving in coastal South Carolina and Georgia by the late eighteenth century. The rise of a lucrative commercial rice industry in the South Carolina and Georgia colonies was due, at least in part, to the skilled labor of enslaved Africans who originated in West Africa's Rice Coast region. What role did the enslaved play in the genesis and evolution of the commercial rice industries in South Carolina, Georgia, Louisiana, and Brazil? This question has simultaneously fascinated and puzzled scholars since Peter Wood's study was published more than three decades ago.

With their tidal rice-growing technology, the inhabitants of West Africa's Rice Coast region produced valuable commodities for the trans-Atlantic slave trade: rice and slaves. The final episode in this story will investigate the ways in which West African rice farmers participated voluntarily and involuntarily in the new markets for rice and slaves. To determine the global impact of coastal dwellers' tidal rice-growing technology, we will follow slaving vessels across the Atlantic Ocean as they purchased rice and/or captives in ports along the West African Rice Coast and disembarked in South Carolina and Georgia.

A Veritable Granary of Rice

In the Rice Coast of West Africa, the trans-Atlantic trade in captives stimulated a twofold demand for provisions. First, coastal ports and factories swelled with the arrival of European, Afro-European, and African traders. In addition, African traders brought captives down from the interior—sometimes traveling in caravans of porters carrying goods for sale at the coast. For the most part, although most caravans brought foodstuffs to be sold in coastal ports, neither traders nor captives produced food in coastal trading centers. The very survival of traders and captives alike thus depended on coastal trade in provisions.

Upon arriving at Walkeria—Dr. Walker's factory at the head of the Rio Nunez region in coastal Guinea—in 1793, Samuel Gamble would have found a quasi-urban center of European, American, and biracial traders and *grumetes,* free Africans in the traders' employ. By the mid-eighteenth century in Saint-Louis—one of two coastal entrepôts in Senegal—each individual in a similar group of African and European dependents of the *Compagnie des In-*

des consumed approximately two pounds of millet daily and eighty tons of millet annually.[1] The size of the populations in coastal ports and their demands for foodstuffs ebbed and waned depending on the season—ebbing in the dry season when coastal trade was in full session and waning in the rainy season when the rains brought coastal trade to a standstill.

Coastal urban communities inhabited by traders and captives in transit to the New World were not the only new market for rice provisions created by the trans-Atlantic slave trade. Captives and crews aboard slave ships bound for New World destinations constituted a larger, more demanding market that consumed far more provisions. Keeping in mind the brutality, horror, and indignity of the trans-Atlantic slave trade and the Middle Passage, slaving vessels housed many people—enslaved and free, white and black, Europeans and Africans. Moving a cargo of human beings against their wills required more crew members than any other trade in the merchant marine. The ratio of captives to crew members averaged out to approximately 8.25 throughout the trans-Atlantic slave trade period. In the mid-seventeenth century, Spanish American ships averaged 7.7 captives per crew member. By the second half of the eighteenth century, increased efficiency of slaving ships[2] was a factor in the ratio rising to 9.5.[3] All of these people—captain, crew, and captive alike—required sustenance.

Captives brought to the coast by African traders, or purchased and held on the coast by European traders, represented a significant segment of nonproducing consumers.[4] Traders along West Africa's coast usually held only small numbers of captives while waiting for arriving ships. Depending on the supply of, and demand for, captives, incoming slavers often waited in port for African traders to bring captives from the interior—a sufficient number to fill their ships. Unfortunately for Gamble and his fever-stricken crew, the full complement of 250 captives, for which he had contracted, was not available when he arrived at Walkeria. As captives became available, Gamble waited for his crew to recover from illness and allowed other ship captains to purchase the slaves. His overall circumstances—being stranded in coastal Guinea for nine months while his crew members recovered, died, and/or required replacement—were exceptional. His experience of waiting on the coast to purchase enough African captives to make a slaving voyage profitable, however, was more the rule than the exception.

Typically, slave traders purchased only a few captives at a time—an average of one or two a day, sometimes as many as eight—from local African and European traders who brought them to coastal factories and ports. The longer captives remained imprisoned on the West African coast, the more likely they were to contract and succumb to disease, either on the coast or during the Middle Passage voyage.[5] On average, a captive spent three months in transit in coastal ports.[6] However, in 1773 the ship *Zanggodin* took 377 days to load 127 captives on the Guinea Coast, a loading rate far above the norm. A second ship traveling to the region, the *Geertruyda & Christina,* had an abnormally long stay on the coast, taking 508 days to load 276 captives.[7] When months passed before slavers could fill their ships, as in the case of Gamble, most traders imprisoned their captives on the coast, as opposed to on board ship, to prevent the outbreak of disease on board. In general, European traders were anxious to purchase their complement of captives quickly. These were worst-case scenarios.

The numbers of captives aboard slaving vessels varied among European nations throughout the trans-Atlantic slave trade. In general during the eighteenth century, the numbers increased but the ratio of captives per ton decreased. Slave traders used vessels with larger capacities to transport more captives. Between 1727 and 1769, British slavers tended to use smaller vessels departing to North America to carry approximately 200 captives per vessel. In the 1780s, British slavers averaged 390 captives per slaving ship en route to the West Indies.[8] Normally, however, slaving vessels traveling to West Africa's Rice Coast were smaller, carrying fewer captives, crew members, and provisions, because of the region's proximity to both Europe and North America. For example, slavers typically operated smaller vessels and purchased fewer captives when traveling between the Rice Coast and North America. Hence, between 1763 and 1768, Grant, Oswald & Co. used larger slaving vessels to fulfill a contract with a French company based in Honfleur—Société pour la Rivière de Sierra lionne. They transported captives from Bance Island to Guadeloupe and Saint Domingue, an average of 346 captives per ship and 969 captives per year totaling 4,847 in all. More commonly, in the 1760s ships traveling between Bance Island and the Americas carried between 219 and 235 captives per voyage.[9] Throughout the trade, the number of crew members rose or fell in direct correlation to the number of captives aboard ship.

In the late seventeenth century, the Portuguese government took the lead in standardizing the amount of provisions slavers transported and fed their captives. Through trial and error, slavers across national boundaries and company affiliations developed guidelines for provisioning slave ships with adequate food and water to deliver the maximum amount of living "cargo" to market. Experienced captains traveled with double the required provisions as a preventative measure against the high rates of mortality that resulted from delays. This all-too-common turn of events threatened to jeopardize the profit margin of the voyage if provisions became depleted and/or captives contracted illnesses.

An average trip from Africa's West Coast to the U.S. South or the Caribbean lasted two months. Each and every day, most slave traders gave their captives two meals, the first consisting mainly of a starch such as rice or yams, and the second consisting of a starchy gruel made of corn, barley, biscuits, and meat or fish. They garnished both meals with palm oil and peppers. In the eighteenth century, a typical French vessel carried forty kilograms of biscuits, beans, and rice for each captive. After the late eighteenth century, most slave captains, regardless of nation, also provided lime juice for the captives to drink—a prophylactic against the spread of scurvy.[10]

Though slave ship captains departed Europe or the U.S. colonies with adequate provisions for the captain and crew's voyage to the New World, it was usually necessary to restock provisions prior to returning to the New World through the Middle Passage. Slavers chose rice as one of the standard provisions for the masses of captives aboard ships.[11] Unlike yams or other possible provisions, rice and legumes could be stored for months at a time in hermetically sealed containers in damp, moldy conditions—in an African farmer's granary throughout the rainy season or in a slaving vessel's hull—then washed and dried before consumption.[12] By the late seventeenth and early eighteenth century, English ships in particular began frequenting West Africa's Rice Coast region to purchase rice before proceeding further down the coast to purchase captives.[13]

Slave ship captains often described the Senegambia, Guinea, Grain, and Windward Coasts, and Cape Mesurado and Cape Mount, as reliable ports where an abundance of rice was available. Sailors whose ships voyaged to the West African Rice Coast reported witnessing an active trade in rice there. According to Captain John Ashley Hall, who had served as third, second, and chief mate on the *Neptune*—which anchored in the Windward Coast to trade for rice prior to sailing on to ports at the Bight of Biafara and Old Calabar to trade for captives—the *Neptune* carried Carolina rice as provisions on the voyage from London to West Africa's coast. Then, prior to sailing to the Bight of Biafara and Old Calabar to purchase captives, the ship anchored at Cape Mount on the Windward Coast where it "procured as much rice, in addition to what we had on board, as we wanted."[14] Alexander Falconbridge, who made five voyages to West Africa's coast, and two voyages to West Africa's Windward Coast, reported purchasing "forty or fifty tons" of rice in the

Windward and Grain Coasts when he served as a surgeon between 1780 and 1787. He also suggested the availability of an inexhaustible amount of rice at coastal ports in present-day Liberia: "[Question] Could you have purchased more [rice] if you had wished it? [Falconbridge] I believe if our business had been to have bought rice, we could have loaded the ship there at Cape Mefurado."[15] Slave ship captains' frequent stops at ports in West Africa's Rice Coast to purchase tons[16] of rice implies two things: increased demand from coastal trading communities and slave ships embarking on the Middle Passage, and also increased supply in surplus rice by the inhabitants of West Africa's Rice Coast. Having investigated the larger demand by urban trading communities, captives waiting to be put aboard slaving vessels, and captives embarking on the voyage across the Atlantic, we will devote the remainder of this section to an examination of increased supply of grains in coastal ports stretching from present-day Senegal in the north to coastal Guinea in the south.

Along West Africa's Atlantic coast in the lower Senegal River valley, the regions of Kajoor-Bawol, Fuuta Tooro, and Gajaga have been called the breadbasket of the Senegambia. Here, Wolof villages in the savanna rather than coastal communities produced grain for subsistence and for sale to both the western Sahara and the Atlantic islands. These three river regions had produced grain for long-standing desert trade networks with merchant-marabouts, trading gum Arabic from the western Sahara for Atlantic imports, cotton cloth, iron, and firearms. Though by the end of the seventeenth century the desert regions of Trarza and Brakna had achieved self-sufficiency in grain production, the desert market still loomed large over the increasing Atlantic-based market.[17] North African traders acted as principal brokers for the grain trade across the Sahara and to Saint-Louis and Gorée. In the early seventeenth century, they successfully exploited urban coastal communities' dependence on imported provisions by both diverting grain to the desert market and by dramatically raising prices on grain sold to Atlantic markets.[18]

In the Senegambia region, particularly in the eighteenth century, drought and famine—caused by both natural disaster and political instability—adversely affected both the trade in captives and in provisions. After the seventeenth century, the nonproducing French trader and free and enslaved African populations in the coastal islands of Gorée and Saint-Louis depended on grain provisions from Kajoor-Bawol, in particular, to feed the expanding slave-holding merchant societies. These demands strained the region's already limited agricultural resources, creating an even larger supply of captives for the trans-Atlantic trade. For example, in 1715–16, grain shortages led to a surplus of captives as slaveholders sold off people whom they could not feed. Free people whose bonds to kin groups and lineages had been loosened by famine became easy prey to kidnappers. However, the unstable conditions did not completely disrupt French traders' abilities to procure grain to feed the increased supply of captives. Between August 1715 and February 1716, the French filled five slaving vessels with 1,190 captives. In 1723–25, drought, locusts, invasions from Moors and Moroccans, and civil wars in Kajoor and Bawol resulted in widespread food shortages and famine. The destruction left Kajoor unsuitable to supply grain for Saint-Louis. Finally, food shortages also led to high rates of mortality of enslaved Africans awaiting embarkation in coastal ports where slavers were unable to purchase adequate provisions. In 1743–44, a total of 25 percent of the captives held in Saint-Louis perished of malnutrition and disease before they could be exported. To alleviate the shortage, the French instituted two strategies: they sent ships to Gorée to purchase provisions, and they expanded the region in which they purchased grain further upriver.[19] Though the Senegambia region was called the breadbasket, the prevalence of famine, drought, and grain shortages, as well as competition from western Sahara trade networks, frequently made it an unreliable source of provisions for the trans-Atlantic trade.

South of Senegal, Balanta-speakers in present-day Guinea-Bissau produced surplus rice as provisions for trans-Atlantic traders in urban coastal communities and for slaving vessels. By the mid-seventeenth century, the trans-Atlantic trade had created rampant violence and chaos in the coastal region. After settling the coastal littoral of Guinea-Bissau in the seventeenth century, the Balanta abandoned yams in favor of cultivating *Oryza glaberrima*, African rice, and began to use age-grades to mobilize young men's labor for performing land-clearing and other heavy agricultural tasks. To protect their villagers, the Balanta simultaneously exchanged captives and paddy rice for iron-edged tools and defensive weapons, particularly knives and swords.

After the abolition of the slave trade, paddy rice remained an important commodity in legitimate trade in the nineteenth century. The Balanta continued to produce surplus paddy rice to satisfy the demands of Cape Verdean traders, whose island homeland was too arid for sustained agricultural production. Cape Verdeans also acted as middlemen between coastal villagers and urban coastal nonproducing communities that still depended on the coast and its hinterland for subsistence. The expansion of rice cultivation and the increased populations strained coastal Guinea-Bissau's economy in ways that manifested differently from the expansion of the grain and slave trades in the lower Senegal valley almost one century earlier. As fertile and low-lying *bolanhas* where paddy rice was cultivated became scarce, inhabitants of coastal societies established new communities by splitting off, or "fissioning," a principal outlet used by decentralized societies to resolve conflict in the absence of permanent, centralized political authority.[20]

The growth of trans-Atlantic trade in coastal Guinea's Rio Nunez region effectively altered the nature of coastal commercial activity. In response to new demands from coastal populations, Luso-African traders reoriented commercial networks between the coast and the interior, which had exchanged rice and salt produced on the coast for dyes and cattle from the interior, toward the Atlantic market up and down the coast, which supplied imported goods in exchange for local commodities such as rice and cattle.[21] Travelers' accounts describe rice—produced on the coast and in the interior—as one commodity available for sale in the Rio Nunez region.[22]

The trade in provisions, like that of slaves, inextricably linked the Rio Nunez region to ports further south. Factories along the coast, including Walkeria, along the Nunez River where Samuel Gamble purchased many captives for his complement, and factories along the Pongo River of Guinea and the Scarcies River and Bance Island in Sierra Leone, hosted large populations of nonproducers, European or Afro-European traders, *grumetes,* caravan traders from the interior, and captives. Unlike the Senegambia and Guinea-Bissau to the north, the ports in Guinea and Sierra Leone to the south served an additional market—the settler population of Freetown—whose demand outpaced all others.

The "Province of Freedom" was founded in 1788 under the leadership of Granville Sharpe and was reincorporated under the leadership of the Sierra Leone Company after the indigenous Temne inhabitants burned down the original settlement. In Freetown, the British resettled several populations—Nova Scotians who had been loyal to the British troops in the American Revolution, the black poor of London, liberated Africans whose slaving vessels had been intercepted in the Atlantic by the British antislavery squadron after the legal trade in slaves was outlawed in 1807, and maroons from Jamaica.[23] By the 1790s, colonists in Freetown came to depend on both the hinterland of Sierra Leone and on coastal ports as far north as the Rio Nunez region for a good portion of their provisions, because poor soil quality limited their agricultural pursuits.[24] From the late eighteenth century into the nineteenth, the Sierra Leone Company, and subsequently the Royal Colony Company, maintained commercial interests in Guinea's coastal ports.[25]

After the establishment of colonial rule in the 1860s, French colonial officials monitored closely the descent of caravans traveling down the Nunez River from the interior to the coast. The arrival of caravans bringing rice, hides, gum, some gold, and captives who served as porters and were available for sale after their service, caught the attention of colonial officers, although coastal farmers laboring in the mosquito-infested swamps did not. The beginning of the dry season, and the return of Fulbe and Susu caravans laden with goods from the interior, marked the advent of regional commercial activity; coastal dwellers' laboring in the rice fields marked the beginning of the rainy season and the cessation of regional trade. In order to predict the profitability of the season's commercial activity, colonial administrators monitored the duration and intensity of rainfall, the progress of the rice cycle, and the infestation of predators such as grasshoppers.[26] In addition, French officials gauged relationships between Fulbe chiefs in the interior and coastal inhabitants to prevent warfare, raiding, and pillaging from interfering with the flow of caravans and commerce.[27] At times, all of these factors could devastate the rice harvests, prevent coastal farmers from selling their rice, and ruin the trade season. A plentiful harvest and open caravan routes meant a profitable commercial season.

French colonial officials observed Fulbe traders buying salt from, as well as selling rice to, Susu middlemen and coastal factories.[28] Peter McLachlan, assistant staff surgeon in the Second West India Regiment who served in both Freetown and the Iles de Los, described baskets six feet long and three feet wide used by Fulbe caravans to transport rice to the coastal Rio Nunez region and salt back to Futa Jallon.[29] Clean rice—which had already been processed—became an important commodity for urban trading communities and for slavers purchasing rice to provision slaving vessels.

In the Rio Nunez region, colonial officials also reported that coastal inhabitants both produced surplus rice for sale and purchased rice from Fulbe traders and European factories at different moments in the agricultural cycle. After the rice harvest, Baga and Nalu rice producers exchanged rice with European factories for manufactured goods. During the "hungry season," the period of the rainy season when stores of the previous year's rice had been expended, coastal farmers often subsequently found themselves in the position of buying rice back from European factories. As he toured coastal villages in the Rio Nunez region, Coffinières de Nordeck reported:

> During the rice harvest, the blacks came to barter in exchange for cloth and other European products; also during the rainy season they don't have anything else to eat; then fatigued, they go to harvest palm nuts, and one gives them the same volume of rice that they had sold [to us] some months before-hand; it is very infantile on the part of the blacks.[30]

Despite the author's biases, his observation reveals coastal farmers' vulnerability to variable harvests that depended on the duration and intensity of rainfall. The new demands of the urban and Atlantic markets laid bare the fissures of a subsistence economy serving a growing commercial demand.

In coastal Guinea, however, the exploitation of captives' labor exemplified the transformative effect that the trans-Atlantic slave trade had on the region. In the interior of the Nunez and Pongo Rivers, and as far south as the Sierra Leone border, local Susu chiefs and traders held large concentrations of captives in villages before boarding them onto slaving vessels, particularly throughout the rainy season when regional commercial traffic slowed to a halt. As traders and chiefs waited to export captives, they used captives' labor to provide security for villages occupied by the enslaved, and to produce surplus rice for sale to slave traders as provisions for their vessels departing from the river in the dry season.[31] In the Rio Nunez region, enslaved populations became heavily concentrated. South of the Iles de Los, near the border between present-day Guinea and Sierra Leone, John Matthews estimated that captives comprised three-fourths of Susu, Bullom, Baga, and Temne villages in 1720, and that the percentage was even higher among the Mande societies in the interior.[32]

On the coast and in Futa Jallon, large-scale unrest and rebellion erupted among captives held in Guinea's villages. In Moria, near the Guinea and Sierra Leone border, enslaved communities mounted a series of revolts lasting thirteen years, from 1783 to 1796. They fought against the cruelty of their owners and the loss of their customary rights, under which some categories of dependents were not eligible for sale.[33] Several decades before the abolition of the trans-Atlantic slave trade, a slave mode of production emerged in parts of Guinea and Sierra Leone when slave labor was used in vital sectors of the economy and slaves were relegated to the bottom of the social order. The high concentration of enslaved people within local societies, as well as the exploitation of the enslaved as laborers in plantation agriculture, including but not limited to rice production, transformed the social institutions of local societies.[34]

The coastal littoral of the Rice Coast is not the only West African region where trade in agricultural surpluses nourished coastal trading communities and captives in transit to the New World. In southeast Nigeria and the Island of Bioko (Fernando Po), yams became important commodities in the trans-Atlantic trade in provisions. In Dahomey, cassava flour was sold as the provision of choice. Plantations in East Africa, particularly at Malindi and Mombasa, produced grains for sale in the trans-Indian Ocean trade to the Arabian Peninsula and the Persian Gulf. In both southeastern Nigeria and East Africa, enslaved labor produced surpluses of valuable agricultural commodities. In these West and East African ports, captives' presence not only heightened the demand for provisions in coastal towns, but their labor also produced agricultural surpluses for sale.[35]

Rice was just one commodity produced by the inhabitants of West Africa's Rice Coast region for the specific demands of European and Afro-European traders during the age of the trans-Atlantic slave trade. Enslaved labor, produced for the specific demands of the New World plantation economy, was the second. The following section examines the impact of the labor of enslaved Africans who originated in West Africa's Rice Coast region and disembarked in South Carolina and Georgia. It begins by posing the important questions: How many captives who embarked slaving vessels in the ports of West Africa's Rice Coast region disembarked in Charleston or Savannah? What was the overall impact of their labor on the rice industry of both colonies?

Counting Captives and Identifying Ports: Charleston-Bound Slaving Voyages and their West African Origins

This final section builds on the work of Daniel Littlefield, the first historian to attempt to quantify the numbers and to identify the origins of enslaved Africans who disembarked in Charleston and Savannah ports. Littlefield's findings were twofold: first, based on records of ports on the Gambia River from 1764—"the only year for which such complete information [had] been uncovered" when his landmark study was published—Littlefield found that more captives from Angola than from the Rice Coast were imported into South Carolina.[36] Second, based on an analysis of newspaper advertisements by South Carolina planters searching for runaway slaves, Littlefield argued that South Carolina planters preferred captives from the Rice Coast.[37] Accordingly, planter preferences explained high percentages of Rice Coast captives, but the availability of large numbers of war captives in Congo-Angola and their acceptability to South Carolina planters explained the high numbers of captives from West Central Africa.

An analysis of newspaper advertisements for the sale of new imports and for the capture of runaways also supports both of Littlefield's conclusions. In newspaper advertisements for slave auctions, slave traders and planters often included information about captives' region of African origin and ethnicity. In newspaper notices of runaways, planters often described runaways' "country marks"—facial scars indicating ethnic identity, status, language, and/or occupational skills in some African societies—to assist other planters and bounty hunters in making a positive identification of the enslaved. Twenty-one percent, or 277 of the colony's runaways advertised between 1730 and 1770, originated in the Windward Coast. Newspaper advertisements described an almost equal number of runaway slaves, 21 percent or 276, as originating in Congo-Angola. The 1730s and 1740s were particularly active decades for runaways described as originating in Congo-Angola. They represented an average of 59 percent of the total. Overall, even though a disproportionate share of enslaved Gambians ran away, planters continued to import them into the colony in large numbers. Littlefield attributed planters' preference for Gambians—despite their penchant for running away, which was disproportionate to bondsmen and women from other regions—to the relatively high value planters placed on Gambians' agricultural skills.[38]

Recent scholarship challenges the notion that enslaved laborers who originated in the Rice Coast made a significant impact on South Carolina and Georgia's commercial rice industries. David Eltis, Philip Morgan, and David Richardson present evidence that West Africa's Rice Coast, which they call the Upper Guinea Coast, was a secondary slaving center producing a small volume of captives. Comparing the proportion of captives arriving from the Upper Guinea Coast into mainland North American ports, including South Carolina and Georgia, their data reveals a fifty-year period—from 1751 to 1800—in which the majority of captives that disembarked in South Carolina and Georgia embarked in the Upper Guinea Coast. This portion of West Africa exported more captives to the tobacco-producing Chesapeake region prior to 1750. Finally, the rice-growing region of Maranhão, Brazil, imported two out of every three of its captives from the Rice Coast region between 1760 and 1810, for reasons which Eltis et al. speculate had little to do with rice.[39]

This latest research is based on an exhaustive compilation of data, heretofore fragmented and scattered in various locations. Almost twenty years after the publication of Littlefield's study, *The Trans-Atlantic Slave Trade: A Database on CD-ROM*, compiled by David Eltis, Stephen D. Behrendt, David Richardson, and Herbert S. Klein has expanded exponentially our knowledge of the trans-Atlantic slave trade, the European and American captains and ship owners who conducted it, and the vessels that transported captives and captors through the Middle Passage. The database brings together a wealth of published and unpublished data on 27,233 slaving voyages, portions of which had been analyzed previously by individual historians. Of the more than 27,000 slaving voyages registered in the compendium, 20,729 voyages embarked with 15.4 million African captives and arrived in New World ports to sell their "cargo." Thus, in contrast to Littlefield's single year of data, we now have historical data for 20,729 slaving voyages from 1527 to 1866—the duration of the trans-Atlantic slave trade—from 54 ports of departure and to the same number of ports of disembarkation. A variable quality and quantity of data is available for the voyages, 14,463 of which exist in the historical record in name only.[40] There remains much that historians still do not know, and unfortunately may never know, about the trans-Atlantic slave trade. However, this new database gives historians valuable tools to begin to answer many questions about the trans-Atlantic slave trade, including whether or not ports in South Carolina and Georgia received a disproportionate number of captives from West Africa's Rice Coast region.

While *The Trans-Atlantic Slave Trade Database* is the largest compendium of documented and studied slaving voyages to date, an unknown number of voyages are not counted because they were not documented. Certain aspects of the trade, such as Portuguese and Brazilian voyages, were disproportionately undocumented and therefore undercounted. Since the original publication, the compilers have been hard at work producing a revised edition that addresses these two shortcomings.[41]

In addition to these two regional trades, the database undercounts direct voyages from regions of Africa to the Americas. Chapter 1 of our text discusses "private" transactions, which were arranged between private coastal traders not affiliated with metropolitan trading firms and island agents. That private voyages were typically not recorded in the métropole explains why they have fallen below historians' radar.[42] Between 1748 and 1784 at Bance Island, private traders purchased an estimated 17 percent of the total number of captives exported by the factory.[43] As a result of the close affiliation between Richard Oswald, owner of Bance Island, and local merchants Henry Laurens in Charleston and John Graham in Savannah, some of the captives aboard private voyages from Bance Island were likely destined for rice plantations in South Carolina and Georgia. These undocumented voyages from the Senegambia and the Windward Coast could thus show an increase in the number of captives imported from the West African Rice Coast region to Charleston and Savannah.

Though Eltis et al. possesses an unprecedented quantity of empirical evidence, he and Littlefield have asked fundamentally different questions. On the one hand, Eltis attempted to quantify the meta-narrative of the trans-Atlantic slave trade, testing whether or not captives originating in West Africa's Upper Guinea Coast constituted a majority of enslaved people imported into rice-growing regions in the New World at any period during the trans-Atlantic trade era. He compared the number of Upper Guinea Coast captives imported into New World rice-growing regions, specifically South Carolina, Georgia, and Maranhão, Brazil, to other North American regions, including nonrice-growing regions, such as the Chesapeake.

On the other hand, Littlefield took a micro-approach and disaggregated the numbers of captives coming from the Rice Coast and the ports located in other Western African subregions. Using a limited amount of data, Littlefield compared the number of captives that disembarked in South Carolina from one Rice Coast port, James Island, to the numbers of captives that disembarked in South Carolina from ports in West-Central Africa. With expanded empirical data for the composition and chronology of the slave trade on the African side of the Atlantic, we can more closely examine the operation of the trans-Atlantic slave trade in South Carolina. With these tools in hand, it is an opportune time to bring Eltis's incomparable data to bear on Littlefield's important question.

Reexamining the volume of Rice Coast captives disembarking in South Carolina and Georgia ports requires more than just an expansion of the data heretofore available to historians for the trans-Atlantic slave trade. It also requires a shift in our understanding of pre-colonial African history. The literature on the American side of the Atlantic has adopted the terminology of slave traders[44] by examining discrete portions of the Rice Coast, such as the Senegambia, Sierra Leone (Bance Island), or the Windward Coast, in an attempt to tie captives from these West African parcels to coastal South Carolina and Georgia. If we continue in this piecemeal fashion, then Littlefield's original analysis is correct. The 44,432 captives who disembarked in the Carolinas from West-Central Africa exceeded the numbers who embarked from individual ports in the Rice Coast. The 26,626 captives from the Senegambia, or 15.2 percent of the total number disembarked in the Carolinas, represent the next largest population. As this study has shown, neither the Atlantic and Mande communities who inhabited this diverse region nor their indigenous rice-growing technology were confined to discrete ports along the West African coast. The remainder of this section will examine both West Africa's Rice Coast and West-Central Africa as distinct regions encompassing several coastal ports.

The latest and most complete data available for the trans-Atlantic slave trade provides empirical confirmation of the importance of the West African Rice Coast and West-Central Africa in supplying captives to the South Carolina and Georgia markets. Of the 171,538 captives who disembarked in the Carolinas, 54,425 or 32 percent of the total embarked slaving vessels in West Africa's Rice Coast region. This figure is larger than the 44,432 captives that originated in West-Central Africa, constituting 26 percent of the total. Of the 15,240 captives to disembark in Georgia, 6,832 (45 percent of the total) originated in West Africa's Rice Coast region. In contrast, West-Central Africa was the region of origination for only 2,803, or 19 percent of African captives imported into Georgia. On the one hand, the volume of trade in Georgia paled in comparison to the trade in South Carolina. On the other hand, the numbers of slaving vessels for which the points of embarkation are known is also significantly smaller. Taking into account the undercount of voyages from the Senegambia, which constituted the northern ports of the West African Rice Coast region, to the Americas and of private voyages, these numbers are likely even higher.

Table 6.1 Total Number/Percentage of Captives Disembarked in South Carolina from All Regions in Africa

SC	Rice Coast: Senegambia, Sierra Leone (including Bance Island), Windward Coast	West-Central Africa	Gold Coast	Bight of Biafra	Bight of Benin	South-east Africa	Africa Unspecified	Total Slaves Imported
1701–1725	1,048 16.1%		195 3%	117 1.8%			5,149 79.1%	6,509
1726–1750	3,075 10.2%	11,887 39.4%		3,366 11.1%			11,862 39.3%	30,190
1751–1775	36,444 50.4%	11,359 15.7%	8,542 11.8%	6,808 9.4%	2,207 3.1%	293 0.4%	6,640 9.2%	72,293
1776–1800	3,145 29.5%	1,740 16.3%	3,317 31.2%	440 4.2%			2,004 18.8%	10.646
1801–1825	10,713 20.6%	19,446 37.3%	6,065 11.6%		764 1.5%	825 1.6%	14,267 27.4%	52,080
Total Slaves Imported to SC, 1701–1825	54,425 31.7%	44,432 25.9%	18,119 10.6%	10,731 6.3%	2,791 1.6%	1,118 0.7%	39,922 23.2%	171,538

Note: Table generated from David Eltis, Stephen Behrendt, David Richardson, Herbert S. Klein, eds., *The Trans-Atlantic Slave Trade: A Database on CD-Rom* (Cambridge: Cambridge University Press, 1999).

Table 6.2 Total Number/Percentage of Captives Disembarked in Georgia from All Regions in Africa

GA	Rice Coast: Senegambia, Sierra Leone (including Bance Island), Windward Coast	West-Central Africa	Gold Coast	Bight of Biafra	Bight of Benin	South-east Africa	Africa Unspecified	Total Slaves Imported
1726–1750	0	252 100.0%	0	0	0	0	0	252
1751–1775	4,180 67.8%	372 6.1%	320 5.2%	0	0	0	1,291 20.9%	6,163
1776–1800	2,652 38.1%	736 10.5%	1,286 18.4%	0	0	0	2,303 33%	6,977
1801–1825	0	1,443 78%	0	0	0	0	405 22%	1,848
Total Slaves Imported to GA, 1726–1825	6,832 44.8%	2,803 18.5%	1,606 10.5%	0	0	0	3,999 26.2%	15,240

Note: Table generated from David Eltis, Stephen Behrendt, David Richardson, Herbert S. Klein, eds., *The Trans-Atlantic Slave Trade: A Database on CD-Rom* (Cambridge: Cambridge University Press, 1999).

As both Eltis and Littlefield have suggested, chronology plays an important role in the volume of Africans imported into South Carolina and Georgia from the Rice Coast and West-Central Africa regions. Prior to 1750, the regions of origin were not specified for the majority of enslaved Africans who disembarked in South Carolina—almost 80 percent between 1701 and 1725 and almost 40 percent between 1726 and 1750.[45] In Georgia, the overwhelming majority—nearly 100 percent between 1726 and 1750—embarked in West Central Africa. In South Carolina, captives originating in the Rice Coast region constituted the majority of the imports between 1751 and 1775, comprising 50 percent of the total or 36,444 captives. In Georgia during the same time period, Rice Coast captives constituted an even larger share of a smaller imported population, 67.8 percent of the total or 4,180 captives. Between 1776 and 1800, Rice Coast captives disembarking in Georgia ports continued to constitute 38 percent of the imports or 2,652 captives. In South Carolina, however, Rice Coast captives slipped to second place: more than 29 percent of the imported population, 3,145 captives, originated in the Rice Coast compared to more than 31 percent of the population, or 3,317 captives who originated in the Gold Coast. Though Rice Coast captives lost market share in South Carolina, their volume was still significant. Throughout the last half of the eighteenth century—a critical period in the development of commercial rice industries in South Carolina and Georgia—their numerical significance cannot be denied.

Up until the early eighteenth century, South Carolina was still a frontier colony searching for a staple crop, a plantation economy, and a cultural identity. During this period, the earliest documented influx of Africans originated in West-Central Africa, though an equivalent percentage—more than 38 percent—of Africans originated in unspecified African regions. Many of the enslaved Africans that embarked in West-Central Africa may have originated in the Kingdom of the Kongo, one of the two areas of western Africa where the Portuguese first made contact. The Portuguese established Catholic churches and schools, became embroiled in local succession disputes, and traded in slaves. The Kingdom of Kongo exported more than 3.5 million captives between 1600 and 1800 as a direct result of its civil wars. A significant number of the West-Central African captives who disembarked in South Carolina before 1739 may have been professional warriors trained in a Kongolese military tradition, which stressed agility, hand-to-hand combat, and even firearms skills. The war captives from the Kingdom of Kongo may have also played a decisive role in the Stono Rebellion.[46]

By the 1730s and 1740s, tidewater rice production perfected water control using floodgates and dams, therefore improving on many of the water-control principles of inland swamp production, increasing the rate of efficiency,

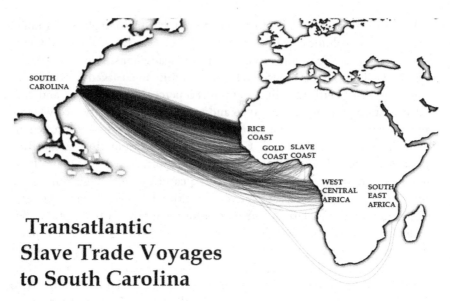

Transatlantic
Slave Trade Voyages
to South Carolina

FIGURE 6.1. Graphic of "Slaving Vessels Disembarking in South Carolina, 1701–1825." Copyright Laura Miller.

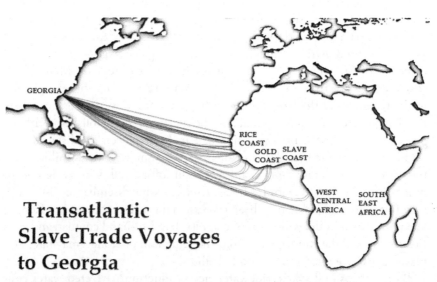

Transatlantic
Slave Trade Voyages
to Georgia

FIGURE 6.2. Graphic of "Slaving Vessels Disembarking in Georgia, 1701–1825." Copyright Laura Miller.

and decreasing the frequency and number of swollen streams called fresh-nets.[47] Chapter 5 discussed the early undocumented period of experimentation in inland swamps, in which enslaved laborers and planters used plug-trunks to channel fresh water into—and brackish water out of—rice fields. These wooden devices made from hollowed-out silk cotton tree trunks acted as precursors for the mechanized irrigation systems used after the mid-eighteenth century on South Carolina and Georgia rice plantations. The wooden material culture also bore striking resemblance to aspects of technology used by coastal farmers in West Africa's Rice Coast region. By the mid-eighteenth century, South Carolina planters had taken the raw materials of West African rice-growing technology and transformed them to suit South Carolina's emerging commercial rice industry. In the mid-eighteenth century, when the numbers of captives from West Africa's Rice Coast region became dominant among slaves imported into South Carolina, rice plantation owners were adopting tidewater rice production, growing rice in salt marshes, tidal rivers, and swamps inundated by brackish water.

Establishing tidewater fields required extensive land clearing and preparation. Enslaved laborers moved tons of earth to build temporary ditches in a corner of the new tidewater rice fields, cleared logs and stumps for the permanent embankment, constructed permanent embankments around the perimeter of the new fields, and installed trunks for water control. For example, to construct an eighty-acre plantation, the enslaved moved "well over 39,000 cubic yards of fine-grained river-swamp muck" and constructed "two-and-a-quarter miles of exterior, interior, and 'check' banks, and twelve to thirteen miles of canals, ditches, and quarterdrains" with axes, shovels, and sheer force.[48] By this stage in the process, the task was only nearly half complete! Enslaved laborers subsequently prepared the land for the establishment of new fields by cleaning and draining acres of land, one section at a time. Enslaved Africans' labor performed the superhuman task of transforming the coastlines of South Carolina and Georgia. Historian S. Max Edelson cautions that after 1730 African agency in transmitting West African rice cultivation and processing techniques to South Carolina should not necessarily be celebrated because of the brutal labor regimes—enforced with violence—imposed by planters who appropriated Africans' skills and transformed them to serve commercial industry.[49]

It is difficult to quantify the toll that reclaiming South Carolina swamps took on the health and well-being of enslaved men and women charged with the back-breaking task and on enslaved communities, because the enslaved left so few written records about their own experiences.[50] However, in their letters and memoirs, planters bear witness to the difficulty of negotiating with freedmen to repair broken embankments after the Civil War.[51] Planters were often unsuccessful in convincing free men and women to continue performing "muck work" in the rice fields. Labor shortages, hurricanes, as well as South Carolina and Georgia plantations' inability to compete with mechanized production and fresh soils west of the Mississippi River, contributed to the demise of South Carolina and Georgia's rice industry.[52]

With access to a seemingly inexhaustible supply of laborers, South Carolina and Georgia planters transformed tidewater rice-growing technology from an art into a science. Of the enslaved Africans imported into South Carolina and Georgia during the foundation and evolution of the commercial rice industry, historians may never be able to ascertain how many who originated in West Africa's Rice Coast region possessed tidal rice-growing skills—skills that planters exploited to fuel the colonies' commercial industries and remake the coastline.

In the mid-eighteenth century, enslaved Africans from the West African Rice Coast region were imported just as the colony of South Carolina was establishing its economic and cultural identity. Between 1751 and 1800, captives from West Africa's Rice Coast/Upper Guinea Coast region constituted the majority of imports into South Carolina and Georgia ports. Between 1751 and 1776 in South Carolina and 1751 and 1800 in Georgia, more enslaved Africans imported into South Carolina and Georgia originated in the West African Rice Coast than any other single region on the African continent. No other region of Africa continued to inject this volume of captives who spoke related languages, possessed similar agricultural technology, and were accustomed to living and laboring in a similar physical environment. Inland swamp and tidal rice-growing technology were not only similar to their region of embarkation—the West African Rice Coast—but also to their region of disembarkation—South Carolina and Georgia. The influx of enslaved labor from West Africa's Rice Coast impacted both the evolution of Gullah and Geechee languages and cultures and of commercial rice industries in South Carolina and Georgia in ways that historians are still working to understand.

Whereas the majority of enslaved Africans imported into South Carolina and Georgia between 1750 and 1800 originated in West Africa's Rice Coast region, the trend reversed itself between 1801 and 1867 when only 10,713, or more than 19 percent, of South Carolina's captives, and 139, or almost 6 percent, of Georgia's captives came from the Rice Coast. Georgia imported the overwhelming majority of its captives from West-Central Africa—1,763—representing 76.7 percent of all its total imports. Relative to Georgia, however, South Carolina imported a smaller plurality of its captives from West-Central Africa—19,446 or more than 35 percent—during the nineteenth century.[53]

By 1800, the commercial rice industries in South Carolina and Georgia, as well as the cultural identity of the colonies' enslaved community were, well-established. However, in West-Central Africa, particularly in the Kingdom of Kongo and Angola, the civil wars that generated almost 3.5 million captives between 1600 and 1800 continued to rage. Throughout the Atlantic World, the British abolition of the slave trade in 1807 marked a turning point. Afterwards, West-Central Africa became almost the singular supplier to ports throughout the New World, particularly during the last years of the clandestine trade in African captives between 1850 and 1867.[54] As a result of smuggling, this abundant supply met elastic demand in places such as Brazil, Cuba, Guadeloupe, Louisiana, Florida, and Texas—regions where planters needed large labor inputs to cultivate untamed lands.

Statistics only tell part of the story, however. They provide an empirical framework from which scholars can begin to engage in a discussion of the human experiences of Africans enslaved in the New World. Scholars can identify African regions supplying captives to regions of the New World at specific moments in time when the discussion is informed by quantitative data. Knowing the trends in trans-Atlantic commerce also enables scholars to bring to bear an understanding of the dynamism inherent in pre-colonial African societies where the captives in question originated. Only with this empirical grounding can we proceed to reconstruct the dynamic processes through which the enslaved created new cultures, skills, and worldviews in the Diaspora and in the contributions that West, West-Central, and in more limited instances, southeastern African societies, made to their transformation.

Conclusion

In 1754, Caleb Godfrey embarked on his first of two voyages as commander of the *Hare,* a sloop owned by Samuel and William Vernon. Godfrey and his crew spent four months purchasing captives in West Africa's Rice Coast, specifically at Bance Island—a major slave-trading fort strategically located at the furthest navigable point of the Sierra Leone River near Freetown, the capital of present-day Sierra Leone—and in the Gold Coast in present-day Ghana. Two months after departing the West African coast, the *Hare* disembarked in Charleston with its cargo of African captives aboard.

A few short months after arriving in Charleston in 1755, Godfrey set off from Rhode Island on a second voyage for Samuel and William Vernon aboard the *Hare.* This time he traveled directly to Bance Island in Sierra Leone, just one of the two ports where he had purchased captives the previous year. Though Godfrey embarked at Bance Island, he traveled as far north as the Rio Nunez region in coastal Guinea to procure his complement of eighty-four captives. Approximately two months after its departure, the *Hare* disembarked its cargo of sixty-three surviving captives in Charleston, including twenty-two children, nine girls and thirteen boys.[55]

In June 1754, a month before the *Hare* set sail for its second voyage, Samuel and William Vernon attempted to insure the ship and its cargo from Rhode Island to the West African Coast, and during its tenure on the African coast. The owners also attempted to insure the ship to its destination, either Jamaica or South Carolina depending on where Godfrey purchased captives. They wrote: "To the Island of Jamaica with Liberty to touch at the Windward Islands *Or Should he make his Trade to Windward then Insured to So. Carolina* [author's emphasis], in which Case Expect the Preem'o [premium] will be the Easier [*sic*]."[56] The notion that Caleb Godfrey would find a ready market for his "cargo" in South Carolina if he purchased his complement of captives in the Windward Coast—located in West Africa's Rice Coast region—is implicit in the information entered on the Vernons' insurance application. In purchasing insurance for Godfrey's second voyage of the *Hare,* the Vernon brothers also assured the underwriters of the likelihood of Godfrey purchasing his entire cargo on the Windward Coast, without proceeding further south to the Gold Coast.[57] Godfrey may have returned to Sierra Leone because he felt he had established an adequate supply of contacts with factors at Bance Island to obtain a sufficient number of captives to fill his ship in a relatively reasonable period of time. The Vernons made no mention of Jamaica—where the ship docked subsequent to Charleston—as a favorable market for captives from the Windward Coast or the Gold Coast.

The Vernon brothers entrusted the sale of the *Hare*'s cargo to Henry Laurens, a successful slave trader and planter who also became a statesman toward the end of his life. By 1756, when the *Hare* returned to Charleston with a cargo of captives for sale, Laurens had established a business relationship with Richard Oswald, the principal partner in the London trading firm that owned Bance Island.[58] From Laurens's own papers, Joseph A. Opala has reconstructed the mechanics of the lucrative business transactions between Laurens and Oswald: Oswald dispatched slaving vessels loaded with between 250 and 350 captives, ivory, and camwood annually to Charleston. Laurens posted advertisements for the sale of Rice Coast captives and auctioned them to local South Carolina planters. With the proceeds of the sale, Laurens purchased locally made commodities, particularly Carolina rice, for sale in England if the ship was returning first to London, or ship-building supplies if the ship was to return directly to Bance Island.[59] By the 1770s, trade in rice

FIGURE 6.3. Image of "Advertisement for the *Hare, South Carolina Gazette*, June 17, 1756" From the Collections of the Charleston Library Society. Copyright Charleston Library Society.

and captives from West Africa's Rice Coast made Laurens one of the wealthiest planters in all of the British colonies.

Samuel and William Vernon wrote to Laurens and his business partner, George Austin, to handle the sale of the *Hare*'s cargo in Charleston. According to Laurens, most area planters were exercising judicious conservatism when it came to capital outlays, because the prices of rice and indigo—the colony's staple crops—were unprofitably low. By the middle of 1756, threats of war with France had dampened the slave markets in South Carolina. Because of the uncertainty of the impending war, most South Carolina planters could not afford to expand their workforces to produce crops that brought only a pittance at market. Though selling captives from the West African Rice Coast to South Carolina planters was an important component of Laurens's business, he did not want the responsibility of selling the *Hare*'s captives. Therefore, he went so far as to suggest that Godfrey take his cargo of Windward Coast captives to a Caribbean market.[60]

Despite Laurens's warnings, the *Hare* did land in Charleston with sixty-three captives aboard. To announce the auction, Laurens placed an advertisement in the *South Carolina Gazette*. Laurens's description in his advertisement of the captives as "healthy" does not in the least match the notes in his private communications about the cargo. In a letter to the Vernon brothers, Laurens expressed his distaste for Godfrey's ability to select prime Africans—only forty-two of his first complement sold on the day of the 1756 auction—or to manage his crew, who deserted him shortly after the ship arrived in Charleston's harbor. Laurens described the remainder of slaves in the cargo as "refuse slaves," too sick, infected with yaws (a contagious and incurable skin disease), too small, or too old to perform heavy agricultural labor: "God knows what we shall do with those that remain, they are a most scabby Flock all of them full of the Crockeraws-several have extream sore Eyes, three very puny Children and add to this the worst infirmity of all Others with which 6 or 8 are attended . . . Old Age [*sic*]."[61]

Though, according to Laurens, several planters expressed displeasure at traveling eighty or ninety miles to bid on such a shabby lot of captives, his brother-in-law, Elias Ball, seemed to have been a satisfied customer. Ball purchased six children, four boys and two girls, and noted their date of purchase, approximate ages, and newly given English first names in his plantation ledger. Ball purchased one girl of approximately ten years of age and named her "Priscilla," whom he took—along with five captives—back to his Comingtee Plantation on the East Branch of South Carolina's Cooper River. Priscilla and her descendants were enslaved on the Ball plantation until emancipation when her great-great-grandson gained his freedom.[62]

This story about Caleb Godfrey and Samuel and William Vernon demonstrates that the enslaved were not the only historical actors in the transmittal of the West African rice-growing technology to South Carolina and Georgia plantations. Newspaper advertisements published after 1760 announcing the arrival of slaving vessels and the sale of cargoes of enslaved Africans support the Vernon brothers' contention that South Carolina was a profitable market for enslaved Africans from West Africa's Rice Coast. Did South Carolina planters prefer captives from West Africa's Rice Coast region? If so, can planters' preferences be attributed to planters' subjective perceptions of physical types, broad cultural areas, labor regimes, and foods eaten in parts of West Africa? From their firsthand experiences of purchasing rice and slaves along the coast and feeding captives in the hulls of slaving vessels, captains of slaving vessels were in the best position to form perceptions about the enslaved and to pass their perceptions on to slave factors in Charleston and Savannah.[63]

Throughout the New World, complex forces shaped the trade in African captives, only one of which was planters' preferences. Planters in South Carolina and Georgia represented a fraction of the southern U.S. market, which absorbed comparatively fewer captives in relation to larger markets in the Caribbean. Here, sugar plantations drove elastic demands for fresh laborers. Thus, South Carolina and Georgia planters occupied the periphery of the periphery. Given North America's small market share, it is unlikely that even if South Carolina planters did prefer enslaved Africans from West Africa's Rice Coast region, their preferences could have shaped the marketplace. Only the preferences of buyers in plantation economies exercising a larger market share, particularly sugar plantations in the Caribbean, actually did.[64]

Although its location was closer to the North American mainland than other West African regions, West Africa's Rice Coast was also a secondary market. In comparison to West African regions south of the Rice Coast, like the Bights of Biafara and Benin, and West-Central Africa, the West African Rice Coast supplied fewer captives to trans-Atlantic markets.[65] The more densely populated regions to its south possessed centralized forms of authority, social, political, and judicial mechanisms, and recurring warfare that generated a larger volume of captives for sale. The Rice Coast region, by comparison, was relatively sparsely populated and had fewer centralized political authorities to exercise control over the trans-Atlantic slave trade. Hence, both rice plantations in South Carolina and Georgia and the West African Rice Coast were peripheral regions with regard to demand and supply respectively. Logistics—such as the size of slaving vessels, the length of the voyage, and the ability to procure one's complement in a timely manner—linked these two secondary and peripheral regions. Together these factors fostered a link between the secondary slave-supplying regions, which did not produce large complements of captives, and secondary slave-buying regions, which could not absorb huge complements of captives.

Overall, the trade was much more idiosyncratic than the relationship between Richard Oswald and Henry Laurens would suggest. Laurens, like Samuel Gamble, was the exception to the rule. Of all of the traders who conducted business in the Rio Nunez region, even of those who purchased surplus rice and therefore depended on the fruits of Africans' labor, Samuel Gamble came closest to investigating and to considering how African farmers produced surplus rice. Unfortunately for historians, coastal Africans' skills remained overwhelmingly invisible to European traders who traveled to the West African Rice Coast and recorded the first written documents for the region. It nourished the bodies of European traders in urban areas and on slaving vessels, the African *grumetes* whom they employed, and the African captives they purchased and forcibly transported to the New World through the Middle Passage. It did not help to shape English slave traders' imaginations about West Africa's Rice Coast region and the ethnic groups inhabiting it, because few actually traveled to coastal areas where and when rice was being cultivated. If, like Gamble, they had, would first-hand experiences have influenced slavers' perceptions? Certainly not. If slavers and planters acknowledged that the enslaved possessed technology with deep roots in West Africa and that enslaved laborers were skilled, not merely brute, laborers, such realizations would have undermined the ideology that justified and perpetuated the institution of enslavement.

Conclusion

"Innovation, Inheritance, and Borrowing: A Theory on Cultural Change in Pre-Colonial Africa and the African Diaspora"

The year 2008, marking the bicentennial of the abolition of trans-Atlantic slave trade in the North American colonies, is an appropriate moment to make a confession that Africanist historians who specialize in the pre-colonial period, such as myself, are usually loath to admit. The forced migration of more than fifteen million Africans from the African continent to the New World—which accelerated the creation of the African Diaspora, was one of many factors leading to the colonization of Africa, and paved the way for the Industrial Revolution—set in motion the most significant social, political, economic, and cultural processes to take place in the last five hundred years of Africa's, and arguably of the world's, history. The occasion of this anniversary is also an appropriate time to reflect on the creation of new cultures in the Diaspora and to consider whether or not they have roots in Africa. Where does Africa end and the African Diaspora begin? What is the relationship between cultural transformation in Africa and the African Diaspora? This concluding chapter will argue that early African history and the methods that this study has used to reconstruct it—particularly the comparative method of historical linguistics—provide tools that can be used to understand processes of cultural change in the African Diaspora.

The introductory chapter of this study laid out the building blocks of the comparative method of historical linguistics—identifying regular sound correspondences established through investigations of core vocabulary and using such correspondences as the first step to identify cognates and to classify cognate cultural vocabulary words as inherited, innovated, or borrowed forms. Speech communities find the information described by inherited vocabulary words relevant enough to pass down to subsequent generations who must find the information sufficiently relevant to retain the vocabulary. These words retain regular sound correspondences. For example, Coastal speech communities in the Rio Nunez region have inherited a word for salt from their distant linguistic ancestors. In addition to inheriting words, linguistic sub-groups also innovate words that cannot be traced to such ancestors. For example, proto-Coastal-speakers in the Rio Nunez region innovated a word for white mangroves which dates back several millennia to their settlement of the region, and proto-Highlands-speakers innovated words for hierarchical social institutions, features of the forest-savanna region, iron, iron cooking pots, and chopping down trees, a process that dates back to c. 500 to 1000 CE and reflects the roots of Highlands-speakers' knowledge about the forest-savanna region. After c. 1000 CE, Coastal daughter speech communities appropriated terminology, such words for chopping down trees, from their Sitem-speaking neighbors and applied it to the coastal environment. Across linguistic speech communities, Coastal and Highlands daughter speech communities in the Rio Nunez region innovated specialized terminology related to rice-growing techniques and material culture. Lastly, speech communities borrowed cultural vocabulary from neighboring speech communities with whom they had regular language contact. Between 1500 and 1800 CE, Atlantic speech communities in coastal Guinea borrowed generic terminology related to rice cultivation—as opposed to the specialized terminology indigenous to their languages—from Susu-speakers.

In coastal Guinea, the comparative method of historical linguistics has provided the tools for this study to trace the development not only of agricultural technology, but also of coastal cultural identities. Its application has revealed intensely localized, highly specialized, and continuously dynamic societies and processes whose deep roots date back millennia into coastal West Africa's ancient past. This rare picture of early coastal West African societies challenges Africanists' assumptions that rice-growing technology diffused from the interior to the coast. It also stands in sharp contrast to Americanists' constructions of a static, undifferentiated pre-colonial Africa that acted as the progenitor of cultures in the African Diaspora.

Embedded in the comparative theory of historical linguistics is a theory of cultural change centered on the core principles of inheritance, innovation, and borrowing. Groups inherit cultural practices, social institutions, and other features from previous generations and subsequent generations continue to retain them as long as they have relevance. New circumstances—a change in existing conditions, migration to a new locale, and/or innovation of new strategies for management and new forms of expression—can spark change from within and cause groups to break from their inherited past. Lastly, interaction with other groups can result in borrowing of cultural practices, forms of cultural expression, and social and political institutions. While applying the comparative method of historical linguistics to Atlantic languages along West Africa's coastal littoral represents a significant achievement in the field of African history, the philosophy underlying the method—inheritance, innovation, and borrowing—holds important lessons for the creation of new cultures in the Diaspora.

Currently, the literature on cultural formation in the African Diaspora privileges either inheritance from Africa or innovation in the New World. Melville Herskovits's *The Myth of the Negro Past* (1958) launched the decades-old debate. Lorenzo Dow Turner first initiated the discussion of "Africanisms," African survivals and retentions in the Gullah language spoken by the enslaved on South Carolina and Georgia rice plantations and their descendants. In his *Africanisms in the Gullah Dialect* (1949), the first scientific and systematic analysis of the Gullah language, Turner correlated Gullah to West African languages by using language to map the origins of Africans enslaved in South Carolina and Georgia's Lowcountry. He described aspects of the Gullah language's syntax, morphology, word formation, pronunciation, and intonation and compiled a long list—which has become the centerpiece of his work—of African-derived vocabulary, personal "basket" or "pet" names, and texts, their meanings, and their translations in West African languages. Whereas Lorenzo Dow Turner examined survivals (inheritance) and transformations (innovation) in the Gullah language, most scholars of communities and cultures in the African Diaspora have only followed along part of the path blazed by Turner and have focused on one or the other.

The past decade has seen a proliferation of studies by scholars specializing in the history and culture of Africa—particularly specialists in pre-colonial West Africa[1]—and scholars of different regions in the New World who also have an interest in African history[2] in what Patrick Manning has termed "Africa-diaspora"—"the interplay of [African] homeland and diaspora, African studies and African-diaspora studies."[3] Recent literature on the African Diaspora has reignited a search for African continuities—inheritance—in New World enslaved societies, introducing new historical approaches to uncover them.

Grounded in the historical sources of a particular region of pre-colonial Africa—West-Central Africa—the work of historians James Sweet and Paul Lovejoy establishes cultural continuities between West-Central Africa and Brazil that are distinguishable from the passive and ahistorical "survivals and retentions" of Herskovits. Lovejoy has argued that enough historical information exists about the trans-Atlantic slave trade and pre-colonial western Africa for scholars to write about the Diaspora, its origins, and the creation of new communities and cultures in the African Diaspora with historical specificity. The UNESCO Slave Route Project—and I would add the Trans-Atlantic Slave Trade database—have added exponentially to scholars' knowledge of the regions of western Africa from which a significant number of African captives originated and of the inner workings of the trans-Atlantic slave trade. Lovejoy proposes a methodology for approaching "African history in the Americas" in a more nuanced way: first, a study of the demography of the trans-Atlantic slave trade to identify the regional origins of African captives who disembarked in specific New World ports at specific moments in time, as well as their age and sex ratios; additional study of biographical accounts of the enslaved to understand the reasons for enslavement—the mechanisms of capture in Africa and sale across the Atlantic—which may assist historians in understanding the processes through which the enslaved privileged certain elements of their complex identities and forged new communities in the New World.

In his work on religion in Afro-Portuguese societies, James Sweet has argued that enslaved populations in Brazil actively maintained connections to the culture of their African homelands in their naming practices, religious observances, ethnic identities, and kinship relations, to cite a few examples. Thus, in West-Central Africa, local worldviews existed and became both regional and influenced by Portuguese Catholicism. In Brazil, these West-Central African features survived until the late eighteenth century, continued to circulate among enslaved and free communities, and were transformed by the institutions of enslavement and emancipation. Though Sweet and Lovejoy have taken a more nuanced and historical approach to the connections between West-Central Africa and New World communities in which large numbers of the enslaved originated from West-Central Africa, they are still only addressing one part of cultural change, inheritance.

Intrinsic to recent African Diaspora studies is a critique of "creolization," innovation. Sidney Mintz and Richard Price's *The Birth of African-American Culture,* one of the best-known studies on creolization, argues that Africans did not share a common culture—only underlying cultural values—prior to their enslavement and involuntary export to the New World. Because there could have been no direct transfer of African cultural traits to enslaved communities in the New World, no African cultural elements survived the institution intact. Sweet, like Lovejoy, argues that the premise of Diasporan cultural forms as diluted or creolized is fundamentally and inherently flawed. Instead, historians should assume that specific African cultural forms survived intact and should analyze the process of creolization that the inherited forms underwent among enslaved communities in the New World. The pendulum continues to swing back and forth between a view that maintains inheritance of African cultural forms and one that claims innovation in the New World.

Because the emerging African Diaspora literature raises questions that originate in Africa, not the African Diaspora, the notion that the African continent, its cultures and inhabitants, are intrinsic to the African Diaspora is fundamental to it. Its proponents would go as far as suggesting that the African Diaspora begins in Africa. On the opposite side of the Atlantic, a second school of thought rejects Africa as the progenitor of the Diaspora and dismisses the notion that Africa played even an important role in the formation of the Diaspora. These literatures operate independently of one another—as if spinning on parallel axes—and are rarely in mutual conversation.

A critique of cultural studies, Paul Gilroy's *The Black Atlantic* represents the extreme polarity of innovation in the New World in the ongoing debate between inheritance and innovation. Published in 1993, this important study ignited discussions—primarily among scholars specializing in literature, arts, and political movements in the Diaspora, as opposed to in Africa—about the relationship of Diaspora communities in Europe to modernity.[4] To Gilroy, modernity began not with the abolition of the trans-Atlantic slave trade and the advent of the Industrial Revolution, but when Africans and Europeans collided—involuntarily and voluntarily—in the Middle Passage. The ship, particularly the slaving vessel, is the transcendent vehicle that transported enslaved Africans from the pre-modern period into Gilroy's modernity, a temporal as well as a physical space. Gilroy uses "Afro-modernity" to describe a counterculture that is a manifestation of Blacks' ambivalence to modernity and that creates trans-national cultural expressions among people of African descent in the Western Hemisphere.

Thus, the oppression of enslavement and the trans-Atlantic slave trade binds blacks in the Western Hemisphere together and relegates them to the margins of Western modernity, though their labor power is critical to the dawning of the modern period in both Western Europe and North America. Gilroy's vision of Afro-modernity represents a break—a violent rupture because of the inherent violence of enslavement—from Africa. Rather than through "roots" and "rootedness" in or inheritance from Africa, the Black Atlantic is born out of the routes moving people of African descent to and within the western hemisphere and the processes of blacks within the Western Hemisphere creating and recreating hybrid trans-national cultures, social and political movements. Within Gilroy's vision of the Black Atlantic—which even takes "Africa" out of the Diaspora—there is no place for pre-modern and dynamic African cultural forms. Gilroy's *Black Atlantic* operates on the premise that pre-modern Africa was traditional, pure, and static prior to the trans-Atlantic slave trade, putting traditional Africa in conflict with—and essentially disqualifying Africa and Africans on the continent from participating in—modernity's complexities.

Contested relationships to the homeland may be one of the mechanisms by which communities in the Diaspora define and distinguish themselves.

Africa is still the blind spot of Diaspora studies: it "appears as a place from which people departed, the memory of which becomes progressively more generalized, rather than as a diverse and changing continent whose inhabitants participated at every stage in creating the world of today."[5] This narrow and one-dimensional view of Africa obscures the very complex and highly localized ways that cultures on the African continent changed from exposure to internal and external stimuli prior to, as well as from a result of the trans-Atlantic slave trade, and the ways that pre-colonial African history could inform the history of the African Diaspora and the New World African cultures created therein. Two hundred years after the abolition of the trans-Atlantic slave trade in the North American colonies, the questions remain: Where does Africa end and the African Diaspora begin? What is the relationship between cultural transformation in Africa and the African Diaspora?

This study used linguistic and technological change as a prism through which to examine cultural formation and transformation in pre-colonial Africa. Its empirical evidence refutes the perceptions of pre-colonial and pre-modern Africa as static and undifferentiated. Outside of African history, scholars often make this assumption based on a lack of what they perceive to be historical source material. By using an interdisciplinary methodology, this study has expanded the concept of historical sources and introduced to a broader audience the tools used by some Africanists to reconstruct the continent's early history. And by taking a deep historical approach to a local region in pre-colonial Africa, this study has revealed the dynamism in Africa's early history—the ways that African societies transformed and local communities privileged aspects of their identity, in response to internal and external stimuli in ancient times—centuries and millennia before interaction with Europeans and/or the advent of the trans-Atlantic slave trade. The process of cultural dynamism—as opposed to stasis—and the highly localized nature of some African identities should inform historians' conceptualization of the ways that African captives transported through the Middle Passage formed new identities, communities, and vehicles for cultural expression in the New World.

Although the comparative method of historical linguistics laid the foundation of the study, the key to the model is its underlying premises—inheritance, innovation, and borrowing—and not the method itself. By conceptualizing the processes of cultural change in the African Diaspora as continuity, change from within, and change from without—inheritance, innovation, and borrowing—within the historical context of local societies, historians could begin to understand the particular social and cultural processes at work at specific points in time within local communities of the African Diaspora.

In 1981, Daniel C. Littlefield wrote: "Without a doubt the African background gave the African immigrant the capability to contribute more than just brawn to the development of plantation society in North America."[6] Without a doubt, this book—with its innovative interdisciplinary methodology and its nontraditional historical sources—has gone deeper than ever before possible into the African background for some of the enslaved Africans who embarked on slaving vessels in the West African Rice Coast region, disembarked in South Carolina and Georgia, and subsequently labored on the colonies' rice plantations. It demonstrates not only the deep roots of agricultural technology in West Africa, but also the deep roots of internal dynamism and transformation among stateless, coastal societies, which have until recently been considered static even by Africanists. The highly localized nature of the African background of this relatively small West African region and relatively small group of enslaved Africans holds lessons for the history of the African Diaspora and its connections to Africa, and for time periods pre-dating written sources. In advocating the transcendence of the dichotomy between inheritance from African or innovation in the New World, this study advances a theory of cultural change that is open and elastic enough to encompass the diversity of communities, cultures, and forms of expression in Africa and the African Diaspora.

Appendix I.

Fieldwork Interviews

El Hadj Abdulaye Bangura, Mbulungish village of Monchon, October 1, 1998.

Aissatu Bangura, Susu village of Missira, December 16 and 17, 1997.

Amara Bangura, Mboteni village of Binari, September 9, 1998; December 4, 1998.

Arbot Bangura, Sitem village of Kuffin, interview conducted in Conakry, November 13, 1998.

Boniface Bangura, Sitem village of Kawass, September 22, 1998; November 28, 1998.

Ibrahima Bangura, Mbulungish village of Monchon, September 29, 1998; December 17, 1998.

M'Baye Ndugu Bangura, Nalu village of, October 9, 1998.

Mohamed DiJongo Bangura, Mboteni village of Binari, April 29 and 30, 1998; May 3, 1998; July 20, 1998; September 9, 1998; December 2 and 4, 1998.

Saliu Bangura, Nalu village of Kukuba, December 12, 1997; May 16 and 27, 1998; July 15 and 17, 1998; December 19, 1998.

Alsenyi Camara, Mbulungish village of Monchon, March 23, 1998; July 5 and 7, 1998; September 27 and 28, 1998; October 1, 1998; December 16, 1998.

Ibrahima Camara, Nalu village of Kukuba, September 17, 1998; December 17, 1998.

Issa Camara, Sitem village of Kawass, November 28, 1998.

El-Hadj Lansana Camara, Mbulungish village of Monchon, December 17, 1998.

Mamadu Camara, Sitem village of Kawass, September 23, 1998.

El Hadj Mamadu Saliu Camara, Jalonke-speaker interview conducted in Conakry, November 12, 1998; December 15, 1998.

Mohammed Camara, Nalu village of Kukuba, May 27, 1998.

Arafan Momo Camara, Mbulungish village of Monchon, March 25, 1998; September 26 and 28, 1998; December 18, 1998.

Usman Camara, Nalu village of Kukuba, May 23, 1998; September 18, 1998; December 9, 1998.

Salifu Camara, Nalu village of Kukuba, September 14, 1998.

Saturnet Camara, Sitem village of Kawass, December 7, 1998.

Seydu Camara, Sitem village of Kawass, March 17, 1998; July 21 and 22, 1998.

Suleyman Camara, Nalu village of Kukuba, September 19, 1998; December 11, 1998.

Mamadu Keita, Nalu village of Kukuba, September 17, 1998.

Thomas Keita, Nalu village of Kukuba, September 17 and 19, 1998.

Mamadu Kompo, Landuma village of Kimiya, May 24, 1998.

Mimo Camara, Kamsar, August 4 and 5, 1998.

Detna Nakodé, Balanta village of Missera, November 9, 1998.

El Hadj Silah, Mbulungish village of Monchon, December 17, 1998.

Ndiaye Sumah, Mbulungish of Boŋkompon, September 29, 1998; October 3, 1998; December 17, 1998; March 27, 1998.

Mamadu Samura, Jalonke-speaker, interview conducted in Conakry, November 12, 1998.

Seydu Muctar Sumah, Mboteni village of Binari, July 28 and 30, 1998; September 8, 10, and 11, 1998; November 9 and 30, 1998; December 2, 1998.

Thierno Tambasa, Landuma village of Kimiya, May 24, 1998.

Appendix 2.

Rice Terminology in Atlantic Languages Spoken in the Coastal Rio Nunez Region[1]

	Nalu	Mbulungish	Mboteni	Sitem
Seasonal stream	*m-tɛsɛ/ a-tɛsɛ*	*bɔlɔŋ/ cubɔlɔŋ; paral cipparaŋ. ipal/ appalleŋ*	*pɔl*	
Small seasonal stream		*masaleŋ*	*ilex/ alexeŋ*	
Tree used to fabricate the short fulcrum shovel and the shovel handle	*m-silaa/ a- silaa*	*ki-mal*		
Red mangrove (*Rhizophora racemosa*) used to fabricate the short or long fulcrum shovel	*m-mak/ a-mak*	*ki-kiNYc/ e-kiNYcil; ku-wɔll a-wɔlleŋ*	*e-ma, ɛ-ma / a-ma*	*a-kinc/ kinc*
Rice cultivated in the red mangroves		*malɔ be kinycilpon/ cimmalɔŋ be kiNYcilpon*	*fɔr ɛma*	
White mangroves (*Avicennia africana*)	*m-yɔcf/ a-yɔcf*	*yɔp/ ki-yɔp*	*e-weleŋ, weleŋ/ awelleŋ*	*kopir/ copir*
Rice cultivated in the white mangroves		*malɔ biyɔppon/ cimalɔ ciyɔppon*	*maafer*	
Order given by the elder to begin fieldwork			*fɔfuduŋ*	*kusɔkɔp*
Enough water in the mangrove field to begin fieldwork			*asɔfsilawola*	*dumun dɛncmɛ dukubora*
Order given by the elder to stop fieldwork			*senden afanc*	*aŋkatefer*

(continued)

Appendix 2 *(continued)*

	Nalu	Mbulungish	Mboteni	Sitem
Harvest ceremony (pre-Islam)			*xesara lemma*	*kuunre malɔ*
Order given to begin the harvest			*ndebe loŋyon*	*kiitel kufɔlɔ*
Fulcrum shovel handle	*m-kuŋgbala/ a-kuŋgbala*	*kur capɔn/ cukurkappon; ki-ti akɔp/ ɛ-ti akɔp*	*ndii kɔp*	
Small pieces of wood used to reinforce shovel foot when tying it to handle (could be bamboo or the stalk of the red mangrove)	*m-ba iŋkifɔblasen/ a-ba iŋkifɔblasen m-caanahsen/ a-caanahsen*	*wacl/ cuwacel*	*i-xarel aŋ-xare*	*me-kɪnc*
Shovel blade	*ma-fancl a-fanc*	*a-fencl e-fenccel*	*i-cell aNY-cel*	
Sculpted blade of fulcrum shovel		*kɔp ŋyetelpon*	*inUmi cel*	
To sharpen the fulcrum shovel blade	*m-namtah/ a-namtah*	*a-fenc gbat*	*aŋrcel*	
Vine used to attach shovel foot to handle	*m-nintampl/ a-nintamp*	*ntell eteellen*		*dɛ-tempal s-tempa*
To clear the red mangroves to make the large dike		*ɛ-cɛp*	*asaBen wucer akuvɔr*	
To burn the rice hay before the rainy season			*muxalɔmppasinal*	*kɪcɔs yikaya malɔ*
To trace the grand dike		*ki-bereŋ uurte*	*wac nxɔfɔrn*	
To cut the earth with the shovel to make the dike		*abereŋ yeket/ cibereŋ yeket*	*ebaxacakea*	

To cut weeds and separate two ridges	m-sɔɔŋ/ a-sɔɔŋ		auwl	kɪ-ces
To walk on the weeds to diminish their size	ma-dakal a-daka		i-camanasen	kɪ-namp
To cut the weeds on the bottom before turning soil with the shovel	ma-cesal/ a-cesa	iŋcepel mɔlɔ inpenna; a-cappa		kɪ-ces yika
First turning of the weeds and soil with fulcrum shovel	m-kes/ a-kes	bɔŋwaca; ki-cɛp/ a-cappa; a-beret/ ɛ-beret	afanc	
One shovelful of earth	ma-bees/ a-bees		for	dambal/ samba
To walk on weeds for a second time	m-ŋakten/ a-ŋakten		elerpernanasɔɔl	
To tuck weeds into the soil with hands or feet		walta	ayixil; ibaxanas (feet are used in the fields) ibaxayekel (hands are used in the nursery)	kɪ-nas anɛk
Second turning of the soil to cover the weeds with fulcrum shovel	m-wupur/ a-wupur	bɔŋkubut; awnpur		
Short fulcrum shovel	ma-kumbal a-kumbal	ki-taŋgbaŋ/ ci-taŋgbaŋŋel	aŋ-kumbɛl; faa-aykumbɛl (for repairing the dikes and other small jobs in the field and around the village)	

(continued)

Appendix 2 (continued)

	Nalu	Mbulungish	Mboteni	Sitem
Long fulcrum shovel (2 to 4 meters long)	m-kɔp lanna/ a-kɔp lanna	kɔp kokilanne/ ci-kɔppel kokilanne	e-lar (for use when turning the earth for the first time)	
Ancestral fulcrum shovel used without metal blade			kɔp amaŋkre cel/ su kɔpamaŋ i-cel	
Dike/mound	ma-bɔŋen/ a-bɔŋen	ki-bereŋ/ ci-bereŋ	axɔBern/ aŋxɔBern	
Ridge	ma-nek/ a-neek	ε-nek/ ki-nek	e-nek/ a-nek	a-nek
Furrow	m-sumuunt/ a-sumuunt	ku-bont/ a-bontol	e-won/ a-won	
To sow in rows	ma-ceep	a-sappa	suk mmao	kɪ-cep tecɪr
To sow in the fields		a-meŋker	mbuŋma asina	
To sow by broadcasting	ma-yara	malɔ pen	mboo mmao	kɪ-glal ka malɔ
To sow directly in the field	ma-yaara		afur mmao	
To sow directly, done tightly	m-dafeet/ a-dafeet		axɔfɛl	kɪ-fɪlfɪl; kɪ-gbɛɛ malɔ
To sow directly, done tightly and then to pull up some seedlings and leave some		malɔ seŋ	mBelmmalon	
To sow directly, done loosely	m-yɔlyolen/ a-yɔlyolen	malɔ bɛ kabateŋŋe bilimpon	maasepna	
To sow on flat land		bɔkitefɛ	maaxɔfɔla	

English				
First rice nursery			tabla mbuŋŋund kamao	kısımı kınmkıɔskɔ cɔkɔ
Second rice nursery			mbuŋŋa asenden	kısımı kamεrεŋ
Too much water beneath the rice nursery			asɔyɔkɔkinin mmao	kiykankla dumun
Normal cycle of the rice nursery			fam mmao	ocɔmas
To wash bottom of germinated rice seedlings before transplanting			abɔɔɔr mmao	ki-yaak malɔ
To attach germinated rice seedlings			εra mmao	ku-kutus malɔ
To put the attached and germinated rice seedlings in water before transplanting			ndεpman asɔla	aŋbe midire
To cover the seeds with banana leaves		malɔ gbopretl cimmallɔŋ gbepret	wofor mmao	kukumpus malɔ
Germinated seedlings	m-kiceepal a-kiceepa	ε-fiebelaŋŋa εcɔlcεn	axɔfεl	malɔ mopoŋ
Seedlings that did not germinate		malɔ tɔtil cim-mallɔŋcɔti; malɔ beabawɔɔce	maamaŋ kulum	malɔ melεcε
To pull up weeds with the hands		ɔtʊlʊt	iŋkur awευεn	
To transplant	m-ceepa	belaŋ ɔcɔlε; a-sappa	iυaaso	pa-cεεp; tɔk-yɔkɔ an luksırne kı-fcɔf mɔ
To weed after replanting			iŋkur aBaBεn	kUwas malɔ

(continued)

Appendix 2 (continued)

	Nalu	Mbulungish	Mboteni	Sitem
To clean the canal to begin fieldwork		bamcaɔtɔ	wuxucer aso	kɨfɨnc kiboŋen
To open the canal	m-bannataŋ/ a-bannataŋ		imuaxurtuŋun	kɨ-ŋer
To evacuate the water when the rice is ripe		wulci; ɔtɔcaŋ	ɛbelaso kamato	malɔ mɔlɔl
To close the canal	m-laŋŋaŋ/ a-laŋŋaŋ		caimuarumtuŋ	kɨ-ŋiri
End of the canal		bampetɔtipote/ cim-bammelpecitɔtɔpete	alubana	
Canal used to evacuate water from field	m-tisɔtɔ/ a-tisɔtɔ; m-sumunt/ a-sumunt	bampetelɔtɔ/ cim-bampetɔtɔ	tuŋ/ suruŋ	dɨk wure du mun; dobo
Principal drain		kubŋkum	tuŋ/ suruŋ	
Secondary drain		mawuŋkummul	fatuŋ/ fam suruŋ	
To guard the rice field from predators during the hungry season	ma-lɛɛm kabafrɛ/ a-lɛɛm kabafrɛ	a-kecek mmel		kɨ-bum
Temporary shelter in the rice field	ma-gbɔɔŋk kamtɔh/ a-gbɔɔŋk kamtɔh	agbɔŋk/ agbɔŋkel	iŋgaNYcaŋ	U-bal dale tetek
To move to the field until the harvest			ncebel asina	siŋkɔdale dikidire
Harvest	ma-bit/ a-bit	malɔ ɛtel	mBer	kɨ-tel ka malɔ
To evacuate the harvested rice to the dike so that it will not get wet			yokon mal awultɔŋ	patel dikiboŋen

English					
Small handful/pile of harvested rice				*era mmao*	*malɔ kɪcaka*
Large pile of rice arranged with the grains on the inside				*maasuŋ saŋ kappa*	*amboc kur*
To fan rice			*kɔ-fuŋŋa*		*kɪ-foy*
To fan rice with fanner			*malɔ petel*	*afoi mmao*	*kɪ-gbap malɔ*
To fan rice with wind			*malɔ fuŋŋa*	*wuluŋ mmao*	*kɪ-foi malɔ*
Rice fanner	*m-fɛntab* [loanword from English]	*m-dɛhɛn*	*kɪ-rɛbɛ/ cɪ-rɛbɛ*	*kebei*	*kɪ-rɛbɛ/ cɪ-rɛbɛ*
To mill rice		*ma-matθ*	*ka-tampa*	*icer*	
To mill rice for first time			*malɔ tampa*	*yuŋkapt mmaun*	*kɪ-sɛpɪr; kɪ koyos*
To mill rice for second time			*malɔ bekebirite*	*wuŋ ailim*	*anxɔ dikseprt*
To mill daily rations of rice with feet			*malɔ ɛɛɛk esupun*	*sux mmao*	
Daily ration of rice				*maɔwl/ maŋalɔ*	*malɔ medi*
Area where rice is beaten		*ma-tana*	*tetek kubɔrton*	*aBoma*	
To cover the rice after beating but before fanning it				*wupurmaayɔŋyɔn*	
To transport the rice to the granary				*suŋ maarun*	*pakis malɔ*
Rice granary for seeds				*tɛle pasansi*	*kɪsare malɔ*
To dry the parboiled rice				*famben mmao aruful*	*kɪ cɛɛs*

(continued)

Appendix 2 (continued)

	Nalu	Mbulungish	Mboteni	Sitem
To distribute cooked rice for consumption			wal malɔn	kiyeres yɛɛc
Calabash in which rice was served			isar mmao	pepe
Wooden bowl in which rice was served			ifɛrl	po-rɔs/ si-rɔs
Rice is spoiled, because it was prepared with too much fire and smoke			mmambɛl fus	yɛɛc yɛntɛɛ
Weeds used to reinforce the big mound	m-hoofl a-boof	kepl ci-keppel	seNYNYɛl uɔn	
Water moss	m-cufran/ a-cufran	a-fucl ku-fuccel	afuNYc	kɪ-foc kadumun
New field with no mounds or ridges	m-bitikl a-bitik		avent	kɪ-pɪr
To make new ridges		abetal abetelaŋ		
Field on high ground whose soil is sandy		cɔ yeibonŋkorolɛ/ cɔ yeibonŋkoroŋ	aninanmces	
Field lying fallow	m-woskamtɔb atilɛbahi a-woskamtɔb watil-ɛbah	cakara ɛnɛkicot; bɔŋ bɛ pepiyecilɛ/ cimbonŋel pepiyecilɛ		
Low-lying area	m-cumbaayl a-cum-baaŋ	timbilɛ apoll citimbilɛŋŋel	iniyapɔŋ	
Rice husk	m-kiseeŋal a-kiseeŋa			U-fɔntal fɔrU
Rice seed	m-kofok ka marol a-kofok ka maro	agba agbalɛŋ	axɔfɔl mmao	

Threshed, unmilled rice	m-maaro tabobor/ a-maaro tabobor	malɔ bipɛcl cimmalɔ ciabɔlɛ	maŋkul	malɔ mɔbomba
Pounded rice	m-maaro ntɔn/ a-maaro ntɔn	caaki cicakileŋ	manduŋyund	malɔ mɔsɔkır
Rice straw	m-maaro nsimaθ/ a-maaro nsimaθ	malɔ baba tampa	mamiŋ kɛlɛcɛr	malɔ ɛtɛw sɛpır
Rice grain	m-maaro yaaŋka/ a-maaro yaaŋka	caaki	maŋkul	malɔ mɛgbıntɛ
Rice broken during processing	m-NYin ka maaro/ a-NYin ka maaro	mɛNYım/ cimmɛNYım	aNYcakas	
Parboiled rice	m-maaro nton/ a-maaro nton	malɔ yıŋyın/ cimmalɔ yıŋyın	aruful	malɔ mɔcıfl talɔ pɔcıf
Cooked rice	m-fɛɛfl a-fɛɛf	ɔro	mandul	yɛc
Rice broth made with rice flour	m-mɔnil a-mɔni	baxa	mbɔs ammasam; alafa	
Rice broth made with rice	m-baba/ a-baba	mɔni	mbɔs; asowasa	
To form grain	m-yeenNYcaŋ	malɔ fuŋŋa		
Head of the rice plant	m-ki ka mba putna/ a-ki ka aba putna	kapa malɔ/ ciŋkapel amalɔ "literally head of rice"	kap mmaol saŋka mmao	do-bomp da malɔ "literally head of rice plant"
Early-maturing rice variety	m-rɛfnaba/ a-rɛfnaba	mabaxa		malɔ mɔkɔ mɔ nunkɛnɛ
Cluster	m-cɔncɔ/ a-tɔncɔ			kı-nɔcnɔl ŋcɔnc

(continued)

Appendix 2 *(continued)*

	Nalu	Mbulungish	Mboteni	Sitem
Beginning of gestation	m-laƒkam laƅ/ alaƒkam laƅ		awal siɲɲapaɲɲal	malɔ melek cor
Rice in gestation period			maavul	malɔ melɛ cor
Rice forming the head			maafutuŋ	malɔ kuwurus
Rice plants in the same field form heads at different times			maalɔ mdafutuɲɲul	kunɔmkul malɔ
Approaching the rainy season			elle leper	malɔfɛ
Rainy season	m-tem kamkaak a-tem kamkaak	temeisa	kuiyoŋ	tem ta kɪfe
Cold season	m-bɔɔb kamcacɲaɓ/ a-bɔɔb kamcacɲaɓ	wcɔppipepi	ccs	
Beginning of the rainy season	ma-lɔfɛ/ a-lɔfɛ	tɔ-lɔfɛ	table eleBerː eleper	
Beginning of fieldwork		kitaŋkemɛc	sux mmao; ku-sɔk mmao	

End of the rainy season		*kayemin/ ci-kayemin*	*elelen*	
End of the rainy season, hungry season	*m-lank/ a-lank*		*elelen; elelaŋ*	
Hungry season	*NYim sabɔk/ NYinnɛ sabɔk*	*tcippelɛmpep wori*	*laŋ*	
Surveillance period			*yilaŋxɔc*	*kɪmɔmɔn kɪbora*
Dry season	*m-hɔɔh kamθabraan/ a-hɔɔh kamθabraan*	*abanam/ tɛmu abanan*		*kɪ-tɪŋ*

1. Because of space considerations, I am publishing selected data for the understudied Nalu, Mbulungish, Mboteni, and Sitem languages. Colleagues who wish to consult unpublished language data from my fieldwork need only contact me personally. Please see Appendix 1 for a complete list of languages and interviews.

Notes

Introduction

1. In 1789–90, Samuel Gamble had been second captain of the *Jemmy*, which departed from Liverpool, purchased slaves primarily in the Banana Islands, and successfully disembarked in Montego Bay, Jamaica. Though the ship's twenty-three crew members disembarked at the end of the fourteen-month voyage, six captives lost their lives during the Middle Passage. David Eltis, Stephen D. Behrendt, David Richardson, and Herbert S. Klein, eds., *The Trans-Atlantic Slave Trade: A Database on CD-Rom* (Cambridge: Cambridge University Press, 1999).

2. Bruce L. Mouser, *A Slaving Voyage to Africa and Jamaica: The Log of the Sandown, 1793–1794* (Bloomington: Indiana University Press, 2002), 38.

3. Ibid., 98.

4. Ibid., xiii.

5. Gamble probably visited Sitem villages along the Dougoubona/Kabouli/Kouli River. Bruce Mouser, "Qui étaient les Baga? Perceptions européennes, 1793–1821," in Gérald Gaillard, *Migrations anciennes et peuplement actuel des Côtes guinéennes* (Paris: L'Harmattan, 2000), 432.

6. Mouser, *A Slaving Voyage*, 86, 98–99.

7. Gamble mistakenly identifies Baga farmers as inhabitants of the Windward Coast, which is located south of coastal Guinea, primarily in present-day Sierra Leone and Liberia. See Daniel C. Littlefield, *Rice and Slaves: Ethnicity and the Slave Trade in Colonial South Carolina* (Baton Rouge: Louisiana State University, 1981), 93–95.

8. Judith A. Carney, "Rice, Slaves, and Landscapes of Cultural Memory," in *Places of Cultural Memory: African Reflections on the American Landscape: Conference Proceedings, May 9–12, 2001, Atlanta, GA* (Washington, D.C.: U.S. Department of the Interior, National Park Service, 2001), 50. North of coastal Guinea, André de Faro described tidal rice farming in Guinea-Bissau. See Paul E. H. Hair, ed., *André de Faro's Missionary Journey to Sierra Leone in 1663–1664* (Freetown: University of Sierra Leone Institute of African Studies, 1982), 24.

9. René Caillé's 1824–28 account describes tidal rice farming, including the building of dikes and bunds with a wooden fulcrum shovel and the transplanting of germinated seedlings among Baga farmers. See René Caillé, *Travels through Central Africa to Timbuctoo* (London: Frank Cass & Co., 1968), 162. John Matthews, in his 1785–87 travelers' account, mentions upland and lowland rice cultivation along the Rio Pongo region of coastal Guinea. See John Matthews, *A Voyage to the River Sierra-Leone* (London: Frank Cass & Co., 1966), 55–56.

10. Edda L. Fields, "Rice Farmers in the Rio Nunez Region: A Social History of

Agricultural Technology and Identity in Coastal Guinea, ca. 2000 BCE to 1880 CE" (Ph.D. diss., University of Pennsylvania, 2001).

11. Walter Hawthorne, "The Interior Past of an Acephalous Society: Institutional Change among the Balanta of Guinea-Bissau, c. 1400–1950" (Ph.D. diss., Stanford University, 1998), 40–48.

12. Peter Mark, *"Portuguese" Style and Luso-African Identity: Precolonial Senegambia, 16th–19th Centuries* (Bloomington: Indiana University Press, 2002); George E. Brooks, *Eurafricans in Western Africa: Commerce, Social Status, Gender, and Religious Observance from the Sixteenth to the Eighteenth Century* (Athens: Ohio University Press, 2003); idem, "The Signares of Saint-Louis and Gorée: Women Entrepreneurs in 18th Century Senegal," in Nancy J. Hafkin, ed., *Women in Africa: Studies in Social and Economic Change* (Stanford, Calif.: Stanford University Press, 1976), 19–44.

13. Hawthorne, "The Interior Past," 12–28; Robin Horton, "Stateless Societies in the History of West Africa," in J. F. A. Ajayi and Michael Crowder, ed., *History of West Africa: Volume I* (London: Longman, 1972), 79.

14. Boubacar Barry, *Senegambia and the Atlantic Slave Trade* (Cambridge: Cambridge University Press, 1998), 96–102; Ismaël Barry, *Le Futa-Jaloo face à la colonisation: conquête et mise en place de l'administration en Guinée* (Paris: L'Harmattan, 1997).

15. Bruce L. Mouser, "Iles de Los as Bulking Center in the Slave Trade 1750–1800," *Revue française d'histoire d'outre-mer* 83: 313 (1996), 77–90; Paul Hair contends that the presence of sand bars was one of the principal reasons why the rivers between the Balola and Nunez were not well known to the Portuguese. See André Alvares de Álmada, *Brief Treatise on the Rivers of Guinea (c. 1594): Part II Notes* (Liverpool: University of Liverpool Department of History, 1986).

16. Mouser, "Iles de Los as Bulking Center," 77–90.

17. Mouser, "Who and Where Were the Baga? European Perceptions from 1793 to 1821," *History in Africa* 29 (2002), 340, 343.

18. In general, Sierra Leone is better documented in European travelers' accounts than Guinea. A few examples are Paul E. H. Hair, "Sources on Early Sierra Leone: (15) Marmol 1573," *Africana Research Bulletin* 9: 3 (1979), 78–9; idem, "Early Sources on Religion and Social Values in the Sierra Leone Region: (1) Cadamosto 1463," *The Sierra Leone Bulletin of Religion* 11: (1969), 51; idem, "Early Sources on Religion and Social Values in the Sierra Leone Region: (2) Eustache de la Fosse 1480," *Africana Research Bulletin* 4: 4 (1974), 50.

19. Bruce L. Mouser, "Trade, Coasters, and Conflict in the Rio Pongo from 1790 to 1808," *Journal of African History* 14: 1 (1973), 53–54.

20. Francisco de Lemos Coelho, *Description of the Coast of Guinea*, edited by Paul E. H. Hair (Liverpool: University of Liverpool Department of History, 1985), 9/2; Paul E. H. Hair, "Sources on Early Sierra Leone: (9) Barreira's Account of the Coast of Guinea, 1606," *Africana Research Bulletin* 7: 1 (1977), 61; idem, "Early Sources on Religion (1) Cadamosto," 54; Bruce L. Mouser and Ramon Sarró, eds., *Travels into the Baga and Soosoo Countries in 1821 by Peter McLachlan* (Leipzig: University of Leipzig African History and Culture Series, 1999), vii, ix.

21. Marie-Christine Cormier-Salem, "À la découverte des mangroves: regards multiples sur un objet de recherche mouvant," in Marie-Christine Cormier-Salem, ed., *Dynamique et usages de la mangrove dans les pays des rivières du Sud (du Sénégal à la Sierra Leone)* (Paris: ORSTOM éditions, 1994), 16–18; Philip D. Curtin, *Death by Migration: Europe's Encounter with the Tropical World in the Nineteenth Century* (Cambridge: Cambridge University Press, 1989), 62–79.

22. Captain Theophilus Conneau, *A Slaver's Log Book or 20 Years' Residence in Africa* (Englewood Cliffs, N.J.: Prentice-Hall, 1976), 99, 107.

23. Ibid., 272; Bruce L. Mouser, ed., *Account of the Mandigoes, Susoos, & Other Nations, c. 1815 by the Reverend Leopold Butscher* (Leipzig: University of Leipzig Papers on Africa, 2000), 5 n.19.

24. André Coffinières de Nordeck, "Voyage aux pays des Bagas et du Rio Nuñez, 1884–1885," *Le tour du monde* 51: 1e semestre (1887), 292.

25. Paul E. H. Hair, "Sources on Early Sierra Leone: [(13) Barreira's] Report of 1607–1608—The Visit to Bena," *Africana Research Bulletin* 8: 2–3 (1978), 98–99.

26. See Hair, *André de Faro's Missionary Journey*, 25, 69; idem, "Sources on Early Sierra Leone: (13)," 78, 99; idem, "Sources on Early Sierra Leone: (9) Barreira," 55–56.

27. Julia Floyd Smith, *Slavery and Rice Culture in Low Country Georgia 1750–1860* (Knoxville: University of Tennessee Press, 1985), 7.

28. Olga Linares de Sapir, "Shell Middens of Lower Casamance and Problems of Diola Protohistory," *West African Journal of Archaeology* 1 (1971), 23–54; Raymond Mauny, *Tableau géographique de l'Ouest Africain au Moyen Âge d'après les sources écrites, la tradition et l'archéologie* (Dakar: Institute français d'Afrique noire, 1961), 172–74; idem, "L'aire des mégalithes 'sénégambiens'," *Notes africaines* 73 (1957), 1–2; idem, "Nouvelles pierres sonnantes d'Afrique occidentale," *Notes africaines* 79 (1958), 65–67.

There are, however, a few archaeological studies of Guinea's interior. See A. Chermette, "Monument monolithique de la région de Kankan (Haute Guinée)," *Notes africaines* 42 (1949), 179; B. A. Gross, "Notes guinéennes," *Notes africaines* 19: 7 (1943), 4; T. Hamy, "Rapport sur une fouille exécutée dans la grotte de Rotoma, près de Konakry," *Revue coloniale* (1899), 497–501; idem, "La Grotte du Kakimbon á Rotoma, près Konakry (Guinée française)," *L'Anthropologie* 12 (1901), 380–95.

29. Hawthorne, "The Interior Past," 40–48.

30. David Berliner, "'Nous sommes les derniers buloNic': Sur une impossible transmission dans une société d'Afrique de l'Ouest (Guinée Conakry)" (Ph.D. diss., Université Libre de Bruxelles, 2003); idem, "An 'Impossible' Transmission: Youth Religious Memories in Guinea-Conakry," *American Ethnologist* 32: 4 (2005), 576–92.

31. For examples of the historical and comparative linguistic method applied to the Bantu language group, see Koen Bostoen, "Linguistics for the Use of African History and the Comparative Study of Bantu Pottery Vocabulary," *Antwerp Papers in Linguistics* 106 (2004), 131–54; Christopher Ehret, "Cattle-Keeping and Milking in Eastern and Southern African History," *Journal of African History* 1: 8 (1967), 1–17; idem, "Sheep and Central Sudanic Peoples in Southern Africa," *Journal of African History* 9: 2 (1968), 213–21; idem, "On the Antiquity of Agriculture in Ethiopia," *Journal of African History* 20: 2 (1979), 161–77; Kairn A. Klieman, *"The Pygmies Were Our Compass": Bantu and Batwa in the History of West Central Africa, Early Times to c. 1900 CE* (Portsmouth: Heinemann, 2003); Derek Nurse, "The Contribution of Linguistics to the Study of History in Africa," *Journal of African History* 38 (1997), 359–91; David Lee Schoenbrun, *A Green Place, A Good Place: Agrarian Change, Gender, and Social Identity in the Great Lakes Region to the 15th Century* (Portsmouth: Heinemann, 1998); idem, "We Are What We Eat: Ancient Agriculture between the Great Lakes," *Journal of African History* 34: 1 (1993), 1–31; Jan Vansina, "New Linguistic Evidence and the 'Bantu Expansion'," *Journal of African History* 36 (1995), 173–95; idem, *Paths in the Rainforest: Toward a History of Political Tradition in Equatorial Africa* (Madison: University of Wisconsin Press, 1990).

32. A few previous studies use historical linguistics to reconstruct portions of West and West-Central Africa's interior, but not the coast. See Klieman, *"The Pygmies Were Our Compass"*; M. E. Kropp-Dakubu, "On the Linguistic Geography of the Area of Ancient Begho," in H. Trutenau, ed., *Languages of the Akan Area: Papers in Western Kwa Linguistics and on the Linguistic Geography of the Area of Ancient Begho* (Basel: Basler Afrika Bibliographien, 1976), 63–91; Tal Tamari, *Les castes de l'Afrique occidentale: artisans et musiciens endogames* (Nanterre: Société d'ethnologie, 1997); Kay Williamson, "Linguistic Evidence for the Use of Some Tree and Tuber Food Plants in Southern Nigeria," in Thurstan Shaw, ed., *The Archaeology of Africa: Foods, Metals and Towns* (New York: Routledge, 1993), 139–53; idem, "Linguistic Evidence for the Prehistory of the Niger Delta," in E. J. Alagoa, F. N. Anozie, and Nwanna Nzewunwa, eds., *The Early History of the Niger Delta* (Hamburg: H. Buske, 1988), 65–119.

33. Marie Yvonne Curtis, "L'art Nalu, l'art Baga de Guinée: approches comparatives" (Ph.D. diss., Université de Paris I Panthéon-Sorbonne, 1996); Marie Paule Ferry, unpublished wordlists (Kogoli, Mboteni, Mbuluŋuc, and Sitem languages); Tina Weller Ganong, "Features of Baga Morphology, Syntax, and Narrative Discourse" (M.A. thesis, University of Texas at Arlington, 1998); Maurice Houis, "La rapport d'annexion en Baga," *Bulletin l'Institut français d'Afrique noire* 15: 1 (1953), 848–54; idem, "Le système pronominal et les classes dans les dialectes Baga," *Bulletin de l'Institut français d'Afrique noire* 15: 1 (1953), 381–404; idem, "Les minorités ethniques de la Guinée côtière, situation linguistique," *Études guinéennes* 4 (1952), 25–48; Sigmund Koelle, *Polyglotta Africana* (London: Church Missionary House, 1854); Frederick Lamp, *Art of the Baga: A Drama of Cultural Reinvention* (New York: The Museum for African Art, 1996); Ramon Sarró-Maluquer, "Baga Identity: Religious Movements and Political Transformation in the Republic of Guinea" (Ph.D. diss., University College London, 1999); Erhard Voeltz, Abouboucar Camara, Tina Weller Ganong, and Martin Ganong, "Baga: Intam kicicis citem (syllabaire de langue baga)," *Cahiers d'étude des langues guinéennes* 3 (1996); idem, "Bibliographie linguistique de la Guinée," *Cahiers d'étude des langues guinéennes* 2 (1996); idem, "Les langues de la Guinée," *Cahiers d'étude des langues guinéennes* 1 (1996); idem, and Mohammed Camara, "Lexique Nalu-Français," unpublished. David Berliner began working in the region after I completed my fieldwork. See Berliner, "'Nous sommes les derniers buloNic'"; idem, "An 'Impossible' Transmission."

34. Mark Durie and Malcolm Ross, "Introduction," in *The Comparative Method Reviewed: Regularity and Irregularity in Language Change* (New York: Oxford University Press, 1996), 16.

35. Fashion and prestige can also play important roles in dialect divergence as individual language speakers imitate the speech patterns of more prestigious people. Though the initial choices are conscious acts, other members of the speech community may subconsciously imitate the language changes. See Charles Barber, *The English Language: A Historical Introduction* (Cambridge: Cambridge University Press, 2000), 59.

36. Bostoen, "Linguistics for the Use of African History," 133.

37. Barber, *The English Language*, 52, 86.

38. David Dalby, "The Mel Languages: A Reclassification of Southern West Atlantic," *African Languages Studies* 6 (1965), 1–17.

39. Jean L. Doneux, "Hypothèses pour la comparative des langues Atlantiques," *Africana linguistica* 6 (1975), 41–129; Konstantin Pozdniakov, *Sravnitel'naia Grammatika Atlantichskikh Iazykov* (Izdatel'skaia Firma, Vostoshnai Literatura, Moscow, 1993) (translated by Lioudmila Selemeneva, Carnegie Mellon University, Department of English);

J. David Sapir, "West Atlantic: An Inventory of Languages, their Noun Class System and Consonant Alternation," in *Current Trends in Linguistics in Sub-Saharan Africa* (The Hague: Mouton, 1971), 45–112.

40. Fields, "Rice Farmers in the Rio Nunez Region," 37–46.

41. Barber, *The English Language,* 40, 43–46.

42. Durie and Ross, "Introduction," 5–6.

43. Once historical linguists have established a genetic relationship among a group of languages, they use "lexicostatistics" to estimate the degree of relationship between daughter languages that descended from a common linguistic ancestor. From 100-word core vocabulary lists, historical linguists identify and count cognates. The presence of two cognates in a pair of genetically related languages implies the existence of an ancestral form of the word in a common linguistic ancestor. Historical linguists confirm the proposed list of cognate vocabulary by comparing sounds and establishing sound correspondences in a broader selection of vocabulary than the 100-word core lists.

44. Important debate continues on this hypothesis, because it has two implications: core vocabulary words are some of the oldest words in a language; and sound changes, which distinguish daughter languages from their linguistic ancestors, are encoded in core vocabulary words. Some linguists resist the notion that one can identify a set of culturally neutral vocabulary words in all of the world's languages. Others have questioned the stability of core vocabulary, demonstrating that both core and non-core vocabulary is affected by borrowing. See C. H. Borland, "Computing African Linguistic Prehistory," in Derek F. Gowlett, ed., *African Linguistic Contributions: Papers in Honour of Ernest Westphal* (Pretoria: Via Afrika Limited, 1992), 6–11; idem, "How Basic Is 'Basic' Vocabulary?", *Current Anthropology* 23: 3 (1982), 315–16.

45. Barber, *The English Language,* 87–92.

45. Ibid., 67–77.

47. Ibid., 146.

48. Christopher Ehret, "Testing the Expectations of Glottochronology against the Correlations of Language and Archaeology in Africa," in Colin Renfrew, April McMahon, and Larry Trask, eds., *Time Depth in Historical Linguistics* (Cambridge: The McDonald Institute for Archaeological Research, 2000), 373.

49. Colin Renfrew, "Introduction: The Problem of Time Depth," in Renfrew et al., *Time Depth in Historical Linguistics,* ix–xiv.

50. Sheila Embleton, "Lexicostatistics/Glottochronology: From Swadesh to Sankoff to Starostin to Future Horizons," in Renfrew et al., *Time Depth in Historical Linguistics,* 143–66.

51. Jan Vansina, *How Societies Are Born: Governance in West-Central Africa before 1600* (Charlottesville: University of Virginia, 2004), 4–5, 8.

52. Ehret, "Testing the Expectations of Glottochronology," 373–99.

53. Vansina, *How Societies Are Born,* 4–5, 8.

54. Ibid. and private communication with Jan Vansina, letter dated December 30, 2004.

1. The Rio Nunez Region

1. Judith A. Carney, *Black Rice: The African Origins of Rice Cultivation in the Americas* (Cambridge, Mass.: Harvard University Press, 2001), 10–30.

2. The "Grain Coast" is located south of the "Rice Coast" between Cape Mount and

Cape Palmas in present-day Liberia. During the pre-colonial period, this forested region produced malaguetta pepper, a prized commodity in both interregional and trans-Atlantic trade networks. It is malaguetta pepper grains and not rice that give the Grain Coast its name. See George E. Brooks, *Landlords & Strangers: Ecology, Society and Trade in Western Africa, 1000–1630* (Boulder, Colo.: Westview, 1993), 5, 14, 24–25; idem, *Eurafricans in Western Africa: Commerce, Social Status, Gender, and Religious Observance from the Sixteenth to the Eighteenth Century* (Athens: Ohio University Press, 2003), 13–15.

3. Walter Rodney, *A History of the Upper Guinea Coast, 1545 to 1800* (Oxford: Clarendon, 1970), 1–38; Brooks, *Landlords & Strangers*, 14, 21–23, 25; idem, *Eurafricans in Western Africa*, 2, 5, 19–20.

4. Carney, *Black Rice*, 57–63; W. Andriesse and L. O. Fresco, "A Characterization of Rice-Growing Environments in West Africa," *Agriculture, Ecosystems and Environment* 33 (1991), 377–95; Paul Richards, *Indigenous Agricultural Revolution: Ecology and Food Production in West Africa* (Boulder, Colo.: Westview, 1985), 74.

5. Peter J. Hogarth, *The Biology of Mangroves* (Oxford: Oxford University Press, 1999), 3, 5.

6. Judith Carney, "Landscapes of Technology Transfer: Rice Cultivation and African Continuities," *Technology and Culture* 37: 1 (1996), 18; H. D. Catling, *Rice in Deep Water* (Manila: International Rice Research Institute, 1992), 372–76; Moormann and Veldkamp identify four different kinds of salinity, of which marine salinity is only one. See F. R. Moormann and N. van Breeman, eds., *Rice: Soil, Water, Land* (Los Baños, Philippines: International Rice Research Institute, 1978), 121–27; F. R. Moorman and W. J. Veldkamp, "Land and Rice in Africa: Constraints and Potentials," in I. W. Buddenhagen and G. J. Presley, eds., *Rice in Africa* (New York: Academic Press, 1978), 38–39.

7. Marie Yvonne Curtis, "L'art Nalu, l'art Baga de Guinée: approches comparatives" (Ph.D. diss., Université de Paris I Panthéon Sorbonne, 1996), 25; A. R. Orme, "Coastal Environments," in W. M. Adams, Andrew S. Goudie, and A. R. Orme, eds., *The Physical Geography of Africa* (Oxford: Oxford University Press, 1996), 254; Brooks, *Landlords & Strangers*, 13.

8. I. W. Buddenhagen, "Rice Ecosystems in Africa," in I. W. Buddenhagen and G. J. Presley, eds., *Rice in Africa* (New York: Academic Press, 1978), 19–22; Moormann and Veldkamp, *Rice*, 29, 33; Richards, *Indigenous Agricultural Revolution*, 44–45.

9. John Ford, *The Role of the Trypanosomiases in African Ecology: A Study of the Tsetse Fly Problem* (Oxford: Clarendon, 1971), 36–37, 54–55.

10. Carney, "Landscapes of Technology Transfer," 55–59.

11. Hogarth, *The Biology of Mangroves*, 3, 5, 11–18; P. B. Tomlinson, *The Botany of Mangroves* (Cambridge: Cambridge University Press, 1986), 121–30.

12. Carney, *Black Rice*, 50; R. Charbrolin, "Rice in West Africa," in C. L. A. Leakey and J. B. Willis, eds., *Food Crops of the Lowland Tropics* (Oxford: Oxford University Press, 1977), 12.

13. Roland Portères, "*African Cereals: Eleusine, Fonio, Black Fonio, Teff,* Brachiaria, paspalum, Pennisetum, *and African Rice,*" in Jack R. Harlan and Jan M. J. De Wet, eds., *Origins of African Plant Domestication* (The Hague: Mouton, 1976), 441–45; idem, "Berceaux agricoles primaires sur le continent Africain," *Journal of African History* 3: 2 (1962), 197–99.

14. Roderick J. McIntosh and Susan Keech McIntosh, "The Inland Niger Delta before the Empire of Mali: Evidence from Jenne-Jeno," *Journal of African History* 22: 1 (1981), 15–16.

15. Jack R. Harlan, "Agricultural Origins: Centers and Noncenters," *Science* 174 (1971), 468–74.

16. Dorian Fuller, "Crop-Cultivation—the Evidence," in Kevin Shillington, ed., *Encyclopedia of African History: Volume 1* (New York: Fitzroy Dearborn, 2005), 326–28.

17. Portères, *"African Cereals,"* 441–45; idem, "Berceaux agricoles primaires," 197–99.

18. Richards, *Indigenous Agricultural Revolution,* 74.

19. Joseph Lauer, "Rice in the History of the Lower Gambia-Geba Area" (M.A. thesis, University of Wisconsin, 1969), 12, 42–43; Orlando Ribeiro, *Aspectos e problemas da expansão portuguesa* (Lisboa: Junta da Investigações do Ultramar, 1962), 49, 88, 116; Auguste Chevalier, "Sur le riz Africains du groupe *Oryza glaberrima,*" *Revue de botanique appliquée et d'agriculture tropicale* 17 (1937), 413–18.

20. Carney, *Black Rice,* 81; Paul Richards, "Natural Symbols and Natural History: Chimpanzees, Elephants and Experiments in Mende Thought," Kay Milton, ed., *Environmentalism: The View from Anthropology* (London: Routledge, 1993), 152.

21. Carney, *Black Rice,* 36, 81; Roland Portères, "Primary Cradles of Agriculture in the African Continent," in J. D. Fage and R. A. Oliver, eds., *Papers in African Prehistory* (Cambridge: Cambridge University Press, 1970), 48–49.

22. Carney, *Black Rice,* 50, 113; idem, "Rice Milling, Gender, and Slave Labour in Colonial South Carolina," *Past and Present* 153 (1996), 108–34; National Research Council, *Lost Crops of Africa* (Washington, D.C.: National Academy Press, 1996), 26–29.

23. G. Bezancon, J. Bozza, G. Koffi, and G. Second, "Genetic Diversity of Indigenous Rice in Africa," in I. W. Buddenhagen and G. J. Presley, eds., *Rice in Africa* (New York: Academic Press, 1978), 45.

24. Bruce L. Mouser, "Trade and Politics in the Nunez and Pongo Rivers, 1790–1865" (Ph.D. diss., Indiana University, 1971), 1–4; Boubacar Barry, *Senegambia and the Atlantic Slave Trade* (Cambridge: Cambridge University Press, 1998), 17.

25. Curtis, "L'art Nalu, l'art Baga," 37.

26. Most linguists agree that the Kalum (Baga Kalum) language is extinct. However, Kalum wordlists are published in Sigmund W. Koelle, *Polyglotta Africana* (London: Church Missionary Society, 1854). Evidence from Koelle's lists will be analyzed in chapters 3, 4, and 5. Mandori (Baga Mandori), Kakissa (Baga Kakissa), and Koba (Baga Koba) will not be covered in this study.

27. Sitem is more closely related to several additional languages spoken in coastal Guinea (which are not examined in this study): Mandori, Kakissa, Koba, and Kalum; and to Temne, spoken in Sierra Leone.

28. Mouser, "Trade and Politics," 7–10; Frederick Lamp, *Art of the Baga: A Drama of Cultural Reinvention* (New York: The Museum for African Art/Prestel-Verlag, 1996), 42–43.

29. Among historical linguists, it is standard practice to identify specific communities with a compound word consisting of the language name and the word *speakers,* joined by a hyphen, i.e., Nalu- and Mboteni-speakers. This format is used for both present-day daughter speech communities and ancestral speech communities of the distant past.

30. G. Tucker Childs, "Language Contact, Language Death, Section V: Language Contact: Atlantic-Mande/Intra-Atlantic," International Workshop The Atlantic Languages: Typological or Genetic Unit? University of Hamburg, Asien-Afrika-Institut, 2007.

31. Ibid.

32. Ibid.

33. Barry, *Senegambia and the Atlantic,* 19.

34. Brooks, *Landlords & Strangers,* 14.

35. Edda L. Fields, "Rice Farmers in the Rio Nunez Region: A Social History of Agricultural Technology and Identity in Coastal Guinea, ca. 2000 BCE to 1880 CE" (Ph.D. diss., University of Pennsylvania, 2001), 7–11.

36. Paul Pélissier, *Les Paysans du Sénégal: les civilisations agraires du Cayor à la Casamance* (Saint-Yrieix: Impr. Fabrègue, 1966), 747–49.

37. Hawthorne, *Planting Rice and Harvesting Slaves,* 159–71; idem, "Nourishing a Stateless Society during the Slave Trade: The Rise of Balanta Paddy-Rice Production in Guinea-Bissau," *Journal of African History* 42 (2001), 1–24.

38. Linares, *Power, Prayer and Production;* Pélissier, *Les Paysans du Sénégal;* Louis-Vincent Thomas, *Les Diola: essai d'analyse fonctionnelle sur une population de Basse-Casamance* (Dakar: Institut français d'Afrique noire, 1959).

39. Childs, "Language Contact, Language Death," 5.

40. Rodney, *A History of the Upper Guinea Coast,* 19–20, 62.

41. Bruce Mouser, ed., *Journal of James Watt: Expedition to Timbo, Capital of the Fula Empire in 1794* (Madison: African Studies Program, University of Wisconsin–Madison, 1994), 8.

42. Ibid., xiv.

43. Ibid., 24–26; Brooks, *Landlords & Strangers,* 197–96; Rodney, *A History of the Upper Guinea Coast,* 200–22.

44. Mouser, "Trade and Politics," 33–39; Barry, *Senegambia and the Atlantic Slave Trade,* 134–36.

45. David Eltis, Philip Morgan, and David Richardson, "The African Contribution to Rice Cultivation in the Americas," Georgia Workshop in Early American History and Culture, University of Georgia, LeConte Hall, 2005, 8–12.

46. David Eltis, Stephen D. Behrendt, David Richardson, and Herbert S. Klein, eds., *The Trans-Atlantic Slave Trade: A Database on CD-Rom* (Cambridge: Cambridge University Press, 1999).

47. Bruce L. Mouser, ed., *Account of the Mandingoes, Susoos, & Other Nations, c. 1815 by the Reverend Leopold Butscher* (Leipzig: University of Leipzig African History and Culture Series, 2000), 5 and n. 16; idem, "Trade, Coasters, and Conflict in the Rio Pongo from 1790 to 1808," *Journal of African History* 14: 1 (1973), 45–64; idem, "Women Slavers of Guinea-Conakry," in Claire C. Robertson and Martin A. Klein, eds., *Women and Slavery in Africa* (Madison: University of Wisconsin Press, 1983), 325–29; Daniel Schafer, *Anna Madgigine Jai Kingsley: African Princess, Florida Slave, Plantation Owner* (Gainesville: University Press of Florida, 2005); idem, "Family Ties that Bind: Anglo-African Slave Traders in Africa and Florida, John Fraser and His Descendants," *Slavery and Abolition: A Journal of Slave and Post-Slave Studies* 20 (1999), 1–21; E. R. Ware, "Enoch Richmond Ware's Voyage to West Africa, 1842–1843," in N. R. Bennett and George E. Brooks, eds., *New England Merchants in Africa: A History through Documents, 1802 to 1865* (Brookline, Mass.: Boston University Press, 1965), 298–313.

48. Gwendolyn Midlo Hall, *Slavery and African Ethnicities in the Americas: Restoring the Links* (Chapel Hill: University of North Carolina Press, 2005), 28; David Hancock, *Citizens of the World: London Merchants and the Intersection of the British Atlantic Community, 1735–1785* (Cambridge: Cambridge University Press, 1995), 204–206.

49. Eltis et al., *The Trans-Atlantic Slave Trade.*

50. Claude Rivière, "Le long des côtes de Guinée avant la phase coloniale," *Bulletin de l'Institut français d'Afrique noire* 30: Ser. B. (1968), 733–35; Mouser, "Trade and Politics," 8; Rodney, *A History of the Upper Guinea Coast*, 21.

51. Daniel C. Littlefield, *Rice and Slaves: Ethnicity and the Slave Trade in Colonial South Carolina* (Baton Rouge: Louisiana State University Press, 1981), 93–95.

52. Carney, *Black Rice*, 19, 63–68; idem and Richard Porcher, "Geographies of the Past: Rice Slaves, and Technological Transfer in South Carolina," *Southeastern Geographer* 33: 2 (1993), 132–47.

53. S. Max Edelson, *Plantation Enterprise in Colonial South Carolina* (Cambridge, Mass.: Harvard University Press, 2006), 47, 54, 59, 68, 70–71, 77.

2. The First-Comers and the Roots of Coastal Rice-Growing Technology

1. André Arcin, *Histoire de la Guinée Française: rivières de Sud, Fouta-Dialo, région du sud, Soudan* (Paris: Augustin Challamel, 1911), 176, 177.

2. M. A. Chevrier, "Relative aux coutumes des adeptes de la société secrète des Scymos, indigènes fétichistes du littoral de la Guinée," *L'Anthropologie* 17 (1906), 365; Edda L. Fields, "Rice Farmers in the Rio Nunez Region: A Social History of Agricultural Technology and Identity in Coastal Guinea, ca. 2000 BCE to 1880 CE" (Ph.D. diss., University of Pennsylvania, 2001); J. Figarol, *Monographie Cercle du Rio Nuñez 1912*, Box 1.42, Conakry, Archives Nationale, 95; Claudius Madrolle, *En Guinée* (Paris: H. Le Soudier, 1895), 216, 264–66; Lucien Marie François Famechon, *Notice sur la Guinée française* (Paris: Alcon-Levy, 1900), 24; Frederick Lamp, *Art of the Baga: A Drama of Cultural Reinvention* (New York: The Museum of African Art/Prestel Verlag, 1996). The distinguished historian Djibril Tamsir Niane also possesses a large collection of Baga oral traditions containing these core elements, which remains unpublished. See also Fernand Rouget, *La Guinée* (Corbeil: Impr. Typ. Crête, 1906), 145–46; Ramon Sarró-Maluquer, "Baga Identity: Religious Movements and Political Transformation in the Republic of Guinea" (Ph.D. diss., University College, London, 1999); Jean Suret-Canale, *La République de Guinée* (Paris: Éditions sociales, 1970), 30–32.

For examples of oral narratives collected among the Nalu in the village of Kukuba, see Fields, "Rice Farmers in the Rio Nuñez Region"; Amélia Frazão Moreira, "Récits de migration entre les Nalou de Cucubaré," in Gèrald Gaillard, ed., *Migrations anciennes et peuplement actuel des Côtes guinéennes* (Paris: L'Harmattan), 403–13; J. Machat, *Guinée française: Les Rivières du sud et le Fouta-Diallon* (Paris: Augustin Challamel, 1906), 238–39; Docteur Méo, "Études sur le Rio-Nunez," *Bulletin du Commission d'Études historiques et scientifique de l'Afrique Occidentale Français* (1919), 281.

3. Figarol, *Monographie Cercle du Rio Nuñez*, 95 (author's translation).

4. Interview with Mamadu Camara, Sitem village of Kawass, July 25, 1998.

5. Lamp, *Art of the Baga*, 49–63; see p. 54 for information about Temne oral traditions.

6. Sarró-Maluquer, "Baga Identity," 47, 50, 53.

7. Fields, "Rice Farmers in the Rio Nunez Region," 82–100, 136–42, 162–75.

8. Sarró-Maluquer, "Baga Identity," 54; Claude Maclaud, "Étude sur la distribution géographique des races sur la côte occidentale d'Afrique de la Gambie à la Mellacorée," *Bulletin de géographie, historique et descriptive* 21: 1 (1899), 114–18.

9. David Berliner, "'Nous sommes les derniers buloNic:' Sur une impossible transmission dans une société d'Afrique de l'Ouest (Guinée Conakry)" (Ph.D. diss., Université Libre de Bruxelles, 2003), 67–73.

10. Edda L. Fields, "Before 'Baga': Settlement Chronologies of the Coastal Rio Nunez Region, Earliest Times to c. 1000 CE," *International Journal of African Historical Studies* 37: 2 (2004), 236–43.

11. It is a standard convention among historical linguists to use "c." as an abbreviation for "circa" to qualify dates generated by glottochronology. This abbreviation denotes that linguistic processes take long periods of time to complete and do not conform to calendar dates found on written documents. In addition, linguistic methods do not yield precise calendar dates, as do diaries, colonial reports, or other written documents. Thus, these dates give readers an approximation of when ancestral languages diverged and ancestral speech communities inherited, innovated, and borrowed words.

12. For the cognate percentages and the calculation of the glottochronological estimates, see Fields, "Before 'Baga'," 239.

13. Maurice Houis, "Les minorités ethniques de la Guinée côtière: Situation linguistique," *Études guinéennes* 4: 25 (1952), 43–46; W. A. A. Wilson, *An Outline of the Temne Language* (London: School of Oriental and African Studies, University of London, 1961), 61.

14. Fields, "Rice Farmers in the Rio Nunez region," 61–64.

15. For an explanation of the theories of fewest moves and greatest diversity, which this study uses to approximate homeland of the proto-Coastal language, see ibid., 246–50.

16. For one example of this large literature, see David W. Phillipson, *The Later Prehistory of Eastern and Southern Africa* (New York: Africana Publishing, 1977), 210–30. For a critique of this literature, see Jan Vansina, "New Linguistic Evidence and the 'Bantu Expansion'," *Journal of African History* 36 (1995), 173–95.

17. Kairn A. Klieman, *'The Pygmies Were Our Compass': Bantu and Batwa in the History of West Central Africa, Early Times to c. 1900 C.E.* (Portsmouth: Heinemann, 2003), 23–24, 60, 72–78, 88–89. In coastal Guinea, Bruce Mouser also discusses "first-comers," "newcomers," and "owners of the land." He uses these concepts to explain customary rights that the Baga possessed between 1793 and 1821 to act as hosts to Susu traders from the interior and Luso-African and European traders. See Bruce L. Mouser, "Who and Where Were the Baga? European Perceptions from 1793 to 1821," *History in Africa* 29 (2002), 337–64.

18. Jan Vansina, *Paths in the Rainforests: Toward a History of Political Tradition in Equatorial Africa* (Madison: University of Wisconsin Press, 1990), 31–33; idem, "Deep-down Time: Political Tradition in Central Africa," *History in Africa* 16 (1989), 341–62.

19. For a list of regular sound correspondences in Coastal languages, see Fields, "Before 'Baga'," 238.

20. For the relationship between the Northern and Southern branches of the Atlantic language group, see the latest and most complete classification of the Atlantic language group by J. David Sapir, "West Atlantic: An Inventory of the Languages, their Noun Class Systems and Consonant Alternation," in *Current Trends in Linguistics in Sub-Saharan Africa* (The Hague: Mouton, 1971), 45–112.

21. Baga salt-making techniques: André Donelha, *Descrição da Serra Leoa e dos Rios de Guiné do Cabo Verde (1625) translated by P. E. H. Hair* (Lisboa: Junta de Investigações Cientificas do Ultramar, 1977), f.9v and note, 99, 215; André Alvares de Álmada, *Brief Treatise on the Rivers of Guinea (c. 1594): Part I, translated by Paul E. H. Hair* (Liverpool: University of Liverpool Department of History, 1984), 13/13, 15/6; René Caillié, *Travels through Central Africa to Timbuctoo* (London: Frank Cass & Co., 1968), 163; Conneau, *A Slaver's Log Book,* 99; Valentim Fernandes, *Description de la côte occidentale d'Afrique*

(Sénégal au Cap de Monte, Archipels), translated by Th. Monod, A. Teixeira da Mota and R. Mauny (Bissau: Publicações do Centro de Estudos da Guiné Portuguesa 11, 1951), f. 124; Sylvan Meinrad Xavier de Goldbery, *Travels in Africa* (London: M. Jones, 1803), vol. 2, 241; John Matthews, *A Voyage to the River Sierra-Leone* (London: Frank Cass & Co., 1966), 12, 15; Denise Paulme, "Des riziculteurs africaines: Les BAGA (Guinée française)," *Cahiers d'Outre-mer* 10 (1957), 274; Duarte Pacheco Pereira, *Esmeraldo de situ orbis* (London: Hakluyt Society, 1961), liv.i, ch. 33.

Salt-making in different regions: Gambia River, see Álmada, *Brief Treatise on the Rivers of Guinea: Part I,* 6/11.

Boiling salt crust: Matthews, *A Voyage to the River Sierra-Leone,* 37; Walter Rodney, *A History of the Upper Guinea Coast, 1545–1800* (Oxford: Clarendon, 1970), 18; Bruce L. Mouser, ed., *Journal of James Watt: Expedition to Timbo Capital of the Fula Empire in 1794* (Madison: African Studies Program, University of Wisconsin–Madison, 1994), 63v–64.

22. Rodney, *A History of the Upper Guinea Coast,* 18–20.

For twentieth-century descriptions of salt production, see Marie-Christine Cormier-Salem, "A la découverte des mangroves: regards multiples sur un objet de recherche mouvant," *Dynamique et usages de la mangrove dans les pays des rivières du Sud, du Sénégal a la Sierra Leone* (Paris: ORSTOM éditions, 1994), 13.

23. Francisco de Lemos Coelho, *Description of the Coast of Guinea (1684), translated by Paul E. H. Hair* (Liverpool: University of Liverpool Department of History, 1985), 25; Álmada, *Brief Treatise on the Rivers of Guinea (c. 1594): Part II Notes, translated by Paul E. H. Hair* (Liverpool: University of Liverpool Department of History, 1986), 15/6.

24. Álmada, *Brief Treatise on the Rivers of Guinea: Part I,* 15/6; idem, *Brief Treatise on the Rivers of Guinea: Part II Notes,* 13/13, 14/3.

25. John Alexander, "The Salt Industries of West Africa: A Preliminary Study," in Thurstan Shaw, ed., *The Archaeology of Africa: Foods, Metals, and Towns* (New York: Routledge, 1993), 652–57; E. Bovill, *The Golden Trade of the Moors* (London: Oxford University Press, 1958); Tadeusz Lewicki and Marion Johnson, *West African Food in the Middle Ages: According to Arabic Sources* (London: Cambridge University Press, 1974); Paul E. Lovejoy, *Salt of the Desert Sun: A History of Salt Production and Trade in the Central Sudan* (Cambridge: Cambridge University Press, 2002); Rodney, *A History of the Upper Guinea Coast,* 19–20.

For descriptions of the salt trade, see: along Nunez River: Coelho, *Description of the Coast,* 58/f.49; Conneau, *A Slaver's Log Book,* 65; Bruce L. Mouser, ed., *Account of the Mandingoes, Susoos, & Other Nations, c. 1815 by the Reverend Leopold Butscher* (Leipzig: University of Leipzig African History and Culture Series, 2000), 21 and n. 83; idem and Ramon Sarró, eds., *Travels into the Baga and Soosoo Countries in 1821 by Peter McLachlan* (Leipzig: University of Leipzig African History and Culture Series, 1999), 10.

Imported from Cacheu: Coelho, *Description of the Coast,* 61/f.52.

From Gambia: Álmada, *Brief Treatise on the Rivers of Guinea: Part I,* 7/11.

Along Rio Pongo and traded by Fula caravans: Alexander Peter Kup, ed., *Adam Afzelius' Sierra Leone Journal 1795–6* (Upsala: Studia Ethnographica Upsaliensia, 1967), ff.2/19v, 2/40, 2/94, 2/104; Thomas Winterbottom, *An Account of the Native Africans in the Neighbourhood of Sierra Leone* (London: C. Whittingham, 1803), 8, 171; Caillé, *Travels through Central Africa,* 171.

From islands along Rio Pongo: Coelho, *Description of the Coast,* 61/f.52.

Along Dubreka River: Goldbery, *Travels in Africa, Volume 2,* 242.

By Bulloms, Pereira, *Esmeraldo de situ orbis*, liv.i, cap.33, 82; Fernandes, *Description de la côte*, f.124.

Along Dubreka River: Goldbery, *Travels in Africa, Volume 2*, 242.

26. Álmada, *Brief Treatise on the Rivers of Guinea: Part I*, 1/23; Coelho, *Description of the Coast*, 61/f.52; Matthews, *A Voyage to the River Sierra Leone*, 146; Donelha, *Descrição da Serra Leoa*, f.30v; Matthews, *A Voyage to the River Sierra Leone*, 146; Rodney, *A History of the Upper Guinea Coast*, 18–20; G. Thilmans and J. P. Rossie, "Le 'Flambeau de la Navigation' de Dierick Ruiters," *Bulletin de l'Institut fondamental d'Afrique noire* 31: Ser. B 1 (1969), 108.

27. Mouser, "Who and Where Were the Baga?," 344–45; Donelha, *Descrição da Serra Leoa*, 99, 214; Álmada, *Brief Treatise on the Rivers of Guinea: Part I*, 13/3; Mouser, *Journal of James Watt*, 4, 8, 21, 22, 74; Kup, *Adam Afzelius' Sierra Leone Journal*, 31.

28. Álmada, *Brief Treatise on the Rivers: Part II*, 15/14, 19/1; Antonio Brásio, *Monumenta missionaria Africana: Africa Ocidental (1570–1600), 2nd Ser., Vol. III* (Lisboa: Agência-Geral do Ultramar, 1968), 422; E. G. R. Fenton, *The Troublesome Voyage of Captain Edward Fenton, 1582–1583; Narratives & Documents* (Cambridge: Hakluyt Society, 1959), 102–103.

29. Mouser, ed., *Journal of James Watt*, 4, 8, 9, 10, 17, 21, 22, 59, 74; idem, "Who and Where Were the Baga?," 344–45; idem, ed., *A Slaving Voyage to Africa and Jamaica: The Log of the Sandown, 1793–1794* (Bloomington: Indiana University Press, 2002), 98, 100; Kup, *Adam Afzelius Sierra Leone Journal*, 15.

30. Conneau, *A Slaver's Log Book*, 103.

31. Both *A. africana* and *Rhizophora racemosa* have seeds, which are poisonous unless properly cured. *L. racemosa* species do not have poisonous seeds. P. B. Tomlinson, *The Botany of Mangroves* (Cambridge: Cambridge University Press, 1986), 24–32, 145–62.

32. Donelha, *Descrição da Serra Leoa*, 99.

According to Teixeira da Mota, Donelha uses a term *tarrafe* in Portuguese Creole, which is derived from the Arabic *tarf*, to describe *A. africana* and *Laguncularia racemosa*, Donelha, *Descrição da Serra Leoa*, f.123. Santo includes *Rhizophora racemosa* on this list; J. do Espirito Santo, "Nomes vernáculos de algumas plantas da Guiné Portuguesa," *Boletim cultural da Guiné portuguesa* 18 (1963), 458.

Burkill et al. also define the Portuguese Creole word *tarrafe* as *A. africana* and describe island people in Western Senegal using the "germinated seeds of *Avicennia* as a famine food, but, these when uncooked or improperly prepared are actually poisonous." See H. M. Burkill, J. M. Dalziel, and J. Hutchinson, eds., *The Useful Plants of West Tropical Africa* (London: Crown Agents for the Colonies, 1937), 453–54, 85–87.

33. For descriptions of *A. africana* north of the Nunez River along the Rio Grande, see Álmada, *Brief Treatise on the Rivers of Guinea: Part I*, 11/1.

34. M. Sow, A. Diallo, N. Diallo, C. A. Dixon, and A. Guisse, "Formations végétales et sols dans les mangroves des Rivières du Sud," in Marie-Christine Cormier-Salem, ed., *Dynamique et usages de la mangrove dans les pays des rivières du Sud* (Paris: ORSTOM éditions, 1994), 51–56; Peter J. Hogarth, *The Biology of Mangroves* (Oxford: Oxford University Press, 1999), 36–45; Tomlinson, *The Botany of Mangroves*, 12–20, 96–98; H. D. Jordan, "The Relation of Vegetation and Soil to Development of Mangrove Swamps for Rice Growing in Sierra Leone," *The Journal of Applied Ecology* 1: 1 (1964), 209–12.

35. Olga Linares de Sapir, "Shell Middens of Lower Casamance and Problems of Diola Protohistory," *West African Journal of Archaeology* 1 (1971), 26.

36. M. Sow, "Formations végétales et sols," 52.

37. Hogarth, *The Biology of Mangroves*, 4–11.

38. Ibid; Tomlinson, *The Botany of Mangroves*, 98–100.

39. Hogarth, *The Biology of Mangroves*, 4–11.

40. Judith Carney and Richard Porcher, "Geographies of the Past: Rice, Slaves, and Technological Transfer in South Carolina," *Southeastern Geographer* 33: 2 (1993), 134–35.

41. David Lee Schoenbrun, *A Green Place, A Good Place: Agrarian Change, Gender, and Social Identity in the Great Lakes Region to the 15th Century* (Portsmouth: Heinemann, 1998), 49.

42. Hogarth, *The Biology of Mangroves*, 36–45; Tomlinson, *The Botany of Mangroves*, 12–20, 96–98; Sow, "Formations végétales et sols," 51–57.

43. Linares, "Shell Middens of Lower Casamance," 41.

44. Álmada, *Brief Treatise on the Rivers of Guinea: Part II*, 15/11, Appendix III, 9/3; John Atkins, *A Voyage to Guinea, Brazil, & the West Indies* (London: Frank Cass & Co., 1970), 47; Joseph Corry, *Observations upon the Windward Coast of Africa* (London: Frank Cass & Co., 1968), 34; Fenton, *The Troublesome Voyage*, 102; Richard Hakluyt, *The Principall Navigations, Voiages and Discoveries of the English Nation* (Cambridge: The Hakluyt Society and the Peabody Museum, 1965), 445–65; Job Hortop and G. R. G. Conway, *The Rare Travailes of Job Hortop* (Mexico: [s.n.], 1928), 5; Matthews, *A Voyage to the River Sierra-Leone*, 49; Winterbottom, *An Account of the Native Africans*, 19, 66.

45. Linares de Sapir, "Shell Middens of the Lower Casamance," 38, 41.

46. Hawthorne, *Planting Rice and Harvesting Slaves*, 35–36.

3. The Newcomers and the Seeds of Tidal Rice-Growing Technology

1. Paul E. H. Hair, "Sources on Early Sierra Leone: (15) Marmol 1573," *Africana Research Bulletin* 9: 3 (1979), 70–84.

2. Valentim Fernandes, *Description de la côte occidentale d'Afrique (Sénégal au Cap de Monte, Archipels)*, translated by Th. Monod, A. Teixeira da Mota and R. Mauny (Bissau: Publicações do Centro Estudos da Guiné Portuguesa, 1951), 167 n.150; Paul E. H. Hair, "Ethnolinguistic Continuity on the Guinea Coast," *Journal of African History* 8: 2 (1967), 253; W. A. A. Wilson, *An Outline of the Temne Language* (London: School of Oriental and African Studies, University of London, 1961), 1.

3. Paul E. H. Hair, "An Ethnolinguistic Inventory of the Upper Guinea Coast before 1700," *African Language Review* 6 (1967), 50.

4. André Alvares de Álmada, *Brief Treatise on the Rivers of Guinea (c. 1594): Part I (translated by Paul E. H. Hair)* (Liverpool: University of Liverpool Department of History, 1984), 15/6; idem, *Brief Treatise on the Rivers of Guinea (c.1594): Part II* (Liverpool: University of Liverpool Department of History, 1986), 15/6; Fernandes, *Description de la côte*, 166–167 n. 150; Hair, "An Ethnolinguistic Inventory of the Upper Guinea Coast," 65 n.61, 69, 50; idem, "Early Sources on Religion and Social Values in the Sierra Leone Region; (1) Cadamosto 1463," *The Sierra Leone Bulletin of Religion* 11 (1969), 55–56; Duarte Pacheco Pereira, *Esmeraldo du situ orbis: Côte occidentale d'Afrique du Sud Marocain au Gabon* (London: Hakluyt Society, 1937, 1961), liv.1, cap.32, 74, 80, 82.

5. Álmada, *Brief Treatise on the Rivers of Guinea (c.1594): Part II*, 15/6; André Donelha, *Descrição da Serra Leoa a dos Rios de Guiné do Cabo Verde* (Lisboa: Junta de Investigações Científicas do Ultramar, 1977), 202–203, 238–39, 258–59, 262–63.

6. For wordlists from and descriptions of Mel languages, see David Dalby, "The Mel Languages in Polyglotta Africana, Part 1: Baga, Landuma, and Temne," *African Language*

Studies 4 (1965), 129–35; idem, "Mel Languages in the Polyglotta Africana: Part II: Bullom, Kissi and Gola," *Sierra Leone Language Review* 5 (1966), 139–51; Tina Weller Ganong, "Features of Baga Morphology, Syntax, and Narrative Discourse" (M.A. thesis, University of Texas at Arlington, 1998); Maurice Houis, "Contes Baga (Dialecte du Koba)," *Études guinéennes* 6 (1950), 3–15; idem, "Les minorités ethniques de la Guinée côtière: Situation linguistique," *Études guinéennes* 4 (1952), 25–48; idem, "Le système pronominale et les classes dans les dialectes baga," *Bulletin de l'Institut français d'Afrique noire* 5: 1 (1953), 381–404; idem, "La rapport d'annexion en baga," *Bulletin de l'Institut français d'Afrique noire* 15: 1 (1953), 848–54; Sigmund Koelle, *Polyglotta Africana* (London: Church Missionary Society, 1854); C. F. Schlenker, *A Collection of Temne Traditions* (London: Church Missionary Society, 1861).

7. For classifications and descriptions of Mel languages, see David Dalby, "The Mel Languages: A Reclassification of Southern West Atlantic," *African Language Studies* 6: (1965), 1–17; Edda L. Fields, "Before 'Baga': Settlement Chronologies of the Coastal Rio Nunez Region, Earliest Times to c. 1000 CE," *International Journal of African Historical Studies* 37: 2 (2004), 240–44; idem, "Rice Farmers in the Rio Nunez Region: A Social History of Agricultural Technology and Identity in Coastal Guinea, ca. 2000 BCE to 1880 CE" (Ph.D. diss., University of Pennsylvania, 2001), 67–70; J. David Sapir, "West Atlantic: An Inventory of Languages, their Noun Class Systems and Consonant Alternation," in *Current Trends in Linguistics in Sub-Saharan Africa* (The Hague: Mouton, 1971), 62–64; W. A. A. Wilson, "Temne and the West Atlantic Group," *Sierra Leone Language Review* 2 (1963), 26; idem, "Temne, Landuma and the Baga Languages," *Sierra Leone Language Review* 1 (1962), 27–38.

8. For cognate percentages and settlement chronology for the Mel subgroup, see Fields, "Before 'Baga'," 240, 249–52; idem, "Rice Farmers in the Rio Nunez Region," 106–10.

9. Paul E. H. Hair, "The History of the Baga in Early Written Sources," *History in Africa* 24 (1997), 385–86.

10. George E. Brooks, *Landlords & Strangers: Ecology, Society, and Trade in Western Africa, 1000–1630* (Boulder, Colo.: Westview, 1993), 13–16.

11. John Ford, *The Role of Trypanosomiases in African Ecology: A Study of the Tsetse Fly Problem* (Oxford: Clarendon, 1971), 2–3, 36–37, 38–39, 54–55, 67.

12. Paul Richards, *Indigenous Agricultural Revolution: Ecology and Food Production in West Africa* (Boulder, Colo.: Westview, 1985), 41, 132–37; Brooks, *Landlords & Strangers*, 4, 12–13; Philip D. Curtin, *Economic Change in Precolonial Africa; Senegambia in the Era of the Slave Trade* (Madison: University of Wisconsin Press, 1975), 218–19.

13. Richards, *Indigenous Agricultural Revolution*, 49–50.

14. Ibid., 63–71.

15. James Fairhead and Melissa Leach, *Misreading the African Landscape: Society and Ecology in a Forest-Savanna Mosaic* (Cambridge: Cambridge University Press, 1996).

16. George E. Brooks, "A Provisional Historical Schema for Western Africa Based on Seven Climate Periods (ca. 9000 B.C. to the 19th Century)," *Cahier d'Études africaines* 101–102: 26-1-2 (1986), 43.

17. Sharon E. Nicholson, "The Methodology of Historical Climate Reconstruction and Its Application to Africa," *Journal of African History* 20: 1 (1979), 33–38; idem, "Saharan Climates in Historic Times," in Martin A. J. Williams and Hugues Faure, eds., *The Sahara and the Nile: Quaternary Environments and Prehistoric Occupation in Northern Africa* (Rotterdam: Balkema, 1980), 173–200.

18. Nicholson, "The Methodology of Historical Climate Reconstruction," 36–37.

19. Brooks, *Landlords & Strangers,* 7, Appendix A.

20. Brooks, "A Provisional Historical Schema," 43–46, 50–53; idem, *Landlords & Strangers,* 7.

James Webb compared Nicholson's and Brooks's schemas and found that they present two diametrically opposed interpretations for the seventeenth and eighteenth centuries. Nicholson proposes one wet period from the late fifteenth to the late eighteenth centuries while Brooks finds one wet period from c. 1500 to c. 1630 and a dry period from c. 1630 to c. 1860. Webb resolves the issue by "abandoning the somewhat artificial construct of wet and dry periods" and instead examining a long-term trend toward aridity beginning in the late sixteenth and early seventeenth century. James L. A. Webb, Jr., *Desert Frontier: Ecological and Economic Change along the Western Sahel, 1600–1850* (Madison: University of Wisconsin Press, 1995), 4–5.

21. Brooks's pioneering study spans the period from 1000 to 1630 and covers the entire West African region. Aside from using climatic studies to establish a chronology of climate change, his study relies most heavily on European travelers' accounts for historical reconstruction. Thus, the majority of the book focuses on the period from 1500 to 1630. See Brooks, *Landlords & Strangers.*

22. Álmada, *Brief Treatise on the Rivers of Guinea (c.1594): Part I,* 14/6.

23. Ibid.

24. Idem, *Brief Treatise on the Rivers of Guinea (c.1594): Part II,* 14/5; Valentim Fernandes also describes kingship among the Temne in the River Scarcies region; see Fernandes, *Description de la Côte,* 83, 172 n.174.

25. René Caillé, *Travels through Central Africa to Timbuctoo* (London: Frank Cass & Co. Ltd., 1968), 166; Bruce L. Mouser, "Trade and Politics in the Nunez and Pongo Rivers, 1790–1865" (Ph.D. diss., Indiana University, 1971), 7; idem and Ramon Sarró, eds., *Travels into the Baga and Soosoo Countries in 1821* (Leipzig: University of Leipzig African History and Culture Series, 1999), 11.

26. Mouser, "Trade and Politics," 9.

27. André Donelha, *Descrição da Serra Leoa e dos rios de Guiné do Cabo Verde (1625) (notas por Avelino Teixiera da Mota, Description de la Serre Leoa et des Rios de Guinée du Cabo Verde (1625) (translated by P. E. H. Hair)* (Lisboa: Junta de Investigações Cientificas do Ultramar, 1977), 12–20, 26–30.

28. Donelha, *Descrição da Serra Leoa,* 81, 13–21, 27–37.

29. For additional descriptions of the diversity of game in Sierra Leone's forest/savanna, see John Matthews, *A Voyage to the River Sierra-Leone* (London: Frank Cass & Co., 1966), 39–40; Paul E. H. Hair, *André de Faro's Missionary Journey to Sierra Leone in 1663–1664* (Freetown: University of Sierra Leone, Institute of African Studies, 1982), 48.

30. Donelha, *Descrição da Serra Leoa,* 79–96.

31. John H. Atherton, "Excavations at Kamabai and Yagala Rock Shelters, Sierra Leone," *The West African Journal of Archaeology* 2 (1972), 39, 61.

32. Álmada, *Brief Treatise on the Rivers of Guinea (c.1594): Part I,* 15/8; Idem, *Brief Treatise on the Rivers of Guinea (c.1594): Part II,* 15/8; Manuel Alvares, *Ethiopia Minor and a Geographical Account of the Province of Sierra Leone* (Liverpool: University of Liverpool Department of History, 1990), f.74; Donelha, *Descrição da Serra Leoa,* ff. 9 and note 10v, 11, 235 note 113; Fernandes, *Description de la côte,* 95, 166, ff.149.

33. Matthews, *A Voyage to the River Sierra-Leone,* 52.

34. Brooks, *Landlords & Strangers*, 170, 174, 198–200; Rodney, *A History of the Upper Guinea Coast*, 272.

35. Theophilous Conneau, *A Slaver's Log Book or 20 Years' Residence in Africa* (Englewood Cliffs, N.J.: Prentice-Hall, 1976), 65; Mouser, ed., *Account of the Mandingoes and Susoos*, 9 and note 38, 20; idem, ed., *Journal of James Watt: Expedition to Timbo Capital of the Fula Empire in 1794* (Madison: African Studies Program, University of Wisconsin–Madison, 1994), 40, 63; idem and Ramon Sarró, *Travels to the Baga and Soosoo Countries in 1821 by Peter McLachlan* (Leipzig: University of Leipzig African History and Culture Series, 1999), 24; Winterbottom, *An Account of the Native Africans*, 54.

36. Álmada, *Brief Treatise on the Rivers of Guinea, (c.1594): Part I*, 15/11.

37. Mouser, "Trade and Politics," 8.

38. Mouser, *Journal of James Watt*, 21–22.

39. Paul Pélissier, *Les Paysans du Sénégal: les civilisations du Cayor a la Casamance* (Saint-Yrieix: Impr. Fabrègue, 1966), 747; Judith A. Carney, *Black Rice: The African Origins of Rice Cultivation in the Americas* (Cambridge, Mass.: Harvard University Press, 2001), 23–24, 28.

40. Olga Linares de Sapir, "Shell Middens of Lower Casamance and Problems of Diola Protohistory," *West African Journal of Archaeology* 1 (1971) 33–35, 41–43.

41. Pélissier, *Les Paysans du Sénégal*, 747–49.

42. Thomas Winterbottom, *An Account of the Native Africans in the Neighbourhood of Sierr Leone* (London: C. Whittingham, 1803), 47–48; Mouser, *Journal of James Watt*, 22, 38–39, 54–56. For descriptions of intercropping, see 56; for descriptions of crop rotation, see Bruce L. Mouser, ed., *Account of the Mandingoes, Susoos, & Other Nations, c. 1815* (Leipzig: University of Leipzig African History and Culture Series, 2000), 5; and for descriptions of sowing in the uplands, see 5.

4. Coastal Collaboration and Specialization

1. David Doar, *Rice and Rice Planting in the South Carolina Low Country* (Charleston: Charleston Museum, 1970), 5, 7, 41.

2. Ibid., 20; Hilliard suggests that planters "were surely cognizant of rice culture [and field flooding] practiced elsewhere," elsewhere, that is, than Africa. See Sam B. Hilliard, "Antebellum Tidewater Rice Culture in South Carolina and Georgia," in James R. Gibson, ed., *European Settlement and Development in North America: Essays on Geographical Change in Honour and Memory of Andrew Hill Clark* (Toronto: University of Toronto Press, 1978), 97.

3. Doar, *Rice and Rice Planting*, 13.

4. Alice R. Huger Smith, Herbert Ravenel Sass, and D. E. Huger Smith, *A Carolina Rice Plantation of the Fifties: 30 Paintings in Water-Colour* (New York: W. Morrow and Co., 1936), 23.

5. Ibid.

6. Walter Hawthorne, *Planting Rice and Harvesting Slaves: Transformations along the Guinea-Bissau Coast, 1400–1900* (Portsmouth: Heinemann, 2003), 155–56; Michel Jajolet, *Premier voyage du sieur de Courbe fait à la coste d'Afrique en 1685* (Paris: E. Chapman, 1913), 208–209.

7. Hawthorne, *Planting Rice and Harvesting Slaves*, 39, 155–56.

8. Joseph Lauer, "Rice in the History of the Lower Gambia-Geba Area" (M. A. thesis,

University of Wisconsin, 1969), 3; Olga Linares, *Power, Prayer and Production: The Jola of Casamance, Senegal* (Cambridge: Cambridge University Press, 1992), 85.

9. Lauer, "Rice in the History," 18.

10. J. David Sapir, "West Atlantic: An Inventory of the Languages, their Noun Class System and Consonant Alternation," in *Current Trends in Linguistics in Sub-Saharan Africa* (The Hague: Mouton, 1971), 45–112; Jean L. Doneux, "Hypothèses pour la comparative des langues Atlantiques," *Africana linguistica* 6 (1975), 41–129; Konstantin Pozdniakov, *Sravnitel'naia Grammatika Atlantichskikh Iazykov* (Izdatel'skaia Firma, Vostoshnai Literatura, Moscow, 1993) (translated by Lioudmila Selemeneva, Carnegie Mellon University, Department of English).

11. Judith A. Carney, *Black Rice: The African Origins of Rice Cultivation in the Americas* (Cambridge, Mass.: Harvard University Press, 2001), 39.

12. Walter Hawthorne, "The Interior Past of an Acephalous Society: Institutional Change among the Balanta of Guinea-Bissau, c. 1400–1950" (Ph.D. diss., Stanford University, 1998), 15.

13. Robin Horton, "Stateless Societies in the History of West Africa," in J. F. A. Ajayi and Michael Crowder, eds., *History of West Africa: Volume I* (London: Longman, 1972), 78.

14. Hawthorne, "The Interior Past," 21–25.

15. Roderick McIntosh and Susan Keech McIntosh, "The Inland Niger Delta before the Empire of Mali: Evidence from Jenne-jeno," *Journal of African History* 22: 1 (1981), 1–22; idem, "Western Representations of Urbanism and Invisible African Towns," in Susan Keech McIntosh, ed., *Beyond Chiefdoms: Pathways to Complexity in Africa* (Cambridge: Cambridge University Press, 1999), 56–65.

16. David Northrup, *Trade without Rulers: Pre-Colonial Economic Development in South-eastern Nigeria* (Oxford: Clarendon, 1978);K. Onwuka Dike, *Trade and Politics in the Niger Delta, 1830–1855: An Introduction to the Economic and Political History of Nigeria* (Westport, Conn.: Greenwood Press, 1981).

17. According to Hawthorne, the Balanta also resisted slave raiding by moving to the rivers along the coast and cultivating rice in the mangroves (as was discussed in chapter 2) and erecting barricades, both wooden palisades and maze-like labyrinths, around their villages. See Hawthorne, *Planting Rice and Harvesting Slaves,* 96.

18. Bruce L. Mouser, "Trade and Politics in the Nunez and Pongo Rivers, 1790–1865" (Ph.D. diss., Indiana University, 1971), 7–10, 15–18.

19. Susan Keech McIntosh, "Pathways to Complexity: An African Perspective," in Susan Keech McIntosh, ed., *Beyond Chiefdoms: Pathways to Complexity in Africa* (Cambridge: Cambridge University Press, 1999), 1–30; Victoria Bomba Coifman, "The People of the African-European Frontier, from the Sahil to Sierra Leone, the Rio Nunez and Rio Pongo of Lower Guinea," in Gérald Gaillard, ed., *Migrations anciennes et peuplement actuel des Côtes guinéennes* (Paris: L'Harmattan, 2000), 508–10; Donald R. Wright, *The World and a Very Small Place in Africa* (Armonk, N.Y.: N. E. Sharpe, 1997), 112–14.

20. Ann B. Stahl, "Perceiving Variability in Time and Space: The Evolutionary Mapping of African Societies," in Susan Keech McIntosh, ed., *Beyond Chiefdoms: Pathways to Complexity in Africa* (Cambridge: Cambridge University Press, 1999), 39–45; Caroline Neale, *Writing "Independent" History: African Historiography, 1960–1980* (Westport. Conn.: Greenwood, 1985), 4.

21. Roland Portères, "Berceaux agricoles primaires sur le continent Africain," *Journal of African History* 3: 2 (1962), 199; Judith A. Carney, "African Rice in the Columbian Exchange," *Journal of African History* 42: 3 (2001), 386.

22. Ibid., 386 note 37.

23. Ibid., 386.

24. Roland Portères, "Les Appellations des céréales en Afrique," *Journal d'agriculture tropicale et de botanique appliquée* 5: 1–11 (1958), 179 (author's translation). Portères published a number of articles of this kind of which this is just one example.

25. Some Atlanticists, however, think these conclusions are premature, especially given the intense contact between Atlantic and Mande speech communities over the past millennium; private communication with G. Tucker Childs, February 2007, Hamburg, Germany.

26. Carlos Lopes, *Kaabunké: espaço, território e poder na Guiné-Bissau, Gâmbia e Casamance pré-colonias* (Lisboa: Comissão Nacional para as Comemorações dos Descobrimentos Portugueses, 1999), 154–55.

27. Walter Hawthorne, "Nourishing a Stateless Society during the Slave Trade: The Rise of Balanta Paddy-Rice Production in Guinea-Bissau," *Journal of African History* 42: (2001), 10.

28. In comparison to Nalu's three noun classes, Sitem has fifteen. *Toŋ-kumbɛl/aŋ-kumbɛ* appears to fit into class five, *t-, tV-, tVŋ-, tıŋ-/m-, mV-, mVŋ-, mıŋ-, m-,* which includes inanimate words like drum, hut, skirt, and seedling. The noun classifiers suggest that *toŋ-kumbɛl* may be a Sitem word. See Tina Weller Ganong, "Features of Baga Morphology: Syntax and Narrative Discourse" (M.A. thesis, University of Texas at Arlington, 1998), 19–22.

29. Linguists agree that Mboteni is one of a few Atlantic languages in which the noun class system does not operate. Thus, based on the morphological evidence, the Mboteni language borrowed *faa-aŋ-kumbel* from Nalu or Sitem, because it exhibits a fossilized noun class. Sapir, "West Atlantic," 95.

30. Interview with Seydu Muctar Sumah, Mboteni village of Binari, September 8, 1998.

31. Interview with Saliu Bangura, Nalu village of Kukuba, May 27, 1998.

32. Interviews with Ibrahima Bangura, Mbulungish village of Monchon, December 17, 1998; Alseni Camara, Mbulungish village of Monchon, July 5, 1998.

33. Interviews with Mohammed DiJongo Bangura, Mboteni village of Binari, December 2 and 4, 1998; Saliu Bangura, December 19, 1999; Ibrahima Camara, Nalu village of Kukuba, December 17, 1998; Suleyman Camara, Nalu village of Kukuba, September 19, 1998.

34. Linares, *Power, Prayer and Production,* 19; ibid., "Diminished Rains and Divided Tasks," in A. Endre Nyerges, ed., *The Ecology of Practice: Studies of Food Crop Production in Sub-Saharan West Africa* (Amsterdam: Gordon and Breach, 1997), 49; Paul Pélissier, *Les Paysans du Sénégal: les civilisations du Cayor à la Casamance* (Saint-Yrieix: Impr. Fabrègue, 1966), 738–41.

35. Hawthorne, *Planting Rice and Harvesting Slaves,* 153; Lauer, "Rice in the History," 12–13.

36. In Guinea-Bissau, some groups of farmers still use fulcrum shovels without metal blades. The Jola, on the other hand, always cap a *kajandu* with a steel blade, which is usually made by a Manding blacksmith. Personal communication with Olga Linares at the 2004 African Studies Association conference in New Orleans and e-mail dated February 11, 2005.

37. Interview with Mohamed DiJongo Bangura, April 29–30, 1998.

38. Hawthorne, *Planting Rice and Harvesting Slaves,* 45–46.

39. René Caillé, *Travels through Central Africa to Timbuctoo* (London: Frank Cass & Co. Ltd., 1968), 162.

40. Marie Yvonne Curtis and Ramon Sarró, "The *Nimba* Headdress: Art, Ritual, and History of the Baga and Nalu Peoples of Guinea," *Museum Studies* 23: 2 (1997), 122; Frederick Lamp, *Art of the Baga: A Drama of Cultural Reinvention* (New York: The Museum for African Art/Prestel Verlag, 1996), 159–62.

41. Lamp, *Art of the Baga,* 171–73; Curtis and Sarró, "The *Nimba* Headdress," 129.

42. Lamp, *Art of the Baga,* 171–73.

43. Ibid., 223–40; David Berliner, " 'Nous sommes les derniers buloNic': Sur une impossible transmission dans une société d'Afrique de l'Ouest (Guinée Conakry)" (Ph.D. diss., Université Libre de Bruxelles, 2003), 9–10.

44. Lamp, *Art of the Baga,* 176–80.

45. Curtis and Sarro, "The *Nimba* Headdress," 130.
Several publications also give details about the centrality of the *D'mba* masquerade among the Nalu. See, for example, Arturo A. da Silva, "Arte Nalu," *Boletim cultural da Guiné portuguesa* 44 (1956), 27–47; Fernando Rogado Quintino, *Práctica e utensilagem agrícolas na Guiné* (Lisboa: Junta de Investigações do Ultramar, 1971).

46. Sapir, "West Atlantic," 51; Erhard Voeltz and Mohammed Camara, "Lexique Nalu-Français" (Unpublished manuscript).

47. Curtis and Sarró, "The *Nimba* Headdress," 130.

48. Peter Mark, *"Portuguese" Style and Luso-African Identity: Precolonial Senegambia, 16th–19th Centuries* (Bloomington: Indiana University Press, 2002), 5, 94, 146.

49. Charles B. Dew, *Bond of Iron: Master and Slave at Buffalo Forge* (New York: W. W. Norton and Company, 1994); Tera W. Hunter, *To 'Joy My Freedom: Southern Black Women's Lives and Labors after the Civil War* (Cambridge, Mass.: Harvard University Press, 1997); Ronald L. Lewis, *Coal, Iron, and Slaves: Industrial Slavery in Maryland and Virginia, 1715–1865* (Westport, Conn.: Greenwood, 1979); Carroll W. Pursell, ed., *A Hammer in Their Hands: A Documentary History of Technology and the African-American Experience* (Cambridge, Mass.: MIT Press, 2005); Leslie A. Schwalm, *'A Hard Fight for We': Women's Transition from Slavery to Freedom in South Carolina* (Urbana: University of Illinois Press, 1997); Bruce Sinclair, ed., *Technology and the African-American Experience: Needs and Opportunities for Study* (Cambridge, Mass.: MIT Press, 2004); Robert Starobin, *Industrial Slavery in the Old South* (New York: Oxford University Press, 1970); Joe William Trotter, Jr., *Coal, Class, and Color: Blacks in Southern West Virginia, 1915–32* (Urbana: University of Illinois Press, 1990); Richard Wade, *Slavery in the Cities: The South, 1820–1860* (New York: Oxford University Press, 1964).

5. The Strangers and the Branches of Coastal Rice-Growing Technology

1. Boubacar Barry, *Senegambia and the Atlantic Slave Trade* (Cambridge: Cambridge University Press, 1998), 133–37.

2. André Coffinères de Nordeck, "Voyage aux pays des Bagas et du Rio-Nunez, *"Le Tour du Monde,* I, le semestre, 1886," 276 (author's translation).

3. P. B. Tomlinson, *The Botany of Mangroves* (Cambridge: Cambridge University Press, 1986), 100.

4. Coffinères de Nordeck, "Voyage aux pays des Bagas, 279–80 (author's translation).

5. Ibid., 284 (author's translation).

6. Peter J. Hogarth, *The Biology of Mangroves* (Oxford: Oxford University Press, 1994), 35.

7. Walter Hawthorne, *Planting Rice and Harvesting Slaves: Transformations along the Guinea-Bissau Coast, 1400–1900* (Portsmouth: Heinemann, 2003), 39. See also George E. Brooks, *Landlords & Strangers: Ecology, Society, and Trade in Western Africa, 1000–1630* (Boulder. Colo.: Westview, 1993), 89; Joseph Lauer, "Rice in the History of the Lower Gambia-Geba Area" (M.A. thesis: University of Wisconsin at Madison, 1969); Olga Linares, "From Tidal Swamp to Inland Valley: On the Social Organization of Wet Rice Cultivation among the Diola of Senegal," *Africa* 51: 2 (1981), 558–61.

8. Hogarth, *The Biology of Mangroves,* 5; M. Sow, A. Diallo, N. Diallo, C. A. Dixon, and A. Guissè, "Formations végétales et sols dans les mangroves des Rivières du Sud," in Marie-Christine Cormier-Salem, ed., *Dynamique et usages de la mangrove dans les pays des rivières du Sud, du Sénégal à la Sierra Leone* (Paris: ORSTOM éditions, 1994), 48–56.

9. Tomlinson, *The Botany of Mangroves,* 96–100; Hogarth, *The Biology of Mangroves,* 4–11.

10. Olga Linares de Sapir, "Shell Middens of Lower Casamance and Problems of Diola Protohistory," *West African Journal of Archaeology* 1 (1971), 33, 36.

11. Friederike Lupke, "A Grammar of Jalonke Argument Structure" (Ph.D. diss., Radboud Universitait Nijmegen, 2005), 14. See also Kent D. Bimson, "Comparative Reconstruction of Proto-Northern-Western Mande" (Ph.D. diss., University of California at Los Angeles, 1978); David Dwyer, "Mande," in John Bendor-Samuel and Rhonda L. Hartell, eds., *The Niger-Congo Languages: A Classification and Description of Africa's Largest Language Family* (Lanham, Md.: University Press of America, 1989), 47–65; Claire Grégoire, "Étude lexicostatistique de quarante-trois langues et dialectes mande," *Africana linguistica* 11 (1994), 53–70; Raimund Kastenholz, "Comparative Mande Studies: State of the Art," *Sprache und Geschichte in Afrika* 12/13 (1991/1992), 107–58; Idem, "Essai de classification des dialectes Mande-Kan," *Sprache und Geschichte in Afrika* (1979), 205–33; Ronald W. Long, "A Comparative Study of the Northern Mande Languages" (Ph.D. diss., Indiana University, 1971); Valentim Vydrine, *Mande-English Dictionary: Maninka, Bamana* (Saint Petersburg: Dimitry Bulanin, 1999), 7–10.

12. Susu and Jalonke share approximately 90 percent of their cognates. Glottochronology would estimate that these two dialects began diverging from their common linguistic ancestor after c. 1500 CE.

13. Erhard Voeltz, "Les Langues de la Guinée," *Cahiers d'étude des langues guinéennes* 1 (1966), 29–30.

14. Bruce Mouser, ed., *Account of the Mandingoes, Susoos, & Other Nations, c. 1815 by the Reverend Leopold Butscher* (Leipzig: University of Leipzig Africa History and Culture Series, 2000), iii; idem, "Qui étaient les Baga? Perceptions européennes, 1793–1821," in Gérald Gaillard, ed., *Migrations anciennes et peuplement actuel des Côtes guinéennes* (Paris: Harmattan, 2000), 436.

15. Lupke, "A Grammar of Jalonke," 12.

16. Barry, *Senegambia and the Atlantic,* 6–8.

17. Ibid., 25, 96; Lupke, "A Grammar of Jalonke," 16–17; Odile Goerg, *Commerce et colonisation en Guinée, 1850–1913* (Paris: Éditions L'Harmattan, 1986), 19–22; Bruce L. Mouser, "Trade and Politics in the Nunez and Pongo Rivers, 1790–1865" (Ph.D. diss., Indiana University, 1971), 18–20.

18. Barry, *Senegambia and the Atlantic,* 35, 100.

19. Brooks, *Landlords & Strangers,* 33.

20. André Alvares de Álmada, *Brief Treatise on the Rivers of Guinea, c. 1594: Part I, translated by Paul E. H. Hair* (Liverpool: University of Liverpool Department of History, 1984), 14/3.

21. Ibid., 14/13.

22. Ibid. André Donelha, *Descrição da Serra Leoa e dos rios de Guiné do Cabo Verde (1625)* (Lisboa: Junta de Investigações Cientificas do Ultramar, 1977), 270–71, note 184.

23. Duarte Pacheco Pereira, *Esmeraldo de situ orbis: Côte occidentale d'Afrique du Sud Marocain au Gabon* (London: Hakluyt Society, 1937, 1961), 98.

24. Paul E. H. Hair, "Sources on Early Sierra Leone: (9) Barreira's 'Account of the Coast of Guinea,' 1606," *Africana Research Bulletin* 7: 1 (1977), 65; André Alvares de Álmada, *Brief Treatise on the Rivers of Guinea (c. 1594): Part II Notes, translated by Paul E. H. Hair* (Liverpool: University of Liverpool Department of History, 1986), 15/8; Olfert Dapper, *Description de l'Afrique* (Amsterdam: Chez Wolfgang, Waesberge, Boom & van Someren, 1686), 246; Paul E. H. Hair, "Sources on Early Sierra Leone: (13) Barreira's Report of 1607–1608—The Visit to Bena," *Africana Research Bulletin* 8: 2–3 (1978), 2–3, 80.

25. Francisco de Lemos Coelho, *Description of the Coast of Guinea (1684)* (Liverpool: University of Liverpool Department of History, 1985), 9/57; Bruce L. Mouser and Ramon Sarró, eds., *Travels into the Baga and Soosoo Countries in 1821 by Peter McLachlan* (Leipzig: University of Leipzig African History and Culture Series, 1999), 16.

26. South of the Nunez River, Luís de Cadamosto, an Italian who worked for the Portuguese, contended that the inhabitants of the Kalum peninsula possessed "no weapons because no iron has been found in their land." Hair questions the authenticity of this account because Cadamosto heard it secondhand from a clerk in Portugal who worked on the expedition. See Paul E. H. Hair, "Early Sources on Religion and Social Values in the Sierra Leone Region: (1) Cadamosto 1463," *The Sierra Leone Bulletin of Religion* 11 (1969), 61, 54–55.

27. Coelho, *Description of the Coast*, 9/8; Mouser, *Travels into the Baga and Soosoo Countries*, 9.

28. Hawthorne, *Planting Rice and Harvesting Slaves*, 38–46.

29. David Lee Schoenbrun, *A Green Place, A Good Place: Agrarian Change, Gender, and Social Identity in the Great Lakes Region to the 15th Century* (Portsmouth: Heinemann, 1998), 48–50.

30. Christopher Ehret, "Agricultural History in Central and Southern Africa ca. 1000 B.C. to A.D 500," *Transafrican Journal of History* 4 (1974), 1–25; idem, "Patterns of Bantu and Central Sudanic Settlement in Central and Southern Africa (C.A.1000 B.C.–500A.D.)," *Transafrican Journal of History* 3 (1973), 1–71; idem, "Language and History," in Bernd Heine and Derek Nurse, eds., *African Languages: An Introduction* (Cambridge: Cambridge University Press, 2000); idem, *An African Classical Age: Eastern and Southern Africa in World History, 1000B.C. to 400A.D.* (Charlottesville: University of Virginia Press, 1998); Kairn A. Klieman, *'The Pygmies Were Our Compass': Bantu and Batwa in the History of West-Central Africa, Early Times to c.1900C.E.*(Portsmouth: Heinemann, 2003), 101–103, 177–83; M. E. Kropp-Dakubu, "On the Linguistic Geography of the Area of Ancient Begho," in H. Trutenau, ed., *Languages of the Akan Area* (Basel: Basler Afrika Bibliographien, 1976), 63–91; Schoenbrun, *A Green Place, A Good Place;* idem, "'We Are What We Eat': Ancient Agriculture between the Great Lakes," *Journal of African History* 34: 1 (1993), 1–31; Kay Williamson, "Linguistic Evidence for the Prehistory of the Niger Delta," in Ebiegberi J. Alagoa, F. N. Anozie, and Nwanna Nzewunwa, eds., *The Early*

History of the Niger Delta (Hamburg: H. Buske, 1988), 65–119; idem, "Linguistic Evidence for the Use of Some Tree and Tuber Food Plants in Southern Nigeria," in Thurstan Shaw, ed., *The Archaeology of Africa: Foods, Metals and Towns* (New York: Routledge, 1993), 139–53; Jan Vansina, *Paths in the Rainforest: Toward a History of Political Tradition in Equatorial Africa* (Madison: University of Wisconsin Press, 1990).

31. C. H. Borland, "Computing African Linguistic Prehistory," in Derek F. Gowlett and Ernest Westphal, eds., *African Linguistic Contributions: Papers in Honour of Ernest Westphal* (Pretoria: Via Afrika, 1992), 6–11; idem, "How Basic is 'Basic' Vocabulary?," *Current Anthropology* 23: 3 (1982), 315–16; Vansina, *Paths in the Rainforest*, 14–16.

32. Interviews with Jalonke-speakers in Conakry: El Hadj Mamadu Saliu Camara on November 12, 1998 and December 15, 1998; Mamadu Samura on November 12, 1998. Also see Lupke, "A Grammar of Jalonke," 109–14.

33. Roland Portéres, "*African Cereals: Eleusine, Fonio, Black Fonio, Teff,* Brachiaria, paspalum, Pennisetum, *and African Rice,*" in Jack R. Harlan and Jan M. DeWet, eds., *Origins of African Plant Domestication* (The Hague: Mouton, 1976), 417–24.

34. Interview with Seydu Camara, Sitem village of Kawass, March 17, 1998.

35. Jack B. Harlan and Jean Pasquereau, "Décrue Agriculture in Mali," *Economic Botany* 23 (1969), 70; André Lericollais and Jean Schmitz, "La Calebasse et le houe," *Cahiers O.R.S.T.O.M.* 20: 3–4 (1984), 430.

36. Yasmine Marzouk-Schmitz, "Instruments aratoires, systèmes de cultures et différenciation intra-ethnique," *Cahiers O.R.S.T.O.M.* 20: 3–4 (1984), 416–23.

37. Vansina, *Paths in the Rainforest*, 61, 86, 211, 214, 217, 227; for farming techniques for cassava, see 88, 215.

38. Personal communication with Erhard Voeltz, June 1996.

39. See also Olga Linares, *Power, Prayer and Production: The Jola of Casamance, Senegal* (Cambridge: Cambridge University Press, 1992), 20.

40. Sam B. Hilliard, "Antebellum Tidewater Rice Culture in South Carolina and Georgia," in James R. Gibson, ed., *European Settlement and Development in North America: Essays on Geographical Change in Honour and Memory of Andrew Hill Clark* (Toronto: University of Toronto Press, 1978), 94; Mart A. Stewart, "Rice, Water, and Power: Landscapes of Domination and Resistance in the Lowcountry, 1790–1880," *Environmental History Review* 15: 3 (1991), 47.

41. S. Max Edelson, *Plantation Enterprise in Colonial South Carolina* (Cambridge, Mass.: Harvard University Press, 2006), 64, 68, 77, 89.

42. Douglas C. Wilms, "The Development of Rice Culture in 18th Century Georgia," *Southeastern Geographer* 12 (1972), 49.

43. Hilliard, "Antebellum Tidewater Rice Culture," 58; idem, "The Tidewater Rice Plantation: An Ingenious Adaptation to Nature," *Geoscience and Man* 12 (1975), 98; Stewart, "Rice, Water, and Power," 49.

44. Judith A. Carney, *Black Rice: The African Origins of Rice Cultivation in the Americas* (Cambridge, Mass.: Harvard University Press, 2001), 12; Orlando Ribeiro, *Aspectos e problemas da expansao portuguesa* (Lisboa: Junta de Investigações do Ultramar, 1962), 49, 88, 116; Auguste Chevalier, "Sur le riz Africains du groupe Oryza glaberrima," *Revue de botanique appliquée et d'agriculture tropicale* 17 (1937), 413–18.

45. G. Bezancon, J. Bozza, G. Koffi, and G. Second, "Genetic Diversity of Indigenous Rice in Africa," in I. W. Buddenhagen and G. J. Presley, eds., *Rice in Africa* (New York: Academic Press, 1978), 45.

46. Interviews in Mboteni village of Binari (Era) with Amara Bangura, September 9,

1998; M'Baye Ndugu Bangura, October 9, 1998; "President" Mohamed DiJongo Bangura, September 9, 1998 and December 2, 1998; Salifu Camara, September 14, 1998; Seydu Muctar Sumah, September 11, 1998 and November 9, 1998.

Interviews in Nalu village of Kukuba with Saliu Bangura, December 10, 1998; Ibrahima Camara, September 17, 1998; Suleyman Camara, September 19, 1998 and December 11, 1998; Usman Camara, September 18, 1998 and December 9, 1998; Mamadu Keita, September 17, 1998; Thomas Keita, September 17, 1998.

Interviews in Sitem village of Kawass with Boniface Bangura, September 22, 1998; Mamadu Camara, September 23, 1998.

Interviews in Mbulungish village of Monchon with El Hadj Abdulaye Bangura, October 1, 1998; Ibrahima Bangura, September 29, 1998 and December 17, 1998; Arafan Momo Camara, September 26, 1998. Interviews in Mbulungish village of Boŋkompon with Ndiaye Sumah, September 29, 1998.

47. Philip D. Curtin, *The Rise and Fall of the Plantation Complex: Essays in Atlantic History* (Cambridge: Cambridge University Press, 1990); Paul E. Lovejoy, *Transformations in Slavery: A History of Slavery in Africa* (Cambridge: Cambridge University Press, 2000).

48. Lauer, "Rice in the History," 9–11.

49. Ibid., 63.

50. Philip Morgan, *Slave Counterpoint: Black Culture in the Eighteenth Century Chesapeake and Lowcountry* (Chapel Hill: University of North Carolina Press, 1998), 151–52, 157; Harlan, "Décrue Agriculture in Mali," 73.

6. Feeding the Slave Trade

1. James Searing, *West African Slavery and Atlantic Commerce: The Senegal River Valley, 1700–1860* (Cambridge: Cambridge University Press, 1993), 84, 61, 75.

2. Throughout the course of the trans-Atlantic slave trade, a number of innovations and advancements helped to reduce captives' mortality, such as air ports, ventilators, windsails, more deck space on slave ships, and improved medical care. Slavers also continued to use nettings to prevent captives from jumping overboard, strong barricades, vigilant watches, and armed guards when captives were brought above deck to prevent insurrection. Marcus Rediker, *The Slave Ship: A Human History* (New York: Viking, 2007).

3. Herbert S. Klein, *The Atlantic Slave Trade* (Cambridge: Cambridge University Press, 1999), 85.

4. Ibid., 92.

5. Ibid., 90–92.

6. Ibid., 122,131.

7. Ibid., 90, 91, 92, 103, 123.

8. Ibid., 142–43, 149–55.

9. David Hancock, *Citizens of the World: London Merchants and the Integration of the British Atlantic Community, 1735–1785* (Cambridge: Cambridge University Press, 1995), 207–14; Gwendolyn Midlo Hall, *Slavery and African Ethnicities in the Americas: Restoring the Links* (Chapel Hill: University of North Carolina Press, 2005), 68, 90–91, 95.

10. Klein, *The Atlantic Slave Trade*, 150, 130, 94, 148, 142–43.

11. Ibid., 93–95.

12. On the other hand, proper storage of yams depends on providing adequate ventilation and avoiding extremely high temperatures. It is preferable that individual yams be stored on racks out of contact with each other to ensure proper ventilation and to prevent

the spread of rodents and insects. See D. G. Coursey, *Yams: An Account of the Nature, Origins, Cultivation and Utilisation of the Useful Members of the Dioscoreaceae* (London: Longmans, 1967), 172–89.

13. Joseph Lauer, "Rice in the History of the Lower Gambia-Geba Area" (M.A. thesis, University of Wisconsin, 1969), 48.

14. Sheila Lambert, ed., *House of Commons Sessional Papers of the Eighteenth Century, Volume 72, George III: Minutes of Evidence on the Slave Trade 1790, Part 2* (Wilmington, Del.: Scholarly Resources, 1975), 533, 513–14; idem, *House of Commons Sessional Papers of the Eighteenth Century, Volume 67, George III: Slave Trade 1788–1790* (Wilmington, Del.: Scholarly Resources, 1975), 23.

15. Idem, *House of Commons Sessional Papers, Volume 72*, 614, 601, 618–20, 624, 630; idem, *House of Commons Sessional Papers, Volume 67*, 23.

See for more references of the trade in provisions along West Africa's coast: idem, *House of Commons Sessional Papers of the Eighteenth Century, Volume 73, George III: Minutes of Evidence on the Slave Trade, 1790* (Wilmington, Del.: Scholarly Resources, 1975), 35, 88, 104, 151, 166; idem, *House of Commons Sessional Papers, Vol. 69*, 65–66, 71–72; idem, *House of Commons Sessional Papers, Volume 71, George III: Minutes of Evidence on the Slave Trade 1790), Part 1* (Wilmington, Del.: Scholarly Resources, 1975), 255.

16. During the era of trans-Atlantic commerce, a ton represented a unit of carrying capacity, not weight. Personal communication with Marcus Rediker, December 31, 2005.

17. James L. A. Webb, *Desert Frontier: Ecological and Economic Change along the Western Sahel, 1600–1850* (Madison: University of Wisconsin Press, 1995), 36–39.

18. Ibid.; Edward Bickersteth, "Journal of the Assistant Secretary," *Missionary Register*, February 1817, 52–53; Searing, *West African Slavery and Atlantic Commerce*, 58, 63, 65, 75, 79, 83.

19. Ibid., 60–65, 79–88.

20. Walter Hawthorne, *Planting Rice and Harvesting Slaves: Transformations along the Guinea-Bissau Coast, 1400–1900* (Portsmouth: Heinemann, 2003), 154, 178, 186–89.

21. Odile Goerg, *Commerce et colonisation en Guinée, 1850–1913* (Paris: L'Harmattan, 1986), 39.

22. Sylvan Meinrad Xavier de Goldbery, *Travels in Africa* (London: M. Jones, 1803), Volume 2, 162–63; Claude Rivière, "Le long des côtes de Guinée avant la phase coloniale," *Bulletin de l'Institut fondamental d'Afrique noire* 30: Ser. B (1968), 735–36.

23. Christopher Fyfe, *A History of Sierra Leone* (Oxford: Oxford University Press, 1962).

24. Suzanne Schwartz, ed., *Zachary Macaulay and the Development of the Sierra Leone Company, 1793–4; Part II: Journal, October–December 1793* (Leipzig: University of Leipzig Papers on African History and Culture Series, 2000), vii–ix; idem, *Zachary Macaulay and the Development of the Sierra Leone Company, 1793–4; Part I: Journal, June–October 1793* (Leipzig: University of Leipzig Papers on African History and Culture Series, 2000), iv, vi, xi.

25. Bruce L. Mouser, "Traders, Coasters, and Conflict in the Rio Pongo from 1790 to 1808," *Journal of African History* 14: 1 (1973), 45–64; idem and Ramon Sarró, eds., *Travels into the Baga and Soosoo Countries in 1821 by Peter McLachlan* (Leipzig: University of Leipzig Papers on African History and Culture Series, 1999), v; A. Demougeot, "Histoire du Nunez," *Bulletin du Comité d'études historiques et scientifique de l'Afrique Occidentale Français* 21: 2 (1938), 195–96; Walter Rodney, *A History of the Upper Guinea Coast, 1545–1800* (Oxford: Clarendon, 1970), 21; Goerg, *Commerce et colonisation en Guinée*, 39.

26. The examples of these reports are too numerous to name. Only a few examples are listed: 2.D.222, No. 67, "Rapport agricole, commerciale et politique" 1.D.3., le 3 Mai 1897; 2.D.30, Boké le 6 Août 1894; "Bulletin agricole, commercial et politique," No. 3, Mars 1895; "Bulletin agricole, commercial et politique," le 30 juin 1895; "Bulletin agricole commercial et politique," Août 1895; 2.D.225, No. 147.

27. For examples, see 2.D.9, "Bulletin agricole, commercial et politique," le 1 Février 1888; 2.D.220, Boké le 20 Août 1877; No. 27, Boké le 23 Septembre 1877; Boké le 20 Septembre 1878; No. 27, Boké le 10 Avril 1879; No. 64, Boké le 5 Octobre 1878; No. 64, Boké le 3 Octobre 1880; "Bulletin agricole, commercial et politique," le 15 Mars 1883; "Bulletin agricole, commercial et politique," le 31 Octobre 1883; 2.D.30, No.2, "Bulletin agricole, commercial et politique," le 1 et 20 Février 1894; Boké, le 16 Avril 1894; Boké, le 10 Juin 1893; 2.D.221, No. 57, le 5 Juin 1888.

28. Mouser and Sarró, *Travels into the Baga and Soosoo Countries,* 15; Matthews, *A Voyage to the River Sierra-Leone,* 14.

29. Mouser and Sarró, *Travels into the Baga and Soosoo Countries,* 24; V. Brousmiche, "Voyage au Rio Nunez," *Bulletin de la société de géographie de Marseille* 1 (1877), 316.

30. Lieutenant André Coffinières de Nordeck, "Voyage aux pays des Bagas et du Rio Nuñez," *Le Tour du Monde* 1: 1e Semestre (1886), 295 (author's translation).

31. Barry, *Senegambia and the Atlantic,* 117.

32. Matthews, *A Voyage to the River Sierra-Leone,* 12, 149; Barry, *Senegambia and the Atlantic,* 121–23; Bronislaw Nowak, "The Slave Rebellion in Sierra Leone in 1785–1786," *Hemispheres* 3 (1986), 151–69; Lord Stanley, "Narrative of William Cooper Thompson's Journey from Sierra Leone to Timbo, Capital of the Futah Jallo in West Africa," *Journal of Royal Geographical Society of London* 16 (1846), 106–38; Mouser quotes Ismail Rashid as estimating the percentage of enslaved within the population to be between 70 and 80 percent. See Bruce L. Mouser, "Rebellion, Marronage, and *Jihad:* Strategies of Resistance to Slavery on the Sierra Leone Coast. 1783–1796," *Journal of African History* 48 (2007), 27–44.

33. Ibid.

34. Paul Lovejoy has argued that the slave mode of production emerges in West Africa after the abolition of the slave trade and the Fulbe jihads. See Paul Lovejoy, *Transformations in Slavery: A History of Slavery in Africa* (Cambridge: Cambridge University Press, 2000).

35. Frederick Cooper, *Plantation Slavery on the East African Coast* (New Haven, Conn.: Yale University Press, 1977), 80–113; Robin Law, "Slave-Raiders and Middlemen, Monopolists and Free-Traders: The Supply of Slaves for the Atlantic Trade in Dahomey c. 1715–1850," *Journal of African History* 30: 1 (1989), 45–68; Joseph C. Miller, *Way of Death: Merchant Capitalism on the Angolan Slave Trade, 1730–1830* (Madison: University of Wisconsin Press, 1988), 393–400; David Northrup, *Trade without Rulers: Pre-Colonial Economic Development in South-eastern Nigeria* (Oxford: Clarendon, 1978), 171–76, 178–82; Searing, *West African Slavery,* 79–80; Jan Vansina, *Paths in the Rainforest: Toward a History of Political Tradition in Equatorial Africa* (Madison: University of Wisconsin Press, 1990), 139, 145.

36. Daniel C. Littlefield, *Rice and Slaves: Ethnicity and the Slave Trade in Colonial South Carolina* (Baton Rouge: Louisiana State University Press, 1981), 21. Elizabeth Donnan attempted to enumerate the total Africans imported into South Carolina between 1730 and 1744 based on the *South Carolina Gazette* and Henry Laurens's letter-books. See Elizabeth Donnan, "The Slave Trade into South Carolina before the Revolution," *The American Historical Review* 33: 4 (1928), 807.

37. Littlefield, *Rice and Slaves,* 109–14; Wood, *Black Majority,* 34–64.

38. Littlefield, *Rice and Slaves,* 118–23, 124.

39. David Eltis, Philip Morgan, and David Richardson, "Agency and Diaspora in Atlantic History: Reassessing the African Contribution to Rice Cultivation in the Americas," *American Historical Review,* December 2007, 1335–43. According to "Table 1," 35,774 slaves from the Upper Guinea Coast, 58.2 percent of the total, disembarked in South Carolina and Georgia between 1751 and 1775; 7,158 slaves from the Upper Guinea Coast disembarked between 1776 and 1800, 50.5 percent of all arrivals from Africa.

40. David Eltis, Stephen D. Behrendt, David Richardson, and Herbert S. Klein, eds., *The Trans-Atlantic Slave Trade: A Database on CD-Rom* (Cambridge: Cambridge University Press, 1999).

41. According to Hall: "Post-publication revisions have already added about 7,000, most of them Portuguese and Brazilian." See Hall, *Slavery and African Ethnicities,* 29.

42. A revised edition also contains "records of 293,000 slaves sailing direct from Africa into the territories that became the United States. Of these, some indication of the African coastal origins exists for 215,306—more than half of the total number of slaves thought to have arrived in mainland North America by this route." David Eltis, Philip Morgan, and David Richardson, "The African Contribution to Rice Cultivation in the Americas," paper presented at the Georgia Workshop in Early American History and Culture, University of Georgia, 2005, 4–5; David Eltis, "The Trans-Atlantic Slave Trade: A Reassessment Based on the Second Edition of the Transatlantic Slave Trade Database," paper presented at the American Historical Association annual conference in January 2006. The revised database is scheduled for release in 2008.

43. Hancock, *Citizens of the World,* 204–207.

44. Whether or not slave traders' perceptions about Africans' ethnicity bore any resemblance to how African captives identified themselves has been an ongoing debate in the literature. See Hall, *Slavery and African Ethnicities,* 23; Manuel Moreno Fraginals, "Africa in Cuba: A Quantitative Analysis of the African Population on the Island of Cuba," in Vera Rubin and Arthur Tuden, eds., *Comparative Perspectives on Slavery in New World Plantation Societies* (New York: New York Academy of Sciences, 1977), 187–201.

45. S. Max Edelson, *Plantation Enterprise in Colonial South Carolina* (Cambridge, Mass.: Harvard University Press, 2006), 60.

46. John K. Thornton, "African Dimensions of the Stono Rebellion," *American Historical Review* 96: 4 (1991), 1102–1103, 1109, 1111–12; idem, "The Art of War in Angola, 1575–1680," in *Comparative Studies in Society and History* 30: 2 (1988), 360–78.

47. Philip D. Morgan, *Slave Counterpoint: Black Culture in the Eighteenth-Century Chesapeake and Lowcountry* (Chapel Hill: University of North Carolina Press, 1998), 156; Sam B. Hilliard, "Antebellum Tidewater Rice Culture in South Carolina and Georgia," in James R. Gibson, ed., *European Settlement and Development in North America: Essays on Geographical Change in Honour and Memory of Andrew Hill Clark* (Toronto: University of Toronto, 1978).

48. Mart A. Stewart, "Rice, Water, and Power; Landscapes of Domination and Resistance in the Lowcountry, 1790–1880," *Environmental History Review* 15: 3 (1991), 50.

49. Edelson, *Plantation Enterprise in Colonial South Carolina,* 62, 158.

50. William Dusinberre, *Them Dark Days: Slavery in the American Rice Swamps* (New York: Oxford University Press, 1996).

51. There are many examples of this phenomenon in both the primary and secondary literature, only one of which is Elizabeth W. Pringle, *A Woman Rice Planter* (Columbia:

University of South Carolina Press, 1992); see also idem, *Chronicles of Chicora Wood* (New York: C. Scribner's Sons, 1990).

52. Pringle, *Chronicles of Chicora Wood*, 58–59; Douglas C. Wilms, "The Development of Rice Culture in 18th Century Georgia," *Southeastern Geographer* 12 (1972), 56.

53. Figures calculated from Eltis et al., *The Trans-Atlantic Slave Trade*.

54. Eltis, "The Trans-Atlantic Slave Trade: A Reassessment" (Table 5); Lovejoy, *Transformations in Slavery*, 122–28; John K. Thorton, *The Kongolese Saint Anthony: Dona Beatriz Kimpa Vita and the Antonian Movement, 1684–1706* (New York: Cambridge University Press, 1998), 203–14; Miller, *Way of Death*.

55. Eltis et al., *The Trans-Atlantic Slave Trade*.

56. Letter "Samuel and William Vernon to Thomlinson, Trecothick, and Company, 1754" in Elizabeth Donnan, ed., *Documents Illustrative of the History of the Slave Trade to America, Volume III: New England and the Middle Colonies* (Washington, D.C.: Carnegie Institution of Washington, 1975), 147.

57. "Samuel and William Vernon to Thomlinson, Trecothick, and Company, 1756," Elizabeth Donnan, ed., *Documents Illustrative of the History of the Slave Trade to America, Volume III: New England and the Middle Colonies*, 168.

58. Hancock, *Citizens of the World*, 82.

59. Joseph A. Opala, *The Gullah: Rice, Slavery and the Sierra Leone-American Connection* (Freetown, Sierra Leone: United States Information Service, 1987), 4–7; Hancock, *Citizens of the World*, 132–33.

60. "Henry Laurens to Samuel and William Vernon, 1756," in Elizabeth Donnan, ed., *Documents Illustrative of the History of the Slave Trade to America, Volume III: New England and the Middle Colonies*, 168–70.

61. Ibid., 174 note 4.

62. Edward Ball, *Slaves in the Family* (New York: Farrar, Straus and Giroux, 1998), 190–95.

63. Littlefield, *Rice and Slaves*, 9, 13, 18–19.

64. David Eltis, "The Volume and Structure of the Transatlantic Slave Trade: A Reassessment," *William and Mary Quarterly*, 58: 1, 3d Series (2001), 33–34, 38; idem, Phillip Morgan, and David Richardson, "Agency and Diaspora in Atlantic History," 1345.

65. Lovejoy, *Transformations in Slavery*, 46–67.

Conclusion

1. Michael A. Gomez, *Black Crescent: The Experience and Legacy of African Muslims in the Americas* (New York: Cambridge University Press, 2005); idem, ed., *Diasporic Africa: A Reader* (New York: Cambridge University Press, 2006); idem, *Exchanging Our Countrymarks: The Transformation of African Identities in the Colonial and Antebellum South* (Chapel Hill: University of North Carolina Press, 1998); idem, *Reversing Sail: A History of the African Diaspora* (New York: Cambridge University Press, 2005); Paul Lovejoy, "The African Diaspora: Revisionist Interpretations of Ethnicity, Culture and Religion under Slavery," *Studies in the World History of Slavery, Abolition and Emancipation* 2: 1 (1997); Kristin Mann and Edna G. Bay, eds., *Rethinking the African Diaspora: The Making of the Black Atlantic in the Bight of Benin* (London: Frank Cass, 2001); John Thornton, *Africa and Africans: The Making of the Atlantic World, 1400–1680* (New York: Cambridge University Press, 1992).

2. James H. Sweet, *Recreating Africa: Culture, Kinship, and Religion in the African-Portuguese World, 1441–1770* (Chapel Hill: University of North Carolina Press,

2003); Colin Palmer, "Defining and Studying the Modern African Diaspora," *Perspectives* 36: 6 (1998), 22–25.

3. Patrick Manning, "Review Article: Africa and the African Diaspora: New Directions of Study," *Journal of African History* 44 (2003), 488.

4. Paul Gilroy, *The Black Atlantic: Modernity and Double Consciousness* (Cambridge, Mass.: Harvard University Press, 1993), 1–71, 187–223; Brent Hayes Edwards, "The Uses of *Diaspora*," *Social Text* 66: 19 (2001), 63; idem, *The Practice of Diaspora: Literature, Translation, and the Rise of Black Internationalism* (Cambridge, Mass.: Harvard University Press, 2003); Michael Hanchard, "Translation, Political Community, and Black Internationalism: Some Comments on Brent Hayes Edwards's *The Practice of Diaspora* 17 (2005), 112–19; idem, "Afro-Modernity: Temporality, Politics, and the African Diaspora," *Public Culture* 11: 1 (1999), 245–68.

5. Manning, "Review Article: Africa and the African Diaspora," 501.

6. Daniel C. Littlefield, *Rice and Slaves: Ethnicity and the Slave Trade in Colonial South Carolina* (Baton Rouge: Louisiana State University Press, 1981), 80.

Bibliography

Adams, W. M., Andrew S. Goudie, and A. R. Orme, eds. *The Physical Geography of Africa*. Oxford: Oxford University, 1996.

Ajayi, J. F. A., and Michael Crowder, eds. *History of West Africa: Volume I*. London: Longman, 1972.

Alagoa, Ebiegberi Joe, F. N. Anozie, and Nwanna Nzewunwa, eds. *The Early History of the Niger Delta*. Hamburg: H. Buske, 1988.

Álmada, André Alvares de. *Brief Treatise on the Rivers of Guinea (c.1594): Part I translated by Paul E. Hair*. Liverpool: University of Liverpool Department of History, 1984.

———. *Brief Treatise on the Rivers of Guinea (c.1594): Part II Notes translated by Paul E. Hair*. Liverpool: University of Liverpool Department of History, 1986.

Alvares, Manuel. *Ethiopia Minor and a Geographical Account of the Province of Sierra Leone*. Liverpool: University of Liverpool Department of History, 1990.

Andriesse, W., and L. O. Fresco. "A Characterization of Rice-Growing Environments in West Africa." *Agriculture, Ecosystems and Environment* 33 (1991): 377–95.

Anttila, Raimo. *Historical and Comparative Linguistics*. Philadelphia: John Benjamin, 1989.

Appia, Beatrice. "Masques de Guinée française et de Casamance." *Journal de la société des africanistes* 13 (1943): 153–82.

———. "Notes sur le génie des eaux en Guinée." *Journal de la société des africanistes* 19 (1944): 33–41.

Arcin, André. *Histoire de la Guinée française: rivières de Sud, Fouta-Dialo, région du sud, Soudan*. Paris: Augustin Challamel, 1911.

———. *La Guinée française: races, religions, coutumes, production, commerce*. Paris: Augustin Challamel, 1907.

Atherton, John H. "Excavations at Kamabai and Yagala Rock Shelters, Sierra Leone." *The West African Journal of Archaeology* 2 (1972): 39–74.

Atkins, John. *A Voyage to Guinea, Brazil, & the West Indies in His Majesty's Ships the "Swallow" and "Weymouth."* London: Frank Cass, 1970.

Bailey, Anne C. *African Voices of the Atlantic Slave Trade: Beyond Silence and Shame*. Boston: Beacon, 2004.

Balandier, G. "Danses de sortie d'excision à Boffa (Guinée française)." *Notes africaines* 38 (1948): 11–12.

———. "Toponymie des îles de Kaback et Kakossa." *Études guinéennes* 8 (1952): 49–54.

Ball, Edward. *Slaves in the Family*. New York: Farrar, Straus and Giroux, 1998.

Barber, Charles L. *The English Language: A Historical Introduction*. Cambridge: Cambridge University Press, 2000.

Barbot, J. *A Description of the Coasts of North and South Guinea, and of Ethiopia Inferior, Vulgarly Angola*. Churchill: Awnsham Comp., 1732.

Barrow, Alfred Henry. *Fifty Years in Western Africa: Being a Record of the Work of the West Indian Church on the Banks of the Rio Pongo*. London: Society for Promoting Christian Knowledge, 1900.

Barry, Boubacar. *Senegambia and the Atlantic Slave Trade*. Cambridge: Cambridge University Press, 1998.

Barry, Ismael. *Le Futa-Jaloo face à la colonisation: conquête et mise en place de l'administration en Guinée*. Paris: L'Harmattan, 1997.

Bastin, Yvonne, André Coupez, and Michael Mann. "Continuity and Divergence in the Bantu Languages: Perspectives from a Lexicostatistic Study." *Annales sciences humaines* 162 (1999): 2–225.

Baum, Robert. *Shrines of the Slave Trade: Diola Religion and Society in the Precolonial Senegambia*. Oxford: Oxford University Press, 1999.

Bendor-Samuel, John, and Rhonda L. Hartell, eds. *The Niger-Congo Languages: A Classification and Description of Africa's Largest Language Family*. Lanham, Md.: University Press of America, 1989.

Bennett, N. R., and George E. Brooks, eds. *New England Merchants in Africa: A History through Documents, 1802 to 1865*. Brookline, Mass.: Boston University Press, 1965.

Bérenger-Féraud, Laurent. "La secte des Simos, chez les peuplades de la côte occidentale compromise entre le Sénégal et le pays de Sierra Leone." *Revue d'anthropologie* 3 (1880): 424–40.

———. *Les peuplades de la Sénégambie: histoire, ethnographie, mœurs, et coutumes, légendes*. Paris: Ernest Leroux, 1879.

Berlin, Ira. *Many Thousands Gone: The First Two Centuries of Slavery in North America*. Cambridge: Belknap, 1988.

———. "Time, Space, and the Evolution of Afro-American Society in British Mainland North America." *The American Historical Review* 85 (1980): 44–78.

Berliner, David. "An 'Impossible' Transmission: Youth Religious Memories in Guinea-Conakry." *American Ethnologist* 32, no. 4 (2005): 576–92.

———. "Nous sommes les derniers buloNic: sur une impossible transmission dans une société d'Afrique de l'Ouest (Guinée Conakry)." Ph.D. diss., Université Libre de Bruxelles, 2003.

Bickersteth, Edward. "Journal of the Assistant Secretary." *Missionary Register* 5, February; March; April (1817): 50–57; 98–113; 159–71.

Bimson, Kent D. "Comparative Reconstruction of Proto-Northern-Western Mande." Ph.D. diss., University of California at Los Angeles, 1978.

Biyi, Esu. "The Temne People and How They Make Their Kings." *Journal of the Royal African Society* 12, no. 46 (1913): 190–99.

Borland, C. H. "How Basic Is 'Basic' Vocabulary?" *Current Anthropology* 23, no. 3 (1982): 315–16.

Bostoen, Koen. "Linguistics for the Use of African History and the Comparative Study of Bantu Pottery Vocabulary." *Antwerp Papers in Linguistics* 106 (2004): 131–54.

Botte, Roger. "Les rapports Nord-Sud, la traite négrière et le Fuuta Jaloo à la fin du XVIIIe siècle." *Annales ESC* 6 (1991): 1411–35.

———. "Révolte, pouvoir, religion: Les Hubbu du Futa-Jalon (Guinée)." *Journal of African History* 29, no. 3 (1988): 391–413.

Bovill, E. *The Golden Trade of the Moors*. London: Oxford University Press, 1958.

Braithwaite, Roderick. *Palmerston in Africa: The Rio Nunez Affair: Competition, Diplomacy, and Justice.* London: British Academic Press, 1996.

———. "The Rio Nunez Affair: New Perspectives on a Significant Event in Nineteenth Century Franco-British Colonial Rivalry." *Revue française d'histoire d'outre-mer* 83, no. 311 (1996): 25–45.

Brásio, António, ed. *Monumenta missionária africana: Africa ocidental (1570–1600).* 2nd Ser., Vol. IV. Lisboa: Agência-Geral do Ultramar, 1968.

———, ed. *Monumenta missionária: Africa ocidental (1570–1600).* 2nd Ser., Vol. III. Lisboa: Agência-Geral do Ultramar, 1968.

Brooks, George E. "Ecological Perspectives on Mande Population Movements, Commercial Networks, and Settlement Patterns from the Atlantic Wet Phase (ca. 5500–2500B.C.) to the Present." *History in Africa* 16 (1989): 23–40.

———. *Eurafricans in Western Africa: Commerce, Social Status, Gender, and Religious Observance from the Sixteenth to the Eighteenth Century.* Athens: Ohio University Press, 2003.

———. *Landlords & Strangers: Ecology, Society, and Trade in Western Africa, 1000–1630.* Boulder. Colo.: Westview, 1993.

———. "A Provisional Historical Schema for Western Africa Based on Seven Climate Periods (ca. 9000B.C. to the 19th Century)." *Cahiers d'Études africaines* 101–102, no. 26-1-2 (1986): 43–62.

———. *Yankee Traders, Old Coasters, & African Middlemen; A History of American Legitimate Trade with West Africa in the Nineteenth Century.* Brookline, Mass.: Boston University, 1970.

Brot, Michel. "Les régions frontalières Guinée/Sierra Leone au début du vingtième siècle aux indépendances." Ph.D. diss., Université de Provence, 1994.

Brousmiche, V. "Voyage au Rio Nunez." *Bulletin de la société de géographie de Marseille* 1 (1877): 313–23.

Brunton, Henry A. *A Grammar and Vocabulary of the Susoo Language.* Edinburgh: J. Richie, 1802.

Buddenhagen, I. W., and G. J. Presley, eds. *Rice in Africa.* New York: Academic Press, 1978.

Burkill, H. M., J. M. Dalziel, and J. Hutchinson, eds. *The Useful Plants of West Tropical Africa being an Appendix to the Flora of West Tropical Africa.* London: Crown Agents for the Colonies, 1937.

Caillié, René. *Travels through Central Africa to Timbuctoo, and Across the Great Desert, to Morocco performed in the years 1824–1828.* London: Frank Cass & Co., 1968.

Carney, Judith A. "African Rice in the Columbian Exchange." *Journal of African History* 42, no. 3 (2001): 377–96.

———. *Black Rice: The African Origins of Rice Cultivation in the Americas.* Cambridge, Mass.: Harvard University Press, 2001.

———. "Landscapes of Technology: Rice Cultivation and African Continuities." *Technology and Culture* 37, no. 1 (1996): 5–35.

———. "Rice Milling, Gender, and Slave Labour in Colonial South Carolina." *Past and Present* 153 (1996): 108–34.

Carney, Judith, and Richard Porcher. "Geographies of the Past: Rice, Slaves, and Technological Transfer in South Carolina." *Southeastern Geographer* 33, no. 2 (1993): 127–47.

Caswall, Henry. *The Martyr of the Pongas: Being a Memoir of the Rev. Hamble James Leacock, Leader of the West Indian Mission to Western Africa.* London: Rivingtons, 1857.

Catling, H. D. *Rice in Deep Water*. Manila: International Rice Research Institute, 1992.

Chermette, A. "Monument néolithique de la région de Kankan (Haute Guinée)." *Notes africaines* 42 (1949): 179.

Chevalier, Auguste. "Études sur les praires de l'Ouest-Africain." *Revue internationale de botanique appliquée et d'agriculture tropicale* 14 (1934): 17–48; 109–37; 1078–81.

———. "Le Sahara, centre d'origines de plantes cultivées." *Mémoires de la société de bio-géographie* 6 (1938): 307–22.

———. "Les petites céréales." *Revue internationale de botanique appliquée et d'agriculture tropicale* 20 (1922): 544–50.

———. "Les ressources ligneuses du Sahara." *Revue internationale de botanique appliquée et d'agriculture tropicale* 12 (1932): 815–24.

———. "Sur le riz Africains du groupe Oryza glaberrima." *Revue de botanique appliquée et d'agriculture tropicale* 17 (1937): 413–18.

Chevrier, M. A. "Relative aux coutumes des adeptes de la société secrète des Scymos, indigènes fétichistes du littoral de la Guinée." *L'Anthropologie* 17 (1906): 359–76.

Childs, G. Tucker. "Language Contact, Language Death, Section V: Language Contact: Atlantic-Mande/intra-Atlantic." International Workshop The Atlantic Languages: Typological or Genetic Unit? University of Hamburg Asien-Afrika-Institut, 2007.

Clark, J. Desmond, and Steven A. Brandt. *From Hunters to Farmers: The Causes and Consequences of Food Production in Africa*. Berkeley: University of California Press, 1984.

Clarke, John. *Specimens of Dialects: Short Vocabularies of Languages, and Notes of Countries & Customs in Africa*. Farnborough, U.K.: Gregg Press, 1972.

Clarke, Mary Lane. *A Limba-English Dictionary or Tampaŋ ta ha Taluŋ ta ka Hulimba ha in Huiŋkilisi ha*. Freetown, Sierra Leone: Printed by the Government Printer, 1929.

Clarke, Robert. *Sierra Leone: A Description of the Manners and Customs of the Liberated Africans; with Observations upon the Natural History of the Colony and a Notice of the Native Tribes*. London: African Publication Society, 1969.

Coclanis, Peter. *The Shadow of a Dream: Economic Life and Death in the South Carolina Low Country, 1670–1920*. New York: Oxford University Press, 1989.

Coelho, Francisco de Lemos. *Description of the Coast of Guinea (1684) (translated by Paul E. H. Hair)*. Liverpool: University of Liverpool Department of History, 1985.

Coffinières de Nordeck, André. "Voyage aux pays des Bagas et du Rio-Nuñez (1884–1885)." *Le Tour du monde* 1, le semestre (1886): 273–304.

Coifman, Victoria Bomba. "West African Women: On the Edges of Jihad in the Early Days of McWorld." *Listening* 33, no. 2 (1998): 111–23.

Conneau, Theophilus. *A Slaver's Log Book or 20 Years' Residence in Africa*. Englewood Cliffs, N.J.: Prentice-Hall, 1976.

Cooper, Frederick. *Plantation Slavery on the East African Coast*. New Haven, Conn.: Yale University Press, 1977.

Cormier-Salem, Marie-Christine, ed. *Dynamique et usages de la mangrove dans les pays des rivières du sud, du Sénégal à la Sierra Leone*. Paris: ORSTOM éditions, 1994.

Corré, A. "Idiomes du Rio Nunez." *Revue de linguistique et de philologie comparée* 10 (1877): 75–97.

———. "Les peuples du Rio Nunez (Côte occidentale d'Afrique)." *Société d'Anthropologie de Paris* 3 (1888): 42–73.

Corry, Joseph. *Observations upon the Windward Coast of Africa (1807)*. London: Frank Cass, 1968.

Coughtry, Jay. *The Notorious Triangle: Rhode Island and the African Slave Trade, 1700–1807*. Philadelphia: Temple University Press, 1981.

Coursey, D. G. *Yams: An Account of the Nature, Origins, Cultivation and Utilisation of the Useful Members of the Dioscoreaceae*. London: Longmans, 1967.

Creel, Margaret Washington. *A Peculiar People: Slave Religion and Community-Culture among the Gullahs*. New York: New York University Press, 1988.

Curtin, Philip D. *The Atlantic Slave Trade; A Census*. Madison: University of Wisconsin Press, 1969.

———. *Death by Migration: Europe's Encounter with the Tropical World in the Nineteenth Century*. Cambridge: Cambridge University Press, 1989.

———. *Economic Change in Precolonial Africa; Senegambia in the Era of the Slave Trade*. Madison: University of Wisconsin Press, 1975.

———. "Epidemiology and the Slave Trade." *Political Science Quarterly* 83, no. 2 (1968): 190–216.

———. *The Rise and Fall of the Plantation Complex: Essays in Atlantic History*. Cambridge: Cambridge University Press, 1990.

Curtis, Marie Yvonne. "L'art Nalu, l'art Baga de Guinée: approches comparatives." Ph.D. diss., Université de Paris I (Panthéon-Sorbonne), 1996.

Curtis, Marie Yvonne, and Ramon Sarró. "The 'Nimba' Headdress: Art, Ritual, and History of the Baga and Nalu Peoples of Guinea." *Museum Studies* 23, no. 2 (1997): 120–33.

Dalby, David. "The Mel Languages in the Polyglotta Africana, Part I: Baga, Landuma and Temne." *African Language Studies* 4 (1965): 129–35.

———. "Mel Languages in the Polyglotta Africana, Part II: Bullom, Kissi and Gola." *Sierra Leone Language Review* 5 (1966): 139–51.

———. "The Mel Languages: A Reclassification of Southern West Atlantic." *African Language Studies* 6 (1965): 1–17.

Dapper, Olfert. *Description de l'Afrique*. Amsterdam: Chez Wolfgang, Waesberge, Boom & van Someren, 1686.

Delafosse, Maurice. *Essai de manuel pratique de la langue Mandé ou Mandingue étude grammaticale de dialecte Dyoula, vocabulaire Français-Dyoula, historié de Samori en Mandé, étude comparée des principaux dialectes Mandé*. Paris: E. Leroux, 1901.

Delange, Jacqueline. "Le Bansonyi du pays Baga." *Objets et Mondes (Musée de l'Homme)* 2, no. 1 (1962): 3–12.

Demougeot, A. "Histoire du Nunez." *Bulletin du Comité d'études historiques et scientifique de l'Afrique occidentale français* 21 (1938): 177–289.

Dew, Charles B. *Bond of Iron: Master and Slave at Buffalo Forge*. New York: W.W. Norton, 1994.

Dike, K. Onwuka. *Trade and Politics in the Niger Delta, 1830–1885: An Introduction to the Economic and Political History of Nigeria*. Oxford: Clarendon, 1956.

Doar, David. *Rice and Rice Planting in the South Carolina Low Country*. Charleston, S.C.: Charleston Museum, 1970.

Donelha, André. *Descrição da Serra Leoa e dos rios de Guiné do Cabo Verde (1625) (notas por Avelino Teixeira da Mota, Description de la Serre Leoa et des rios de Guinée du Cabo Verde (1625) (translated by P. E. H. Hair)*. Lisboa: Junta de Investigações Cientificas do Ultramar, 1977.

Doneux, Jean L. "Hypothèses pour la comparative des langues Atlantiques." *Africana linguistica* 6 (1975): 41–129.

Donnan, Elizabeth. "The Slave Trade in South Carolina before the Revolution." *American Historical Review* 33, no. 4 (1928): 804–28.

———, ed. *Documents Illustrative of the History of the Slave Trade to America: Volume III. New England and the Middle Colonies.* Washington, D.C.: Carnegie Institution of Washington, 1932.

———, ed. *Documents Illustrative of the History of the Slave Trade to America: Volume IV. The Border Colonies and the Southern Colonies.* Washington, D.C.: Carnegie Institution of Washington, 1935.

Durie, Mark, and Malcolm Ross, eds. *The Comparative Method Reviewed: Regularity and Irregularity in Language Change.* New York: Oxford University Press, 1995.

Dusinberre, William. *Them Dark Days: Slavery in the American Rice Swamps.* New York: Oxford University Press, 1996.

Edelson, S. Max. *Plantation Enterprise in Colonial South Carolina.* Cambridge, Mass.: Harvard University Press, 2006.

Edwards, Brent Hayes. *The Practice of Diaspora: Literature, Translation, and the Rise of Black Internationalism.* Cambridge, Mass.: Harvard University Press, 2003.

———. "The Uses of 'Diaspora'." *Social Text* 66, no. 19 (2001): 45–73.

Ehret, Christopher. *An African Classical Age: Eastern and Southern Africa in World History, 1000 B.C. to 400 A.D.* Charlottesville: University of Virginia Press, 1998.

———. "Agricultural History in Central and Southern Africa ca. 1000 B.C. to A.D. 500." *Transafrican Journal of History* 4 (1974): 1–25.

———. "Cattle-keeping and Milking in Eastern and Southern African History." *Journal of African History* 1, no. 8 (1967): 1–17.

———. "The Establishment of Iron-Working in Eastern, Central, and Southern Africa: Linguistic Inferences on Technological History." *Sprache und Geschichte in Afrika* 16/17 (1995/1996): 125–75.

———. "On the Antiquity of Agriculture in Ethiopia." *Journal of African History* 20, no. 2 (1979): 161–77.

———. "Patterns of Bantu and Central Sudanic Settlement in Central and Southern Africa (ca. 1000B.C. B.C.–500A.D.)." *Transafrican Journal of History* 3 (1973): 1–71.

———. "Sheep and Central Sudanic Peoples in Southern Africa." *Journal of African History* 9, no. 2 (1968): 213–21.

Elbl, Ivana. "The Volume of the Early Atlantic Slave Trade, 1450–1521." *Journal of African History* 38, no. 1 (1997): 31–75.

Eltis, David. "The Trans-Atlantic Slave Trade: A Reassessment Based on the Second Edition of the Transatlantic Slave Trade Database." American Historical Association Annual Conference, 2006.

———. "The Volume and Structure of the Transatlantic Slave Trade: A Reassessment." *William and Mary Quarterly* 3rd Series 58, no. 1 (2001): 17–46.

Eltis, David, Philip Morgan, and David Richardson. "The African Contribution to Rice Cultivation in the Americas." Georgia Workshop in Early American History and Culture, University of Georgia, Le Conte Hall, 2005.

———. "Agency and Diaspora in Atlantic History: Reassessing the African Contribution to Rice Cultivation in the Americas." *American Historical Review* 112 (December 2007): 1329–58.

Eltis, David, Stephen D. Behrendt, David Richardson, and Herbert S. Klein, eds. *The Trans-Atlantic Slave Trade: A Database on CD-Rom.* Cambridge: Cambridge University Press, 1999.

Embleton, Sheila M. *Statistics in Historical Linguistics*. Bochum, Germany: Brockmeyer, 1986.

Fage, J. D., and R. A. Oliver, eds. *Papers in African Prehistory*. Cambridge: Cambridge University Press, 1970.

Fagg, William. "A Colossal Mask from the Baga of Guinea." *British Museum Quarterly* 25 (1961): 61–65.

———. "Two Woodcarvings from the Baga of French Guinea." *Man* 47 (August 1947): 113–25.

Fairhead, James, and Melissa Leach. *Misreading the African Landscape: Society and Ecology in a Forest-Savanna Mosaic*. Cambridge: Cambridge University Press, 1996.

Famechon, Lucien Marie François. *Notice sur la Guinée française*. Paris: Alcon-Levy, 1900.

Fenton, E. G. R. *The Troublesome Voyage of Captain Edward Fenton, 1582–1583; Narratives and Documents*. Cambridge: Hakluyt Society, 1959.

Fernandes, Jaime Coutinho. "A habitação dos Nalús." *Memória Centro de Estudos da Guine Portuguesa* 7 (1948): 437–54.

Fernandes, Valentim. *Description de la côte occidentale d'Afrique (Sénégal au Cap de Monte, Archipels), translated by Th. Monod, A. Teixeira da Mota and R. Mauny*. Bissau, Guinea-Bissau: Publicaçóes do Centro Estudos da Guiné Portuguesa, 1951.

Ferry, Marie-Paule. "Konyagui/Kogoli-French (Unpublished wordlist)."

———. "Le passé des ethnies: Tyapi autrefois, Kogoli aujourd'hui (Unpublished article)."

———. "Les Baga de Guinée côtière, des langues ou un groupe? (Unpublished article)."

———. "Mboteni-French wordlist (Unpublished wordlist)."

———. "Mbuluŋuc-French (Unpublished wordlist)."

———. "Sitem-French (Unpublished wordlist)."

Fields, Edda L. "Before 'Baga:' Settlement Chronologies of the Coastal Rio Nunez Region, Earliest Times c. 1000 c.e.." *International Journal of African Historical Studies* 37, no. 2 (2004): 229–53.

———. "Rice Farmers in the Rio Nunez Region: A Social History of Agricultural Technology and Identity in Coastal Guinea, ca. 2000 b.c.e. to 1880 c.e." Ph.D. diss., University of Pennsylvania, 2001.

Figarol, J. "Monographie du Cercle du Rio Nunez." In *Box 1.42, Archives nationale de la République de Guinée*. Conakry, 1907–1912.

Ford, John. *The Role of the Trypanosomiases in African Ecology: A Study of the Tsetse Fly Problem*. Oxford: Clarendon, 1971.

Foulché-Delbosc, R. "Voyage à la côte occidentale d'Afrique, en Portugal et en Espagne (1479–1480)." *Revue hispanique* 4 (1897): 175–201.

Frazier, E. Franklin. *The Negro in the United States*. New York: Macmillan, 1957.

Fyfe, Christopher. *A History of Sierra Leone*. Oxford: Oxford University Press, 1962.

Fyle, Cecil Magbaily. "Solimana and Its Neighbors: A History of the Solima Yalunka from the Mid-Seventeenth Century to the Start of the Colonial Period." Ph.D. diss., Northwestern University, 1976.

Gaillard, Gérald, ed. *Migrations anciennes et peuplement actuel des côtes Guinéennes: Actes du colloque international de l'Université de Lille 1, les 1er, 2 et 3 décembre 1997*. Paris: L'Harmattan, 2000.

Ganong, Tina Weller. "Features of Baga Morphology, Syntax, and Narrative Discourse." M.A. thesis. University of Texas at Arlington, 1998.

Gauthier, M. "Colonie de la Guinée française: Cercle du Rio Nuñez (l'Adjoint des Affaires Indigènes Commandant le Cercle du Rio Nuñez p. i. a Monsieur le Gouverneur de la Guinée Française)." *Revue coloniale* Juillet-Juin (1902–1903): 388–400.

Gavinet, M. "Les Baga du village de Taigbé." *Études guinéennes* 2 (1947): 7–22.

Gibson, James R., ed. *European Settlement and Development in North America: Essays on Geographical Change in Honour and Memory of Andrew Hill Clark.* Toronto: University of Toronto Press, 1978.

Gilroy, Paul. *The Black Atlantic: Modernity and Double Consciousness.* Cambridge, Mass.: Harvard University Press, 1993.

Goerg, Odile. *Commerce et colonisation en Guinée, 1850–1913.* Paris: Éditions L'Harmattan, 1986.

———. *Pouvoir colonial municipalités et espaces urbains: Conakry-Freetown des années 1880 à 1914.* Paris: L'Harmattan, 1997.

Goldbery, Sylvan Meinrad Xavier de. *Travels in Africa: Performed during the Years 1785, 1786, and 1787 in the Western Countries of that Continent.* London: M. Jones, 1803.

Gomez, Michael A. *Black Crescent: The Experience and Legacy of African Muslims in the Americas.* New York: Cambridge University Press, 2005.

———. *Diasporic Africa: A Reader.* New York: Cambridge University Press, 2006.

———. *Exchanging Our Countrymarks: The Transformation of African Identities in the Colonial and Antebellum South.* Chapel Hill: University of North Carolina Press, 1998.

———. *Reversing Sail: A History of the African Diaspora.* New York: Cambridge University Press, 2005.

Gowlett, Derek F., and Ernst Westphal, eds. *African Linguistic Contributions: Papers in Honor of Ernst Westphal.* Pretoria: Via Afrika, 1992.

Grace, John. *Domestic Slavery in West Africa, with Particular Reference to the Sierra Leone Protectorate, 1896–1927.* London: Muller, 1975.

Greene, Sandra. *Gender, Ethnicity, and Social Change on the Upper Slave Coast: A History of the Anlo-Ewe.* Portsmouth: Heinemann, 1996.

Grégoire, Claire. "Étude lexicostatistique de quarante-trois langues et dialectes Mande." *Africana linguistica* 11 (1994): 53–70.

Gross, B. A. "Notes guinéennes." *Notes africaines* 19 (1943): 4.

Guerreiro, Fernão. *Relação anual das coisas que fizeram os padres da Companhia de Jesus.* Coimbra, Portugal: Impr. de Universidade, 1930–42.

Hafkin, Nancy J., ed. *Women in Africa: Studies in Social and Economic Change.* Stanford, Calif.: Stanford University Press, 1976.

Hair, Paul E. H. *Africa Encountered: European Contacts and Evidence 1450–1700.* Hampshire, England: Variorum, 1997.

———. *André de Faro's Missionary Journey to Sierra Leone in 1663–1664: A Shortened Version in English Translation, of André de Faro Relacem.* Freetown: University of Sierra Leone, Institute of African Studies, 1982.

———. "Early Sources on Religion and Social Values in the Sierra Leone Region: (1) Cadamosto 1463." *The Sierra Leone Bulletin of Religion* 11 (1969): 51–64.

———. "Early Sources on Religion and Social Values in the Sierra Leone Region: (2) Eustache de la Fosse 1480." *Africana Research Bulletin* 4, no. 4 (1974): 49–54.

———. "Ethnolinguistic Continuity on the Guinea Coast." *Journal of African History* 8, no. 2 (1967): 247–68.

———. "An Ethnolinguistic Inventory of the Upper Guinea Coast before 1700." *African Language Review* 6 (1967): 32–70.

———. "The History of the Baga in Early Written Sources." *History in Africa* 24 (1997): 381–91.

———. "An Introduction to John Clarke's 'Specimens of Dialects,' 1848/9." *African Language Review* 5 (1966): 72–82.

———. "Some Minor Sources for Guinea, 1519–1559: Enciso and Alfonce/Fonteneau." *History in Africa* 3 (1976): 19–46.

———. "Sources on Early Sierra Leone: (1) Beaulieu 1619." *African Research Bulletin* 4, no. 4 (1974): 41–50.

———. "Sources on Early Sierra Leone: (3) Sandoval (1627)." *Africana Research Bulletin* 5, no. 2 (1975): 78–92.

———. "Sources on Early Sierra Leone: (5) Barreira." *Africana Research Bulletin* 5, no. 4 (1975): 81–118.

———. "Sources on Early Sierra Leone: (9) Barreira's 'Account of the Coast of Guinea', 1606." *Africana Research Bulletin* 7, no. 1 (1977): 50–70.

———. "Sources on Early Sierra Leone: (13) Barreira's Report of 1607–1608—The Visit to Bena." *Africana Research Bulletin* 8, no. 2–3 (1978): 64–108.

———. "Sources on Early Sierra Leone: (15) Marmol 1573." *Africana Research Bulletin* 9, no. 3 (1979): 70–84.

———. "Sources on Early Sierra Leone: (18) Barbot 1678." *Africana Research Bulletin* 11, no. 3 (1981): 46–60.

———. "Susu Studies and Literature: 1799–1900." *Sierra Leone Language Review* 4 (1965): 38–53.

Hair, Paul E. H., Adam Jones, and Robin Law, eds. *Barbot on Guinea: The Writings of Jean Barbot on West Africa.* London: Hakluyt Society, 1992.

Hakluyt, Richard, David B. Quinn, and R. A. Skeleton, eds. *The Principall Navigations, Voiages and Discoveries of the English Nation.* Cambridge: The Hakluyt Society and the Peabody Museum, 1965.

Hall, Gwendolyn Midlo. *Slavery and African Ethnicities in the Americas: Restoring the Links.* Chapel Hill: University of North Carolina Press, 2005.

Hamy, T. "La grotte du Kakimbon à Ratoma, près Konakry (Guinée française)." *L'Anthropologie* 12 (1901): 380–95.

———. "Rapport sur une fouille exécutée dans la grotte de Ratoma, près de Konakry." *Revue coloniale* (1899): 497–501.

Hanchard, Michael. "Afro-Modernity: Temporality, Politics, and the African Diaspora." *Public Culture* 11, no. 1 (1999): 245–68.

———. "Translation, Political, and Black Internationalism: Some Comments on Brent Hayes Edwards's 'The Practice of Diaspora'." *Small Axe* 17 (2005): 112–19.

Hancock, David. *Citizens of the World: London Merchants and the Integration of the British Atlantic Community, 1735–1785.* Cambridge: Cambridge University Press, 1995.

Harlan, Jack, and Jean Pasquereau. "*Décrue* Agriculture in Mali." *Economic Botany* 23 (1969): 70–74.

Harlan, Jack R. "Agricultural Origins: Centers and Noncenters." *Science* 174 (1971): 468–74.

Harlan, Jack R., and Jan M. J. De Wet, eds. *Origins of African Plant Domestication.* The Hague: Mouton, 1976.

Harms, Robert, and Jan Vansina, eds. *Paths toward the Past: African Historical Essays in Honor of Jan Vansina.* Atlanta: African Studies Association, 1994.

Hawthorne, Walter. "The Interior Past of an Acephalous Society: Institutional Change among the Balanta of Guinea-Bissau, c. 1400–1950." Ph.D. diss., Stanford University, 1998.

———. "Nourishing a Stateless Society during the Slave Trade: The Rise of Balanta Paddy-Rice Production in Guinea-Bissau." *Journal of African History* 42 (2001): 1–24.

———. *Planting Rice and Harvesting Slaves: Transformations along the Guinea-Bissau Coast, 1400–1900.* Portsmouth: Heinemann, 2003.

Heine, Bernd, and Derek Nurse, eds. *African Languages: An Introduction.* Cambridge: Cambridge University Press, 2000.

Herskovits, Melville J. *The Myth of the Negro Past.* Gloucester, England: Peter Smith, 1970.

Hilliard, Sam B. "The Tidewater Rice Plantation: An Ingenious Adaptation to Nature." *Geoscience and Man* 12 (1975): 57–60.

Hodge, Carleton T., ed. *Papers on the Mandinga.* Bloomington: Indiana University Press, 1971.

Hogarth, Peter J. *The Biology of Mangroves.* Oxford: Oxford University Press, 1999.

Holas, Bohumil. "Danses masquées de la Basse-Côte." *Études guinéennes* 6 (1950): 61–67.

Holm, John. "Variability of the Copula in Black English and Its Creole Kin." *American Speech* 59, no. 4 (1984): 291–309.

Hopkins, A. G. *An Economic History of West Africa.* New York: Columbia University Press, 1973.

Hortop, Job, and G. R. G. Conway. *The Rare Travailes of Job Hortop.* Mexico: [s.n.], 1928.

Houis, Maurice. "Contes Baga (Dialecte du Koba)." *Études guinéennes* 6 (1950): 3–15.

———. "La rapport d'annexion en Baga." *Bulletin de l'Institut français d'Afrique noire* 15, no. 1 (1953): 848–54.

———. "Le genre animé en Baga." *Notes africaines* 57 (1953): 25–27.

———. "Le système pronominal et les classes dans les dialectes Baga." *Bulletin de l'Institut français d'Afrique noire* 15, no. 1 (1953): 381–404.

———. "Les minorités ethniques de la Guinée côtière: situation linguistique." *Études guinéennes* 4 (1952): 25–48.

———. "Les peuples de la Guinée française." *Cahiers Charles de Foucauld* 44 (1956): 27–34.

———. "Remarques sur la voix passive en Baga." *Notes africaines* 55 (1952): 91–92.

Hunter, Tera W. *To 'Joy My Freedom: Southern Black Women's Lives and Labors after the Civil War.* Cambridge, Mass.: Harvard University Press, 1997.

Inkori, Joseph E. "Measuring the Atlantic Slave Trade: An Assessment of Curtin and Anstey." *Journal of African History* 17, no. 2 (1976): 197–223.

Innes, Gordon. *A Mende-English Dictionary.* London: Cambridge University Press, 1969.

Jajolet, Michel. *Premier voyage du sieur de La Courbe fait à la coste d'Afrique en 1685.* Paris: E. Chapman, 1913.

Joire, Jean. *La préhistoire de Guinée française: inventaire et mise au point de nos connaissances.* Lisboa: Ministério das Colónias, Junta de Investigaçoes Colonias, 1947.

Jordan, H. D. "The Relation of Vegetation and Soil to Development of Mangrove Swamps for Rice Growing in Sierra Leone." *The Journal of Applied Ecology* 1, no. 1 (1964): 209–12.

Joyner, Charles. *Down by the Riverside: A South Carolina Slave Community.* Urbana: University of Illinois Press, 1984.

Kastenholz, Raimund. "Comparative Mande Studies: State of the Art." *Sprache und Geschichte in Afrika* 12/13 (1991/1992): 107–58.

———. "Essai de classification des dialectes Mande-Kan." *Sprache und Geschichte in Afrika* (1979): 205–33.

Kilham, Hannah. *Specimens of African Languages Spoken in the Colony of Sierra Leone.* London: Committee of the Society of Friends, 1828.

Kilson, Martin L., and Robert I. Rotberg, eds. *The African Diaspora: Interpretive Essays.* Cambridge, Mass.: Harvard University Press, 1976.

Klein, Herbert S. *The Atlantic Slave Trade.* Cambridge: Cambridge University Press, 1999.

Klein, Martin. "The Slave Trade and Decentralized Societies." *Journal of African History* 42, no. 1 (2000): 49–65.

Klieman, Kairn A. *'The Pygmies Were Our Compass:' Bantu and Batwa in the History of West Central Africa, Early Times to c. 1900 C.E.* Portsmouth: Heinemann, 2003.

Koelle, Sigmund W. *Polyglotta Africana: or a Comparative Vocabulary of Nearly Three Hundred Words and Phrases in More Than One Hundred Distinct African Languages.* London: Church Missionary Society, 1854.

Kropp-Dakubu, M. E. *West African Language Data Sheets.* Leiden: West African Linguistic Society, 1980.

Kup, Alexander Peter, and C. G. Widstrand, eds. *Adam Afzelius Sierra Leone Journal 1795–6.* Upsala: Studia Ethnographica Upsaliensia, 1967.

Labat, Père Jean-Baptiste. *Nouvelle relations de l'Afrique occidentale contenant une description exacte du Sénégal et des pais situés entre le Cap-Blanc et la rivière de Serralionne jusqu'a plus de 300 lieues en avant dans les terres.* Paris: Chez G. Cavalier, 1728.

Lambert, Sheila, ed. *House of Commons Sessional Papers of the Eighteenth Century, Volume 67, George III: Slave Trade (1788–1790).* Wilmington. Del.: Scholarly Resources, 1975.

———, ed. *House of Commons Sessional Papers of the Eighteenth Century, Volume 69, George III: Report of the Lords of Trade on the Slave Trade 1789, Part 1.* Wilmington, Del.: Scholarly Resources, 1975.

———, ed. *House of Commons Sessional Papers of the Eighteenth Century, Volume 72, George III: Minutes of Evidence on the Slave Trade 1790, Part 2.* Wilmington, Del.: Scholarly Resources, 1975.

———, ed. *House of Commons Sessional Papers of the Eighteenth Century, Volume 73, George III: Minutes of Evidence on the Slave Trade, 1790.* Wilmington, Del.: Scholarly Resources, 1975.

———, ed. *House of Commons Sessional Papers, George III: Minutes of Evidence on the Slave Trade, 1790, Part 1, Volume 71.* Wilmington, Del.: Scholarly Resources, 1975.

Lamp, Frederick. *Art of the Baga: A Drama of Cultural Reinvention.* New York: The Museum for African Art/Prestel-Verlag, 1996.

Lampreia, José D. "Máscaras ritualistas dos Nalus da Guiné Portuguesa." *Actas do Congresso Internacional da Etnografia* 4 (1963): 141–49.

Landerset Simões, Armando de. *Babel Negra.* Lisboa: Ofic. gráf. de O Comercio do Pôrto, 1936.

Lauer, Joseph. "Rice in the History of the Lower Gambia-Geba Area." Master's thesis, University of Wisconsin, 1969.

Laughton, John R. *Gambia: Country, People, and Church in the Diocese of Gambia and the Rio Pongas.* London: Society for the Propagation of the Gospel, 1938.

Lavau, G. de. "Boké (Guinée française)." *Annales africaines* (1958): 245–58.

Law, Robin. "Slave-Raiders and Middlemen, Monopolists and Free-Traders: The Supply of Slaves for the Atlantic Trade in Dahomey c. 1715–1850." *Journal of African History* 30, no. 1 (1989): 45–68.

Leakey, C. L. A., and J. B. Willis, eds. *Food Crops of the Lowland Tropics*. Oxford: Oxford University Press, 1977.

Leprince, Jules. "Ethnographie Les Bagas-Foreh (Mœurs et coutumes)." *Revue scientifique* 14, no. 2 (1900): 47–49.

Lericollais, André, and Jean Schmitz. "La Calebasse et la houe." *Cahiers O.R.S.T.O.M.* 20, no. 3–4 (1984): 427–52.

Lespinay, Charles. "Dictionnaire Baynunk (gu[ny]un-gujaxer-guhaca-guboy): Français (Unpublished manuscript)." 1992.

Lestrange, Monique de. "Génies de l'eau et de la brousse en Guinée française." *Études guinéennes* 4 (1950): 1–24.

Lewicki, Tadeusz, and Marion Johnson. *West African Food in the Middle Ages: According to Arabic Sources*. London: Cambridge University Press, 1974.

Lewis, Earl. "To Turn as on a Pivot: Writing African Americans into a History of Overlapping Diasporas." *The American Historical Review* 100, no. 3 (1995): 765–87.

Lewis, Ronald L. *Coal, Iron, and Slaves: Industrial Slavery in Maryland and Virginia, 1715–1865*. Westport, Conn.: Greenwood, 1979.

Linares de Sapir, Olga F. "Shell Middens of Lower Casamance and Problems of Diola Protohistory." *West African Journal of Archaeology* 1 (1971): 23–54.

Linares, Olga. "African Rice (*Oryza glaberrima*): History and Future Potential." *PNAS* 99, no. 25 (2002): 16360–65.

———. "From Tidal Swamp to Inland Valley: On the Social Organization of Wet Rice Cultivation among the Diola of Senegal." *Africa* 51, no. 2 (1981): 557–595.

———. *Power, Prayer and Production: The Jola of Casamance, Senegal*. Cambridge: Cambridge University Press, 1992.

Littlefield, Daniel C. *Rice and Slaves: Ethnicity and the Slave Trade in Colonial South Carolina*. Baton Rouge: Louisiana State University Press, 1981.

Long, Ronald W. "A Comparative Study of the Northern Mande Languages." Ph.D. diss., Indiana University, 1971.

Lopes, Carl. *Kaabunké: espaço, território e poder na Guiné-Bissau, Gâmbia e Casamance pré-colonias*. Lisboa: Comissão Nacional para as Comemorações dos Descobrimentos Portugueses, 1999.

Lovejoy, Paul E. "The African Diaspora: Interpretations of Ethnicity, Culture and Religion under Slavery." *Studies in the World History of Slavery, Abolition and Emancipation* II, no. 1 (1997).

———. *Salt of the Desert Sun: A History of Salt Production and Trade in the Central Sudan*. Cambridge: Cambridge University Press, 2002.

———. *Transformations in Slavery: A History of Slavery in Africa*. Cambridge: Cambridge University Press, 2000.

Lupke, Friederike. "A Grammar of Jalonke Argument Structure." Ph.D. diss., Radboud Universität Nijmegen, 2005.

Machat, J. *Guinée française: Les Rivières du sud et le Fouta-Diallon: géographie physique et civilisations indigènes*. Paris: Augustin Challamel, 1906.

Maclaud, Claude. "Étude sur la distribution géographique des races sur la côte occidentale d'Afrique de la Gambie à la Mellacorée." *Bulletin de géographie historique et descriptive* 21, no. 1 (1899): 82–119.

Madrolle, Claudius. *En Guinée*. Paris: H. Le Soudier, 1895.

Mann, Kristin, and Edna Bay, eds. *Rethinking the African Diaspora: The Making of the Black Atlantic*. London: Frank Cass, 2001.

Manning, Patrick. "Review Article: Africa and the African Diaspora New Directions of Study." *Journal of African History* 44 (2003): 487–506.

Mark, Peter. *'Portuguese' Style and Luso-African Identity: Precolonial Senegambia, 16th–19th Centuries*. Bloomington: Indiana University Press, 2002.

Marzouk-Schmitz, Yasmine. "Instruments aratoires, systèmes de cultures et différenciation intra-ethnique." *Cahiers O.R.S.T.O.M.* 20, no. 3–4 (1984): 399–425.

Matory, J. Lorand. *Black Atlantic Religion: Tradition, Transnationalism, and Matriarchy in the Afro-Brazilian Candomblé*. Princeton, N.J.: Princeton University Press, 2005.

Matthews, John. *A Voyage to the River Sierra-Leone, containing an account of the Trade and Production of the Country and of the Civil and Religious Customs and Manners of the People*. London: Frank Cass & Co., 1966.

Mauny, Raymond. "Essai sur l'histoire des métaux en Afrique occidentale." *Bulletin d'Institut fondamental d'Afrique noire* Ser. A, 14 (1952): 545–95.

———. "L'aire des mégalithes 'sénégambiens'." *Notes africaines* 73 (1957): 1–2.

———. "Nouvelles pierres sonnantes d'Afrique occidentale." *Notes africaines* 79 (1958): 65–67.

———. *Tableau géographique de l'ouest Africain au moyen âge d'après les sources écrites, la tradition et l'archéologie*. Dakar: Institut français d'Afrique noire, 1961.

Mayer, Brantz. *Captain Canot; or, 20 Years of an African Slaver*. New York: Arno, 1968.

McIntosh, Roderick J. "The Pulse Model: Genesis and Accommodation of Specialization in the Middle Niger." *Journal of African History* 34, no. 2 (1993): 181–220.

McIntosh, Roderick J., and Susan Keech McIntosh. "The Inland Niger Delta before the Empire of Mali: Evidence from Jenne-Jeno." *Journal of African History* 22, no. 1 (1981): 1–22.

McIntosh, Susan Keech, ed. *Beyond Chiefdoms: Pathways to Complexity in Africa*. Cambridge: Cambridge University Press, 1999.

McNaughton, Patrick R. *The Mande Blacksmiths: Knowledge, Power, and Art in West Africa*. Bloomington: Indiana University Press, 1988.

Méo, Docteur. "Études sur le Rio-Nunez." *Bulletin de la commission d'études historiques et scientifique de l'Afrique occidentale français* (1919): 281–317; 341–69.

Mille, Katherine Wyly, and Michael B. Montgomery, eds. *Africanisms in the Gullah Dialect by Lorenzo Dow Turner*. Columbia: University of South Carolina Press, 2002.

Miller, Joseph C. *Way of Death: Merchant Capitalism on the Angolan Slave Trade, 1730–1830*. Madison: University of Wisconsin Press, 1988.

Milton, Kay, ed. *Environmentalism: The View from Anthropology*. London: Routledge, 1993.

Mintz, Sidney, and Richard Price. *The Birth of African-American Culture: An Anthropological Perspective*. Boston: Beacon, 1992.

Moormann, F. R., and N. van Breeman, eds. *Rice, Soil, Water, Land*. Los Baños, Philippines: International Rice Research Institute, 1978.

Morgan, Philip D. *Slave Counterpoint: Black Culture in the Eighteenth-Century Chesapeake and Lowcountry*. Chapel Hill: University of North Carolina Press, 1998.

Mota, Avelino Teixeira da. "A viagem do navio Santiago a Serra Leoa e rio de S. Domingos em 1526—livro de armacao." *Boletim cultural da Guiné portuguesa* 24 (1969): 529–79.

———. *Guiné portuguesa.* Lisboa: Agência Geral do Ultramar, 1954.

Mouser, Bruce L. "The 1805 Forékariah Conference: A Case of Political Intrigue, Economic Advantage, Network Building." *History in Africa* 25 (1998): 219–62.

———. *Guinea Journal: Journeys into Guinea—Conakry during the Sierra Leone Phase, 1800–1821.* Washington, D.C.: University Press of America, 1979.

———. "Iles de Los as Bulking Center in the Slave Trade 1750–1800." *Revue française d'histoire d'outre-mer* 83, no. 313 (1996): 77–90.

———. "Rebellion, Marronage, and Jihad: Strategies of Resistance to Slavery on the Sierra Leone Coast, c. 1783–1796." *Journal of African History* 48 (2007): 27–44.

———. "Trade and Politics in the Nunez and Pongo Rivers, 1790–1865." Ph.D. diss., Indiana University, 1971.

———. "Trade, Coasters, and Conflict in the Rio Pongo from 1790 to 1808." *Journal of African History* 14, no. 1 (1973): 45–64.

———. "Who and Where Were the Baga? European Perceptions from 1793 to 1821." *History in Africa* 29 (2002): 337–64.

———, ed. *Account of the Mandingoes, Susoos, & Other Nations, c. 1815 by the Reverend Leopold Butscher.* Leipzig: University of Leipzig African History and Culture Series, 2000.

———, ed. *Journal of a Missionary Tour to the Labaya Country (Guinea/Conakry) in 1850 by John Ulrich Graf.* Leipzig: University of Leipzig African History and Culture Series, 1998.

———, ed. *Journal of James Watt: Expedition to Timbo, Capital of the Fula Empire in 1794.* Madison: African Studies Program, University of Wisconsin–Madison, 1994.

———, ed. *A Slaving Voyage to Africa and Jamaica: The Log of the Sandown, 1793–1794.* Bloomington: Indiana University Press, 2002.

Mouser, Bruce L., and Ramon Sarró, eds. *Travels into the Baga and Soosoo Countries in 1821 by Peter McLachlan.* Leipzig: University of Leipzig African History and Culture Series, 1999.

Museum of Primitive Art. *Sculpture from Three African Tribes: Senufo, Baga, Dogon.* New York: Museum of Primitive Art, 1959.

National Research Council. *Lost Crops of Africa.* Washington, D.C.: National Academy Press, 1996.

Neale, Caroline. *Writing "Independent" History: African Historiography, 1960–1980.* Westport, Conn.: Greenwood, 1985.

Niane, Djibril Tamsir. "Nimba, décesse de la fécondité en pays Baga." *Afrique histoire* 1, no. 1 (1982): 63–64.

———. "Un masque pour rire." *Afrique histoire* 1, no. 1 (1982): 65.

Niane, Djibril Tamsir, and Joseph Ki-Zerbo, eds. *Histoire générale de l'Afrique: Vol. IV: L'Afrique du XIIe au XVIe siècle.* Paris: UNESCO/NEA, 1985.

Nicholson, Sharon E. "The Methodology of Historical Climate Reconstruction and Its Application to Africa." *Journal of African History* 20, no. 1 (1979): 31–49.

Nicolai, Robert, and Franz Rottlend, eds. *Actes du cinquième de linguistique Nilo-Saharienne.* Köln: Rudiger Koppe Verlag, 1995.

Noirot, Ernest. *À travers le Fouta-Diallon et le Bambouc (Soudan occidental).* Paris: Marpon et Flammarion, 1885.

Northrup, David. *Trade without Rulers: Pre-Colonial Economic Development in South-eastern Nigeria.* Oxford: Clarendon, 1978.

Nowak, Bronislaw. "The Slave Rebellion in Sierra Leone in 1785–1786." *Hemispheres* 3 (1986): 151–69.

Nuijten, Edwin. *Farmer Management of Gene Flow: The Impact of Gender and Breeding System on Genetic Diversity and Crop Improvement in the Gambia.* Wageningen, Netherlands: Wageningen Universiteit, 2005.

Nurse, Derek. "The Contribution of Linguistics to the Study of History in Africa." *Journal of African History* 38 (1997): 359–91.

———. *The Swahili: Reconstructing the History and Language of an African Society, 800–1500.* Philadelphia: University of Pennsylvania Press, 1985.

Nyerges, A. Endre, ed. *The Ecology of Practice: Studies of Food Crop Production in Sub-Saharan West Africa.* Amsterdam: Gordon and Breach, 1997.

Opala, Joseph A. *The Gullah: Rice, Slavery and the Sierra Leone-American Connection.* Freetown, Sierra Leone: United States Information Services, 1987.

Pacheco Pereira, Duarte. *Esmeraldo de situ orbis: côte occidentale d'Afrique du sud Marocain au Gabon.* London: Hakluyt Society, 1937, 1961.

Pales, Léon, and Marie Tassin de Saint Pereuse. *L'Alimentation en A.O.F.: milieux-enquêtes-techniques-rations.* Dakar: O.R.A.N.A., 1955.

Palmer, Colin. "Defining and Studying the Modern African Diaspora." *Perspectives* 36, no. 6 (1998): 22–25.

Paroisse, Georges. "De Conakry au Fouta Djalon." *Bulletin de la société géographie commercial de Paris* (1892–1893): 512–29.

———. "Le Rio Pongo." *Revue économique française* 14, no. 2 (1892): 125–37.

———. "Notes sur les peuplades autochtones de la Guinée française (Rivières du Sud)." *L'Anthropologie* 7 (1896): 428–42.

Paulme, Denise. "Des riziculteurs africains: Les BAGA (Guinée française)." *Les Cahiers d'Outre-mer* 10 (1957): 257–80.

———. "La notion de sorcier chez les Baga." *Bulletin de l'Institut fondamental d'Afrique noire* 20 Ser. B, no. 3–4 (1958): 406–16.

———. "Structures sociales en pays baga (Guinée française)." *Bulletin de l'Institut fondamental d'Afrique noire* 18 Ser. B, no. 1–2 (1956): 98–116.

Paulme-Schaeffner, Denise. "'Elek,' a Ritual Sculpture of the Baga of French Guinea." *Man* 59 (1959): 28–29.

Pélissier, Paul. "Les DIOLA: étude sur l'habitat des riziculteurs de Basse-Casamance." *Les Cahiers d'Outre-mer* 11 (1958): 334–88.

———. *Les Paysans du Sénégal: les civilisations du Cayor à la Casamance.* Saint-Yrieix: Impr. Fabrègue, 1966.

Person, Yves. "Ethnic Movements and Acculturation in Upper Guinea since the Fifteenth Century." *International Journal of African Historical Studies* 4, no. 3 (1971): 669–89.

Phillipson, David W. *The Later Prehistory of Eastern and Southern Africa.* New York: Africana Publishing Co., 1977.

Piacentini, René. *Missionnaire le père Mell, apôtre de la Guinée française, 1880–1921.* Paris: Dillen, 1935.

Portères, Roland. "Berceaux agricoles primaires sur le continent Africain." *Journal of African History* 3, no. 2 (1962): 195–210.

———. "Les Appellations des céréales en Afrique." *Journal d'agriculture tropicale et de botanique appliquée* 5, no. 1–11 (1958): 178–220.

————. "Les noms des riz en Guinée: introduction générale." *Journal d'agriculture tropicale et de botanique appliquée* 9, no. 10 (1965): 369–402.

————. "Les noms des riz en Guinée: les noms des riz en Guinée côtière." *Journal
d'agriculture tropicale et de botanique appliquée* 13, no. 12 (1966): 641–700.

————. "Les noms des riz en Guinée: Oryza-Sativa." *Journal d'agriculture tropicale et de
botanique appliquée* 12, no. 11 (1965): 595–638.

————. "Un problème d'ethno-botanique: relations entre le riz flottant du Rio-Nunez
et l'origine médinigérienne des Baga de la Guinée française." *Journal d'agriculture
tropicale et de botanique appliquée* 11, no. 10–11 (1955): 538–42.

————. "Vielles agricultures de l'Afrique intertropicale: centres d'origine et de diversification variétale primaire et berceaux d'agriculture antérieurs au XVIe siècle."
L'Agronomie tropicale 5, no. 9–10 (1950): 489–507.

Poujade, Jean. "Technologie." *Études guinéennes* 2 (1947): 85–89.

Pozdniakov, Konstantin. *Sravnitel'naia Grammatika Atlantichskikh Iazykov.* Moscow:
Izdatel'skaia Firma, Vostoshnai Literatura, 1993.

Pringle, Elizabeth W. *Chronicles of Chicora Wood.* New York: Charles Scribner's Sons,
1990.

————. *A Woman Rice Planter.* Columbia: University of South Carolina Press, 1992.

Pursell, Carroll W., ed. *A Hammer in Their Hands: A Documentary History of Technology
and the African-American Experience.* Cambridge, Mass.: MIT Press, 2005.

Raimbault, Le R. P. *Dictionnaire Français-Soso et Soso-Français.* Conakry: Société Africaine d'édition et de communication, 1900.

Raulin, Henri. *La dynamique des techniques agraires en Afrique tropicale du Nord.* Paris:
Éditions centre national de la recherche scientifique, 1967.

Rediker, Marcus. "Images of the Slave Ship." Lecture presented at University of Pitts-
burgh, Department of Art and Art History, 2005.

————. *The Slave Ship: A Human History.* New York: Viking, 2007.

Renfrew, Colin, April McMahon, and Larry Trask, eds. *Time Depth in Historical Linguistics.* Cambridge: The McDonald Institute for Archaeological Research, 2000.

Ribeiro, Orlando. *Aspectos e problemas da expansão portuguesa.* Lisboa: Junta da Investigações do Ultramar, 1962.

*Rice, Slaves, and Landscapes of Cultural Memory. Places of Cultural Memory: African
Reflections on the American Landscape: Conference Proceedings,* May 9–12, 2001, Atlanta, Ga. Washington, D.C.: U.S. Department of Interior-National Park Service,
2001.

Richards, Paul. *Coping with Hunger: Hazard and Experiment in an African Rice-Farming
System.* London: Allen and Unwin, 1986.

————. *Indigenous Agricultural Revolution: Ecology and Food Production in West Africa.*
Boulder, Colo.: Westview, 1985.

Ringe, Donald A., Jr. "On Calculating the Factor of Chance in Language Comparison."
Transactions of the American Philosophical Society 82, no. 1 (1992): 1–109.

Rivière, Claude. "La Toponymie de Conakry et du Kaloum." *Bulletin de l'Institut fondamental d'Afrique noire* 28, no. Ser. B 3–4 (1966): 1009–18.

————. "Le long des côtes de Guinée avant la phase coloniale." *Bulletin de l'Institut
fondamental d'Afrique noire* 30, no. Ser. B (1968): 727–50.

Robertson, Claire C., and Martin A. Klein, eds. *Women and Slavery in Africa.* Madison:
University of Wisconsin Press, 1983.

Rodney, Walter. *A History of the Upper Guinea Coast, 1545–1800.* Oxford: Clarendon, 1970.

————. "A Reconsideration of the Mane Invasions of Sierra Leone." *Journal of African History* 8, no. 2 (1967): 219–46.

Rouch, Jules A. *Sur les côtes du Sénégal et de la Guinée: voyage du 'Chevigné'*. Paris: Société d'éditions géographiques, maritimes et coloniales, 1925.

Rouget, Fernand. *La Guinée*. Corbeil: Impr. Typl E. Crête, 1906.

Rubin, Vera, and Arthur Tuden, eds. *Comparative Perspectives on Slavery in New World Plantation Societies*. New York: New York Academy of Sciences, 1977.

Saint-Père, M. "Petit historique des Sossoe du Rio Pongo." *Bulletin de comité d'études historiques et scientifiques de l'Afrique occidentale française* 13, no. 1 (1930): 26–47.

Santo, J. do Espirito. "Nomes vernáculos de algumas plantas da Guiné portuguesa." *Boletim cultural da Guiné portuguesa* 18 (1963): 405–510.

————. "Notas sobre a cultural do arroz entre Os Balantas." *Boletim cultural da Guiné portuguesa* 4 (1949): 192–231.

Sapir, J. David. "West Atlantic: An Inventory of Languages, Their Noun Class System and Consonant Alternation." In *Current Trends in Linguistics in Sub-Saharan Africa*, 45–112. The Hague: Mouton, 1971.

Sarró-Maluquer, Ramon. "Baga Identity: Religious Movements and Political Transformation in the Republic of Guinea." Ph.D. diss., University of London, 1999.

Schafer, Daniel. *Anna Madgigine Jai Kingsley: African Princess Florida Slave, Plantation Owner*. Gainesville: University Press of Florida, 2003.

————. "Family Ties that Bind: Anglo-African Slave Traders in Africa and Florida, John Fraser and His Descendants." *Slavery and Abolition: A Journal of Slave and Post-Slave Studies* 20 (1990): 1–21.

Schlenker, C. F. *A Collection of Temne Traditions, Fables and Proverbs, with an English Translation and also some Specimens of the Author's Own Temne Compositions and Translations to which is appended a Temne-English Vocabulary*. London: Church Missionary Society, 1861.

Schnell, R. "Esquisse de la végétation côtière de la basse Guinée française." *Comptes rendus; première conférence internationale des africanistes de l'ouest* (1947): 203–14.

————. "La fête rituelle de sortie des jeunes excisées en pays Baga (Basse-Guinée)." *Notes africaines* 43 (1949): 84–86.

————. "Noms vernaculaires et usages indigènes de plantes d'Afrique occidentale." *Études guinéennes* 4 (1950): 57–80.

Schoenbrun, David Lee. "Early History in Eastern Africa's Great Lakes Region: Linguistic, Ecological, and Archaeological Approaches, ca. 500 BC to ca. AD 1000." Ph.D. diss., University of California at Los Angeles, 1990.

————. *A Green Place, A Good Place: Agrarian Change, Gender, and Social Identity in the Great Lakes Region to the 15th Century*. Portsmouth: Heinemann, 1998.

————. "We Are What We Eat: Ancient Agriculture between the Great Lakes." *Journal of African History* 34, no. 1 (1993): 1–31.

Schwalm, Leslie A. *A Hard Fight for We: Women's Transition from Slavery to Freedom in South Carolina*. Urbana: University of Illinois Press, 1997.

Schwartz, Suzanne. *Zachary Macaulay and the Development of the Sierra Leone Company, 1793–4; Part II: Journal, October–December 1793*. Leipzig: University of Leipzig Papers on African History and Culture Series, 2000.

————, ed. *Zachary Macaulay and the Development of the Sierra Leone Company, 1793–4, Part I: Journal, June–October 1793*. Leipzig: University of Leipzig Papers on Africa History and Culture Series, 2000.

Searing, James F. *West African Slavery and Atlantic Commerce: The Senegal River Valley, 1700–1860*. Cambridge: Cambridge University Press, 1993.

Segerer, Guillame. *La Langue Bijogo de Bubaque (Guinée Bissau)*. Louvain, Belgium: Peeters, 2002.

Seignobos, Christian, Yasmine Marzouk, and François Sigaut, eds. *Outils aratoires en Afrique: innovations, normes et traces*. Paris: Karthala, 2000.

Seydou, Christiane. *Dictionnaire pluridialectal des racines verbales du Peul: Peul-Français-Anglais*. Paris: Éditions Karthala, 1998.

Shaw, Rosalind. "The Production of Witchcraft/Witchcraft as Production: Memory, Modernity, and the Slave Trade in Sierra Leone." *American Ethnologist* 24, no. 4 (1997): 856–76.

Shaw, Thurstan, ed. *The Archaeology of Africa: Foods, Metals, and Towns*. New York: Routledge, 1993.

Shillington, Kevin, ed. *Encyclopedia of African History*. New York: Fitzroy Dearborn, 2005.

Silva, Artura A. da. "Arte Nalu." *Boletim cultural da Guiné portuguesa* 44, no. 27–47 (1956).

Sinclair, Bruce, ed. *Technology and the African-American Experience: Needs and Opportunities for Study*. Cambridge, Mass.: MIT Press, 2004.

Sinyako, Sacoba. "Quelques coutumes 'Baga Fore'." *L'éducation africaine* (1937): 220–25.

——— . "Une page d'histoire du pays Baga." *L'éducation africaine* Juillet–Décembre (1938): 57–63.

Skinner, David. "Sierra Leone Relations with the Northern Rivers and the Influence of Islam in the Conakry." *International Journal of Sierra Leone Studies* 1 (1988): 91–113.

Smith, Alice R. Huger, Herbert Ravenel Sass, and D. E. Huger Smith. *A Carolina Rice Plantation of the Fifties: 30 Paintings in Water-Colour*. New York: W. Morrow and Co., 1936.

Smith, Julia Floyd. *Slavery and Rice Culture in Low Country Georgia, 1750–1860*. Knoxville: University of Tennessee Press, 1985.

Stanley, Lord. "Narrative of William Cooper Thompson's Journey from Sierra Leone to Timbo, Capital of the Futah Jallo in West Africa." *Journal of the Royal Geographical Society of London* 16 (1846): 106–38.

Starobin, Robert S. *Industrial Slavery in the Old South*. New York: Oxford University Press, 1970.

Stewart, Mart A. "Rice, Water, and Power: Landscapes of Domination and Resistance in the Lowcountry, 1790–1880." *Environmental History Review* 15, no. 3 (1991): 47–64.

Suret-Canale, Jean. *La République de Guinée*. Paris: Éditions sociales, 1970.

Swadesh, Morris. "Lexico-statistic Dating of Prehistoric Ethnic Contacts: With Special Reference to North American Indians and Eskimos." *Proceeding of the American Philosophical Society* 96, no. 4 (1952): 452–65.

——— . "Towards Greater Accuracy in Lexicostatistic Dating." *International Journal of American Linguistics* 21 (1955): 121–37.

Sweet, James H. *Recreating Africa: Culture, Kinship, and Religion in the African-Portuguese World, 1441–1770*. Chapel Hill: University of North Carolina Press, 2003.

Sy, Sékhou Bounama. "Monographie du Rio Pongo." *Recherches africaines* 1 (1969): 30–57.

Tamari, Tal. *Les castes de l'Afrique occidentale: artisans et musiciens endogames*. Nanterre, France: Société d'ethnologie, 1997.

Thiam, Bodiel. "'Nimba', décesse de la fécondité des Baga et Nalou (basse côte de Gui-néenne)." *Notes africaines* 108 (1965): 128–30.

Thilmans, G., and J. P. Rossie. "Le 'Flambeau de la Navigation' de Dierick Ruiters." *Bulletin de l'Institut fondamental d'Afrique noire* 31, no. Ser. B 1 (1969): 106–19.

Thilmans, G., and N. I. de Moraes. "La description de la côte de Guinée du père Baltasar Barreira (1606)." *Bulletin de l'Institut fondamental d'Afrique noire* 34, no. Ser. B (1972): 1–49.

———. "Le Routier de la côte de Guinée de Francisco Pirez de Carvalho." *Bulletin de l'Institut fondamental d'Afrique noire* 32, no. Ser. B (1970): 343–60.

Thomas, Louis-Vincent. *Les Diola; essai d'analyse fonctionnelle sur une population de Basse-Casamance.* Dakar: Institut français d'Afrique noire, 1959.

Thomas, Northcote W. *An Anthropological Report on Sierra Leone.* London: Harrison and Sons, 1916.

———. "Who Were the Manes?" *Journal of the Royal African Society* 19 (1919): 33–42.

———. "Who Were the Manes?" *Journal of the Royal African Society* 20 (1921): 176–88.

Thornton, John. *Africa and Africans: The Making of the Atlantic World, 1400–1680.* New York: Cambridge University Press, 1992.

———. "African Dimensions of the Stono Rebellion." *American Historical Review* 96, no. 4 (1991): 1101–13.

———. "The Art of War in Angola, 1575–1680." *Comparative Studies in Society and History* 30, no. 2 (1988): 360–78.

———. *The Kongolese Saint Anthony: Dona Beatriz Kimpa Vita and the Antonian Movement, 1684–1706.* New York: Cambridge University Press, 1998.

Tomlinson, P. B. *The Botany of Mangroves.* Cambridge: Cambridge University Press, 1986.

Trigo, António Baptista. "Nalús de Cacine." *Boletim cultural da Guiné portuguesa* 5 (1947): 273.

Trotter, Joe William, Jr. *Coal, Class, and Color: Blacks in Southern West Virginia, 1915–32.* Urbana: University of Illinois Press, 1990.

Trutenau, H., ed. *Languages of the Akan Area: Papers in Western Kwa Linguistics and on the Linguistic Geography of the Area of Ancient Begho.* Basel: Basler Afrika Bibliographien, 1976.

Turay, A. K. "Language Contact: Mende and Temne—A Case Study." *Africana Marburgensia* 11, no. 1 (1978): 55–73.

Van Geertruyen, Godelieve. "La fonction de la sculpture dans une société africaine: les Baga, Nalu et Landuma (Guinée)." *Africana candensia* 1 (1976): 63–113.

Vansina, Jan. "Deep-down Time: Political Tradition in Central Africa." *History in Africa* 16 (1989): 341–62.

———. *How Societies Are Born: Governance in West Central Africa before 1600.* Charlottesville: University of Virginia Press, 2004.

———. "New Linguistic Evidence and the 'Bantu Expansion'." *Journal of African History* 36 (1995): 173–95.

———. *Oral Tradition as History.* Madison: University of Wisconsin Press, 1985.

———. *Paths in the Rainforest: Toward a History of Political Tradition in Equatorial Africa.* Madison: University of Wisconsin Press, 1990.

———. "Review Article: Linguistic Evidence and Historical Reconstruction." *Journal of African History* 40 (1999): 469–73.

Villault, N. *Relation des costes d'Afrique appelées Guinée.* Paris: Denis Thierry, 1669.

Voeltz, Erhard. "Bibliographie linguistique de la Guinée." *Cahiers d'étude les langues guinéennes* 2 (1996).

———. "Les Langues de la Guinée." *Cahiers d'étude les langues guinéennes* 1 (1996).

Voeltz, Erhard, Aboubacar Camara, Tina Ganong, and Martin Ganong. "Baga: Intam kicicis citem (syllabaire de langue baga)." *Cahiers d'étude les langues guinéennes* 3 (1997).

Voeltz, Erhard, and Mohammed Camara. "Lexique Nalu-Français" (Unpublished manuscript).

Vogel, Joseph O., ed. *Ancient African Metallurgy: The Sociocultural Context.* Walnut Creek, Calif.: AltaMira, 2000.

———, ed. *Encyclopedia of Precolonial Africa: Archaeology, History, Languages, Cultures, and Environments.* Walnut Creek, Calif.: AltaMira, 1997.

Vydrine, Valentin. *Mande-English Dictionary: Maninka, Bamana.* Saint Petersberg: Dimitry Bulanin, 1999.

Wade, Richard C. *Slavery in the Cities: The South, 1820–1860.* New York: Oxford University Press, 1964.

Walker, Samuel Abraham. *Missions in Western Africa, among the Soosoos, Bulloms, & c.* Dublin: William Curry, Jun and Company, 1845.

Webb, James L. A. *Desert Frontier: Ecological and Economic Change along the Western Sahel, 1600–1850.* Madison: University of Wisconsin Press, 1995.

Williams, Martin A. J., and Hughes Faure, eds. *The Sahara and the Nile: Quaternary Environments and Prehistoric Occupation in Northern Africa.* Rotterdam: Balkema, 1980.

Williamson, J. A. *Sir John Hawkins: The Time and the Man.* Oxford: Clarendon, 1927.

Wilms, Douglas C. "The Development of Rice Culture in 18th Century Georgia." *Southeastern Geographer* 12 (1972): 45–57.

Wilson, W. A. A. *An Outline of the Temne Language.* London: School of Oriental and African Studies, University of London, 1961.

———. "Temne and the West Atlantic Group." *Sierra Leone Language Review* 2 (1963): 26–29.

———. "Temne, Landuma and the Baga Languages." *Sierra Leone Language Review* 1 (1962): 27–38.

Winterbottom, Thomas. *An Account of the Native Africans in the Neighbourhood of Sierra Leone.* London: C. Whittingham, 1803.

Wondji, Christophe. *La côte ouest-africaine, du Sénégal à la Côte d'Ivoire: géographie, sociétés, histoire, 1500–1800.* Paris: Éditions L'harmattan, 1985.

Wood, Betty. *Slavery in Colonial Georgia, 1730–1775.* Athens: University of Georgia Press, 1984.

Wood, Peter. *Black Majority; Negroes in Colonial South Carolina from 1670 through the Stono Rebellion.* New York: Knopf, 1974.

Wright, Donald R. *The World and a Very Small Place in Africa.* Armonk, N.Y.: M. E. Sharpe, 1997.

Index

Page numbers in *italics* indicate illustrations.

swamps (*continued*)
  inland swamps, 32, 51, 126, 157–58, 159, 177, 179, 180; mangrove swamps, 2, 22, 26, 30, 31, 33, 36–37, 80, 89, 105, 132, 145–46, 147, 158; reclaiming, 36, 76, 108; reclamation in South Carolina, 158; "sweet" swamps, 37. *See also* mangrove rice farming
Sweet, James, 189, 190

tarrafe, 220n32
  Temne language, 33, 35, 63, 82
  borrowing from Fulbe language, 101
  core vocabulary list for, 15
  cultural vocabulary list for, 16
  divergence of, 84, 120
  as a "Highland" subgroup of Atlantic language group, 15
  linguistic analysis of: bird, 98; blood, 98; bow, 98; chains/fetters, 94; chopping trees, 104, 126–27; coal, 100; dew, 98; female slave, 94; fish, 98; goat, 98; iron, 99–100, 153; iron cooking pot, 100, 153; ivory, 97, 98; king, 94; loop/noose, 98; male slave, 94; meat/beef, 98; office of the king, 94; oil palm, 98; one who tends cattle, 102; rain, 98; rainy season, 98; rearing/tending cattle, 102; salt, 64; serpent, 98; slavery/bondage, 94; smoke, 100; stranger/ visitor, 94; tooth, 98; very elderly and respected man, 94; wild animal/venison, 98
  relationship to Sitem, 215n27
  sharing cognates with other Highland languages, 86
Temne-speakers, 81, 103–104; sharing oral traditions with Sitem, 58; as source of slaves, 170, 233n32
Texas, 9, 181
tidal flow, 26, 32
tidal rice-farming system, 4, 22, 23, 29, 46, 51–52, 56, 104, 121, 142, 154, 209n9; and the Atlantic speech communities, 61, 80, 105, 111, 115, 120, 123, 125, 126, 132, 154, 155–56; as collaborative effort of Coastal and Highland language speakers, 22, 84, 88, 107–34, 156; compared to *décrue* farming, 149; evolution of, 8–9, 10, 32, 61, 115, 132, 141, 160; rice growing techniques, 36–46, 156; Mande speech communities as a source of, 56, 117, 133; roots of in Rio Nunez region, 8–9, 22, 25–53, 62, 75, 77, 80, 121, 133, 142; Sitem-speaking newcomers contributions to, 22, 81, 92, 125, 127, 146; specialized terminology for, 75, 77, 119, 120, 127, 131, 152, 153, 154, 156; use of for tidewater rice

farming in Georgia and South Carolina, 50, 51, 158, 180. *See also* irrigation and drainage; rice cultivation; salinity
tidewater rice-farming in South Carolina and Georgia, 157, 158, 159, 162; flooding fields, 224n2; land clearing and preparation, 179–80; mirror image of tidal rice-farming in Africa, 50; use of floodgates and dams, 177, 179; using West African skills and technology, 50, 51, 158, 180
Timbo in Futa Jallon, 66
Tinoco, Antonio Velho, 96
ton, representing carrying capacity not weight, 232n15
tooth, linguistic analysis of, 98
Toure, Sekou, 11, 57
trade: caravan traders, 2, 5, 6, 7, 47, 65, 66, 144, 145, 162, 168–69; coastal trade, 5, 23, 142, 162–63, 166, 170, 173; Fulbe-speakers as traders, 35, 41, 47, 65, 66, 101; and Futa Jallon, 47, 65–66, 144, 169; grain trade, 166–67; interregional trade, 5, 6, 46, 47, 65, 88, 89, 97, 101, 105, 112, 113, 142, 144–46, 213–14n2; iron used in interregional trade, 47, 144–46; long-distance trade, 114–15; Luso-Africans as traders, 7, 8, 31, 47, 64–65, 118, 168, 218n17; malaguetta pepper used in trade, 213–14n2; Portuguese traders, 26, 81, 136; salt used in trade, 33, 35, 46–47, 55, 65, 66, 95, 168, 169; and Sierra Leone, 5, 6, 96, 168; Susu-speakers as traders, 6, 35, 46–47, 218n17; trans-Saharan trade, 5, 112–13, 116. *See also* slave traders; trans-Atlantic slave trade
trans-Atlantic slave trade, 5, 23; abolition of the slave trade, 167, 168, 170, 181, 187, 191, 192, 233n34; Balanta trading captives for iron, 145–46; binding blacks in Western Hemisphere together, 191; Caleb Godfrey and voyage of *Hare*, 181–84; count of slaves and identifying ports, 171–81; Hawthorne study of, 76; Igbo peoples as regional actors in, 113–14; maps of voyages to Georgia and South Carolina, *178*; need to trade for salt, 66; poor records on voyages, 48; positive impact of, 187; provisions and water for slaves, 170; rice as provision for slave trading vessels, 161, 162–63, 164–67, 171; ratio of captives to crew, 163, 164; and the Rio Nunez region, 46–49, 66, 168; as source of slaves for, 170, 233n32; ton representing carrying capacity not weight, 232n15
The Trans-Atlantic Slave Trade: A Database, 23, 48, 172–73, 189

EDDA L. FIELDS-BLACK
is an associate professor at Carnegie Mellon
University, specializing in pre-colonial and
West African history. With research interests
extending into the African Diaspora, Fields-
Black has conducted research and lived in
Guinea, Sierra Leone, South Carolina, and
Georgia to uncover the history of African rice
farmers and rice cultures.

CPSIA information can be obtained at www.ICGtesting.com
Printed in the USA
LVOW03s0156110315

429969LV00013B/52/P

9 780253 016102